KT-571-980

Unit/Objective/Sub-objective	Page
Domain 2.0 - Protocols and Standards	
2.15 Identify the basic characteristics of the following Internet access technologies: xDSL (Digital Subscriber Line), Broadband Cable (Cable modem), POTS/PSTN (Plain Old Telephone Service/Public Switched Telephone Network), Satellite, Wireless	**143**
2.16 Define the functions of the following remote access protocols and services: RAS, PPP, SLIP, PPPoE PPTP, VPN, RDP	**143**
2.17 Identify the following security protocols and describe their purposes and functions: IPSec, L2TP, SSL, WEP, WPA, 802.1x	**143**
2.18 Identify authentication protocols (for example, CHAP, MS-CHAP, PAP, RADIUS, Kerberos and EAP)	**143**
Domain 3.0 - Network Implementation	
3.1 Identify the basic capabilities (for example, client support, interoperability, authentication, file and print services, application support and security) of the following server operating systems to access network resources: UNIX/Linux/Mac OS X Server, NetWare, Windows, Appleshare IP (Internet Protocol)	**177**
3.2 Identify the basic capabilities needed for client workstations to connect to and use network resources (for example, media, network protocols, and peer and server services)	**177**
3.3 Identify the appropriate tool for a given wiring task (for example, wire crimper, media tester/certifier, punch down tool, or tone generator)	**177**
3.4 Given a remote connectivity scenario comprised of a protocol, an authentication scheme, and physical connectivity, configure the connection—includes connection to the following servers: UNIX/Linux/Mac OS X Server, NetWare, Windows, Appleshare IP (Internet Protocol)	**177**
3.5 Identify the purpose, benefits, and characteristics of using a firewall	**217**
3.6 Identify the purpose, benefits, and characteristics of using a proxy service	**217**
3.7 Given a connectivity scenario, determine the impact on network functionality of a particular security implementation (for example, port blocking/filtering, authentication and encryption)	**217**
3.8 Identify the main characteristics of VLANs (Virtual Local Area Networks)	**241**
3.9 Identify the main characteristics and purpose of extranets and intranets	**217**
3.10 Identify the purpose, benefits, and characteristics of using antivirus software	**241**
3.11 Identify the purpose and characteristics of fault tolerance: power, link redundancy, storage services	**241**
3.12 Identify the purpose and characteristics of disaster recovery: backup/restore, offsite storage, hot and cold spares, Hot, warm and cold sites	**241**

(continues)

Unit/Objective/Sub-objective	Page
Domain 4.0 - Network Support	
4.1 Given a troubleshooting scenario, select the appropriate network utility from the following: **tracert/traceroute**, **ping**, **arp**, **netstat**, **nbtstat**, **ipconfig/ ifconfig**, **winipcfg**, **nslookup/dig**	271
4.2 Given output from a network diagnostic utility (for example, those utilities listed in objective 4.1), identify the utility and interpret the output	271
4.3 Given a network scenario, interpret visual indicators (for example, link LEDs (Light Emitting Diode) and collision LEDs (Light Emitting Diode)) to determine the nature of a stated problem	271
4.4 Given a troubleshooting scenario involving a client accessing remote network services, identify the cause of the problem (for example, file services, print services, authentication failure, protocol configuration, physical connectivity, and SOHO (Small Office/Home Office) router)	271
4.5 Given a troubleshooting scenario between a client and the following server environments, identify the cause of a stated problem: UNIX/Linux/ Mac OS X Server, NetWare, Windows, Appleshare IP Problems	271
4.6 Given a scenario, determine the impact of modifying, adding or removing network services (for example, DHCP (Dynamic Host Configuration Protocol), DNS (Domain Name Service), and WINS (Windows Internet Name Server)) for network resources and users	317
4.7 Given a troubleshooting scenario involving a network with a particular physical topology (for example, bus, star, mesh, or ring) and including a network diagram, identify the network area affected and the cause of the stated failure	317
4.8 Given a network troubleshooting scenario involving an infrastructure (for example, wired or wireless) problem, identify the cause of a stated problem (for example, bad media, interference, network hardware, or environment)	317
4.9 Given a network problem scenario, select an appropriate course of action based on a logical troubleshooting strategy. This strategy can include the following steps: 1. Identify the symptoms and potential causes 2. Identify the affected area 3. Establish what has changed 4. Select the most probable cause 5. Implement an action plan and solution including potential effects 6. Test the result 7. Identify the results and effects of the solution 8. Document the solution and process	317

Network+

Drew Bird

Mike Harwood

CERTIFICATION

Network+ Exam Cram 2

Copyright © 2005 by Que Publishing

All rights reserved. No part of this book shall be reproduced, stored in a retrieval system, or transmitted by any means, electronic, mechanical, photocopying, recording, or otherwise, without written permission from the publisher. No patent liability is assumed with respect to the use of the information contained herein. Although every precaution has been taken in the preparation of this book, the publisher and author assume no responsibility for errors or omissions. Nor is any liability assumed for damages resulting from the use of the information contained herein.

International Standard Book Number: 0-7897-3254-8

Library of Congress Catalog Card Number: 2004118400

Printed in the United States of America

First Printing: June 2005

08 07 06 05   4 3 2 1

Trademarks

All terms mentioned in this book that are known to be trademarks or service marks have been appropriately capitalized. Que Publishing cannot attest to the accuracy of this information. Use of a term in this book should not be regarded as affecting the validity of any trademark or service mark.

Warning and Disclaimer

Every effort has been made to make this book as complete and as accurate as possible, but no warranty or fitness is implied. The information provided is on an "as is" basis. The author(s) and the publisher shall have neither liability nor responsibility to any person or entity with respect to any loss or damages arising from the information contained in this book or from the use of the CD or programs accompanying it.

Bulk Sales

Que Publishing offers excellent discounts on this book when ordered in quantity for bulk purchases or special sales. For more information, please contact

> **U.S. Corporate and Government Sales**
> **1-800-382-3419**
> **corpsales@pearsontechgroup.com**

For sales outside the U.S., please contact

> **International Sales**
> **international@pearsoned.com**

Publisher
Paul Boger

Executive Editor
Jeff Riley

Acquisitions Editor
Jeff Riley

Development Editor
Steve Rowe

Managing Editor
Charlotte Clapp

Project Editor
Mandie Frank

Copy Editor
Rhonda Tinch-Mize

Indexer
Ken Johnson

Proofreader
Tracy Donhardt

Technical Editor
David Prowse

Publishing Coordinator
Pamalee Nelson

Multimedia Developer
Dan Scherf

Page Layout
Kelly Maish

Que Certification • 800 East 96th Street • Indianapolis, Indiana 46240

A Note from Series Editor Ed Tittel

You know better than to trust your certification preparation to just any-body. That's why you, and more than 2 million others, have purchased an Exam Cram book. As Series Editor for the new and improved Exam Cram 2 Series, I have worked with the staff at Que Certification to ensure you won't be disappointed. That's why we've taken the world's best-selling certification product—a two-time finalist for "Best Study Guide" in CertCities' reader polls—and made it even better.

As a two-time finalist for the "Favorite Study Guide Author" award as selected by CertCities readers, I know the value of good books. You'll be impressed with Que Certification's stringent review process, which ensures the books are high quality, relevant, and technically accurate. Rest assured that several industry experts have reviewed this material, helping us deliver an excellent solution to your exam preparation needs.

Exam Cram 2 books also feature a preview edition of MeasureUp's powerful, full-featured test engine, which is trusted by certification students throughout the world.

As a 20-year-plus veteran of the computing industry and the original creator and editor of the Exam Cram Series, I've brought my IT experience to bear on these books. During my tenure at Novell from 1989 to 1994, I worked with and around its excellent education and certification department. At Novell, I witnessed the growth and development of the first really big, successful IT certification program—one that was to shape the industry forever afterward. This experience helped push my writing and teaching activities heavily in the cer-tification direction. Since then, I've worked on nearly 100 certification related books, and I write about certification topics for numerous Web sites and for *Certification* magazine.

In 1996, while studying for various MCP exams, I became frustrated with the huge, unwieldy study guides that were the only preparation tools available. As an experienced IT professional and former instructor, I wanted "nothing but the facts" necessary to prepare for the exams. From this impetus, Exam Cram emerged: short, focused books that explain exam topics, detail exam skills and activities, and get IT professionals ready to take and pass their exams.

In 1997 when Exam Cram debuted, it quickly became the best-selling computer book series since "...*For Dummies*," and the best-selling certification book series ever. By maintaining an intense focus on subject matter, tracking errata and updates quickly, and following the certi-fication market closely, Exam Cram established the dominant position in cert prep books.

You will not be disappointed in your decision to purchase this book. If you are, please contact me at etittel@jump.net. All suggestions, ideas, input, or constructive criticism are welcome!

Ed Tittel

This book is dedicated to life outside the office window.

 za

About the Author

Mike Harwood (MCSE, A+, Network+, Server+, Linux+) has held a number of roles in the computer field including PC repair, network management, consulting, and technical writing. Mike is also the coauthor of numerous computer books, including the *Network+ Exam Prep* from Que Publishing. He is also a courseware developer, and a regular technology presenter for CBC Radio. When not working, Mike stays as far away from keyboards as possible.

Drew Bird (MCSE, MCNE, Network+, Linux+, Server+) has been in the IT industry since 1988. Over the years he has designed, implemented, and administered networks of all shapes and sizes. In addition to technical training and consulting assignments, Drew has authored a number of technical articles and is a frequent contributor to technology websites. Away from work, Drew enjoys most outdoor activities but is especially keen on mountain biking, kayaking, and skiing.

About the Technical Reviewers

David L. Prowse is owner of TSR Data, a technology solutions company focusing on security and data communications. He is also the creator of TechnicalBlog.Com, an IT support site.

David has more than a dozen IT certifications, including the CompTIA Network+, which he has beta tested twice since its inception. He has also taught the Net+ course to the FAA, CompUSA, Sungard, and many other companies. His vision is of a world where he can sleep more than a few hours a day.

Acknowledgments

The creation of a book is not a simple process and requires the talents and dedication from many people to make it happen. With this in mind, we would like to thank the folks at Que for their commitment to this project.

Specifically, we would like to say thanks to Steve Rowe, Rhonda Tinch-Mize, and Mandie Frank for keeping the ball rolling, the sentences legible, and of course spotting our mistakes. And finally, thanks to Jeff Riley for overseeing the project with enthusiasm and a sense of humour. We only wish we understood it. Let's not forget the technical editor—David Prowse—who checked and rechecked to ensure that the project stayed on target technically, which was a difficult task considering the number of facts presented and the conflicting information that seems to be part of the networking world. Thanks also to Nathan Cable for jumping in on short notice and providing contributions for the Macintosh and AppleShare sections.

Finally, we are very thankful to our family and friends who once again had to put up with us while we worked our way through this project. And as we said last time (but this time we mean it), "we'll make it up to you."

We Want to Hear from You!

As the reader of this book, *you* are our most important critic and commentator. We value your opinion and want to know what we're doing right, what we could do better, what areas you'd like to see us publish in, and any other words of wisdom you're willing to pass our way.

As an executive editor for Que Publishing, I welcome your comments. You can email or write me directly to let me know what you did or didn't like about this book—as well as what we can do to make our books better.

Please note that I cannot help you with technical problems related to the topic of this book. We do have a User Services group, however, where I will forward specific technical questions related to the book.

When you write, please be sure to include this book's title and author as well as your name, email address, and phone number. I will carefully review your comments and share them with the author and editors who worked on the book.

Email: feedback@quepublishing.com

Mail: Jeff Riley
          Executive Editor
          Que Publishing
          800 East 96th Street
          Indianapolis, IN 46240 USA

For more information about this book or another Que Certification title, visit our website at www.examcram2.com. Type the ISBN (excluding hyphens) or the title of a book in the Search field to find the page you're looking for.

Contents at a Glance

Table of Contents

Chapter 5
TCP/IP (Transmission Control Protocol/Internet Protocol) **111**

Introduction

Welcome to the *Network+ Exam Cram*. This book is designed to prepare you to take—and pass—the CompTIA Network+ exam. The Network+ exam has become the leading introductory-level network certification available today. It is recognized by both employers and industry giants (such as Microsoft and Novell) as providing candidates with a solid foundation of networking concepts, terminology, and skills. The Network+ exam covers a broad range of networking concepts to prepare candidates for those technologies they are likely to be working with in today's network environments.

About *Network+ Exam Cram*

Exam Crams are specifically designed to give you the "what-you-need-to-know" information to prepare for the Network+ exam. They cut through the extra information, focusing on the areas you need to get through the exam. With this in mind, the elements within the *Exam Cram* titles are aimed directly at providing the exam information you need in the most succinct and accessible manner.

In this light, this book is organized to closely follow the actual CompTIA objectives. As such, it is easy to find the information required for each of the specified CompTIA Network+ objectives. The objective focus design used by this Exam Cram is an important feature because the information you need to know is easily identifiable and accessible. To see what we mean, compare the CompTIA objectives to the book's layout, and you will see that the facts are right where you would expect them to be.

Within the chapters themselves, potential exam hotspots are clearly highlighted with *Exam Alerts*. Exam Alerts have been carefully placed to let you know that the surrounding discussion is an important area for the exam. To further help you prepare for the exam, a Cram Sheet is included that can be used in the final stages of test preparation. Be sure to pay close attention to the bulleted points provided in the Cram Sheet, as they pinpoint the technologies and facts you are likely going to encounter on the test.

Finally, great effort has gone into the end-of-chapter questions and practice tests to ensure that they accurately represent the look and feel of the ones you will have on the real Network+ exam. Be sure, before taking the exam, that you are comfortable with both the format and content of the questions provided in this book.

About the Network+ Exam

The Network+ N10-003 exam is a revised version of the original exam. The new Network+ objectives are aimed toward those who have nine months experience in network support and administration. CompTIA believes that new Network+ candidates will require more hands-on experience in network administration and troubleshooting, but this should not discourage those who do not. Quite simply, the nature of the questions on the new exam is not dissimilar to the old, and you can get by without the actual hands-on experience. Still, a little hands-on experience never hurt anyone and will certainly add to your confidence going into the exam.

You will have a maximum of 90 minutes to answer the 72 questions on the exam. The allotted time is quite generous, and, by the time you are finished, you are likely going to have time to double-check a few of the answers you are unsure of. By the time the dust settles, you will need a minimum score of 646 to pass the Network+ exam. This is on a scale of 100 to 900.

One of the best things about the Network+ certification is that after you pass the exam, you are certified for life. There is no need to ever recertify. This fact can make the cost of taking the Network+ exam a little easier to swallow. For more information on the specifics of the Network+ exam, refer to CompTIA's main website at http://www.comptia.org/certification/.

Booking and Taking the Network+ Certification Exam

Unfortunately, testing is not free. You'll be charged $207 for each test you take, whether you pass or fail. In the United States and Canada, tests are administered by Sylvan Prometric or VUE testing services. To book a test with Prometric or locate a Prometric testing center near you, refer to the website at www.2test.com or call directly at 1-800-776-4276. To access the VUE contact information and book an exam, refer to the website at www.vue.com or call directly at 1-877-551-7587. When booking an exam, you will need to identify the following information:

➤ Your name as you would like to have it appear on your certificate.

➤ Your Social Security or Social Insurance number.

➤ Contact phone numbers (to be called in case of a problem).

➤ Mailing address, which identifies the address at which you would like your certificate to be mailed.

➤ Exam number and title.

➤ Email address, once again for contact purposes. This often is the fastest and most effective means of contacting you. Many clients require it for registration.

➤ Credit-card payment to pay online. Vouchers can be redeemed by calling the respective testing center.

What to Expect from the Exam

For those who have not taken a certification test, the process can be a little unnerving. For those who have taken numerous tests, it is not much better. Mastering the inner mental game often can be as much of the battle as knowing the material itself. Knowing what to expect before heading in can make the process a little more comfortable.

Certification tests are administered on a computer system at a Prometric or VUE authorized testing center. The format of the exams is straightforward: Each question has several possible answers to choose from. In fact, the questions in this book provide a very good example of the types of questions you can expect on the actual exam. If you are comfortable with them, the test should hold few surprises. Many of the questions vary in terms of length; some of them are longer scenario questions, whereas others are short and right to the point. Read the questions carefully; the longer questions often have a key point in them that will lead you to the correct answer.

Most of the questions on the Network+ exam require you to choose a single correct answer, but a few will require multiple answers. When there are multiple correct answers, a message at the bottom of the screen prompts you to "choose all that apply." Be sure to read the messages.

A Few Exam Day Details

It is recommended to get to the examination room at least 15 minutes early, although a few minutes earlier certainly would not hurt. This is good strategy used to prepare yourself and to allow the test administrator time to answer any questions you might have before the test begins. Many people suggest that you review the most critical information about the test you're taking just before the test. (*Exam Cram* books provide a reference—the Cram Sheet, located inside the front of this book—that lists the essential information from the book in distilled form.) Arriving a few minutes early will give you some time to compose yourself and to mentally review this critical information.

You will be asked to provide two forms of ID, with one of those being photo ID. Both of the identifications you choose should have a signature. You also might need to sign in when you arrive and sign out when you leave.

Be warned: The rules are very clear about what you can and cannot take into the examination room. Books, laptops, note sheets, and so on, are not allowed in the examination room with you. The test administrator will hold these items, to be returned after you complete the exam. You might receive either a wipe board or a pen and a single piece of paper for making notes during the exam. The test administrator will ensure that no paper is removed from the examination room.

After the Test

Whether you want it or not, as soon as you finish your test, your score is displayed on the computer screen. In addition to the results appearing on the computer screen, a hard copy of the report is printed for you. Like the onscreen report, the hard copy displays the results of your exam and provides a summary of how you did on each section of the exam and on each technology. If you were unsuccessful, this summary can help you determine the areas that you need to brush up on.

When you pass the Network+ exam, you will have earned the Network+ certification and your certificate will be mailed to you within a few weeks. Should you not receive your certificate and information packet within five weeks of passing your exam, please contact CompTIA at fulfillment@comptia.org or call 1-630-268-1818 and ask for the fulfillment department.

Last Minute Exam Tips

Studying for a certification exam really is no different from studying for any other exam, but a few hints and tips can give you the edge come exam day:

➤ **Read all the material**—CompTIA has been known to include material not expressly specified in the objectives. This book has included additional information not reflected in the objectives in an effort to give you the best possible preparation for the examination.

➤ **Watch for the Exam Tips and Notes**—The Network+ objectives include a wide range of technologies. Exam Tips and Notes found throughout each chapter are designed to pull out exam-related hotspots. These can be your best friends when preparing for the exam.

➤ **Use the questions to assess your knowledge**—Don't just read the chapter content; use the exam questions to find out what you know and what you don't. If you are struggling, study some more, review, and then assess your knowledge again.

➤ **Review the exam objectives**—Develop your own questions and examples for each topic listed. If you can develop and answer several questions for each topic, you should not find it difficult to pass the exam.

Remember, at the end of the day, the primary object is not just to pass the exam—it is to understand the material. After you understand the material, passing the exam should be simple. Knowledge is a pyramid; to build upward, you need a solid foundation. This book and the Network+ certification are designed to ensure that you have that solid foundation.

Good luck!

Self-Assessment

We included a self-assessment in this *Exam Cram* to help you evaluate your readiness to tackle the Network+ certification. It is also designed to assist you in understanding the skills and experience needed to successfully pass the CompTIA Network+ certification exam.

Network+ Professionals in the Real World

The next section describes an ideal Network+ candidate, although we know full well that not all candidates will meet this ideal. In fact, the description of that ideal candidate might seem downright scary. But take heart: Increasing numbers of people are attaining CompTIA certifications, so the goal is within reach. You can get all the real-world motivation you need from knowing that many others have gone before you, so you will be able to follow in their footsteps. If you're willing to tackle the process seriously and do what it takes to obtain the necessary experience and knowledge, you can take—and pass—the certification test involved in obtaining a Network+ certification. In fact, we've designed this *Exam Cram* to make it as easy on you as possible to prepare for the exam. But prepare you must!

The same, of course, is true for other CompTIA certifications, including

➤ **A+ certification**—A testing program that certifies the competency of entry-level service technicians in the computer industry. It consists of a core exam and a DOS/Windows exam. It is targeted at computer technicians with six months of experience.

➤ **Linux+ Certification**—Linux continues to develop and expand and today is a common sight in networks of all sizes. The Linux+ certification introduces students to this open source operating system and provides a solid background in Linux including installation, file systems, OS navigation, troubleshooting, managing services, and so on.

➤ **Server+**—The Server+ certification is designed to test a candidate's knowledge of server hardware, server best practices, and server maintenance. Some of the technologies covered include upgrading and repairing server hardware and software, troubleshooting hardware configurations, and best practices when working in the server room.

The Ideal Network+ Candidate

The following list describes some relevant statistics about the background and experience an ideal individual might have. Don't worry if you don't meet these qualifications or don't come that close—this is a far from ideal world, and where you fall short is simply where you'll have more work to do.

➤ Academic or professional training in network theory, concepts, and operations. This includes everything from networking media and transmission techniques to network operating systems, services, and applications.

➤ Between 9 and 24 months of networking experience, including experience with Ethernet, routers, and modems, with particular emphasis on the TCP/IP suite. This must include installation, configuration, upgrading, and troubleshooting experience.

➤ Two-plus years in an internetwork environment that includes hands-on experience with Web servers, email servers, database servers, and DHCP and DNS servers. A solid understanding of each system's architecture, installation, configuration, maintenance, and troubleshooting is also essential.

➤ Experience with the Internet, intranets, and extranets.

➤ Familiarity with client and network operating systems.

➤ Experience working with networking protocols, specifically TCP/IP.

If you were to review all the criteria that go into making an ideal Network+ candidate, you will find that it boils down to practical experience in a technical position involving installation, configuration, and maintenance of networks. We believe that well under half of all certification candidates meet these requirements, and that, in fact, most meet fewer than half of these requirements—at least, when they begin the certification process. But because others who already have been certified have survived this ordeal, you can survive it too—especially if you heed what our self-assessment can tell you about what you already know and what you need to learn.

Put Yourself to the Test

The following series of questions and observations is designed to help you determine how much work you must do to pursue CompTIA Network+ certification and what kinds of resources you may consult on your quest. Be absolutely honest in your answers, or you'll end up wasting money on an exam you're not yet ready to take. There are no right or wrong answers, only steps along the path to certification. Only you can decide where you really belong in the broad spectrum of aspiring candidates.

Two things should be clear from the outset, however:

➤ Even a modest background in computer science will be helpful.

➤ Hands-on experience using network technologies is an important ingredient to certification success—but not mandatory.

Educational Background

1. Have you ever taken any networking concepts or technologies classes? [Yes or No]

   If Yes, proceed to question 2; if No, you might want to augment the material in the *Exam Cram* with a book that approaches the topic of network from an independent point of view and not from a certification point of view. When looking for a suitable title, look for those that explain technologies such as TCP/IP, routing, network design, and others in a clear and concise manner.

2. Do you have experience using and working with a network? [Yes or No]

   If Yes, you will probably be able to better understand CompTIA's Network+ objectives. Even being around networks as a user makes you familiar with how they are designed to function. If you're rusty, brush up on basic networking concepts and terminology—especially networking media as it relates to the TCP/IP suite, network security, dial-up fundamentals, and remote connectivity. Then, proceed to question 3.

   If No, you might need to delve a little deeper into networking concepts. This is as simple as taking a trip to the local bookstore and getting an easy-to-read, up-to-date networking basics title.

3. Do you have experience working with network and client operating systems? [Yes or No]

   If Yes, you are on the right track. Network+ requires knowledge of working with both client-side operating systems such as Windows 98/Me and network-operating systems such as Windows 2000. Knowing how to navigate such OSs can be a benefit when configuring and troubleshooting network connectivity from within an operating system.

If No, crank up a computer with an OS on it and start going through it. Look for the network configuration screens. Look to the help file within the OS for quick tutorials and for help in configuring the client system for network connectivity.

If this sounds like a lot, it isn't. Perhaps the single most important element for the successful completion is a desire to learn all about networking. It is, after all, really quite interesting. Once the desire to learn kicks in, the test becomes that much easier.

Hands-on Experience

CompTIA cites hands-on experience as a key to success on the CompTIA Network+ test. This is true because hands-on experience reinforces what is written in the book. However, Network+ covers a broad range of networking technologies—some of which you might never see in your networking career. In such a case, all you can do is rely on the book knowledge. So can you pass the exam without reinforcing knowledge with practical hands-on experience? Yes. Is it advised? No. Bottom line—the more experience, the better. If we leave you with only one realization after taking this self-assessment, it should be that there's no substitute for time spent installing, configuring, and using the various networking products upon which you'll be tested repeatedly and in depth. If you have never worked with any of the networking products or operating systems mentioned earlier, you would be well advised to review this work at least three or four times.

Testing Your Exam Readiness

Whether you attend a formal class on a specific topic to get ready for an exam or use written materials to study on your own, some preparation for the Network+ certification exam is essential. At $207 a try ($155 for CompTIA members), pass or fail, you want to do everything you can to pass on your first try. That's where studying comes in.

For any given subject, consider taking a class if you've tackled self-study materials, taken the test, and failed anyway. The opportunity to interact with an instructor and fellow students can make all the difference in the world, if you can afford that privilege.

If you can't afford to take a class, try the Training Resources link at www.comptia.com for any pointers to free practice exams. And even if you can't afford to spend much at all, you should still invest in some low-cost practice exams from commercial vendors because they can help you assess your readiness to pass a test better than any other tool.

We have included practice questions at the end of each chapter, plus two practice exams at the end of the book. If you don't do that well on the questions at the end of the chapters, you can study more and then tackle the practice exams. From there, feel free to surf the Web and do a little research on the Network+ exam. Newsgroups are a good place to look because there are a number of people willing to chat about their experiences studying and taking the Network+ exam.

If you take the practice tests and score 85 percent or better, you're probably ready to tackle the real thing. If your score isn't above that crucial threshold, obtain all the free and low-budget practice tests you can find and get to work. Keep at it until you can break the passing threshold comfortably.

When it comes to assessing your test readiness, there is no better way than to take a good-quality practice exam and pass with a score of 85 percent or better. When we're preparing ourselves, we shoot for 90-plus percent, just to leave room for the "weirdness factor" that sometimes shows up on CompTIA exams.

Because the Internet is the most rapidly changing segment of Information Technology (IT), the test might change, but this book's material is sufficiently comprehensive that it will be a good preparation tool regardless. Also, you should be aware that CompTIA and other certifications reserve the right to a function known as *slipstreaming*, in which questions are removed and new ones are added without announcement. We scoured the latest trends and interviewed many industry veterans in an attempt to prepare you for the inevitable changes that will occur.

Onward, Through the Fog!

Once you've assessed your readiness, undertaken the right background studies, obtained the hands-on experience that will help you understand the technologies at work, and reviewed the many sources of information to help you prepare for a test, you'll be ready to take a round of practice tests. When your scores come back positive enough to get you through the exam, you're ready to go after the real thing. If you follow our assessment regime, you'll not only know what you need to study, but also when you're ready to make a test date at Prometric or VUE.

Good luck!

Introduction to Networking

Objectives

1.1 Recognize the following logical or physical network topologies given a diagram, schematic, or description:

- ✓ Star
- ✓ Bus
- ✓ Mesh
- ✓ Ring
- ✓ Wireless

1.2 Specify the main features of 802.2 (Logical Link Control), 802.3 (Ethernet), 802.5 (token ring), 802.11 (wireless), and FDDI (Fiber Distributed Data Interface) networking technologies, including

- ✓ Speed
- ✓ Access method (CSMA/CA (Carrier Sense Multiple Access/Collision Avoidance) and CSMA/CD(Carrier Sense Multiple Access/Collision Detection))
- ✓ Topology
- ✓ Media

1.7 Specify the general characteristics (for example, carrier speed, frequency, transmission type, and topology) of the following wireless technologies:

- ✓ 802.11 (Frequency hopping spread spectrum)
- ✓ 802.11x (Direct sequence spread spectrum)
- ✓ Infrared
- ✓ Bluetooth

1.8 Identify factors that affect the range and speed of wireless service (for example, interference, antenna type, and environmental factors)

What you need to know

- ✓ Understand the differences between local area networks (LANs), wide area networks (WANs), and personal area networks (PANs)
- ✓ Identify the characteristics between peer-to-peer and client/server networking
- ✓ Identify the characteristics of various network topologies
- ✓ Understand the characteristics of the following IEEE standards: 802.2, 802.3, 802.5, and 802.11
- ✓ Identify the characteristics of Fiber Distributed Data Interface (FDDI)
- ✓ Understand the impact of interference on Wireless communications

Introduction

There are a variety of physical and logical network layouts in use today. As a network administrator, you might find yourself working on these different network layouts or topologies and, as such, will require knowledge of how they are designed to function.

This chapter reviews general network considerations such as the various topologies used on today's networks, LANs, PANs, and WANs, and the IEEE standards.

LANs, WANs, and PANs

Networks are classified according to their geographical coverage and size. The two most common network classifications are local area networks (LANs) and wide area networks (WANs).

LANs

A *LAN* is a data network that is restricted to a single geographical location and typically encompasses a relatively small area such as an office building or school. The function of the LAN is to interconnect workstation computers for the purposes of sharing files and resources. Because of its localized nature, the LAN is typically high speed and cheaper to set up than a WAN. Figure 1.1 shows an example of a LAN.

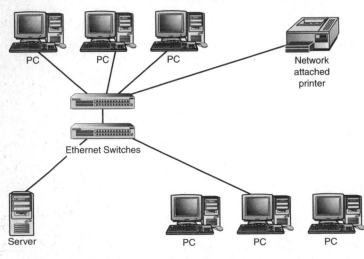

Figure 1.1 Local area network.

WANs

A *WAN* is a network that spans more than one geographical location often connecting separated LANs. WANs are slower than LANs and often require additional and costly hardware such as routers, dedicated leased lines, and complicated implementation procedures. Figure 1.2 shows an example of a WAN.

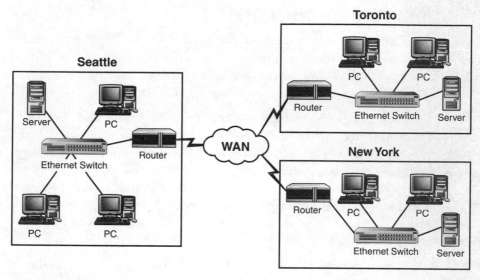

Figure 1.2   Wide area network.

PANs

Wireless technologies have introduced a new term—Wireless Personal Area Networks (WPAN). WPAN refers to the technologies involved in connecting devices in very close proximity to exchange data or resources. An example of this can be seen through connecting a laptop with a PDA to synchronize an address book. Because of their small size and the nature of the data exchange, WPAN devices lend themselves well to ad hoc networking. Ad hoc networks are those that have devices connect directly to each other and not through a wireless access point. Ad hoc wireless networks are discussed later in this chapter.

Because of the close proximity of WPAN networking, short-range wireless technologies are typically used. This includes Bluetooth and Infrared. The key WPAN technology supported in Windows XP Professional, for example, is Infrared Data Association (IrDA). In addition, the IEEE wireless standards, including 802.11b/g, can be used to create a WPAN.

Network Models

There are two basic wired network models from which to choose—the peer-to-peer network model and the client/server model. The model used for a network is determined by several factors, including how the network will be used, how many users will be on the network, and budgetary considerations.

Peer-to-peer Networking

A *peer-to-peer network* is a decentralized network model offering no centralized storage of data or centralized control over the sharing of files or resources. All systems on a peer-to-peer network can share the resources on their local computer as well as use resources of other systems.

Peer-to-peer networks are cheaper and easier to implement than client/server networks, making them an ideal solution for environments in which budgets are a concern. The peer-to-peer model does not work well with large numbers of computer systems. As a peer-to-peer network grows, it becomes increasingly complicated to navigate and access files and resources connected to each computer because they are distributed throughout the network. Further, the lack of centralized data storage makes it difficult to locate and back up key files.

Peer-to-peer networks are typically found in small offices or in residential settings where only a limited number of computers will be attached and only a few files and resources shared. A general rule of thumb is to have no more than 10 computers connected to a peer-to-peer network.

Client/Server Networking Model

The client/server networking model is, without question, the most widely implemented model and the one you are most likely to encounter when working in real-world environments. The advantages of the client/server system stem from the fact that it is a centralized model. It allows for centralized network management of all network services, including user management, security, and backup procedures.

A client/server network often requires technically skilled personnel to implement and manage the network. This and the cost of a dedicated server hardware and software increase the cost of the client/server model. Despite this, the advantages of the centralized management, data storage, administration, and security make it the network model of choice. Table 1.1 summarizes the characteristics of the peer-to-peer and client/server network models.

The role of the client computer in the client/server model is to request the data from the server and present that data to the users.

Table 1.1 Comparison of Networking Models		
Attribute	**Peer-to-Peer Network**	**Client/Server Network**
Size	Restricted to a maximum of 10 computers.	The size of the network is limited only by server size and network hardware, and it can have thousands of connected systems.
Administration	Each individual is responsible for the administration of his or her own system. A administrator is not needed.	A skilled network administrator is often required to maintain and manage the network.
Security	Each individual is responsible for maintaining security for shared files or resources connected to the system.	Security is managed from a central location but often requires a skilled administrator to correctly configure.
Cost	Minimal startup and implementation cost.	Requires dedicated equipment and specialized hardware and administration, increasing the cost of the network.
Implementation	Easy to configure and set up.	Often requires complex setup procedures and skilled staff to set up.

Centralized and Distributed Computing

The terms centralized and distributed computing are used to describe where the network processing takes place. In a *centralized computing model*, one system provides both the data storage and the processing power for client systems. This networking model is most often associated with computer mainframes and dumb terminals, where no processing or storage capability exists at the workstation. These network environments are rare, but they do still exist.

A distributed network model has the processing power distributed between the client systems and the server. Most modern networks use the distributed network model, where client workstations share in the processing responsibilities.

Network Topologies

A *topology* refers to both the physical and logical layout of a network. The *physical* topology of a network refers to the actual layout of the computer cables and other network devices. The *logical* topology of a network, on the other hand, refers to the way in which the network appears to the devices that use it.

Several topologies are in use for networks today. Some of the more common include the bus, ring, star, mesh, and wireless topologies. The following sections provide an overview of each.

Bus Topology

A *bus network* uses a trunk or backbone to which all of the computers on the network connect. Systems connect to this backbone using *T connectors* or taps. To avoid signal reflection, a physical bus topology requires that each end of the physical bus be terminated. Figure 1.3 shows an example of a physical bus topology.

Loose or missing terminators from a bus network will disrupt data transmissions.

Figure 1.3 Physical bus topology.

The most common implementation of a linear bus is the IEEE 802.3 standard. Table 1.2 summarizes the advantages and disadvantages of the bus topology.

Table 1.2 Advantages and Disadvantages of the Bus Topology	
Advantages	**Disadvantages**
Compared to other topologies, a bus is cheap and easy to implement.	There might be network disruption when computers are added or removed.
Requires less cable than other topologies.	Because all systems on the network connect to a single backbone, a break in the cable will prevent all systems from accessing the network.
Does not use any specialized network equipment.	Difficult to troubleshoot.

Ring Topology

The *ring topology* is actually a logical ring, meaning that the data travels in circular fashion from one computer to another on the network. It is not a physical ring topology. Figure 1.4 shows the logical layout of a ring network.

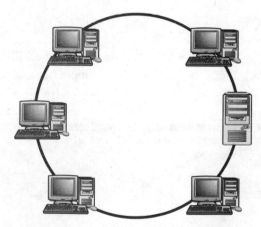

Figure 1.4   Logical design of the ring network.

In a true ring topology, if a single computer or section of cable fails, there is an interruption in the signal. The entire network becomes inaccessible. Network disruption can also occur when computers are added or removed from the network, making it an impractical network design in environments where there is constant change to the network.

Ring networks are most commonly wired in a star configuration. In a Token Ring network, a multistation access unit (MSAU) is equivalent to a hub or switch on an Ethernet network. The MSAU performs the token circulation internally. To create the complete ring, the ring in (RI) port on each MSAU is connected to the ring out (RO) port on another MSAU. The last MSAU in the ring is then connected to the first, to complete the ring. Table 1.3 summarizes the advantages and disadvantages of the ring topology.

Table 1.3 Advantages and Disadvantages of the Ring Topology	
Advantages	**Disadvantages**
Cable faults are easily located, making troubleshooting easier.	Expansion to the network can cause network disruption.
Ring networks are moderately easy to install.	A single break in the cable can disrupt the entire network.

Star Topology

In the *star topology*, all computers and other network devices connect to a central device called a *hub* or *switch*. Each connected device requires a single cable to be connected to the hub, creating a point-to-point connection between the device and the hub.

Using a separate cable to connect to the hub allows the network to be expanded without disruption to the network. A break in any single cable will not cause the entire network to fail. Figure 1.5 provides an example of a star topology.

Among the network topologies discussed in this chapter, the star topology is the easiest to expand in terms of the number of devices connected to the network.

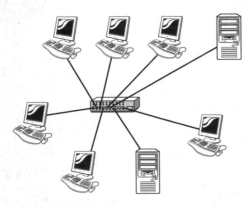

Figure 1.5 Star topology.

The star topology is the most widely implemented network design in use today, but it is not without its shortcomings. Because all devices connect to a centralized hub, this creates a single point of failure for the network. If the hub fails, any device connected to it will not be able to access the network. Because of the number of cables required and the need for network devices, the cost of a star network is often higher than other topologies. Table 1.4 summarizes the advantages and disadvantages of the star topology.

Table 1.4 Advantages and Disadvantages of the Star Topology	
Advantages	Disadvantages
Star networks are easily expanded without disruption to the network.	Requires more cable than most of the other topologies.
Cable failure affects only a single user.	A central connecting device allows for a single point of failure.
Easy to troubleshoot and isolate problems.	More difficult than other topologies to implement.

Mesh Topology

The *mesh topology* incorporates a unique network design in which each computer on the network connects to every other, creating a point-to-point connection between every device on the network. The purpose of the mesh design is to provide a high level of *redundancy*. If one network cable fails, the data always has an alternative path to get to its destination. Figure 1.6 shows the mesh topology.

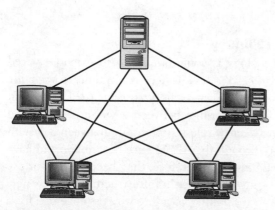

Figure 1.6   Mesh topology.

As you can see from Figure 1.6, the wiring for a mesh network can be very complicated. Further, the cabling costs associated with the mesh topology can be high, and troubleshooting a failed cable can be tricky. Because of this, the mesh topology is rarely used. A variation on a true mesh topology is the hybrid mesh. It creates a redundant point-to-point network connection between only specific network devices. The hybrid mesh is most often seen in WAN implementations. Table 1.5 summarizes the advantages and disadvantages of the mesh topology.

 Because of the redundant connections, the mesh topology offers better fault tolerance than other topologies.

Table 1.5   Advantages and Disadvantages of the Mesh Topology

Advantages	Disadvantages
Provides redundant paths between devices.	Requires more cable than the other LAN topologies.
The network can be expanded without disruption to current users.	Complicated implementation.

Wireless Topology

Wireless networks are typically implemented using one of two wireless topologies: the *infrastructure*, or managed, wireless topology and the *ad-hoc*, or unmanaged, wireless topology.

Infrastructure Wireless Topology

The infrastructure wireless topology is commonly used to extend a wired LAN to include wireless devices. Wireless devices communicate with the wired LAN through a base station known as an *access point (AP)* or *wireless access point (WAP)*. The AP forms a bridge between a wireless and wired LAN, and all transmissions between wireless stations, or between a system and a wired network client, go through the AP. APs are not mobile and have to stay connected to the wired network; therefore, they become part of the wired network infrastructure—thus the name. In infrastructure wireless networks, there might be several access points providing wireless coverage for a large area or only a single access point for a small area such as a single home or small building.

Ad Hoc Wireless Networking

In a wireless ad hoc topology, devices communicate directly between themselves without using an access point. This peer-to-peer network design is commonly used to connect a small number of computers or wireless devices. As an example, an ad hoc wireless network may be set up temporarily between laptops in a boardroom or to connect to systems in a home instead of a wired solution. The ad-hoc wireless design provides a quick method to share files and resources between a small number of systems. Figure 1.7 compares the ad hoc and infrastructure wireless network designs.

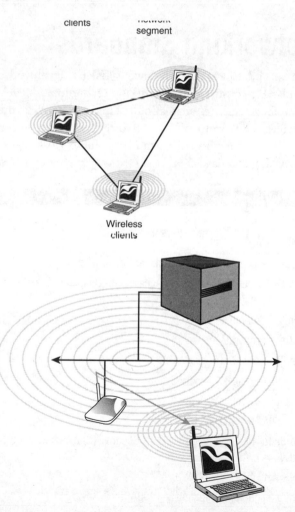

Figure 1.7 Comparing wireless topologies.

Ad hoc Wireless Topology The ad hoc, or unmanaged, network design does not use an AP. All wireless devices connect directly to each other.

In an infrastructure Wireless network, devices use a wireless access point (WAP) to connect to the network.

IEEE and Networking Standards

The Institute of Electrical and Electronic Engineers (IEEE) developed a series of networking standards to ensure that networking technologies developed by respective manufacturers are compatible. This means that the cabling, networking devices, and protocols are all interchangeable when designed under the banner of a specific IEEE standard. Table 1.6 summarizes the IEEE 802 networking standards.

Table 1.6 IEEE 802 Networking Standards	
Specification	**Name**
802.1	Internetworking
802.2	The LLC (Logical Link Control) sublayer
802.3	CSMA/CD (Carrier Sense Multiple Access with Collision Detection) for Ethernet networks
802.4	A token passing bus
802.5	Token Ring networks
802.6	Metropolitan Area Network (MAN)
802.7	Broadband Technical Advisory Group
802.8	Fiber-Optic Technical Advisory Group
802.9	Integrated Voice and Data Networks
802.10	Standards for Interoperable LAN/MAN Security (SILS) (Network Security)
802.11	Wireless networks
802.12	100Mbps technologies, including 100BASEVG-AnyLAN

Only a few of the standards listed in Table 1.6 are tested on the CompTIA exam. The standards that are specifically included in the CompTIA objectives are 802.2, 802.3, 802.5, and 802.11. Each of these IEEE specifications outlines specific characteristics for LAN networking, including the speed, topology, cabling, and access method. The following sections outline the key features of these IEEE specifications and the specific characteristics of each.

802.2 IEEE Standard

The 802.2 standard, referred to as the Logical Link Control (LLC), manages data flow control and error control for the other IEEE LAN standards. Data flow control regulates how much data can be transmitted in a certain amount of time. Error control refers to the recognition and notification of damaged signals. The LLC layer is discussed more in Chapter 4, "OSI Model and Network Protocols."

802.3 IEEE Standard

The IEEE 802.3 standard defines the characteristics for Ethernet networks. Ethernet networking is by far the most widely implemented form of local area networking. Several Ethernet LAN characteristics are identified in the 802.3 standard.

Since the development of the original 802.3 standards, there have also been several additions that have been assigned new designators. These standards are often referred to as the 802.3x standards. Some of the newer standards include 802.3u for Fast Ethernet, 802.3z for Gigabit Ethernet, and 802.3ae for 10-Gigabit Ethernet. The features for 802.3 are listed here:

➤ **Speed**—The original IEEE 802.3 standard specified a network transfer rate of 10Mbps. There have been modifications to the standard, the result being Fast Ethernet (802.3u), which can transmit network data up to 100Mbps and higher, as well as Gigabit Ethernet (802.3z), which can transmit at speeds up to 1000Mbps. 802.3ae is a very fast 803.3 standard. Known as 10-Gigabit Ethernet, it offers speeds 10 times that of Gigabit Ethernet.

➤ **Topology**—The original Ethernet networks used a bus or star topology because the original 802.3 standard included specifications for both twisted pair and coaxial cabling. The IEEE 802.3u and 802.3z specify twisted pair cabling and use a star topology. Remember that even when Ethernet uses a physical star topology, it uses a logical bus topology.

➤ **Media**—The media refers to the physical cabling used to transmit the signal around the network. The original 802.3 specifications identified coaxial and twisted pair cabling to be used. The more modern standards specify twisted pair and fiber-optic cable. 802.3ae currently only supports fiber media.

➤ **Access method**—The access method refers to the way that the network media is accessed. Ethernet networks use a system called *Carrier Sense Multiple Access with Collision Detection (CSMA/CD)*. CSMA/CD works by monitoring the computers that are sending data on the network. If two computers transmit data at the same time, a data collision will occur. To prevent collisions, the systems sending the data will be required to wait a period of time and then retransmit the data to avoid the collision. 10-Gigbit Ethernet only operates in full-duplex mode and, as such, does not need to use the traditional Ethernet CSMA/CD access method.

One of the shortcomings of CSMA/CD is that as more systems are added to the network, the likelihood of collisions increases and the network becomes slower.

802.5 IEEE Standard

The IEEE 802.5 standard specifies the characteristics for Token Ring networks. Token Ring was introduced by IBM in the mid-1980s and quickly became the network topology of choice until the rise in popularity of Ethernet. It is unlikely that you will encounter a ring network in your travels and even more unlikely that you will be implementing a ring network as a new installation. For what it's worth, Token Ring is a solid network system, but Ethernet has all but eliminated it.

The following is a list of the specific characteristics specified in the 802.5 standard:

➤ **Speed**—The 802.5 Token Ring specifies network speeds of 4 and 16Mbps.

➤ **Topology**—Token Ring networks use a logical ring topology and most often a physical star. The logical ring is often created in the multistation access unit (MSAU).

➤ **Media**—Token Ring networks use unshielded twisted pair cabling or shielded twisted pair. More information on the specific characteristics of twisted pair cabling is covered in Chapter 2, "Cabling and Connectors."

➤ **Access method**—802.5 specifies an access method known as *token passing*. On a Token Ring network, only one computer at a time can transmit data. When a computer has data to send, it must use a special type of packet known as a *token*. The token travels around the network looking for computers with data to send. The computer's data is passed along with the token until it gets to the destination computer—at which point, the data is removed from the token and the empty token placed back on the ring.

All network cards on a Token Ring network must operate at the same speed.

FDDI

The American National Standards Institute (ANSI) developed the *Fiber Distributed Data Interface (FDDI)* standard in the mid-1980s to meet the growing need for a reliable and fast networking system to accommodate distributed applications. FDDI uses a ring network design, but, unlike the traditional 802.5 standard, FDDI uses a dual ring technology for fault tolerance. Because of the dual ring design, FDDI is not susceptible to a single cable failure like the regular 802.5 IEEE standard. Figure 1.8 shows an FDDI network with a dual ring configuration.

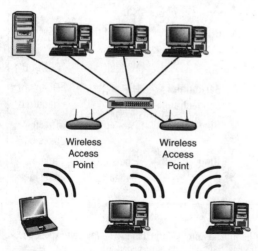

Wireless Access Point   Wireless Access Point

Computer

Figure 1.8   FDDI network.

As with any of the other standards, FDDI has specific characteristics:

➤ **Speed**—FDDI transmits data at 100Mbps and higher.

➤ **Topology**—FDDI uses a dual ring topology for fault-tolerant reasons.

➤ **Media**—FDDI uses fiber-optic cable that enables data transmissions that exceed two kilometers. Additionally, it is possible to use FDDI protocols over copper wire known as the Copper Distributed Data Interface (CDDI).

➤ **Access method**—Similar to 802.5, FDDI uses a token-passing access method.

Table 1.7 summarizes each of the wired standards discussed in the previous sections.

Table 1.7	IEEE 802 Network Standards				
Standard	**Speed**	**Physical Topology**	**Logical Topology**	**Media**	**Access Method**
802.3	10Mbps		Bus and Star	Coaxial and twisted pair	CSMA/CD
802.3u	100Mbps (Fast Ethernet)	Star	Bus	Twisted pair	CSMA/CD
802.3z	1000Mbps	Star	Bus	Twisted pair	CSMA/CD
802.3ae	10-Gigabit		Backbone connections	N/A	Fiber/Not Required
802.5	4Mbps and 16Mbps	Star	Ring	Twisted pair	Token passing
FDDI	100Mbps	Dual ring	Ring	Fiber-optic Twisted pair (CDDI) .	Token passing

Pay close attention to the information provided in Table 1.7. You can expect questions on the Network+ exam based on the details provided in the table.

802.11 IEEE Standards

The 802.11 standards specify the characteristics of wireless LAN Ethernet networks. Under the banner of 802.11, there are four common wireless standards. These include 802.11, 802.11a, 802.11b and 802.11g. Each of these wireless standards identifies several characteristics. Here is a review of the 802.11 wireless standards and characteristics:

➤ **Speed**—802.11 standards are measured in Mbps and vary between network standards.

➤ **Media**—The 802.11 standards use radio frequency (RF) as a transmission media. Depending on the standard, radio frequencies include 2.4GHz and 5GHz.

➤ **Topology**—802.11 wireless standards can be implemented in an ad-hoc or infrastructure topology.

➤ **Access method**—802.11 uses Carrier Sense Multiple Access/Collision Avoidance (CSMA/CA). CSMA/CA is a variation on the CSMA/CD access method. CSMA/CA access method uses a "listen before talking" strategy. Any system wanting to transmit data must first verify that the channel is clear before transmitting, thereby avoiding potential collisions.

➤ **Spread Spectrum**—Spread spectrum refers to the manner in which data signals travel through a radio frequency. Spread spectrum requires that data signals either alternate between carrier frequencies or constantly change their data pattern. Spread spectrum is designed to trade off bandwidth efficiency for reliability, integrity, and security.

➤ **Range**—802.11 wireless standards each specify a transmission range. The range is influenced by many factors such as obstacles or weather.

The following is a look at the various 802.11 standards and their characteristics.

IEEE 802.11—There were actually two variations on the initial 802.11 standard. Both offered 1 or 2Mbps transmission speeds and the same Radio Frequency (RF) of 2.4GHz. The difference between the two was in the way in which data traveled through the RF media. One used frequency hopping spread spectrum (FHSS), and the other, direct sequence spread spectrum (DSSS).

IEEE 802.11a—In terms of speed, the 802.11a standard was far ahead of the original standards. 802.11a specified speeds of up to 54Mbps in the 5GHz band; but most commonly, communications takes place at 6Mbps, 12Mbps, or 24Mbps. 802.11a is not compatible with other wireless standards 802.11b and 802.11g. These standards are heavily favored to the 802.11a standard.

IEEE 802.11b—The 802.11b standard provides for a maximum transmission speed of 11Mbps. However, devices are designed to be backward compatible with previous standards that provided for speeds of 1-, 2-, and 5.5Mbps. 802.11b uses a 2.4GHz RF range and is compatible with 802.11g.

IEEE 802.11g—802.11g is a popular wireless standard today. 802.11g offers wireless transmission over distances of 150 feet and speeds up to 54Mbps compared with the 11 megabits per second of the 802.11b standard. Like 802.11b, 802.11g operates in the 2.4GHz range, and is thus compatible with it.

Each wireless standard has an associated speed. For instance, 802.11g lists a speed of up to 54Mbps. This number represents the pure data rate. However, in network data transmissions, many factors prevent the actual speeds from reaching this rate including data packet information, number of systems, and collisions on the network and interference. Once these are applied to the data rate, the actual speed is often less than half the data rate. Throughput represents the actual speed to expect from wireless transmissions.

Infrared Wireless Networking

Infrared has been around for a long time; perhaps our first experience with it was the TV remote. The command entered onto the remote control travels over an infrared light wave to the receiver on the TV. Infrared technology has progressed, and today infrared development in networking is managed by the Infrared Data Association (IrDA).

IrDA wireless networking uses infrared beams to send data transmissions between devices. Infrared wireless networking offers higher transmission rates reaching 10Mbps to 16Mbps.

Infrared provides a secure, low-cost, convenient cable replacement technology. It is well suited for many specific applications and environments. Some of the key infrared points are included here:

➤ Infrared provides adequate speeds, up to 16Mbps.

➤ A directed infrared system provides a very limited range of approximately 3 feet and typically is used for a PAN.

➤ Infrared devices use less power and a decreased drain on batteries.

➤ Infrared is a secure medium. Infrared signals typically travel short range between devices, which eliminates the problem of eavesdropping or signal tampering.

➤ Infrared is a proven technology. Infrared devices have been available for quite some time and, as such, are a proven, non-proprietary technology with an established user and support base.

➤ Infrared has no radio frequency interference issues or signal conflicts.

➤ Infrared replaces cables for many devices such as keyboards, mice, and other peripherals.

➤ Infrared uses a dispersed mode or a direct line of sight transmission.

Infrared is designed for point-to-point cable replacement.

Bluetooth

Bluetooth is a wireless standard used for many purposes including connecting peripheral devices to a system. Bluetooth uses a low-cost, short-range radio link to create a link to replace many of the cords that used to connect devices.

Bluetooth-enabled devices support transmissions distances of up to 10 or so meters using an ad-hoc network design. Bluetooth establishes the link using an RF-based media and does not require a direct line of sight to make a connection. The Bluetooth Standard defines a short RF link capable of voice or data transmission up to a maximum capacity of 720Kb/s per channel.

Bluetooth operates at 2.4 to 2.48GHz and uses a spread spectrum, frequency-hopping technology. The signal hops can hop between 79 frequencies at 1MHz intervals to give a high degree of interference immunity.

For implementation purposes, Bluetooth provides solutions for three primary areas—cable replacement, ad-hoc networking, and data and access points.

As an established technology, Bluetooth has many advantages, but the speed of 720Kbps is limiting. The newest version of Bluetooth, Bluetooth 2.0, will increase overall speed to a data rate of 3Mbps. This speed might still be significantly slower than 802.11b or g, but for an easily configured, cable replacement technology, it is an attractive option.

Spread Spectrum Technology

Spread spectrum refers to the manner in which data signals travel through a radio frequency. Spread spectrum requires that data signals either alternate between carrier frequencies or constantly change their data pattern. Although the shortest distance between two points is a straight line (narrowband), spread spectrum is designed to trade-off bandwidth efficiency for reliability, integrity, and security. There are two types of spread spectrum radio: frequency hopping and direct sequence.

FHSS requires the use of narrowband signals that change frequencies in a predictable pattern. The term *frequency hopping* refers to hopping of data signals between narrow channels. Somewhere between 20 and several hundred milliseconds, the signal hops to a new channel following a predetermined cyclic pattern.

Because data signals using FHSS switch between RF bands, they have a strong resistance to interference and environmental factors. The constant hopping between channels also increases security as signals are harder to eavesdrop on.

DSSS transmissions spread the signal over a full transmission frequency spectrum. For every bit of data that is sent, a redundant bit pattern is also sent. This 32-bit pattern is called a *chip*. These redundant bits of data provide for both security and delivery assurance. Transmissions are so safe and reliable simply because the system sends so many redundant copies of the data and only a single copy is required to have complete transmission of the data or information. DSSS can minimize the effects of interference and background noise.

Lesser known than DSSS and FHSS RF technologies is OFDM. OFDM is associated with 802.11a wireless networks and is a method of modulation in which a signal is split into several narrowband channels at different frequencies.

FHSS, DSSS, and 802.11 Standards

The original 802.11 standard had two variations—both offering the same speeds but differing in the RF spread spectrum used. One of the 802.11 used FHSS. This 802.11 variant used the 2.4GHz radio frequency band and operated with a 1 or 2Mbps data rate. Since this original standard, wireless implementations have favored DSSS.

The second 802.11 variation used DSSS and specified a 2Mbps-peak data rate with optional fallback to 1Mbps in very noisy environments. 802.11, 802.11b, and 802.11g use the DSSS spread spectrum. This means that the underlying modulation scheme is very similar between each standard, enabling all DSSS systems to coexist with 2, 11, and 54Mbps 802.11

standards. Because of the underlying differences between 802.11a and the 802.11b/g, they are not compatible.

Table 1.8 summarizes each of the wired standards discussed in the previous sections.

Table 1.8	IEEE 802 Wireless Network Standards					
IEEE Standard	**Frequency/ Media**	**Speed**	**Topology**	**Transmission Range**	**Access Method**	**Spread Spectrum**
802.11	2.4GHz RF	1 to 2Mbps	Ad-hoc/ infra-structure		CSMA/CA	DSSS
802.11	2.4GHz RF	1 to 2Mbps	Ad-hoc/ infra-structure		CSMA/CA	FHSS
802.11a	5GHz	Up to 54Mbps	Ad-hoc/ infra-structure	25 to 75 feet indoors range can be affected by building materials	CSMA/CA	OFDM
802.11b	2.4GHz	Up to 11Mbps	Ad-hoc/ infra-structure	Up to 150 feet indoors; range can be affected by building materials	CSMA/CA	DSSS
802.11g	2.4GHz	Up to 54Mbps	Ad-hoc/ infra-structure	Up to 150 feet indoors; range can be affected by building materials	CSMA/CA	DSSS
IrDA	Infrared light beam	Up to 16Mbps	Ad-hoc	1 meter	N/A	N/A
Bluetooth	2.4GHz RF	720Kbps	Ad-hoc	10 meters	N/A	FHSS

Pay close attention to the information provided in Table 1.8. You can expect questions on the Network+ exam based on the details provided in the table.

Establishing Communications Between Wireless Devices

Infrastructure Wireless communication involves the use of two major components—the client device and an access point, or AP. The AP acts as a bridge between the client or station and the wired network.

As with other forms of network communication, before transmissions between devices can occur, the wireless access point and the client must first begin to talk to each other. In the wireless world, this is a two-step process involving association and authentication.

The association process occurs when a wireless adapter is first turned on. The client adapter will immediately begin to scan across the wireless frequencies for wireless APs or if using ad hoc mode, other wireless devices. When the wireless client is configured to operate in infrastructure mode, the user can choose a wireless AP with which to connect. The wireless adapter switches to the assigned channel of the selected wireless AP and negotiates the use of a port.

The authentication process requires that a keyed security measure be negotiated between the AP and the client. The keyed authentication setting can be set to either shared key authentication or open authentication. On many wireless devices, the default setting is set to open authentication. Open authentication requires identity verification between the wireless client and the AP. When set to shared key mode, the client must meet security requirements before communication with the AP can occur.

NOTE | The 802.11 standard allows a wireless client to roam between multiple APs. An AP will transmit a beacon signal every so many milliseconds and includes a time stamp for client synchronization and an indication of supported data rates. A client system will use the beacon message to identify the strength of the existing connection to an AP. If the connection is too weak, the roaming client will attempt to associate itself with a new AP. This allows the client system to roam between distances and APs.

Several components combine to enable wireless communications between devices. Each of these must be configured on both the client and the AP.

➤ **The Service Set Identifier (SSID)**—Whether your wireless network is using infrastructure mode or ad-hoc mode, an SSID is required. The SSID is a configurable client identification that allows clients to communicate to a particular base station. Only clients systems that are configured with the same SSID as the AP can communicate with it. SSIDs provide a simple password arrangement between base stations and clients.

➤ **Wireless Channel**—RF channels are important parts of wireless communications. A channel refers to the band of frequency used for the wireless communication. Each standard specifies the channels that can be used. The 802.11a standard specifies radio frequencies ranges between 5.15 and 5.875GHz. In contrast, 802.11b and 802.11g standards operate between the 2.4 to 2.497GHz ranges. Fourteen channels are defined in the IEEE 802.11b/g channel set; 11 of which are available in North America.

➤ **Security Features**—IEEE 802.11 provides for security using two methods, authentication and encryption. Authentication refers to the verification of client system. In the infrastructure mode, authentication is established between an AP and each station. Wireless encryption services must be the same on the client and the AP for communication to occur.

NOTE Wireless devices ship with default SSIDs, security settings, channels, passwords, and usernames. To protect yourself, it is strongly recommended to change these default settings. Today, many Internet sites list the default settings used by manufacturers with their wireless devices. This information is used by people who want to gain unauthorized access to your wireless devices.

Factors Affecting Wireless Signals

Because wireless signals travel through the atmosphere, they are susceptible to different types of interference than with standard wires networks. Interference weakens wireless signals and is therefore an important consideration when working with wireless networking.

Interference Types

Wireless interference is an important consideration when planning a wireless network. Interference is unfortunately inevitable, but the trick is to minimize the levels of interference. Wireless LAN communications are typically based on radio frequency signals that require a clear and unobstructed transmission path.

What are some of the factors that cause interference?

➤ **Physical objects**—Trees, masonry, buildings, and other physical structures are some of the most common sources of interference. The density of the materials used in a building's construction determines the number of walls the RF signal can pass through and still maintain adequate coverage. Concrete and steel walls are particularly difficult for a signal to pass through. These structures will weaken or, at times, completely prevent wireless signals.

➤ **Radio frequency interference**—Wireless technologies such as 802.11b/g use RF range of 2.4GHz, and so do many other devices such as cordless phones, microwaves, and so on. Devices that share the channel can cause noise and weaken the signals.

➤ **Electrical interference**—Electrical interference comes from devices such as computers, fridges, fans, lighting fixtures, or any other motorized devices. The impact that electrical interference has on the signal depends on the proximity of the electrical device to the wireless access point. Advances in wireless technologies and in electrical devices have reduced the impact these types of devices have on wireless transmissions.

➤ **Environmental factors**—Weather conditions can have a huge impact on wireless signal integrity. Lighting, for instance, can cause electrical interference, and fog can weaken signals as they pass through.

Some of the equipment and materials that can interfere with wireless LAN transmissions include

Equipment such as cordless phones or microwaves that produce radio waves in the 2.4 or 5.2GHz range

RF noise caused by two wireless LANs operating in close proximity

Outdoor broadcast television used by mobile television cameras

Uninterruptible power supply (UPS) devices

Large objects such as pine trees

Fluorescent lights

Heavy machinery

Heavy-duty motors found in elevators or other large devices

Plants and trees

Close proximity to smaller electric devices such as computers or air conditioners

Transformers

This is not an exhaustive list, but it shows how wireless signals can be influenced by many different factors.

Wireless Antennas

A wireless antenna is an integral part of the overall wireless communication. Antennas come in many different shapes and sizes with each one designed for a specific purpose. Selecting the right antenna for a particular network implementation is a critical consideration and one that could ultimately decide how successful a wireless implementation will be. In addition, using the right antennas can save money as networking costs because you'll need fewer antennas and access points.

When a wireless signal is low and being influenced by heavy interference, it might be possible to upgrade the antennas to create a more solid wireless connection. To determine the strength of an antenna, we refer to its gain value.

An antenna's *gain* is a measure of how well the antenna will send or pick up a radio signal. The gain value is measured in decibels-isotropic, or dBi. The gain value of an antenna is a unit of comparison to a reference—that reference being an isotropic antenna. An *isotropic* antenna is an antenna that sends signals equally in all directions (including up and down). An antenna that does this has a 0dBi gain.

An antenna's rating (gain) is the difference between the 0db isotropic antenna and the actual antenna rating. As an example, a wireless antenna advertised as a 15-dBi antenna is 15 times stronger than the hypothetical isotropic antenna.

The initials "dB" reference decibels, and the "i" references the isotropic antenna. dBi is a unit measuring how much better the antenna is compared to isotropic signals.

When looking at wireless antennas, remember that a higher gain rating means stronger sent and received signals. In terms of performance, the rule of thumb is that every 3dBi of gain added doubles the effective power output of an antenna.

Antenna Coverage

When selecting an antenna for a particular wireless implementation, it is necessary to determine the type of coverage used by an antenna. In a typical configuration, a wireless antenna can be either omni directional or directional.

An omni directional antenna is designed to provide a 360-degree dispersed wave pattern. This type of antenna is used when coverage in all directions from the antenna is required. Omni directional antennas are good to use when a broad-based signal is required. Because of the dispersed nature of omni directional antennas, the signal is weaker overall and therefore accommodates shorter signal distances. Omni directional antennas are great in an environment in which there is a clear line of path between the senders and receivers. The power is evenly spread to all points, making omni directional antennas well suited for linking several home and small office users.

Omni directional antennas provide a wide coverage but weaker signal strength in any one direction than a directional antenna.

Directional antennas are designed to focus the signal in a particular direction. This focused signal allows for greater distances and a stronger signal between two points. The greater distances enabled by directional antennas allow a viable alternative for connecting locations, such as two offices, in a point-to-point configuration.

Directional antennas are also used when you need to tunnel or thread a signal through a series of obstacles. This concentrates the signal power in a specific direction and allows you to use less power for a greater distance than an omni directional antenna.

In the wireless world, polarization refers to the direction that the antenna radiates wavelengths. This direction can either be vertical, horizontal, or circular. Today, vertical antennas are perhaps the most common type. As far as configuration is concerned, both the sending and receiving antennas should be set to the same polarization.

Review and Test Yourself

The following sections provide you with the opportunity to review what you learned in this chapter and to test yourself.

The Facts

For the exam, don't forget these important key concepts:

➤ In a star topology, each device on the network connects to a centralized device via a single cable.

➤ Computers in a star network can be connected and disconnected from the network without affecting any other systems.

➤ In a star configuration, all devices on the network connect to devices that act as connectivity points for the network, and these devices create a single point of failure on the network.

➤ The most common implementation of the physical star topology is the Ethernet 10BaseT standard, although most new installations are 100BaseT, at a minimum.

➤ In the ring topology, the network layout forms a complete ring. Computers connect to the network cable directly or, far more commonly, through a specialized network device.

➤ Breaking the loop of a ring network disrupts the entire network. Even if network devices are used to create the ring, the ring must still be broken if a fault occurs or the network needs to be expanded.

➤ The mesh topology requires each computer on the network be connected to each device. This configuration provides maximum reliability and redundancy for the network.

➤ 802.3 defines the Carrier Sense Multiple Access with Collision Avoidance Detection (CSMA/CA) media access method used in Ethernet networks. This is the most popular networking standard used today.

➤ 802.5 defines Token Ring networking.

➤ All cards in a Token Ring network must operate at the same speed.

➤ Ring networks are most commonly wired in a star configuration. In a Token Ring network, a multistation access unit (MSAU) is equivalent to a hub or switch on an Ethernet network.

➤ To connect MSAUs, the ring in and ring out configuration must be properly set.

➤ FDDI uses a dual-ring configuration for fault tolerance.

➤ Four wireless standards are found under the IEEE 802.11 designation; these include 802.11, 802.11a, 802.11b, and 802.11g.

➤ Wireless standards use radio frequency as the transmission media, and they all use the CSMA/CA access method.

➤ Wireless antennas are typically measured in dBi and are either omni-directional or directional. Wireless antennas boost the range and compensate for interference affecting a wireless signal.

➤ Infrastructure wireless topology uses an access point to extend the standard wired LAN. Wireless clients communicate with the AP to access the wires LAN. Ad-hoc networking is the connecting of wireless devices together without using a wireless access point.

➤ Communication between a client and the AP requires both to use a common SSID, wireless channel, and security channel.

Key Terms

- LANs, WANs, and PANs
- Peer-to-peer and client/server networking models
- Physical topology
- Logical topology
- Bus
- Ring
- Star
- Mesh
- Wireless

- IEEE 802.2, 802.3, 802.5, and 802.11
- FDDI
- Infrastructure topology
- Ad hoc topology
- 802.11, 802.11a, 802.11b, 802.11g
- Wireless antenna
- SSID
- Wireless channel

Exam Prep Questions

1. Which of the following standards uses a dual ring configuration for fault tolerance?
   - ❏ A. 802.3
   - ❏ B. FDDI
   - ❏ C. 802.5
   - ❏ D. 802.2

2. Which of the following access methods is associated with Ethernet networks?
   - ❏ A. CSMA/CD
   - ❏ B. CSMA/CA
   - ❏ C. Token Passing
   - ❏ D. Demand Polling

3. You have been asked to install a network that will provide the network users with the greatest amount of fault tolerance. Which of the following network topologies would you choose?
   - ❏ A. Star
   - ❏ B. Ring
   - ❏ C. Mesh
   - ❏ D. Bus

4. Which of the following access methods is associated with the 802.11b standard?
   - ❏ A. CSMA/CD
   - ❏ B. CSMA/CA
   - ❏ C. Token Passing
   - ❏ D. Radio Waves

5. Which of the following topologies allow for network expansion with the least amount of disruption for the current network users?
   - ❏ A. Bus
   - ❏ B. Ring
   - ❏ C. 802.5
   - ❏ D. 802.4
   - ❏ E. Star

6. Which of the following are functions of the LLC? (Choose all that apply.)
   - ❏ A. Data flow control
   - ❏ B. Data fault tolerance
   - ❏ C. Error control
   - ❏ D. Token passing

7. Which of the following statements are associated with a bus LAN network? (Choose all correct answers.)

   ❑ A. A single cable break can cause complete network disruption.

   ❑ B. All devices connect to a central device.

   ❑ C. Uses a single backbone to connect all network devices.

   ❑ D. Uses a dual ring configuration.

8. Which of the following is associated with 802.3u?

   ❑ A. Gigabit Ethernet

   ❑ B. Fast Ethernet

   ❑ C. FDDI

   ❑ D. 802.2

9. What is the maximum speed for the 802.11b IEEE standard?

   ❑ A. 100Mbps

   ❑ B. 40Mbps

   ❑ C. 11Mbps

   ❑ D. 32Mbps

10. As a network administrator, you are called in to troubleshoot a problem on a token ring network. The network uses two MSAUs connected using the ring in ports on both devices. All network cards are set at the same speed. What is the likely cause of the problem?

   ❑ A. Bad network card

   ❑ B. Faulty cabling

   ❑ C. MSAU configuration

   ❑ D. Network card configuration

Answers to Exam Prep Questions

1. The correct answer is B. FDDI uses a ring network design but uses dual rings for fault tolerance. If there is disruption in one of the rings, network traffic can use the other ring. Answer A is incorrect, as the 802.3 specifies Ethernet networks and does not use a ring design. Answer C is incorrect, as 802.5 only defines a single ring. Answer D is incorrect, as 802.2 is the IEEE standard for the Logical Link Layer.

2. The correct answer is A. CSMA/CD works by monitoring the computers that are sending data on the network. If two computers transmit data at the same time onto the network, a data collision will occur. Answer B is incorrect; CSMA/CA uses collision avoidance as an access method. Answer C is incorrect; token passing is associated with ring networks. Demand polling is an access method based on priority and is not used on Ethernet networks; therefore, answer D is incorrect.

3. The correct answer is C. A mesh network uses a point-to-point connection to every device on the network. This creates multiple points for the data to be transmitted around the network and therefore creates a high degree of redundancy. The star, ring, and bus topologies do not offer fault tolerance.

4. The correct answer is B. 802.11b specifies CSMA/CA as the access method for wireless networks. CSMA/CD is the access method associated with the IEEE 802.3 standards and is therefore incorrect. Token passing is an access method but is not used for wireless networks, making answer C incorrect. Answer D is incorrect, as radio waves represent the media used by wireless, not the access method.

5. The correct answer is E. On a star network, each network device uses a separate cable to make a point-to-point connection to a centralized device such as a hub. With such a configuration, a new device can be added to the network by attaching the new device to the hub with its own cable. This process does not disrupt the users who are currently on the network. Answers A, B, C, and D are incorrect because the addition of new network devices on a ring or bus network can cause a disruption in the network and cause network services to be unavailable during the installation of a new device. 802.5 is the IEEE specification for a ring network, and 802.4 is the IEEE specification for a token bus.

6. The correct answers are A and C. The LLC manages both the data flow control and error control for LAN networking standards such as 802.3, 802.5, and 802.11b. The function of the LLC is not to provide fault tolerance; therefore, answer B is incorrect. Similarly, the function of LLC is not associated with token passing.

7. The correct answers are A and C. In a bus network, a single break in the network cable can disrupt all the devices on that segment of the network, a significant shortcoming. A bus network also uses a single cable as a backbone to which all networking devices attach. A star network requires networked devices to connect to a centralized device such as a hub or MSAU. Therefore, answer B is incorrect. A dual ring topology is associated with FDDI, not a bus network.

8. The correct answer is B. 802.3u is the specification for Fast Ethernet under the original 802.3 IEEE standard. 802.3z is the specification for Gigabit Ethernet; therefore, answer A is incorrect. FDDI is not associated with 802.3u; FDDI uses a dual ring network design. 802.2 is the IEEE standard for the LLC sublayer.

9. The correct answer is C. 802.11b allows for a transfer rate of 11Mbps. None of the other answers represent wireless speeds.

10. The correct answer is C. To create the complete ring, the ring in (RI) port on each MSAU is connected to the ring out (RO) port on another MSAU. The last MSAU in the ring is then connected to the first, to complete the ring.

Need to Know More?

Bird, Drew and Harwood, Mike. *Network+ Exam Prep*, Que Publishing, 2004.

Habraken, Joe. *Absolute Beginner's Guide to Networking, Fourth Edition*. Que Publishing, 2003.

Davis, Harold. *Absolute Beginner's Guide to Wi-Fi Wireless Networking*. Que Publishing, 2004.

Cabling and Connectors

Objectives

1.3 Specify the characteristics (for example, speed, length, topology, and cable type) of the following cable standards:

- ✓ 10BaseT and 10BaseFL
- ✓ 100BaseTX and 100BaseFX
- ✓ 1000BaseTX, 1000BaseCX, 1000BaseSX, and 1000BaseLX
- ✓ 10GBaseSR, 10GBaseLR, and 10GBaseER

1.4 Recognize the following media connectors and describe their uses:

- ✓ RJ-11 (Registered Jack)
- ✓ RJ-45 (Registered Jack)
- ✓ F-Type
- ✓ ST (Straight Tip)
- ✓ SC (Standard Connector)
- ✓ IEEE1394 (FireWire)
- ✓ LC (Local Connector)
- ✓ MTRJ (Mechanical Transfer Registered Jack)
- ✓ USB (Universal Serial Bus)

1.5 Recognize the following media types and describe their uses:

- ✓ Category 3, 5, 5e, and 6
- ✓ UTP (Unshielded Twisted Pair)
- ✓ STP (Shielded Twisted Pair)
- ✓ Coaxial cable
- ✓ SMF (Single Mode Fiber) optic cable
- ✓ MMF (Multimode Fiber) optic cable

What you need to know

- ✓ Identify common media considerations
- ✓ Understand the relationship between media and bandwidth
- ✓ Identify the two signaling methods used on networks
- ✓ Understand the three media dialog methods
- ✓ Identify the characteristics of IEEE standards including 802.3, 802.3u, 802.3z, and 802.3ae
- ✓ Identify the commonly implemented network media
- ✓ Identify the various connectors used with network media

Introduction

When it comes to working with an existing network or implementing a new network, you need to be able to identify the characteristics of network media and their associated cabling. This chapter focuses on the media and connectors used in today's networks.

In addition to media and connectors, this chapter identifies the characteristics of the IEEE 802.3 standard and its variants.

General Media Considerations

In addition to identifying the characteristics of network media and their associated cabling, the Network+ exam requires knowledge of some general terms and concepts that are associated with network media. Before looking at the individual media types, it is a good idea to first have an understanding of some general media considerations.

Broadband Versus Baseband

Networks employ two types of signaling methods: baseband and broadband. *Baseband transmissions* use digital signaling over a single wire. Communication on baseband transmissions is bidirectional, allowing signals to be sent and received but not at the same time. To send multiple signals on a single cable, baseband uses something called *Time Division Multiplexing (TDM)*. TDM divides a single channel into time slots.

In terms of LAN network standards, broadband transmissions, on the other hand, use analog transmissions. For broadband transmissions to be sent and received, the media has to be split into two channels. Multiple channels are created using Frequency Division-Multiplexing (FDM).

Simplex, Half Duplex, and Full Duplex

Simplex, half duplex, and full duplex are referred to as dialog modes, and they determine the direction in which data can flow through the network media.

Simplex allows for one-way communication of data through the network, with the full bandwidth of the cable being used for the transmitting signal. One-way communication is of little use on LANs, making it unusual at best for network implementations. Far more common is the *half-duplex* mode, which accommodates transmitting and receiving on the network but not at the same time. Many networks are configured for half-duplex communication.

The preferred dialog mode for network communication is the *full-duplex* mode. To use full duplex, both the network card and the hub or switch must support full duplexing. Devices configured for full duplexing are capable of transmitting and receiving simultaneously. This means that 100Mbps network cards are capable of transmitting at 200Mbps using full-duplex mode.

Media Interference

Depending on where network cabling (commonly referred to as media) is installed, *interference* can be a major consideration. Two types of media interference can adversely affect data transmissions over network media: electro-magnetic interference (EMI) and crosstalk.

EMI is a problem when cables are installed near electrical devices, such as air conditioners or fluorescent light fixtures. If a network media is placed close enough to such a device, the signal within the cable might become corrupt. Network media vary in their resistance to the effects of EMI. Standard UTP cable is susceptible to EMI, whereas fiber cable with its light transmissions is resistant to EMI. When deciding on a particular media, consider where it will run and the impact EMI can have on the installation.

A second type of interference is *crosstalk*. Crosstalk refers to how the data signals on two separate media interfere with each other. The result is that the signal on both cables can become corrupt. As with EMI, media varies in its resistance to crosstalk, with fiber-optic cable being the most resistant.

 For the Network+ exam, remember that fiber-optic cable offers the greatest resistance to EMI and crosstalk.

Attenuation

Attenuation refers to the weakening of data signals as they travel through a respective media. Network media varies in its resistance to attenuation. Coaxial cable is generally more resistant than UTP, STP is slightly more resistant than UTP, and fiber-optic cable does not suffer from attenuation at all. That's not to say that a signal does not weaken as it travels over fiber-optic cable, but the correct term for this weakening is 'chromatic dispersion,' rather than attenuation.

It's important to understand attenuation or chromatic dispersion and the maximum distances specified for network media. Exceeding a media's distance without using repeaters can cause hard-to-troubleshoot network problems. Most attenuation or chromatic dispersion related difficulties on a network require using a network analyzer to detect them.

Data Transmission Rates

One of the more important media considerations is the supported data transmission rate or speed. Different media types are rated to certain maximum speeds, but whether or not they are used to this maximum depends on the networking standard being used and the network devices connected to the network.

The transmission rate of media is sometimes referred to incorrectly as the *bandwidth*. In truth, the term bandwidth refers to the width of the range of electrical frequencies or amount of channels that the media can support.

Transmission rates are normally measured by the number of data bits that can traverse the media in a single second. In the early days of data communications, this measurement was expressed as bits per second (bps), but today's networks are measured in Mbps (megabits per second) and Gbps (gigabits per second).

The different network media vary greatly in the transmission speeds they support. Many of today's application-intensive networks require more than the 10Mbps offered by the older networking standards. In some cases, even 100Mbps, which is found in many modern LANs, is simply not enough to meet current network needs. For this reason, many organizations deploy 1Gbps networks, and some now even go for 10Gbps implementations.

Network Media

Whatever type of network is used, some type of network media is needed to carry signals between computers. Two types of media are used in networks: cable-based media, such as twisted pair, and the media types associated with wireless networking, such as radio waves.

In networks using cable-based media, there are three basic choices:

➤ Twisted pair

➤ Coaxial

➤ Fiber-optic

Twisted-pair and coaxial cables both use copper wire to conduct the signals electronically; fiber-optic cable uses a glass or plastic conductor and transmits the signals as light.

For many years, coaxial was the cable of choice for most LANs. Today, however (and for the past 10 years), twisted pair has proved to be far and away the cable media of choice, thus retiring coax to the confines of storage closets. Fiber-optic cable has also seen its popularity rise but—because of cost—has been primarily restricted to use as a network backbone where segment length and higher speeds are needed. That said, fiber is now increasingly common in server room environments as a server to switch connection method, and in building to building connections in what are termed as metropolitan area networks (MANs).

The following sections summarize the characteristics of each of these cable types.

Twisted-pair Cabling

Twisted-pair cabling has been around a very long time. It was originally created for voice transmissions and has been widely used for telephone communication. Today, in addition to telephone communication, twisted pair is the most widely used media for networking.

The popularity of twisted pair can be attributed to the fact that it is lighter, more flexible, and easier to install than coaxial or fiber-optic cable. It is also cheaper than other media alternatives and can achieve greater speeds than its coaxial competition. These factors make twisted pair the ideal solution for most network environments.

Two main types of twisted-pair cabling are in use today: *Unshielded Twisted Pair (UTP)* and *Shielded Twisted Pair (STP)*. UTP is significantly more commonplace than STP and is used for most networks. Shielded twisted pair is used in environments in which greater resistance to EMI and attenuation is required. The greater resistance comes at a price, however. The additional shielding, plus the need to ground that shield (which requires special connectors), can significantly add to the cost of a cable installation of STP.

NOTE

A third type of twisted pair cable, called Screened Twisted Pair (ScTP) , is available, though not widely deployed. ScTP encases all of the wires in the cable within a single shield. This is in contrast to standard STP cable, which uses the same shield, but also encases each individual wire with shielding. ScTP is cheaper than STP, but it is still more expensive than UTP.

STP provides the extra shielding by using an insulating material that is wrapped around the wires within the cable. This extra protection increases the distances that data signals can travel over STP but also increases the cost of the cabling. Figure 2.1 shows STP and UTP cabling.

STP

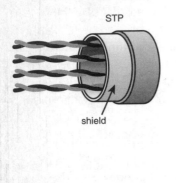

shield

UTP

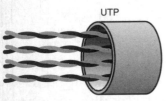

Figure 2.1 STP and UTP cabling. (Reproduced with permission from Computer Desktop Encyclopedia.© 1981-2005 The Computer Language Company Inc. All rights reserved.)

There are several categories of twisted-pair cabling, with the early categories most commonly associated with voice transmissions. The categories are specified by the Electronics Industries Association/Telecommunications Industries Association (EIA/TIA). Table 2.1 shows the categories along with the speeds that they are used to support in common network implementations.

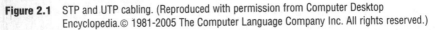

Table 2.1	UTP Cable Categories
Category	**Common Application**
1	Analog voice applications
2	1Mbps

(continued)

Table 2.1 UTP Cable Categories *(continued)*	
Category	**Common Application**
3	16Mbps
4	20Mbps
5	100Mbps
5e	1000Mbps
6	1000Mbps +

NOTE   It should be noted that the figures provided in Table 2.1 refer to speeds that these cables are commonly used to support. Ratified standards for these cabling categories might actually specify lower speeds than those listed, but cable and network component manufacturers are always pushing the performance envelope in the quest for greater speeds. The ratified standards define minimum specifications. For more information on cabling standards, visit the TIA website at http://www.tiaonline.org/.

Coaxial

Coaxial cable, or *coax* as it is commonly referred to, has been around for a long time. Coax found success in both TV signal transmission as well as in network implementations. Coax is constructed with a copper core at the center that carries the signal, plastic insulation, braided metal shielding, and an outer plastic covering. Coaxial cable is constructed in this way to add resistance to *attenuation* (the loss of signal strength as it travels over distance), *crosstalk* (the degradation of a signal caused by signals from other cables running close to it), and EMI (electromagnetic interference). Figure 2.2 shows the construction of coaxial cabling.

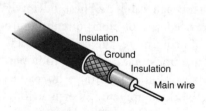

Figure 2.2   Coaxial cabling.

Networks can use two types of coaxial cabling: thin coaxial and thick coaxial. Both have fallen out of favor, but you might still encounter thin coax in your travels.

Thin Coax

Thin coax is much more likely to be seen than thick coax in today's networks, but it isn't common, either. Thin coax is only .25 inches in diameter, making it fairly easy to install. Unfortunately, one of the disadvantages of all thin coax types are that they are prone to cable breaks, which increase the difficulty when installing and troubleshooting coaxial-based networks.

There are several types of thin coax cable, each of which has a specific use. Table 2.2 summarizes the categories of thin coax.

Table 2.2 Thin Coax Categories	
Cable	**Type**
RG-58 /U	Solid copper core
RG-58 A/U	Stranded wire core
RG-58 C/U	Military specification
RG-6	Used for cable TV and cable modems

Fiber-optic Cable

In many ways, fiber-optic media addresses the shortcomings associated with copper-based media. Because fiber-based media use light transmissions instead of electronic pulses, threats such as EMI, crosstalk, and attenuation become a nonissue. Fiber is well suited for the transfer of data, video, and voice transmissions. In addition, fiber-optic is the most secure of all cable media. Anyone trying to access data signals on a fiber-optic cable must physically tap into the media. Given the composition of the cable, this is a particularly difficult task.

Unfortunately, despite the advantages of fiber-based media over copper, it still does not enjoy the popularity of twisted-pair cabling. The moderately difficult installation and maintenance procedures of fiber often require skilled technicians with specialized tools. Furthermore, the cost of a fiber-based solution limits the number of organizations that can afford to implement it. Another sometimes hidden drawback of implementing a fiber solution is the cost of retrofitting existing network equipment. Fiber is incompatible with most electronic network equipment. This means that you have to purchase fiber-compatible network hardware.

Fiber-optic cable, although still more expensive than other types of cable, is well suited for high-speed data communications. It eliminates the problems associated with copper-based media, such as near-end crosstalk, electromagnetic interference (EMI), and signal tampering.

Fiber-optic cable itself is composed of a core glass fiber surrounded by *cladding*. An insulated covering then surrounds both of these within an outer protective sheath. Figure 2.3 shows the composition of a fiber-optic cable.

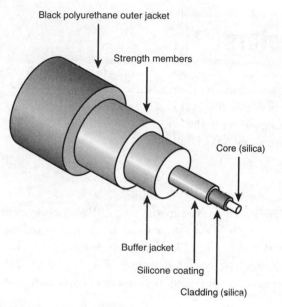

Black polyurethane outer jacket

Strength members

Core (silica)

Buffer jacket

Silicone coating

Cladding (silica)

Figure 2.3 Fiber-optic cable.

Two types of fiber-optic cable are available: single and multimode fiber. In multimode fiber, many beams of light travel through the cable bouncing off of the cable walls. This strategy actually weakens the signal, reducing the length and speed the data signal can travel. Single-mode fiber uses a single direct beam of light, thus allowing for greater distances and increased transfer speeds. Some of the common types of fiber-optic cable include the following:

➤ 62.5 micron core/125 micron cladding multimode

➤ 50 micron core/125 micron cladding multimode

➤ 8.3 micron core/125 micron cladding single mode

In the ever-increasing search for bandwidth that will keep pace with the demands of modern applications, fiber-optic cables are sure to play a key role.

Understanding the types of fiber optics available, as well as their advantages and their limitations, is important for real-world application, as well as the Network+ exam.

Media Connectors

A variety of connectors are used with the associated network media. Media connectors attach to the transmission media and allow the physical connection into the computing device. For the Network+ exam, it is necessary to identify the connectors associated with the specific media. The following sections identify the connectors and associated media.

BNC Connectors

BNC connectors are associated with coaxial media and 10Base2 networks. BNC connectors are not as common as they once were, but still are used on some networks, older network cards, and older hubs. Common BNC connectors include a barrel connector, T-connector, and terminators. Figure 2.4 shows two terminators (top and bottom) and two T-connectors (left and right).

Figure 2.4 BNC connectors.

Although CompTIA does not include BNC connectors in the updated Network+ objectives, we have included them in this chapter to provide complete coverage of the commonly used connectors. In addition, CompTIA has been known to include questions in the exam that are not included in the objectives, and we think it wise to prepare for any eventuality.

RJ-11 Connectors

RJ (Registered Jack) -11 connectors are small plastic connectors used on telephone cables. They have capacity for six small pins. However, in many cases, not all the pins are used. For example, a standard telephone connection only uses two pins, while a cable used for a DSL modem connection uses four.

RJ-11 connectors are somewhat similar to RJ-45 connectors, which are discussed next, though they are a little smaller. Both RJ-11 and RJ-45 connectors have small plastic flange on top of the connector to ensure a secure connection. Figure 2.5 shows two views of an RJ-11 connector.

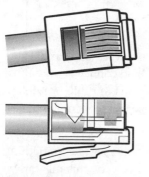

Figure 2.5   RJ-11 connectors.

RJ-45 Connectors

RJ-45 connectors are the ones you are most likely going to encounter in your network travels. RJ-45 connectors are used with twisted-pair cabling, the most prevalent network cable in use today. RJ-45 connectors resemble the aforementioned RJ-11 phone jacks, but support up to eight wires instead of the six supported by RJ-11 connectors. RJ-45 connectors are also larger. Figure 2.6 shows the RJ-45 connectors.

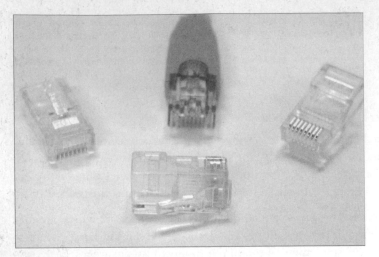

Figure 2.6   RJ-45 connectors.

F-Type

F-Type connectors are screw on connections used for attaching coaxial cable to devices. In the world of modern networking, F-Type connectors are most commonly associated with connecting Internet modems to cable or satellite Internet provider's equipment. However, they are also used for connecting to some proprietary peripherals.

F-Type connectors have a 'nut' on the connection that provides something to grip as the connection is tightened by hand. If necessary, this nut can be also be lightly gripped with pliers to aid disconnection. Figure 2.7 shows an example of an F-Type connector.

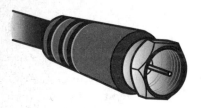

Figure 2.7   F-Type connector.

For the Network+ exam, you are expected to identify the connectors discussed in this chapter by their appearance.

Fiber Connectors

A variety of connectors are associated with fiber cabling, and there are several ways of connecting these connectors. These include bayonet, snap-lock, and push-pull connectors. Figure 2.8 shows the fiber connectors identified in the CompTIA Network+ objectives.

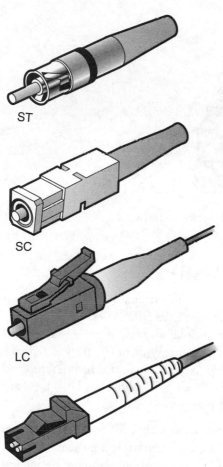

The ST connector uses a half-twist bayonet type of lock.

ST

The SC uses a push-pull connector similiar to common audio and video plugs and sockets.

SC

LC connectors have a flange on top, similar to an RJ-45 connector, that aids secure connection.

LC

MT-RJ is a popular connector for two fibers in a very small form factor.

MT-RJ

Figure 2.8   Fiber connectors. (Reproduced with permission from Computer Desktop Encyclopedia. © 1981-2005 The Computer Language Company Inc. All rights reserved.)

As with the other connectors discussed in this section, be prepared to identify fiber connectors by their appearance and by how they are physically connected.

IEEE1394

The IEEE1394 interface, also known as FireWire, is more commonly associated with the attachment of peripheral devices, such as digital cameras or printers, than network connections. However, it is possible to create small networks with IEEE1394 cables. The IEEE1394 interface comes in a 4- or 6-pin version, both of which are shown in Figure 2.9

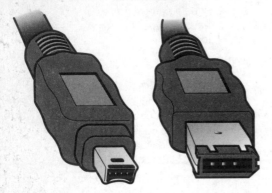

Figure 2.9   4-pin (left) and 6-pin (right) IEEE1394 (FireWire) connectors.

Universal Serial Bus (USB)

Universal Serial Bus (USB) ports are now an extremely common sight on both desktop and laptop computer systems. Like IEEE1394, USB is associated more with connecting consumer peripherals such as MP3 players and digital cameras than networking. However, many manufacturers now make wireless network cards that plug directly in to a USB port. Most desktop and laptop computers have between two and four USB ports, but USB hubs are available that provide additional ports if required.

There are a number of connectors associated with USB ports, but the two most popular are Type A and Type B. Type A connectors are the more common of the two and are the type used on PCs. Although many peripheral devices also use a Type A connector, an increasing number now use a Type B. Figure 2.10 shows a Type A connector (left) and a Type B connector (right) .

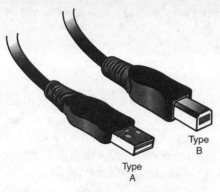

Figure 2.10   Type A (left) and Type B (right) USB connectors.

IEEE 802.3 Standards

The IEEE 802.3 standards define a range of networking systems that are based on the original Ethernet standard. The variations include speed, physical topology, and implementation considerations. The following sections describe these standards.

10 Mbps Networking Standards

There is no specific designation called 'standard Ethernet,' but if there were, it would be assigned to the 10Mbps variants of the IEEE 802.3 standards. Although 10Mbps is now considered too slow for most new networks, there are a large number of existing networks operating at 10Mbps. A number of 10Mbps standards exist, with 10BaseT now being the most common. In the following sections, we discuss a number of the 10Mbps standards.

NOTE

Even though it is not specifically stated in the CompTIA Network+ objectives, we have included coverage on 10Base2 because there is still a chance that you will encounter it in the real world.

10Base2

10Base2, which is defined as part of the IEEE 802.3a standard, specifies data transmission speeds of 10Mbps and a total segment length of 185 meters using RG-58 coaxial cable. The 10Base2 standard specifies a physical bus topology and uses BNC connectors with 50-ohm terminators at each end of the cable. One of the physical ends of each segment must be grounded.

When discussing network standards, the word 'base,' as in 10Base2, defines that the media can only carry one data signal per wire, or channel, at one time.

10Base2 networks allow a maximum of five segments with only three of those segments populated. Each of the three populated segments can have a maximum of 30 nodes attached. 10Base2 requires that there is a minimum of .5 meters between nodes. For the network to function properly, the segment must be complete. With this in mind, the addition or removal of systems might make the network unusable.

The coax cable used in 10Base2 networks is prone to cable breaks. A break anywhere in the cable will make the entire network inaccessible.

Coaxial and the 5-4-3 Rule

When working with Ethernet networks that use coaxial media, the 5-4-3 rule applies. The rule specifies that the network is limited to a total of five cable segments. These five segments can be connected using no more than four repeaters, and only three segments on the network can be populated.

10BaseT

The 10BaseT standard is another 10Mbps standard using UTP cabling. 10BaseT networks have a maximum segment length of 100 meters, and up to a total of five physical segments per network.

10BaseT networks use a star topology with a point-to-point connection between the computer and the hub or switch. 10BaseT can use different categories of UTP cabling, including 3, 4, 5. It can also be used with category 5e and category 6 cabling, but that is a little like renting the Daytona speedway for the day and then cycling around it.

UTP and the 5-4-5 Rule

As with coaxial implementations, there are rules governing UTP networks. UTP Ethernet networks use the 5-4-3 rule, but in a slightly modified form. As with coaxial, a total of five physical segments can be used on the network and these five physical segments can be connected using four repeaters, but all five physical segments can be populated.

10BaseFL

10BaseFL is an implementation of 10Mbps Ethernet over fiber-optic cabling. Its primary benefit, over 10BaseT, is that it can be used in distances up to 2km. However, given the availability of other faster networking standards, such as 100BaseFX (discussed next), you are unlikely to encounter a large number of 10BaseFL implementations.

Table 2.3 summarizes the characteristics of the 10Mbps networking standards discussed in this section.

Table 2.3	10Mbps Network Comparison			
Standard	**Cable Type**	**Segment Length**	**Connector**	**Topology**
10Base2	Thin coaxial	185 meters	BNC	Physical bus
10BaseT	Category 3, 4, 5 twisted pair	100 meters	RJ-45	Physical star
10BaseFL	Fiber Optic	2000 Meters	SC/ST	Physical star

Ensure that you understand the information provided in Table 2.3; there will certainly be questions on the exam that come directly from this information.

Fast Ethernet

Many of the applications used on modern networks demand more bandwidth than what's provided by the 10Mbps network standards. To address this need for faster networks, the IEEE has developed the IEEE 802.3u specifications, of which there are three variations:

➤ 100BaseTX

➤ 100BaseT4

➤ 100BaseFX

Of the three, 100BaseT4 is not listed in the latest version of the CompTIA Network+ objectives. However, we have chosen to include information on it in this section to provide rounded coverage of this topic.

100BaseTX

100BaseTX is the most widely implemented of the Fast Ethernet standards. 100BaseTX uses two pairs of wire in Category 5 UTP cabling and can also use STP cable when a more resistant cable is required. 100BaseTX uses 100Mbps transmission and a total segment length of 100 meters.

100BaseT4

The advantage to 100BaseT4 is its capability to use older categories of UTP cable to perform 100Mbps transfer. In environments already wired with Category 3 or 4 cable, 100BaseT4 can be used instead of replacing the existing cable.

100BaseT4 uses all four pairs of wire of Category 3, 4, and 5 twisted pair and, as such, is prevented from using full-duplex transmissions. The other characteristics of standard 100BaseTX are in effect with 100BaseT4.

100BaseFX

The IEEE 100BaseFX standard specifies 100Mbps transmissions speeds over fiber-optic cable. 100BaseFX can use both multimode and single mode fiber. It has a maximum segment length of 412 meters when used over multimode fiber and 10,000 meters when used over single-mode fiber. Table 2.4 summarizes the characteristics of Fast Ethernet.

Table 2.4	Fast Ethernet			
Standard	Cable Type	Segment Length	Connector	Topology
100BaseTX	Category 5 UTP	100 meters	RJ-45	Physical star
100BaseT4	Category 3, 4, 5 UTP	100 meters	RJ-45	Physical star
100BaseFX	Multimode/ single-mode fiber-optic cable	412/multimode fiber-optic 10,000/ single-mode fiber-optic	SC, ST	Physical star

Be sure that you understand the information provided in Table 2.4, as there will be questions on the exam that are derived from this information.

Gigabit Ethernet

Gigabit Ethernet networking, which is becoming increasingly common as a backbone connection method and for a server to switch connectivity, is achieved using either copper-based media or fiber optic cabling. The two IEEE standards that specify Gigabit transfer are 802.3z and 802.3ab.

802.3z

Three distinct standards are specified under the 802.3z standard; they are referred to collectively as 1000BaseX.

The three standards are 1000BaseLX, 1000BaseSX, and 1000BaseCX. 1000BaseLX and 1000BaseSX use long wavelength laser and short wavelength laser, respectively. Both 1000BaseSX and 1000BaseLX can be supported over two types of multimode fiber—62.5 and 50 micron-diameter fibers. Only long wave lasers support the use of single-mode fiber.

The 1000BaseCX standard specifies Gigabit Ethernet over STP cabling. Segment length of 1000BaseCX is extremely limited, reaching a maximum of 25 meters. 1000BaseCX is not widely implemented.

802.3ab

The 802.3ab standard specifies Gigabit Ethernet transfer over Category 5 UTP cable. To achieve the 1000Mbps speeds, each of the four pairs of wires in a twisted-pair cable can transmit 250Mbps. Table 2.5 summarizes the characteristics of the Gigabit standards.

Table 2.5 Gigabit Ethernet			
Standard	**Cable Type**	**Segment Length**	**Connector**
1000BaseLX	Multimode/single-mode fiber	550/multimode 5000/ single-mode	Fiber connectors
1000BaseSX	Multimode fiber	550 meters using 50 Micron multimode fiber	Fiber connectors
1000BaseCX	STP	25 meters	9-pin shielded connector, 8-pin fiber channel type 2 connector
1000BaseT	UTP	75 meters	RJ-45

Ensure that you understand the information provided in Table 2.5; there will be questions on the exam that are derived from this information.

10 Gigabit Ethernet

As the name suggests, 10 Gigabit Ethernet, which is referred to as 10GbE, has the capability to provide data transmission rates of up to 10 Gigabits per second. 10 Gigabit Ethernet is defined in the IEEE 802.3ae standard.

There are a number of 10GbE implementations, though CompTIA chooses to focus on 10GBaseSR, 10GBaseLR, and 10GBaseER in the objectives for the Network+ exam. Of these standards, 10BaseSR is designed for LAN or MAN implementations, with a maximum distance of 300 meters using 50 micron multimode fiber-optic cabling. 10BaseSR can also be implemented with 62.5 micron multimode fiber, but is limited to 33 meters in this configuration.

10GBaseLR and 10GBaseER are designed for use in MAN and WAN implementations, and are implemented using single mode fiber-optic cabling. 10GBaseLR has a maximum distance of 10km, whereas 10GBaseER has a maximum distance of 40km. Table 2.6 summarizes the characteristics of 10 Gigabit Ethernet standards relevant to the Network+ exam.

Table 2.6 Summary of IEEE 802.3ae 10 Gigabit Ethernet Characteristics			
	10GBaseSR	**10GBaseLR**	**10GBaseER**
Transmission Method	Baseband	Baseband	Baseband
Speed	10000Mbps	10000Mbps	10000Mbps
Distance Cable Type	33m/300m	10,000m	40,000m
	50 or 62.5 micron	Single Mode	Single Mode
	multimode	fiber	fiber
	Fibre/50 Micron		
	Multimode fiber		
Connector Type	Fiber connectors	Fiber connectors	Fiber connectors

Review and Test Yourself

The following sections provide you with the opportunity to review what you learned in this chapter and to test yourself.

The Facts

For the exam, don't forget these key concepts:

➤ RJ-11 connectors are used with standard phone lines and are similar in appearance to RJ-45 connectors. However, RJ-11 connectors are smaller.

➤ RJ-45 connectors are used with UTP cabling.

➤ F-type connectors are used to connect coaxial cable to devices such as Internet modems.

➤ Fiber-optic cabling uses a variety of connectors, but SC and ST are more commonly used than others.

➤ SC and ST connectors are associated with fiber cabling. ST connectors offer a twist type attachment, whereas SCs have a push-on connector.

➤ LC and MTRJ are other types of fiber-optic connectors.

➤ UTP cabling is the most common type used on today's networks. For greater speeds, distances, and resistance to interference, fiber-optic cable provides an increasingly affordable alternative.

➤ 10Base2, sometimes called Thinnet or Thin Ethernet, is the 802.3 specification for a network that uses thin coaxial cable (that is, RG-58 cable).

➤ 10BaseT networks use UTP cable and RJ-45 connectors to transfer data at up to 10Mbps.

➤ 10BaseFL networks use fiber-optic cabling and can span distances of up to 2km.

➤ 100BaseTX networks use RJ-45 connectors and use Category 5 STP or UTP cable.

➤ 100BaseT4 networks use Category 3, 4, and 5 cable with RJ-45 connectors.

➤ 100BaseFX uses fiber-optic cable and often uses SC or ST connectors

➤ 1000BaseSX and 1000BaseLX offer 1000Mbps transfer speed using fiber-optic cable.

➤ 1000BaseCX offers 1000Mbps transfer speed over shielded copper cable. Distances are restricted to 25 meters.

➤ 1000BaseTX offers 1000Mbps transfer speed over UTP cable up to a maximum of 100 meters.

➤ 10Gbps networks are defined by the IEEE 802.3ae standard.

➤ 10GBaseSR is designed for use over short distances up to 300 meters with 50 micron multimode fiber.

➤ 10GBaseLR uses single mode fiber-optic cable and can be used up to 10km.

➤ 10GBaseER uses single mode fiber-optic cable and can be used up to 40km.

Key Terms

➤ Media

➤ Bandwidth

➤ Baseband/broadband

➤ Duplexing

➤ Thin coax/Twisted pair/Fiber-optic cable

➤ 10BaseT/10Base2/100BaseTX/100BaseFX/Gigabit Ethernet/10Gb Ethernet (10GbE)

➤ RJ-11/RJ-45/F-type/ST/SC/LC/MTRJ/BNC connectors

➤ Crosstalk

➤ Attenuation

➤ EMI

Exam Prep Questions

1. You are troubleshooting a network using 1000BaseCX cable and suspect that the maximum length has been exceeded. What is the maximum length of 1000BaseCX cable?
   - ❑ A. 1,000 meters
   - ❑ B. 100 meters
   - ❑ C. 25 meters
   - ❑ D. 10,000 meters

2. As system administrator, you find yourself working on a legacy 10Base2 network. Which of the following technologies would you be working with? (Choose three.)
   - ❑ A. UTP
   - ❑ B. RG-58
   - ❑ C. BNC connectors
   - ❑ D. Terminators
   - ❑ E. RJ-45 connectors

3. Your manager has asked you to specify a high speed 10GbE link to provide connectivity between two buildings 3km from each other. Which of the following IEEE standards are you likely to recommend?
   - ❑ A. 10GBaseLR
   - ❑ B. 10GBaseSR
   - ❑ C. 10GBaseT4
   - ❑ D. 10GBaseFL

4. Which of following connectors are commonly used with fiber cabling?
   - ❑ A. RJ-45
   - ❑ B. BNC
   - ❑ C. SC
   - ❑ D. RJ-11

5. Which of the following definitions describe the loss of signal strength as a signal travels through a particular media?
   - ❑ A. Attenuation
   - ❑ B. Crosstalk
   - ❑ C. EMI
   - ❑ D. Chatter

6. What kind of cable would you associate with an F-type connector?
   - ❑ A. Fiber optic
   - ❑ B. UTP
   - ❑ C. Coaxial
   - ❑ D. STP

7. In a 100BaseT network environment, what is the maximum distance between the device and the networking equipment, assuming that no repeaters are used?

- ❏ A. 1,000 meters
- ❏ B. 100 meters
- ❏ C. 500 meters
- ❏ D. 185 meters

8. A user calls to report that he is experiencing periodic problems connecting to the network. Upon investigation, you find that the cable connecting the user's PC to the switch is close to a fluorescent light fitting. What condition is most likely causing the problem?

- ❏ A. Crosstalk
- ❏ B. EMI
- ❏ C. Attenuation
- ❏ D. Faulty cable

9. Which of the following is NOT a type of fiber-optic connector used in network implementations?

- ❏ A. MTRJ
- ❏ B. SC
- ❏ C. BNC
- ❏ D. LC

10. Which of the following fiber connectors uses a twist-type connection method?

- ❏ A. ST
- ❏ B. SC
- ❏ C. BNC
- ❏ D. SA

Answers to Exam Prep Questions

1. The correct answer is C. The 1000BaseCX standard specifies Gigabit Ethernet transfer over Category 5 UTP cable. It uses STP twisted-pair cable and has a 25-meter length restriction. All of the other answers are incorrect.

2. The correct answers are B, C, and D. 10Base2 networks use thin coax (RG-58) media, BNC connectors, and a terminator at each end of the bus to dampen the signal reflection. Answers A and E are incorrect, as they are used by other network standards such as 10BaseT and 100BaseTX.

3. The correct answer is A. 10GBaseLR can be used over distances up to 10km. 10GBaseSR can only be used up to a maximum distance of 300 meters. 10GBaseT4 and 10GBaseFL are not recognized 10 Gigabit Ethernet standards.

4. The correct answer is C. SC connectors are used with fiber-optic cable. RJ-45 connectors are used with UTP cable, BNC is used for thin coax cable, and RJ-11 is used for regular phone connectors.

5. The correct answer is A. The term used to describe the loss of signal strength for media is attenuation. Crosstalk refers to the interference between two cables, EMI is electromagnetic interference, and chatter is not a valid media interference concern.

6. The correct answer is C. F-type connectors are used with coaxial cables. They are not used with fiber-optic, Unshielded Twisted Pair (UTP) or Shielded Twisted Pair (STP) cabling.

7. The correct answer is B. 100BaseT networks use UTP cabling, which has a maximum cable length of 100 meters. Answer A is incorrect. This distance could only be achieved with UTP cabling by using repeaters. Answer C specifies the maximum cable length for 10Base5 networks; and answer D specifies the maximum cable length for 10Base2 networks.

8. The correct answer is B. EMI is a type of interference that is often seen when cables run too closely to electrical devices. Answer A is incorrect; crosstalk describes the interference whereby two cables interfere with each other. Attenuation identifies the loss of signal strength. Answer D is incorrect also. It may be that a faulty cable is causing the problem; however, the question asks for the most likely cause and because the cable is running near the fluorescent lights, the problem is more likely associated with EMI.

9. The correct answer is C. BNC is a connector type used with coaxial cabling. It is not used as a connector for fiber-optic cabling. MTRJ, SC, and LC are all recognized types of fiber-optic connectors.

10. The correct answer is A. ST fiber connectors use a twist-type connection method. Answer B is incorrect as SC connectors use a push-type connection method. The other choices are not valid fiber connectors.

Need to Know More?

 Bird, Drew and Harwood, Mike. *Network+ Exam Prep 2*, Que Publishing, 2005.

 Comer, Douglas I. *Computer Networks and Internets*, Prentice Hall, 1999.

 Tulloch, Mitch and Tulloch, Ingrid. *Microsoft Encyclopedia of Networking, Second Edition*. Microsoft Press. 2002.

Networking Devices

Objectives

1.6 Identify the purposes, features, and functions of the following network components:

- ✓ Hubs
- ✓ Switches
- ✓ Bridges
- ✓ Routers
- ✓ Gateways
- ✓ CSU/DSU (Channel Service Unit/Data Service Unit)
- ✓ NICs (Network Interface Card)
- ✓ ISDN (Integrated Services Digital Network) adapters
- ✓ WAPs (Wireless Access Point)
- ✓ Modems
- ✓ Transceivers (media converters)
- ✓ Firewalls

2.1 Identify a MAC (Media Access Control) address and its parts

What you need to know

- ✓ Describe how hubs and switches work
- ✓ Explain how hubs and switches can be connected to create larger networks
- ✓ Describe how bridges, routers, and gateways work
- ✓ Describe how routing protocols are used for dynamic routing
- ✓ Explain the purpose of other networking components such as Channel Service Unit/Digital Service Unit (CSU/DSU) and gateways
- ✓ Describe the purpose and function of network cards
- ✓ Describe how to identify a MAC address
- ✓ Understand the function of a transceiver
- ✓ Describe the purpose of a firewall

Introduction

All but the most basic of networks require devices to provide connectivity and functionality. Understanding how these networking devices operate and identifying the functions they perform are essential skills for any network administrator and requirements for a Network+ candidate.

This chapter introduces commonly used networking devices, and, although it is true that you are not likely to encounter all of the devices mentioned in this chapter on the exam, you can be assured of working with at least some of them.

Hubs

At the bottom of the networking food chain, so to speak, are hubs. Hubs are used in networks that use twisted-pair cabling to connect devices. Hubs can also be joined together to create larger networks. *Hubs* are simple devices that direct data packets to all devices connected to the hub, regardless of whether the data package is destined for the device. This makes them inefficient devices and can create a performance bottleneck on busy networks.

In its most basic form, a hub does nothing except provide a pathway for the electrical signals to travel along. Such a device is called a *passive* hub. Far more common nowadays is an *active* hub, which, as well as providing a path for the data signals, regenerates the signal before it forwards it to all of the connected devices. A hub does not perform any processing on the data that it forwards, nor does it perform any error checking.

Hubs come in a variety of shapes and sizes. Small hubs with five or eight connection ports are commonly referred to as *workgroup hubs*. Others can accommodate larger numbers of devices (normally up to 32). These are referred to as *high-density devices*. Because hubs don't perform any processing, they do little except enable communication between connected devices. For today's high-demand network applications, something with a little more intelligence is required. That's where switches come in.

MSAU

In a Token Ring network, a multistation access unit (MSAU) is used in place of the hub that is used on an Ethernet network. The MSAU performs the token circulation inside the device, giving the network a physical star appearance. Each MSAU has a Ring In (RI) port on the device, which is connected to the Ring Out (RO) port on another MSAU. The last MSAU in the ring is then connected to the first to complete the ring. Because Token Ring networks are few and far between nowadays, it is far more likely that you will find yourself working with Ethernet hubs and switches.

Multistation access unit is sometimes written as MSAU however, it is commonly referred to as an MAU. Both are acceptable acronyms.

Even though MSAU and Token Ring networks are not common, you can expect a few questions on them on the exam.

Switches

Like hubs, *switches* are the connectivity points of an Ethernet network. Devices connect to switches via twisted-pair cabling, one cable for each device. The difference between hubs and switches is in how the devices deal with the data that they receive. Whereas a hub forwards the data it receives to all of the ports on the device, a switch forwards it only to the port that connects to the destination device. It does this by *learning* the MAC address of the devices attached to it, and then by matching the destination MAC address in the data it receives. Figure 3.1 shows how a switch works.

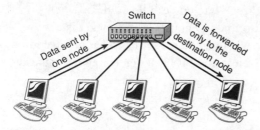

Figure 3.1 How a switch works.

By forwarding data only to the connection that should receive it, the switch can improve network performance in two ways. First, by creating a direct path between two devices and controlling their communication, it can greatly reduce the number of collisions on the network. As you might recall, collisions occur on Ethernet networks when two devices attempt to transmit at exactly the same time. In addition, the lack of collisions enables switches to

UNIVERSITY OF HERTFORDSHIRE LRC

communicate with devices in full-duplex mode. In a full-duplex configuration, devices can send and receive data from the switch at the same time. Contrast this with half-duplex communication, in which communication can occur in only one direction at a time. Full-duplex transmission speeds are double that of a standard, half-duplex, connection. So, a 10Mbps connection becomes 20Mbps, and a 100Mbps connection becomes 200Mbps.

The net result of these measures is that switches can offer significant performance improvements over hub-based networks, particularly when network use is high.

Irrespective of whether a connection is at full or half duplex, the method of switching dictates how the switch deals with the data it receives. The following is a brief explanation of each method:

➤ **Cut-through**—In a cut-through switching environment, the packet begins to be forwarded as soon as it is received. This method is very fast, but creates the possibility of errors being propagated through the network, as there is no error checking.

➤ **Store-and-forward**—Unlike cut-through, in a store-and-forward switching environment, the entire packet is received and error checked before being forwarded. The upside of this method is that errors are not propagated through the network. The downside is that the error checking process takes a relatively long time, and store-and-forward switching is considerably slower as a result.

➤ **FragmentFree**—To take advantage of the error checking of store-and-forward switching, but still offer performance levels nearing that of cut-through switching, FragmentFree switching can be used. In a FragmentFree-switching environment, enough of the packet is read so that the switch can determine whether the packet has been involved in a collision. As soon as the collision status has been determined, the packet is forwarded.

Hub and Switch Cabling

In addition to acting as a connection point for network devices, hubs and switches can also be connected to create larger networks. This connection can be achieved through standard ports with a special cable or by using special ports with a standard cable.

UNIVERSITY OF HERTFORDSHIRE LRC

The ports on a hub to which computer systems are attached are called *Medium Dependent Interface-Crossed (MDI-X)*. The crossed designation is derived from the fact that two of the wires within the connection are crossed so that the send signal wire on one device becomes the receive signal of the other. Because the ports are crossed internally, a standard or *straight-through* cable can be used to connect devices.

Another type of port, called a *Medium Dependent Interface (MDI)* port, is often included on a hub or switch to facilitate the connection of two switches or hubs. Because the hubs or switches are designed to see each other as simply an extension of the network, there is no need for the signal to be crossed. If a hub or switch does not have an MDI port, hubs or switches can be connected by using a *crossover* cable between two MDI-X ports. The crossover cable serves to uncross the internal crossing. You can see diagrams of the cable pinouts for both a straight-through and crossover cable in Figures 3.2 and 3.3, respectively.

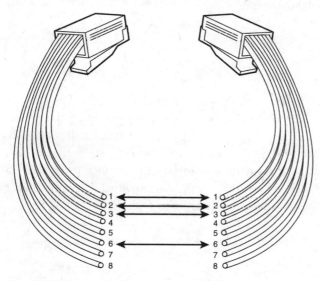

Figure 3.2   The pinouts for a straight-through cable.

In a crossover cable, wires 1 and 3 and wires 2 and 6 are crossed.

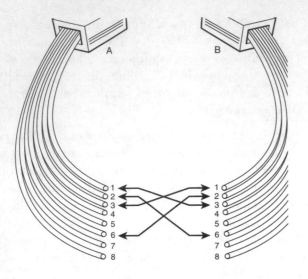

Figure 3.3 The pinouts for a crossover cable.

Bridges

Bridges are used to divide larger networks into smaller sections. They do this by sitting between two physical network segments and managing the flow of data between the two. By looking at the MAC address of the devices connected to each segment, bridges can elect to forward the data (if they believe that the destination address is on another interface), or block it from crossing (if they can verify that it is on the interface from which it came). Figure 3.4 shows how a bridge can be used to segregate a network.

 NOTE | Bridges can also be used to connect two physical LANs into a larger logical LAN.

When bridges were introduced, the MAC addresses of the devices on the connected networks had to be entered manually, a time-consuming process that had plenty of opportunity for error. Today, almost all bridges can build a list of the MAC addresses on an interface by watching the traffic on the network. Such devices are called *learning bridges* because of this functionality.

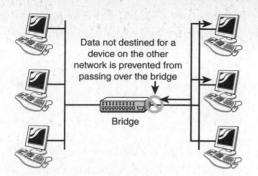

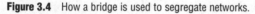

Figure 3.4 How a bridge is used to segregate networks.

Bridge Placement and Bridging Loops

There are two issues that you must consider when using bridges. The first is the bridge placement, and the other is the elimination of bridging loops:

➤ **Placement**—Bridges should be positioned in the network using the 80/20 rule. This rule dictates that 80% of the data should be local and that the other 20% should be destined for devices on the other side of the bridge.

➤ **Bridging loops**—Bridging loops can occur when more than one bridge is implemented on the network. In this scenario, the bridges can confuse each other by leading one another to believe that a device is located on a certain segment when it is not. To combat the bridging loop problem, the IEEE 802.1d Spanning Tree protocol enables bridge interfaces to be assigned a value that is then used to control the bridge-learning process.

Types of Bridges

Three types of bridges are used in networks:

➤ **Transparent bridge**—Derives its name from the fact that the devices on the network are unaware of its existence. A transparent bridge does nothing except block or forward data based on the MAC address.

➤ **Source route bridge**—Used in Token Ring networks. The source route bridge derives its name from the fact that the entire path that the packet is to take through the network is embedded within the packet.

➤ **Translational bridge**—Used to convert one networking data format to another; for example, from Token Ring to Ethernet and vice versa.

Today, bridges are slowly but surely falling out of favor. Ethernet switches offer similar functionality; they can provide logical divisions, or segments, in the network. In fact, switches are sometimes referred to as multiport bridges because of the way they operate.

Routers

In a common configuration, routers are used to create larger networks by joining two network segments. Such as a SOHO router used to connect a user to the Internet. A router can be a dedicated hardware device or a computer system with more than one network interface and the appropriate routing software. All modern network operating systems include the functionality to act as a router.

 Routers will normally create, add, or divide on the Network Layer as they are normally IP-based devices.

A router derives its name from the fact that it can route data it receives from one network onto another. When a router receives a packet of data, it reads the header of the packet to determine the destination address. Once it has determined the address, it looks in its routing table to determine whether it knows how to reach the destination and, if it does, it forwards the packet to the next hop on the route. The next hop might be the final destination, or it might be another router. Figure 3.5 shows, in basic terms, how a router works.

As you can see from this example, routing tables play a very important role in the routing process. They are the means by which the router makes its decisions. For this reason, a routing table needs to be two things. It must be up-to-date, and it must be complete. There are two ways that the router can get the information for the routing table—through static routing or dynamic routing.

Static Routing

In environments that use *static routing*, routes and route information are entered into the routing tables manually. Not only can this be a time-consuming task, but also errors are more common. Additionally, when there is a change in the layout, or topology, of the network, statically configured routers must be manually updated with the changes. Again, this is a time-consuming and potentially error-laden task. For these reasons, static routing is suited to only the smallest environments with perhaps just one or two routers. A far more practical solution, particularly in larger environments, is to use dynamic routing.

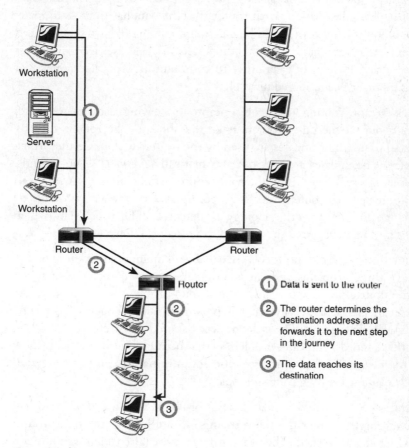

Workstation

Server

Workstation

Router   Router

Router   ① Data is sent to the router

② The router determines the destination address and forwards it to the next step in the journey

③ The data reaches its destination

Figure 3.5   How a router works.

Dynamic Routing

In a *dynamic routing* environment, routers use special routing protocols to communicate. The purpose of these protocols is simple; they enable routers to pass on information about themselves to other routers so that other routers can build routing tables. There are two types of routing protocols used—the older distance vector protocols and the newer link state protocols.

Distance Vector Routing

The two most commonly used distance vector routing protocols are both called Routing Information Protocol (RIP). One version is used on networks running TCP/IP. The other, sometimes referred to as IPX RIP, is designed for use on networks running the IPX/SPX protocol.

RIP works on the basis of *hop counts*. A hop is defined as one step on the journey to the data's destination. Each router that the data has to cross to reach its destination constitutes a hop. The maximum number of hops that RIP can accommodate is 15. That is to say that in a network that uses RIP, all routers must be within 15 hops of each other to communicate. Any hop count that is in excess of 15 is considered unreachable.

Distance vector routing protocols operate by having each router send updates about all the other routers it knows about to the routers directly connected to it. These updates are used by the routers to compile their routing tables. The updates are sent out automatically every 30 or 60 seconds. The actual interval depends on the routing protocol being used. Apart from the periodic updates, routers can also be configured to send a *triggered update* if a change in the network topology is detected. The process by which routers learn of a change in the network topology is known as *convergence*.

Although distance vector protocols are capable of maintaining routing tables, they have three problems. The first is that the periodic update system can make the update process very slow. The second problem is that the periodic updates can create large amounts of network traffic—much of the time unnecessarily as the topology of the network should rarely change. The last, and perhaps more significant, problem is that because the routers only know about the next hop in the journey, incorrect information can be propagated between routers, creating routing loops.

Two strategies are used to combat this last problem. One, *split horizon*, works by preventing the router from advertising a route back to the other router from which it was learned. The other, *poison reverse* (also called split horizon with poison reverse), dictates that the route *is* advertised back on the interface from which it was learned, but that it has a metric of 16. Recall that a metric of 16 is considered an unreachable destination.

Link State Routing

Link state routing works quite differently from distance vector-based routing. Rather than each router telling each other connected router about the routes it is aware of, routers in a link state environment send out special packets, called *link state advertisements (LSA)*, which contain information only about that router. These LSAs are forwarded to all the routers on the network, which enables them to build a map of the entire network. The advertisements are sent when the router is first brought onto the network and when a change in the topology is detected.

Of the two (distance vector and link state), distance vector routing is better suited to small networks and link state routing to larger ones. Link state protocols do not suffer from the constant updates and limited hop count, and they are also quicker to correct themselves (to converge) when the network topology changes.

On TCP/IP networks, the most commonly used link state routing protocol is the Open Shortest Path First (OSPF). On IPX networks, the NetWare Link State Protocol (NLSP) is used. Table 3.1 summarizes the distance vector and link state protocols used with each network protocol.

 It is necessary to know which distance vector and link state routing protocols are associated with which network protocols.

Table 3.1   Routing Protocols

Network Protocol	Distance Vector	Link State
TCP/IP	RIP	OSPF
IPX/SPX	RIP*	NLSP

IPX RIP

Sometimes, to distinguish between the versions of RIP for IP and IPX, the version for IPX is referred to as IPX RIP.

Gateways

Any device that translates one data format to another is called a *gateway*. Some examples of gateways include a router that translates data from one network protocol to another, a bridge that converts between two networking systems, and a software application that converts between two dissimilar formats. The key point about a gateway is that only the data format is translated, not the data itself. In many cases, the gateway functionality is incorporated into another device.

Gateways and Default Gateways

Don't confuse a gateway with the term *default gateway*, which is discussed in Chapter 6, "WAN Technologies, Remote Access, and Security Protocols." The term default gateway refers to a router to which all network transmissions not destined for the local network are sent.

CSU/DSU

A Channel Service Unit/Digital Service Unit (CSU/DSU), sometimes called Data Service Unit, is a device that converts the digital signal format used on LANs into one used on WANs. Such translation is necessary because the networking technologies used on WANs are different from those used on LANs.

The CSU/DSU sits between the LAN and the access point provided by the telecommunications company. Many router manufacturers are now incorporating CSU/DSU functionality into their products.

Network Cards

Network cards, also called Network Interface Cards, are devices that enable computers to connect to the network.

When specifying or installing a NIC, you must consider the following issues:

➤ **System bus compatibility**—If the network interface you are installing is an internal device, bus compatibility must be verified. The most common bus system in use is the Peripheral Component Interconnect (PCI) bus, but some older systems might still use Industry Standard Architecture (ISA) expansion cards.

➤ **System resources**—Network cards, like other devices, need IRQ and memory I/O addresses. If the network card does not operate correctly after installation, there might be a device conflict.

➤ **Media compatibility**—Today, the assumption is that networks use twisted-pair cabling, so if you need a card for coaxial or fiber-optic connections, you must specify this. Wireless network cards are also available.

Even more than the assumption you are using twisted-pair cabling is that the networking system being used is Ethernet. If you require a card for another networking system such as Token Ring, this must be specified when you order.

ALERT When working on a Token Ring network, you have to ensure that all network cards are set to transmit at the same speeds. NICs on an Ethernet network can operate at different speeds.

To install or configure a network interface, you will need drivers of the device, and might need to configure it, although many devices are now plug and play. Most network cards are now software configured. Many of these software configuration utilities also include testing capabilities. The drivers and software configuration utilities supplied with the cards are often not the latest available, so it is best practice to log on to the Internet and download the latest drivers and associated software.

ISDN Adapters

Integrated Services Digital Network (ISDN) is a remote access and WAN technology that can be used in place of a Plain Old Telephone Service (POTS) dial-up link if it is available. The availability of ISDN depends on whether your local telecommunications service provider offers the service, the quality of the line to your premises, and your proximity to the provider's location. ISDN offers greater speeds than a modem and can also pick up and drop the line considerably faster.

If ISDN is available and you do elect to use it, a special device called an *ISDN terminal adapter* is needed to connect to the line. ISDN terminal adapters can be add-in expansion cards, external devices that connect to the serial port of the system, or specialized interfaces built in to routers or other networking equipment. The ISDN terminal adapter is necessary because, although it uses digital signals, the signals are formatted differently from those used on a LAN. In addition, ISDN can create multiple communication channels on a single line. Today, ISDN is not widely deployed and has been replaced by faster and often cheaper technologies.

Wireless Access Points

Wireless access points (APs) are a transmitter and receiver (transceiver) device used to create a wireless LAN (WLAN). APs are typically a separate network device with a built-in antenna, transmitter, and adapter. APs use the wireless infrastructure network mode to provide a connection point between WLANs and a wired Ethernet LAN. APs also typically have several ports allowing a way to expand the network to support additional clients.

Depending on the size of the network, one or more APs might be required. Additional APs are used to allow access to more wireless clients and to expand the range of the wireless network. Each AP is limited by a transmissions range—the distance a client can be from a AP and still get a useable signal. The actual distance depends on the wireless standard being used and the obstructions and environmental conditions between the client and the AP.

A WAP can operate as a bridge connecting a standard wired network to wireless devices or as a router passing data transmissions from one access point to another.

Saying that an AP is used to extend a wired LAN to wireless clients doesn't give you the complete picture. A wireless AP today can provide different services in addition to just an access point. Today, the APs might provide many ports that can be used to easily increase the size of the network. Systems can be added and removed from the network with no affect on other systems on the network. Also, many APs provide firewall capabilities and DHCP service. When they are hooked up, they will provide client systems with a private IP address and then prevent Internet traffic from accessing client systems. So in effect, the AP is a switch, a DHCP Server, router, and a firewall.

APs come in all different shapes and sizes. Many are cheaper and designed strictly for home or small office use. Such APs have low powered antennas and limited expansion ports. Higher end APs used for commercial purposes have very high powered antennas enabling them to extend the range that the wireless signal can travel.

APs are used to create a wireless LAN and to extend a wired network. APs are used in the infrastructure wireless topology.

Modems

A *modem*, short for modulator/demodulator, is a device that converts the digital signals generated by a computer into analog signals that can travel over conventional phone lines. The modem at the receiving end converts the signal back into a format the computer can understand. Modems can be used as a means to connect to an ISP or as a mechanism for dialing up to a LAN.

Modems can be internal add-in expansion cards, external devices that connect to the serial or USB port of a system, PCMCIA cards designed for use in laptops, or proprietary devices designed for use on other devices such as portables and handhelds.

The configuration of a modem depends on whether it is an internal or external device. For internal devices, the modem must be configured with an interrupt request (IRQ) and a memory I/O address. It is common practice, when installing an internal modem, to disable the built-in serial interfaces and assign the modem the resources of one of those (typically COM2). Table 3.2 shows the resources associated with serial (COM) port assignments.

Table 3.2 Common Serial (COM) Port Resource Assignments			
Port ID	IRQ	I/O Address	Associated Serial I/F Number
COM1	4	03F8	1
COM2	3	02F8	2
COM3	4	03E8	1
COM4	3	02E8	2

For external modems, you need not concern yourself directly with these port assignments, as the modem connects to the serial port and uses the resources assigned to it. This is a much more straightforward approach and one favored by those who work with modems on a regular basis. For PCMCIA and USB modems, the plug-and-play nature of these devices makes them simple to configure, and no manual resource assignment is required. Once the modem is installed and recognized by the system, drivers must be configured to enable use of the device.

Two factors directly affect the speed of the modem connection—the speed of the modem itself and the speed of the Universal Asynchronous Receiver/Transmitter (UART) chip in the computer that is connected to the modem. The UART chip controls the serial communication of a computer, and although modern systems have UART chips that can accommodate far greater speeds than the modem is capable of, older systems should be checked to make sure that the UART chip is of sufficient speed to support the modem speed. The UART chip installed in the system can normally be determined by looking at the documentation that comes with the system. Table 3.3 shows the maximum speed of the commonly used UART chip types.

Table 3.3 UART Chip Speeds	
UART Chip	**Speed (Kbps)**
8250	9600
16450	9600
16550	115,200
16650	430,800
16750	921,600
16950	921,600

NOTE

Keep in mind that Internal modems have their own UARTs, but External modems use the UART that works with the Com Port.

ALERT

If you have installed an internal modem and are experiencing problems with other devices such as a mouse, there might be a resource conflict between the mouse and the modem. Also, legacy ISA NICs often use IRQ3 and might conflict with the modems.

Transceivers (Media Converters)

The term transceiver does describe a separate network device, but it can also be technology built and embedded in devices such as network cards and modems. In a network environment, a transceiver gets its name from being both a transmitter and a receiver of signals—thus the name transceivers. Technically, on a LAN, the transceiver is responsible for placing signals onto the network media and also detecting incoming signals traveling through the same wire. Given the description of the function of a transceiver, it makes sense that that technology would be found with network cards.

Although transceivers are found in network cards, they can be external devices as well. As far as networking is concerned, transceivers can ship as a module or chip type. Chip transceivers are small and are inserted into a system board or wired directly on a circuit board. Module transceivers are external to the network and are installed and function similarly to other computer peripherals, or they can function as standalone devices.

There are many types of transceivers—RF transceivers, fiber optic transceivers, Ethernet transceivers, wireless (WAP) transceivers, and more. Though each of these media types are different, the function of the transceiver remains the same. Each type of the transceiver used has different characteristics, such as the number of ports available to connect to the network and whether full-duplex communication is supported.

Listed with transceivers in the CompTIA objectives are media converters. Media converters are a technology that allows administrators to interconnect different media types—for example, twisted pair, fiber, and Thin or thick coax—within an existing network. Using a media converter, it is possible to connect newer 100Mbps, Gigabit Ethernet, or ATM equipment to existing networks such as 10BASE-T or 100BASE-T. They can also be used in pairs to insert a fiber segment into copper networks to increase cabling distances and enhance immunity to electromagnetic interference (EMI).

Firewalls

A *firewall* is a networking device, either hardware or software based, that controls access to your organization's network. This controlled access is designed to protect data and resources from an outside threat. To do this, firewalls are typically placed at entry/exit points of a network—for example, placing a firewall between an internal network and the Internet. Once there, it can control access in and out of that point.

Although firewalls typically protect internal networks from public networks, they are also used to control access between specific network segments within a network—for example, placing a firewall between the Accounts and the Sales departments.

As mentioned, firewalls can be implemented through software or through a dedicated hardware device. Organizations implement software firewalls through network operating systems (NOS) such as Linux/UNIX, Windows servers, and Mac OS servers. The firewall is configured on the server to allow or permit certain types of network traffic. In small offices and for regular home use, a firewall is commonly installed on the local system and configured to control traffic. Many third-party firewalls are available.

Hardware firewalls are used in networks of all sizes today. Hardware firewalls are often dedicated network devices that can be implemented with very little configuration and protect all systems behind the firewall from outside sources. Hardware firewalls are readily available and often combined with other devices today. For example, many broadband routers and wireless access points have firewall functionality built in. In such case, the router or WAP might have a number of ports available to plug systems in to.

Firewalls are discussed in greater detail in Chapter 8, "Configuring Network Security."

Table 3.4 provides a summary of the networking devices identified in this chapter.

Table 3.4	Network Devices Summary	
Device	**Function/Purpose**	**Key Points**
Hub	Connects devices on a twisted-pair network.	A hub does not perform any tasks besides signal regeneration.
Switch	Connects devices on a twisted-pair network.	A switch forwards data to its destination by using the MAC address embedded in each packet.
Bridge	Divides networks to reduce overall network traffic.	A bridge allows or prevents data from passing through it by reading the MAC address.
Router	Connects networks together.	A router uses the software-configured network address to make forwarding decisions.
Gateway	Translates from one data format to another.	Gateways can be hardware or software based. Any device that translates data formats is called agateway.
CSU/DSU	Translates digital signals used on a LAN to those used on a WAN.	CSU/DSU functionality is sometimes incorporated into other devices, such as a router with a WAN connection.
Network card	Enables systems to connect to the network.	Network interfaces can be add-in expansion cards, PCMCIA cards, or built-in interfaces.
ISDN terminal adapter	Connects devices to ISDN lines.	ISDN is a digital WAN technology often used in place of slower modem links. ISDN terminal adapters are required to reformat the data format for transmission on ISDN links.
WAP	Provides network capabilities to wireless network devices.	A WAP is often used to connect to a wired network, thereby acting as a link between wired and wireless portions of the network.

(continued)

Table 3.4	Network Devices Summary *(continued)*	
Device	**Function/Purpose**	**Key Points**
Modem	Provides serial communication capabilities across phone lines.	Modems modulate the digital signal into analog at the sending end and perform the reverse function at the receiving end.
Transceiver	Coverts one media type to another, such as UTP to fiber.	A device that functions as a transmitter and a receiver of signals such as analog or digital.
Firewall	Provides controlled data access between networks.	Firewalls can be hardware or software based and are an essential part of a networks security strategy.

MAC Addresses

A *MAC address* is a unique 6-byte address that is burned into each network interface or more specifically, directly into the PROM chip on the NIC. The number must be unique, as the MAC address is the basis by which almost all network communication takes place. No matter which networking protocol is being used, the MAC address is still the means by which the network interface is identified on the network. Notice that I say network interface. That's very important, as a system that has more than one network card in it will have more than one MAC address.

MAC addresses are expressed in six hexadecimal values. In some instances, the six values are separated by colons (:); in others, hyphens (-) are used; and in still others, a space is simply inserted between the values. In any case, because the six values are hexadecimal, they can only be numbers 0–9 and the letters A–F. So, a valid MAC address might be 00-D0-56-F2-B5-12 or 00-26-DD-14-C4-EE. There is a way of finding out whether a MAC address exists through the IEEE, which is responsible for managing MAC address assignment. The IEEE has a system in place that lets you identify the manufacturer of the network interface by looking at the MAC address.

For example, in the MAC address 00-80-C8-E3-4C-BD, the 00-80-C8 portion identifies the manufacturer and the E3-4C-BD portion is assigned by the manufacturer to make the address unique. The IEEE is the body that assigns manufacturers their IDs, called Organizationally Unique Identifiers, and the manufacturer then assigns the second half, called the Universal LAN MAC address. From the IEEE's perspective, leaving the actual assignment of addresses to the manufacturers significantly reduces the administrative over-head for the IEEE.

As discussed, MAC addresses are expressed in hexadecimal format. For that reason, they can only use the numbers 0–9 and the letters A–F. There are only six bytes, so a MAC address should be six groups of two characters. Any other number of characters or any answer that contains a letter other than those described can be immediately discounted as an answer.

The method by which you can discover the MAC address of the network interfaces in your equipment depends on which operating system is being used. Table 3.5 shows you how to obtain the MAC address on some of the more common platforms.

Be prepared to identify the commands used to view a MAC address as shown in Table 3.5. You might be asked to identify these commands on the Network+ exam.

Table 3.5 Commands to Obtain MAC Addresses	
Platform	**Method**
Windows 95/98/Me	Run the **winipcfg** utility.
Windows NT/2000	Run **ipconfig /all** from a command prompt.
Linux/Some UNIX	Run the **ifconfig -a** command.
Novell NetWare	Run the **config** command.
Cisco Router	Run the **sh int** *<interface name>* command.

As you work with network interfaces more, you might start to become familiar with which ID is associated with which manufacturer. Although this is a skill that might astound your friends and impress your colleagues, it won't help you with the Network+ exam. Just knowing what does, and doesn't, represent a valid MAC address will be sufficient on the exam.

Review and Test Yourself

The following sections provide you with the opportunity to review what you learned in this chapter and to test yourself.

The Facts

➤ Both hubs and switches are used in Ethernet networks. Token Ring networks, which are few and far between, use special devices called multistation access units (MSAUs) to create the network.

➤ The function of a hub is to take data from one of the connected devices and forward it to all the other ports on the hub.

➤ Most hubs are considered *active* because they regenerate a signal before forwarding it to all the ports on the device. In order to do this, the hub needs a power supply.

➤ Rather than forwarding data to all the connected ports, a switch forwards data only to the port on which the destination system is connected.

➤ Switches make forwarding decisions based on the Media Access Control (MAC) addresses of the devices connected to them to determine the correct port.

➤ In cut-through switching, the switch begins to forward the packet as soon as it is received.

➤ In a store-and-forward configuration, the switch waits to receive the entire packet before beginning to forward it.

➤ FragmentFree switching works by reading only the part of the packet that enables it to identify fragments of a transmission.

➤ Hubs and switches have two types of ports: Medium Dependent Interface (MDI) and Medium Dependent Interface-Crossed (MDI-X).

➤ A straight-through cable is used to connect systems to the switch or hub using the MDI-X ports.

➤ In a crossover cable, wires 1 and 3 and wires 2 and 6 are crossed.

➤ Both hubs and switches come in managed and unmanaged versions. A managed device has an interface through which it can be configured to perform certain special functions.

➤ Bridges are used to divide up networks and thus reduce the amount of traffic on each network.

➤ Unlike bridges and switches, which use the hardware-configured MAC address to determine the destination of the data, routers use the software-configured network address to make decisions.

➤ With distance-vector routing protocols, each router communicates all the routes it knows about to all other routers to which it is directly attached.

➤ RIP is a distance routing protocol for both TCP and IPX.

➤ Link state protocols communicate with all other devices on the network to build complete maps of the network. They generate less network traffic than distance vector routing protocols but require more powerful network hardware.

➤ Open Shortest Path First (OSPF) and NetWare Link State Protocol (NLSP) are the most commonly used link state routing protocols used on IP and IPX networks respectively.

➤ The term *gateway* is applied to any device, system, or software application that can perform the function of translating data from one format to another.

➤ A CSU/DSU acts as a translator between the LAN and the WAN data formats.

➤ Wireless network devices gain access to the network via Wireless Access Points.

➤ Wireless Access Points provide additional functionality such as DHCP, router, firewall, and hub/switch.

➤ Modems translate digital signals from a computer into analog signals that can travel across conventional phone lines.

➤ Transceivers are devices on the network that both transmit and receive data signals.

➤ Media converters are used to convert between one media type and another.

Key Terms

- Hub
- Bridge
- Gateway
- Network Interface Cards
- ISDN adapters
- Switch
- Router
- CSU/DSU
- System area network cards
- Wireless Access Points (WAPs)
- Modems
- MAC addresses

- Distance vector
- Link state
- Dynamic routing
- Static routing
- NLSP
- OSPF
- RIP
- Convergence
- Bridging loops
- Transceivers
- Media converters

Exam Prep Questions

1. Users are complaining that the performance of the network is not satisfactory. It takes a long time to pull files from the server, and, under heavy loads, workstations can become disconnected from the server. The network is heavily used, and a new video conferencing application is about to be installed. The network is a 100BaseT system created with Ethernet hubs. Which of the following devices are you most likely to install to alleviate the performance problems?

   ❑ A. Switch
   ❑ B. Router
   ❑ C. Bridge
   ❑ D. Gateway

2. Which of the following devices forwards data packets to all connected ports?

   ❑ A. Router
   ❑ B. Switch
   ❑ C. Bridge
   ❑ D. Hub

3. Of the following routing methods, which is likely to take the most amount of administration time in the long term?

   ❑ A. Static
   ❑ B. Link state
   ❑ C. Distance vector
   ❑ D. Dynamic

4. Your manager asks you to look into some upgrades for your network. The current network is a 10Base2 system, and you have been experiencing numerous hard-to-track-down cable problems. As a result, you have decided to upgrade to a 10BaseT system. On the networking vendor's price list are both active and passive hubs. The passive hubs are considerably cheaper than the active ones, and you are tempted to opt for them so that you come in under budget. A colleague advises you against the purchase of passive hubs. What is the primary difference between an active and a passive hub?

   ❑ A. Passive hubs do not offer any management capabilities.
   ❑ B. Passive hubs cannot be used in full-duplex mode.
   ❑ C. Passive hubs do not regenerate the data signal.
   ❑ D. Passive hubs forward data to all ports on the hub, not just the one for which they are intended.

5. Which of the following statements best describes a gateway?

□ A. It is a device that enables data to be routed from one network to another.

□ B. It is a term used to refer to any device that resides at the entrance of a network.

□ C. It is a device, system, or application that translates data from one format to another.

□ D. It is a network device that can forward or block data based on the MAC address embedded within the packet.

6. You have a thin coaxial-based Ethernet network and are experiencing performance problems on the network. By using a network performance-monitoring tool, you determine that there are a large number of collisions on the network. In an effort to reduce the collisions, you decide to install a network bridge. What kind of bridge are you most likely to implement?

□ A. Collision bridge

□ B. Transparent bridge

□ C. Visible bridge

□ D. Translational bridge

7. Which of the following represents a valid MAC address?

□ A. **00-D0-56-F2-B5-12**

□ B. **00-63-T6-4H-7U-78**

□ C. **00-62-DE-6F-D2**

□ D. **000-622-DE5-75E-EA6**

8. Which of the following devices passes data based on the MAC address?

□ A. Hub

□ B. Switch

□ C. MSAU

□ D. Router

9. What is the speed of the 16550 UART chip?

□ A. 921,600

□ B. 430,800

□ C. 115,200

□ D. 9,600

10. Which of the following devices would you find only on a Token Ring network?

□ A. Hub

□ B. Switch

□ C. MSAU

□ D. Router

Answers to Exam Prep Questions

1. The correct answer is A. Replacing Ethernet hubs with switches can yield significant performance improvements. Of the devices listed, they are also the only one that can be substituted for hubs. Answer B, router, is incorrect as a router is used to separate networks, not as a connectivity point for workstations. A bridge could be used to segregate the network and so improve performance, but a switch is a more obvious choice in this example. Therefore, answer C is incorrect. Answer D, gateway, is incorrect. A gateway is a device, system, or application that translates data from one format to another.

2. The correct answer is D. Hubs are inefficient devices that send data packets to all connected devices. Many of today's networks are upgrading to switches that pass data packets to the specific destination device. This method significantly increases network performance.

3. The correct answer is A. Static routing will take more time to administer in the long term, as any changes to the network routing table must be entered manually. Answers B and C are incorrect. Distance vector and link state are both dynamic routing methods. Answer D is also incorrect. Dynamic routing might take more time to configure initially; but in the long term, it will require less administration time. It can adapt to changes in the network layout automatically.

4. The correct answer is C. An active hub regenerates the data signal before forwarding, it a passive hub does not. Answer A is incorrect. The management capabilities of a hub have nothing to do with the active/passive aspect of the device. Answer B is incorrect. Hubs are not capable of operating in full-duplex mode. Only network switches are capable of performing this function in this context. Answer D describes the function of a switch, not a hub.

5. The correct answer is C. A gateway can be a device, system, or application that translates data from one format to another. Answers B and D are more likely to describe a router than a gateway. Answer D describes a bridge. A bridge is a device that is used to segregate a network. It makes forwarding or blocking decisions based on the MAC address embedded within the packet.

6. The correct answer is B. A transparent bridge can be used to segment a network, which reduces the amount of collisions and the overall network traffic. It is called transparent because the other devices on the network do not need to be aware of the device and will, in fact, operate as if it wasn't there. Answer D is incorrect as a translational bridge is

used in environments where it is necessary to translate from one data format to another. Such a conversion is not necessary in this scenario. Answers A and C are invalid. There is no such thing as a collision bridge or a visible bridge.

7. The correct answer is A. A MAC address is a 6-byte address that is expressed in hexadecimal format. Answer B contains the letters T and U, which are not valid. Hexadecimal format uses only numbers and the letters A through F. For this reason, answer B is incorrect. Answer C is only five bytes, so it is incorrect. Answer D is incorrect because a byte in hexadecimal is expressed in two characters and the answer uses three.

8. The correct answer is B. When determining the destination for a data packet, the switch learns the MAC address of all devices attached to it and then matches the destination MAC address in the data it receives. None of the other devices pass data based solely on the MAC address.

9. The correct answer is C. 115,200 is the speed of the 16550 UART chip. Answer A is incorrect as 921,600 is the speed of the 16750 and 16950 UART chips. Answer B is incorrect as 430,800 is the speed of the 16650 UART chip and 9600 is the speed of the 8250 UART chip.

10. The correct answer is C. A Multistation Access Unit (MSAU) is used as the connectivity point on a Token Ring network. Answers A and B are incorrect. Switches and hubs are associated with Ethernet networks. Answer D is incorrect. Routers can be found on both Token Ring and Ethernet networks.

Need to Know More?

 Olexa, Ron. *Implementing 802.11, 802.16, and 802.20 Wireless Networks: Planning, Troubleshooting, and Operations.* Communications Engineering. Newnes Publishing, 2004.

 Computer networking products and information—www. alliedtelesyn.com.

Computer networking device information—www.3com.com.

 "Computer Networking Tutorials and Advice"—compnetworking. about.com.

OSI Model and Network Protocols

Objectives

2.2 Identify the seven layers of the OSI (Open Systems Interconnect) model and their functions

2.3 Identify the OSI (Open Systems Interconnect) layers at which the following network components operate:

✓ Hubs
✓ Switches
✓ Bridges
✓ Routers
✓ NICs (Network Interface Card)
✓ WAPs (wireless access point)

2.4 Differentiate between the following network protocols in terms of routing, addressing schemes, interoperability, and naming conventions:

✓ IPX/SPX (Internetwork Packet Exchange/Sequence Packet Exchange)
✓ NetBEUI (Network Basic Input/Output System Extended User Interface)
✓ AppleTalk/AppleTalk over IP (Internet Protocol)
✓ TCP/IP (Transmission Control Protocol/Internet Protocol)

What you need to know

✓ Identify the seven layers of the OSI model
✓ Identify the function of each of the layers in the OSI model
✓ Identify the layer at which networking devices function
✓ Identify the various common protocol suites used with networks
✓ Understand the basic characteristics of common protocol suites

Introduction

One of the most important networking concepts to understand is the *Open Systems Interconnect (OSI)* reference model. This conceptual model, created by the *International Organization for Standardization (ISO)* in 1978 and revised in 1984, describes a network architecture that allows data to be passed between computer systems.

This chapter looks at the OSI model and describes how it relates to real-world networking. It also examines how common network devices relate to the OSI model. Even though the OSI model is conceptual, an appreciation of its purpose and function can help you better understand how protocol suites and network architectures work in practical applications.

OSI Seven Layer Model

As shown in Figure 4.1, the OSI reference model is built, bottom to top, in the following order: physical, data-link, network, transport, session, presentation, and application. The physical layer is classified as layer 1 and the top layer of the model, the application layer, as layer 7.

On the Network+ exam, you may either see an OSI layer referenced by its name, such as data-link, or by its layer number. For instance, you might find that a router is referred to as a layer 3 device.

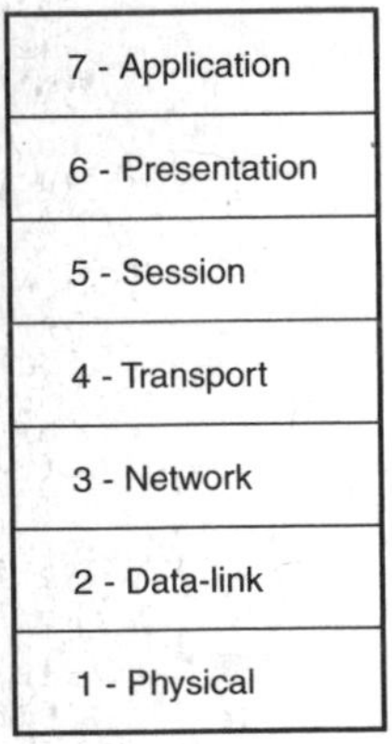

| 7 - Application |
| 6 - Presentation |
| 5 - Session |
| 4 - Transport |
| 3 - Network |
| 2 - Data-link |
| 1 - Physical |

Figure 4.1   The OSI seven layer model.

Each layer of the OSI model has a specific function. The following sections describe the function of each layer, starting with the physical layer and working up the model.

Physical Layer (Layer 1)

The physical layer of the OSI model identifies the physical characteristics of the network, including the following specifications:

➤ **Hardware**—The type of media used on the network such as type of cable, type of connector, and pinout format for cables.

➤ **Topology**—The physical layer identifies the topology to be used in the network. Common topologies include ring, mesh, star, and bus.

In addition to these, the physical layer also defines the voltage used on a given media and the frequency at which the signals that carry the data move from one state to another. These characteristics dictate the speed and bandwidth of a given media as well as the maximum distance over which a certain media type can be used.

Data-link Layer (Layer 2)

The data-link layer is responsible for getting data to the physical layer so that it can be transmitted over the network. The data-link layer is also responsible for error detection, error correction, and hardware addressing. The term *frame* is used to describe the logical grouping of data at the data-link layer.

The data-link layer has two distinct sublayers—the *Media Access Control* (*MAC*) sublayer and the *Logical Link Control* (*LLC*) sublayer.

➤ **MAC layer**—The MAC address is defined at this layer. The MAC address is the physical or hardware address burned into each NIC. The MAC sublayer also controls access to network media. The MAC layer specification is included in the IEEE802.1 standard.

➤ **LLC layer**—The LLC layer is responsible for the error and flow-control mechanisms of the data-link layer. The LLC layer is specified in the 802.2 standard.

Network Layer (Layer 3)

The primary responsibility of the network layer is *routing*—providing mechanisms by which data can be passed from one network system to another. It does not specify how the data is passed, but rather provides the mechanisms to do so. Functionality at the network layer is provided through protocols, which are software components.

Protocols at the network layer are also responsible for *route selection*, which refers to determining the best path for the data to take throughout the network. In contrast to the data-link layer, which uses MAC addresses to communicate on the LAN, network protocols use software configured addresses and special routing protocols to communicate on the network. The term *packet* is used to describe the logical grouping of data at the data-link layer.

 When working with networks, there are two ways in which routes can be configured: *statically* or *dynamically*. In a static routing environment, routes are added manually to the routing tables. In a dynamic routing environment, routing protocols such as *Routing Information Protocol* (*RIP*) and *Open Shortest Path First* (*OSPF*) are used. These protocols communicate routing information between networked devices on the network.

Transport Layer (Layer 4)

The basic function of the transport layer is to provide mechanisms to transport data between network devices. Primarily it does this in three ways:

➤ **Error checking**—Protocols at the transport layer ensure that data is sent or received correctly.

➤ **Service addressing**—Protocols such as TCP/IP support many network services. The transport layer makes sure that data is passed to the right service at the upper layers of the OSI model.

➤ **Segmentation**—To traverse the network, blocks of data need to be broken down into packets that are of a manageable size for the lower layers to handle. This process, called *segmentation*, is the responsibility of the transport layer.

Protocols at the Transport Layer

Protocols that operate at the transport layer can either be connectionless, such as the User Datagram Protocol (UDP) , or connection oriented, such as *Transmission Control Protocol* (*TCP*). For a further discussion of these protocols, and of the difference between connection oriented and connectionless protocols, refer to the information on network protocols later in this chapter.

Flow Control

The transport layer is also responsible for *data flow control*, which refers to the way in which the receiving device can accept data transmissions. There are two common methods of flow control used, *buffering* and *windowing*:

➤ **Buffering**—When buffering flow control is used, data is temporarily stored and waits for the destination device to become available. Buffering can cause a problem if the sending device transmits data much faster than the receiving device is able to manage it.

➤ **Windowing**—In a windowing environment, data is sent in groups of segments that require only one acknowledgment. The size of the window (that is, how many segments fit into one acknowledgment) is defined at the time the session between the two devices is established. As you can imagine, the need to have only one acknowledgment for every, say, five segments can greatly reduce overhead.

Session Layer (Layer 5)

The session layer is responsible for managing and controlling the synchronization of data between applications on two devices. It does this by establishing, maintaining, and breaking sessions. Whereas the transport layer is responsible for setting up and maintaining the connection between the two nodes, the session layer performs the same function on behalf of the application.

Presentation Layer (Layer 6)

The presentation layer's basic function is to convert the data intended for or received from the application layer into another format. Such conversion is necessary because of the way in which data is formatted, so it can be transported across the network. This conversion is not necessarily readable by applications. Some common data formats handled by the presentation layer include the following:

➤ **Graphics files**—JPEG, TIFF, GIF, and so on are graphics file formats that require the data to be formatted in a certain way.

➤ **Text and data**—The presentation layer can translate data into different formats such as American Standard Code for Information Interchange (ASCII) and the Extended Binary Coded Decimal Interchange Code (EBCDIC).

▶ **Sound/video**—MPEGs, QuickTime video, and MIDI files all have their own data formats to and from which data must be converted.

Another very important function of the presentation layer is *encryption*, which is the scrambling of data so that it can't be read by anyone other than the intended recipient. Given the basic role of the presentation layer—that of data-format translator—it is the obvious place for encryption and decryption to take place.

Application Layer (Layer 7)

In simple terms, the function of the application layer is to take requests and data from the users and pass them to the lower layers of the OSI model. Incoming information is passed to the application layer, which then displays the information to the users. Some of the most basic application-layer services include file and print capabilities.

The most common misconception about the application layer is that it represents applications that are used on a system such as a Web browser, word processor, or a spreadsheet. Instead, the application layer defines the processes that enable applications to use network services. For example, if an application needs to open a file from a network drive, the functionality is provided by components that reside at the application layer.

OSI Model Summary

In summary, Table 4.1 lists the seven layers of the OSI model and describes some of the most significant points of each layer.

Table 4.1	OSI Model Summary
OSI Layer	**Major Functions**
Physical (Layer 1)	Defines thephysical structure of the network and the topology.
Data-link (Layer 2)	Provides error detection and correction. Uses two distinct sublayers: the Media Access Control (MAC) and Logical Link Control (LLC) layers. Identifies the method by which media is accessed. Defines hardware addressing through the MAC sublayer.
Network (Layer 3)	Handles the discovery of destination systems and addressing. Provides the mechanism by which data can be passed from one network system to another.

(continued)

Table 4.1   OSI Model Summary *(continued)*

OSI Layer	Major Functions
Transport (Layer 4)	Provides connection services between the sending and receiving devices and ensures reliable data delivery. Manages flow control through buffering or windowing. Provides segmentation, error checking, and service identification.
Session (Layer 5)	Synchronizes the data exchange between applications on separate devices.
Presentation (Layer 6)	Translates data from the format used by applications into one that can be transmitted across the network. Handles encryption and decryption of data. Provides compression and decompression functionality. Formats data from the application layer into a format that can be sent over the network.
Application (Layer 7)	Provides access to the network for applications.

Identifying the OSI Layers at Which Various Network Components Operate

When you have an understanding of the OSI model, it is possible to relate network connectivity devices discussed in Chapter 3, "Networking Devices," to the appropriate layer of the OSI model. Knowing at which OSI level a device operates allows you to better understand how it functions on the network. Table 4.2 identifies various network devices and maps them to the OSI model.

For the Network+ exam, you are expected to be able to identify at which layer of the OSI model certain network devices operate.

Table 4.2   Mapping Network Devices to the OSI Model

Device	OSI Layer
Hub	Physical (Layer 1)
Switch	Data-link (Layer 2)
Bridge	Data-link (Layer 2)
Router	Network (Layer 3)
NIC	Data-link (Layer 2)
WAP	Data-link (Layer 2)

Differentiating Among Protocols

You might find yourself working with a number of protocols in today's networked environments. The primary function of these protocols is to facilitate communication between network devices. This section reviews the main characteristics of the most widely used protocols.

Connectionless and Connection-oriented Protocols

Before getting into the characteristics of the various network protocols and protocol suites, it's important to first identify the difference between connection-oriented and connectionless protocols.

In a *connection-oriented* communication, there is guaranteed delivery of the data. Any packet that is not received by the destination system is resent by the sending device. Communication between the sending and receiving devices continues until the transmission has been verified. Because of this, connection-oriented protocols have a higher overhead and place greater demands on bandwidth.

 Connection-oriented protocols such as TCP (Transmission Control Protocol) are capable of accommodating lost or dropped packets by asking the sending device to retransmit them. They are capable of doing this because they wait for all the packets in an entire message to be received before considering the transmission complete. On the sending end, connection-oriented protocols also assume that a lack of acknowledgment is sufficient reason to retransmit.

In contrast to connection-oriented communication, *connectionless* protocols offer only a *best-effort* delivery mechanism. Basically, the information is sent—there is no confirmation that the data has been received. If there is an error in the transmission, there is no mechanism to resend the data, so transmissions made with connectionless protocols are not guaranteed. Connectionless communication requires far less overhead than connection-oriented communication, so it is popular in applications such as streaming audio and video where a small number of dropped packets might not represent a significant problem.

 As you work through the various protocols, keep an eye out for the protocols that are connectionless and those that are connection-oriented.

Internetwork Packet Exchange/Sequenced Packet Exchange

Like TCP/IP and AppleTalk that are also discussed in this chapter, IPX/SPX is not a single protocol but rather a protocol suite. IPX/SPX was created by Novell for use on Novell networks. When Novell had a larger presence in the network arena, so too did the IPX/SPX protocol suite. Today, the popularity of IPX/SPX has yielded to TCP/IP although it is still used in some network environments—enough at least to include it in the CompTIA exam objectives. TCP/IP's suitability for large multisite networks and its general acceptance has now even led Novell to adopt TCP/IP as the protocol of choice. Table 4.3 shows some of the protocols that comprise the IPX/SPX suite and their functions.

Table 4.3   IPX/SPX Protocols and Their Functions

Protocol	Function	Related OSI Layer(s)
Internetwork Packet Exchange (IPX)	A connectionless transport protocol that is primarily responsible for logical network addressing, route selections, and connection services.	Network, Transport
NetWare Link State Protocol (NLSP)	NLSP uses a link-state route discovery method to build routing tables.	Network
NetWare Core Protocol (NCP)	NCP is a connection-oriented protocol that provides the connection between clients and services.	Application, Presentation, Session
Routing Information Protocol (RIP)	Similar to the routing protocol used with TCP/IP, RIP is responsible for the routing of packets on an IPX/SPX network.	Network
Service Advertising Protocol (SAP)	SAP allows systems providing services to the network, such as file and print services, to announce their services and addresses to the network.	Application, Presentation, Session
Sequenced Packet Exchange (SPX)	SPX is a connection-based protocol used when guaranteed message delivery is required on the network.	Transport

IPX Addressing

An example of an IPX address is 0BAD33CE:0003FE7C06EC. The 0BAD33CE portion represents the IPX address for the network, which is also sometimes referred to as the network number. The part 0003FE7C06EC is the MAC address of the node, which is used for the second part of the address. The node MAC address is derived directly from the MAC address burned on to each network card, but in IPX addressing, it is expressed without the colons (:). In addition to this format, IPX addresses can also be written with each group of four hexadecimal characters separated by colons—for example, 0000:0007:003C:7F53:04CF. In some cases, any leading 0s on the network address portion are dropped. For example, 00000007 can be expressed simply as 7. The address would then be 7:003C:7F53:04CF.

Because IPX addresses are expressed in hexadecimal, they can only contain the letters A through F and the numbers 0 through 9. There can be a maximum of 8 characters in the segment portion and 12 characters in the MAC address portion. You should be prepared to identify how IPX addressing works for the Network+ exam.

IPX Interoperability

As you might expect, the IPX/SPX protocol suite is fully supported by Novell NetWare, but it can also be used in a Microsoft Windows environment. Microsoft includes its own version of the IPX/SPX protocol, NWLink, which provides this interoperability. Using the NWLink protocol and the Microsoft Client for NetWare, Windows systems can connect to a NetWare server using IPX/SPX.

Because of the prevalence of TCP/IP, interoperability with the IPX/SPX protocol has become less important. For some time now, TCP/IP has been used as the default protocol on Novell networks. As far as Linux is concerned, there is a way to use the IPX/SPX protocol on a Linux system, but TCP/IP is the protocol of choice there too.

IPX/SPX Naming

Unlike TCP/IP, which is discussed later, there are few issues with IPX/SPX naming because servers are normally the only parts of a network that are assigned names. These names, which are sometimes referred to as addresses, can be up to 47 characters (in current versions of NetWare). Workstations do not need such names and instead just use IPX addresses.

NetBEUI Protocol

NetBEUI was once a popular protocol for smaller networks. It is fast and easy to configure but has one significant drawback in that it is not routable. This one fact limits NetBEUI to a single network segment far too restrictive for the majority of today's networking environments.

NetBEUI Addressing

In terms of addressing, NetBEUI is perhaps the simplest of all the protocols discussed here. For this reason, it is still sometimes used on very small simple networks such as those found in a home or on very small business networks. Computers on a NetBEUI network are identified by NetBIOS names. The NetBIOS name can be no longer than 15 characters and must be unique to the network. Using the 15 characters, you can assign the computers descriptive names such as *workstation*, *student1*, or *secretary2*.

Interoperability with NetBEUI

The discussion on interoperability with NetBEUI is a short one; it is used on Windows platforms exclusively.

AppleTalk

AppleTalk is a protocol associated with Apple networks. The AppleTalk protocol is an established protocol, having been introduced in the early 1980s, and continued development toward the end of the 1980s enabled it to become a viable internet-working protocol.

Like the IPX/SPX and TCP/IP protocol suites, the AppleTalk protocol suite is composed of several protocols. Table 4.4 lists the protocols within the AppleTalk protocol suite and their functions.

Table 4.4	AppleTalk Protocols and Their Functions	
Protocol	**Function**	**OSI Layer**
AppleShare	AppleShare provides application layer services, including file and print sharing.	Application (Layer 7)
AppleTalk Address Resolution Protocol (AARP)	AARP is used to map AppleTalk addresses to Ethernet and Token Ring physical addresses.	Network (Layer 3)

(continued)

Table 4.4   AppleTalk Protocols and Their Functions *(continued)*

Protocol	Function	OSI Layer
AppleTalk Data Stream Protocol (ADSP)	ADSP is a session layer protocol used to establish connections between network devices. It also functions at the transport layer and manages flow control.	Session (Layer 5)
AppleTalk Filing Protocol (AFP)	The AFP protocol manages file sharing for the network.	Presentation (Layer6)/ Application (Layer 7)
AppleTalk Session Protocol (ASP)	Similar to the ADSP protocol, ASP works at the session layer of the OSI model and establishes and releases connections between networked devices.	Session (Layer 5)
AppleTalk Transaction Protocol (ATP)	ATP establishes a connectionless session between networked systems. ATP functions at the transport layer.	Transport (Layer 4)
Datagram Delivery Protocol (DDP)	Performs datagram delivery and also handles routing functions.	Network (Layer 3)
EtherTalk Link Access Protocol (ELAP)	ELAP is a variation of the AppleTalk protocol that is compatible with the Ethernet protocol.	Data-Link (Layer 2)
Name Binding Protocol (NBP)	The NBP protocol is used to map computer hostnames to network layer addresses.	Transport (Layer 4)
Printer Access Protocol (PAP)	PAP is a session layer protocol used to provide printing services on an AppleTalk network.	Session (Layer 5)
Routing Table Maintenance Protocol (RTMP)	RTMP is the protocol on AppleTalk networks that maintains the routing tables for the network.	Transport (Layer 4)
TokenTalk Link Access Protocol (TLAP)	TLAP is a variation on the AppleTalk protocol that is compatible with the Token Ring protocol.	Data-Link (Layer 2)
Zone Information Protocol (ZIP)	ZIP is used to divide network devices into logical groups called *zones*.	Session (Layer 5)

Be prepared to identify the protocols found within the AppleTalk protocols suite for the Network+ exam.

The CompTIA objective for this topic cites AppleTalk over IP under the same heading as AppleTalk. In reality, AppleTalk over IP is just the use of the AppleTalk Filing Protocol (AFP) over a TCP/IP connection.

AppleTalk Addressing

Like the other protocols discussed, the AppleTalk protocol uses a two-part addressing scheme—a node and a network section. The node portion of the address is assigned automatically when the system is first brought up onto the network. It is a randomly generated number and then broadcast to the entire network. If a duplicate node address is assigned, another will be assigned and rebroadcast to the network. The network portion of the address is assigned by the network administrator.

The actual AppleTalk address is 24 bits long with 16 bits used for the network address and 8 bits for the node address. AppleTalk addresses are expressed in decimal format, with the network and node addresses separated by a period. An example of an AppleTalk address might be 4.67. The 4 represents the network number, and 67 is the node number.

When working with AppleTalk networks, you will work with *zones*. Zones are a method used to group devices and systems together into logical units. Zones are similar in function to workgroups on Windows systems, and make it easier for users and administrators alike to locate resources.

AppleTalk Interoperability

AppleTalk was designed for the purpose of being used on Apple networks and, as such, is not natively supported by most of the other major operating systems. Because of this, today, other protocols such as TCP/IP are a more common choice, even for Apple-based networks. In fact, Macintosh systems themselves support the use of TCP/IP. AppleTalk can be configured to work with other platforms, but, given the proliferation of TCP/IP, this is not widely done.

AppleTalk Routing

The earliest implementations of AppleTalk were not routable, but later versions were. Routing functionality for AppleTalk is provided by the RTMP protocol. RTMP provides similar functionality to the RIP protocol used with IPX/SPX and TCP/IP networks.

AppleTalk Naming

AppleTalk networks use logical hostnames, making systems readily recognizable on the network. The network address-to-hostname resolution is handled by the NBP protocol in the AppleTalk protocol suite. It performs a similar function to that provided by DNS on a TCP/IP network.

The TCP/IP Protocol Suite

Quite often, TCP/IP is referred to as a network protocol, although that's not entirely accurate. Like IPX/SPX and AppleTalk, TCP/IP is actually a protocol suite comprised of many separate protocols—each of which has its own purpose and function. Combined, they all provide the TCP/IP functionality. The following list contains some of the more well-known protocols found within the TCP/IP protocol suite:

➤ Address Resolution Protocol (ARP)

➤ File Transfer Protocol (FTP)

➤ Internet Control Message Protocol (ICMP)

➤ Internet Protocol (IP)

➤ Reverse Address Resolution Protocol (RARP)

➤ Simple Mail Transfer Protocol (SMTP)

➤ Transmission Control Protocol (TCP)

This is just an introduction to the protocols found within the TCP/IP protocol suite. Chapter 5, "TCP/IP (Transmission Control Protocol/Internet Protocol)," as well as objectives 2.5 through 2.12, discuss TCP/IP in much more detail.

TCP/IP Standards

One of the strengths of the TCP/IP protocol suite is that it is not owned by any one party and is not licensed. This is in contrast to protocols such as AppleTalk and IPX/SPX, which are owned by Apple and Novell, respectively. Because of its non-proprietary nature, TCP/IP has an *open development model* with its standards published in documents known as *Requests for Comments (RFCs)*. RFCs are maintained by the *Internet Engineering Task Force (IETF)*. You can find RFCs pertaining to TCP/IP on IETF's website at www.ietf.org.

TCP/IP Addressing

Anyone who has worked with TCP/IP knows that TCP/IP addressing can be a complex topic. This section provides an overview of TCP/IP addressing to compare how other protocols handle addressing. However, Chapter 5 provides a detailed look at the TCP/IP protocol including addressing.

In the most commonly deployed version of TCP/IP, version 4, (IPv4) addresses are composed of four sets of 8 bits referred to as *octets*. These are expressed in numbers and separated by periods. An example of a TCP/IP address is 192.168.3.2. This format is often referred to as a 32-bit dotted decimal.

A single TCP/IP address represents both the IP address of an individual system and the network to which the system is attached. Determining which part of the IP address belongs to the network and which belongs to the node is the responsibility of the *subnet mask*. If part of the address refers to the network, it is assigned a binary value of 1 within the subnet mask. If it is the node address, it's assigned a binary value of 0 within the subnet mask.

For example, if you had a subnet mask of 255.255.255.0, the first two octets refer to the network and the second refer to the node address. So using the previous IP address as an example, the 192.168.3 portion of the address represents the network ID, and the .2 portion of the address represents the node ID. Table 4.5 shows default subnet masks and addressing examples.

You can expect to have to identify the parts of an IP address for the exam.

Table 4.5   Determining Network and Node Addresses

Subnet Mask	IP Address	Network Address	Node Address
255.0.0.0	192.168.10.100	192	168.10.100
255.255.0.0	192.168.10.100	192.168	10.100
255.255.255.0	192.168.10.100	192.168.10	100

As previously mentioned, more information on TCP/IP addressing is provided in Chapter 5.

TCP/IP Interoperability

Of all the protocols used on today's networks, TCP/IP is by far the most versatile and interoperable. All of the popular operating systems today not only support TCP/IP, but the vast majority also use it as the default protocol. This means that in any network environment, you can have Linux, Windows, and NetWare servers and clients all communicating using TCP/IP.

TCP/IP Naming

Systems on a TCP/IP network can be accessed from the network either by their IP address or by a hostname. Hostnames are the names assigned to the system to make them easier to remember. For instance, the secretary's computer might have the address of 192.168.4.23, but you can access it using its hostname of *secretary1* or whatever name you assign it.

The name-resolution process from IP address to hostname is often performed dynamically through a *Domain Name Server* (*DNS*). It can also be done statically using a text file called 'Hosts,' which is stored on each system. More information on name resolution is provided in Chapter 5.

TCP/IP Routing

TCP/IP is a fully routable protocol, making it a natural choice for large networks and those that span multiple locations. As mentioned previously, TCP/IP is a protocol suite; there are two primary protocols within TCP/IP that provide the routing functionality—*Routing Information Protocol* (*RIP*) and *Open Shortest Path First* (*OSPF*) .

Protocol Summary

To help you in your exam preparations, the most pertinent information from this section is listed in Table 4.6.

Table 4.6 Comparison of the Various Protocols Discussed in This Chapter			
Protocol	**Overview**	**Routable**	**Addressing**
IPX/SPX	Used to be the default protocol for NetWare, but now TCP/IP is preferred. Still supported by Netware, Windows, and Linux. Simplest addressing scheme of routable protocols discussed here.	Yes	Uses the MAC address to identify the node, and an eight-character (4-byte) hexadecimal address to identify the network.
NetBEUI	Used by Windows.	No	Uses NetBIOS names to identify systems on the network.

(continued)

Table 4.6	Comparison of the Various Protocols Discussed in This Chapter *(continued)*		
Protocol	**Overview**	**Routable**	**Addressing**
AppleTalk	Used by Macintosh with some support on other platforms.	Yes	Uses a two-part addressing scheme. The first is a randomly generated number for the node address, and the second an administrator assigned number for the network address.
TCP/IP	Used by default with UNIX, Linux, NetWare and Windows systems. Also supported by Macintosh systems and practically every other computing platform. The most inter-operable of all protocols.	Yes	Uses four sets of 8 bits referred to as *octets*. A subnet mask is used to define what parts of the address refer to the network, and what parts refer to the node.

Review and Test Yourself

The following sections provide you with the opportunity to review what you learned in this chapter and to test yourself.

The Facts

➤ The application layer provides access to the network for applications and certain user functions. Displays incoming information and prepares outgoing information for network access.

➤ The presentation layer converts data from the application layer into a format that can be sent over the network. Converts data from the session layer into a format that can be understood by the application layer. Handles encryption and decryption of data. Provides compression and decompression functionality.

➤ The session layer synchronizes the data exchange between applications on separate devices. Handles error detection and notification to the peer layer on the other device.

➤ The transport layer establishes, maintains, and breaks connections between two devices. Determines the ordering and priorities of data. Performs error checking and verification and handles retransmissions, if necessary.

➤ The network layer provides mechanisms for the routing of data between devices across single or multiple network segments. Handles the discovery of destination systems and addressing.

➤ The data-link layer has two distinct sublayers: LLC and MAC. It performs error detection and handling for the transmitted signals and defines the method by which the medium is accessed. Finally, it defines hardware addressing through the MAC sublayer.

➤ The physical layer defines the physical structure of the network. It defines voltage/signal rates and the physical connection methods as well as the physical topology.

➤ Application protocols map to the application, presentation, and session layers of the OSI model. These include AFP, FTP, TFTP, NCP, SMTP, HTTP and SNMP.

➤ Transport protocols map to the transport layer of the OSI model and are responsible for the transporting of data across the network. These include ATP, NetBEUI, SPX, TCP, and UDP.

➤ The NetBEUI protocol uses names as addresses and is not routable.

➤ Network protocols are responsible for providing the addressing and routing information. These include IP, IPX, and DDP.

➤ RIP is routing protocol. There are versions of RIP for both IPX/SPX and TCP/IP networks.

Key Terms

➤ OSI

➤ Physical layer

➤ Data-link layer

➤ Network layer

➤ Transport layer

➤ Session layer

➤ Presentation layer

➤ Application layer

➤ LLC

➤ MAC

➤ Static routing

➤ Dynamic routing

➤ TCP

➤ UDP

➤ SPX

➤ Connectionless protocols

➤ Connection-oriented protocols

➤ NetBEUI

➤ AppleTalk

➤ Protocol suite

➤ Application protocol

➤ Transport protocol

➤ Network protocol

➤ Packet

➤ ATP

➤ FTP

➤ SNMP

➤ SMTP

➤ TCP

➤ UDP

➤ SPX

➤ IPX

➤ IP

➤ TCP/IP addressing

➤ Routing protocols

➤ OSPF

➤ RIP

Exam Prep Questions

1. Which of the following protocols provide network routing functionality? (Choose two.)

   ❑ A. NBP
   ❑ B. RIP
   ❑ C. RTMP
   ❑ D. NCP

2. Which of the following protocols uses the MAC address as part of the addressing scheme?

   ❑ A. IPX/SPX
   ❑ B. TCP/IP
   ❑ C. AppleTalk
   ❑ D. NetBEUI

3. At which OSI layer does a WAP operate?

   ❑ A. Network
   ❑ B. Physical
   ❑ C. Data-link
   ❑ D. Session

4. Which of the following are sublayers of the data-link layer? (Choose two.)

   ❑ A. MAC
   ❑ B. LCL
   ❑ C. Session
   ❑ D. LLC

5. Which of the following protocols uses names as network addresses?

   ❑ A. NetBEUI
   ❑ B. TCP/IP
   ❑ C. IPX/SPX
   ❑ D. AppleTalk

6. Which of the following characteristics best describe the SPX protocol? (Choose two.)

   ❑ A. Provides a connectionless communication between network devices.
   ❑ B. Provides connection-oriented communication between network devices.
   ❑ C. Functions at the network layer of the OSI model.
   ❑ D. Functions at the transport layer of the OSI model.

7. Which of the following OSI layers is responsible for establishing connections between two devices?

   ❑ A. Network
   ❑ B. Transport
   ❑ C. Session
   ❑ D. Data-link

8. Which of the following protocol suites uses ZIP?

   ❑ A. TCP/IP
   ❑ B. IPX/SPX
   ❑ C. NetBEUI
   ❑ D. AppleTalk

9. Which of the following protocols offer guaranteed delivery? (Choose two.)

   ❑ A. SPX
   ❑ B. IPX
   ❑ C. IP
   ❑ D. TCP

10. At which OSI layer does a switch operate?

    ❑ A. Layer 1
    ❑ B. Layer 2
    ❑ C. Layer 3
    ❑ D. Layer 4

Answers to Exam Prep Questions

1. The correct answers are B and C. RIP is a distance-vector routing protocol used on TCP/IP and IPX/SPX networks. RTMP is a routing protocol used on AppleTalk networks. Answer A, NBP, is incorrect. The NBP protocol is used to map computer hostnames to network layer addresses on AppleTalk networks. Answer D is incorrect—NCP is a part of the IPX/SPX protocol suite that makes network services available to clients.

2. The correct answer is A. IPX/SPX uses the MAC address to identify the node and network addresses. TCP/IP, answer B, uses a four octet address to identify the node and network. AppleTalk uses a 24-bit address—part of which is randomly generated and part of which is manually assigned. NetBEUI uses alphanumeric names to refer to devices.

3. The correct answer is C. A wireless access point (WAP) operates at the data-link layer of the OSI model. An example of a network layer device is a router. An example of a physical layer device is a hub. Session layer components are normally software, not hardware.

4. The correct answers are A and D. The data-link layer is broken into two distinct sublayers, the Media Access Control (MAC) and the Logical Link Control (LLC). LCL is not a valid term, and session is another of the OSI model layers.

5. The correct answer is A. NetBEUI uses names as network addresses. All the other network protocols listed use numbered addressing schemes at the network layer to identify systems.

6. The correct answers are B and D. SPX is a connection-oriented protocol that operates at the transport layer of the OSI model. IPX is an example of a connectionless protocol. Network layer protocols are most commonly associated with route discovery and datagram delivery.

7. The correct answer is B. The transport layer is responsible for establishing a connection between networked devices. The Network layer is most commonly associated with route discovery and datagram delivery. Protocols at the Session layer synchronize the data exchange between applications on separate devices. Protocols at the Data-link layer perform error detection and handling for the transmitted signals and define the method by which the medium is accessed.

8. The correct answer is D. The Zone Information Protocol (ZIP) is used to divide AppleTalk network devices into logical groups called *zones*. None of the other protocol suites listed use ZIP or zones. TCP/IP uses network numbers to define logical areas of a network, as does IPX/SPX. NetBEUI uses workgroup names, which are similar to zones, but it does not use ZIP.

9. The correct answers are A and D. Both SPX and TCP are connection-oriented protocols, which guarantee delivery of data. IPX is a connectionless transport protocol, and IP is a network layer protocol that's responsible for tasks such as addressing and route discovery.

10. The correct answer is B. A switch uses the MAC addresses of connected devices to make its forwarding decisions. Therefore, it is referred to as a data-link, or Layer 2, network device. Devices or components that operate at Layer 1 are typically media based, such as cables or connectors. An example of a Layer 3 device would be a router. Layer 4 components are typically software based, not hardware.

Need to Know More?

 Bird, Drew and Harwood, Mike. *Network+ Exam Prep 2*. Que Publishing, 2005.

Ogletree, Terry William. *Upgrading and Repairing Networks, Fourth Edition*. Que Publishing, 2003.

Tulloch, Mitch, Ingrid Tulloch. *Microsoft Encyclopedia of Networking, Second Edition*. Microsoft Press. 2002.

5

TCP/IP (Transmission Control Protocol/Internet Protocol)

Objectives

2.5 Identify the components and structure of IP (Internet Protocol) addresses (IPv4, IPv6), and the required setting for connections across the Internet

2.6 Identify classful IP (Internet Protocol) ranges and their subnet masks (for example, Class A, B, and C)

2.7 Identify the purpose of subnetting

2.8 Identify the differences between private and public network addressing schemes

2.9 Identify and differentiate between the following IP (Internet Protocol) addressing methods:
- ✓ Static
- ✓ Dynamic
- ✓ Self-assigned (APIPA [Automatic Private Internet Protocol Addressing])

2.10 Define the purpose, function, and use of the following protocols used in the TCP/IP (Transmission Control Protocol/Internet Protocol) suite:
- ✓ TCP (Transmission Control Protocol)
- ✓ UDP (User Datagram Protocol)
- ✓ FTP (File Transfer Protocol)
- ✓ SFTP (Secure File Transfer Protocol)
- ✓ TFTP (Trivial File Transfer Protocol)
- ✓ SMTP (Simple Mail Transfer Protocol)
- ✓ HTTP (Hypertext Transfer Protocol)
- ✓ HTTPS (Hypertext Transfer Protocol Secure)
- ✓ POP3/IMAP4 (Post Office Protocol version 3/Internet Message Access Protocol version 4)
- ✓ Telnet

✓ SSH (Secure Shell)
✓ ICMP (Internet Control Message Protocol)
✓ ARP/RARP (Address Resolution Protocol/Reverse Address Resolution Protocol)
✓ NTP (Network Time Protocol)
✓ NNTP (Network News Transport Protocol)
✓ SCP (Secure Copy Protocol)
✓ LDAP (Lightweight Directory Access Protocol)
✓ IGMP (Internet Group Multicast Protocol)
✓ LPR (Line Printer Remote)

2.11 Define the function of TCP/UDP (Transmission Control Protocol/User Datagram Protocol) ports

2.12 Identify the well-known ports associated with the following commonly used services and protocols:

✓ 20 FTP (File Transfer Protocol)
✓ 21 FTP (File Transfer Protocol)
✓ 22 SSH (Secure Shell)
✓ 23 Telnet
✓ 25 SMTP (Simple Mail Transfer Protocol)
✓ 53 DNS (Domain Name Server)
✓ 69 TFTP (Trivial File Transfer Protocol)
✓ 80 HTTP (Hypertext Transfer Protocol)
✓ 110 POP3 (Post Office Protocol version 3)
✓ 119 NNTP (Network News Transport Protocol)
✓ 123 NTP (Network Time Protocol)
✓ 143 IMAP4 (Internet Message Access Protocol version 4)
✓ 443 HTTPS (Hypertext Transfer Protocol Secure)

2.13 Identify the purpose of network services and protocols (for example, DNS (Domain Name Service), NAT (Network Address Translation), ICS (Internet Connection Sharing), WINS (Windows Internet Name Service), SNMP (Simple Network Management Protocol), NFS (Network File System), Zeroconf (Zero configuration), SMB (Server Message Block), AFP (Apple File Protocol) and LPD (Line Printer Daemon))

What you need to know

✓ Understand IPv4 and IPv6 addressing
✓ Understand the function of default gateways
✓ Identify the function and purpose of subnetting
✓ Identify the differences between public and private networks
✓ Identify the function of protocols within the TCP/IP protocol suite
✓ Identify the ports associated with common network services
✓ Understand the function of various network services

Introduction

Without question, the TCP/IP protocol suite is the most widely implemented protocol on networks today. As such, it is a focus on the Network+ exam. To pass the exam, you will definitely need to understand the material presented in this chapter.

This chapter deals with the individual protocols within the protocol suite. The chapter looks at the function of the individual protocols and their purposes. It starts by discussing one of the more complex facets of TCP/IP—addressing.

IP Addressing

IP addressing is one of the most challenging aspects of TCP/IP and one that can leave even the most seasoned network administrators scratching their heads. Fortunately, the Network+ exam requires only a fundamental knowledge of IP addressing. The following sections look at how IP addressing works for both IPv4 and the newest version of the IP, IPV6.

To communicate on a network using the TCP/IP protocol, each system has to be assigned a unique address. The address defines both the number of the network to which the device is attached and the number of the node on that network. In other words, the IP address provides two pieces of information. It's a bit like a street name and a house number of a person's home address.

Each device on a logical network segment must have the same network address as all the other devices on the segment. All the devices on that network segment must then have different node addresses.

In IP addressing, another set of numbers, called a subnet mask, is used to define which portion of the IP address refers to the network address and which refers to the node address.

IP addressing is different in IPv4 and IPv6. We'll begin our discussion by looking at IPv4, as IPv6 networks are still few and far between.

IPv4

An IPv4 address is composed of four sets of 8 binary bits, which are referred to as *octets*. The result is that IP addresses are 32 bits in length. Each bit in each octet is assigned a decimal value. The leftmost bit has a value of 128, followed by 64, 32, 16, 8, 4, 2, and 1, left to right.

Each bit in the octet can be either a 1 or a 0. If the value is 1, it is counted as its decimal value, and if it is 0, it is ignored. If all the bits are 0, the value of the octet is 0. If all the bits in the octet are 1, the value is 255, which is 128+64+32+16+8+4+2+1.

By using the set of 8 bits and manipulating the 1s and 0s, you can obtain any value between 0 and 255 for each octet.

Table 5.1 shows some examples of decimal-to-binary value conversions.

Table 5.1 Decimal-to-Binary Value Conversions		
Decimal Value	Binary Value	Decimal Calculation
10	00001010	8+2=10
192	11000000	128+64=192
205	11001101	128+64+8+4+1=205
223	11011111	128+64+16+8+4+2+1=223

IP Address Classes

IP addresses are grouped into logical divisions called *classes*. In the IPv4 address space, there are five address classes (A through E), although only three (A, B, C) are used for assigning addresses to clients. Class D is reserved for multicast addressing, and Class E is reserved for future development.

Of the three classes available for address assignments, each uses a fixed-length subnet mask to define the separation between the network and the node address. A Class A address uses only the first octet to represent the network portion, a Class B address uses two octets, and a Class C address uses the first three octets. The upshot of this system is that Class A has a small number of network addresses, but each class A address has a very large number of possible host addresses. Class B has a larger number of networks, but each class B address has a smaller number of hosts. Class C has an even larger number of networks, but each Class C address has an even smaller number of hosts. The exact numbers are provided in Table 5.2.

Table 5.2 IPv4 Address Classes and the Number of Available Network/Host Addresses				
Address Class	Range	Number of Networks	Number of Hosts per Network	Binary Value of First Octet
A	1–126	126	16,777,214	0xxxxxxx
B	128–191	16384	65,534	10xxxxxx

(continued)

Table 5.2 **IPv4 Address Classes and the Number of Available Network/Host Addresses** *(continued)*

Address Class	Range	Number of Networks	Number of Hosts per Network	Binary Value of First Octet
C	192–223	2,097,152	254	110xxxxx
D	224–239	NA	NA	1110xxxx
E	240–255	NA	NA	1111xxxx

Notice in Table 5.2 that the network number 127 is not included in any of the ranges. The 127 network ID is reserved for the local loopback. The local loopback is a function of the protocol suite used in the troubleshooting process.

For the Network+ exam, you should be prepared to identify into which class a given address falls. You should also be prepared to identify the loopback address.

Subnet Mask Assignment

Like an IP address, a *subnet mask* is most commonly expressed in a 32-bit dotted-decimal format. Unlike an IP address, though, a subnet mask performs just one function: It defines which parts of the IP address refer to the network address and which refer to the node address. Each of the classes of IP address used for address assignment has a standard subnet mask associated with it. The default subnet masks are listed in Table 5.3.

Table 5.3 **Default Subnet Masks Associated with IP Address Classes**

Address Class	Default Subnet Mask
A	255.0.0.0
B	255.255.0.0
C	255.255.255.0

Default Gateways

Default gateways are the means by which a device can access hosts on other networks for which it does not have a specifically configured route. Most workstation configurations actually just use a default gateway rather than having any static routes configured. Such a configuration is practical because workstations are typically only connected to one network, and thus have only one way off that network.

When a system wants to communicate with another device, it first determines whether the host is on the local network or a remote network. If the host is on a remote network, the system looks in the routing table to determine whether it has an entry for the network that the remote host is on. If it does, it uses that route. If it does not, the data is sent to the default gateway.

In essence, the default gateway is simply the path out of the network for a given device.

If a system is not configured with any static routes or a default gateway, it is limited to operating on its own network segment.

IPv6 Addressing

Although IPv4 has served us well for a number of years, it is finally starting to reach its end. The main problem with IPv4 is simply that the demand for IP addresses outweighs what IPv4 is capable of providing. That is where IPv6 comes in.

By far, the most significant aspect of IPv6 is its addressing capability. The address range of IPv4 is nearly depleted, and it is widely acknowledged that we are just at the beginning of the digital era. Therefore, we need an addressing scheme that offers more addresses than can possibly be used in the foreseeable future. IPv6 delivers exactly that. Whereas IPv4 uses a 32-bit address, IPv6 uses a 128-bit address that yields a staggering 340,282,366,920,938,463,463,374,607,431,768,211,456 possible addresses!

IPv6 addresses are expressed in a different format from those used in IPv4. An IPv6 address is composed of eight octet pairs expressed in hexadecimal, separated by colons. The following is an example of an IPv6 address:

```
42DE:7E55:63F2:21AA:CBD4:D773:CC21:554F
```

Be ready to identify both a valid IPv4 and IPv6 address for the Network+ exam.

Subnetting

Now that you have looked at how IP addresses are used, you can learn the process of subnetting. *Subnetting* is a process by which the node portions of an IP address are used to create more networks than you would have if you used the default subnet mask.

To illustrate subnetting, let's use an example. Suppose that you have been assigned the Class B address 150.150.0.0. Using this address and the default subnet mask, you could have a single network (150.150) and use the rest of the address as node addresses. This would give you a large number of possible node addresses, which in reality is probably not very useful. With subnetting, you use bits from the node portion of the address to create more network addresses. This reduces the number of nodes per network, but chances are, you will still have more than enough.

There are two main reasons for subnetting. First, it allows you to use IP address ranges more effectively. Second, it provides increased security and manageability to IP networking by providing a mechanism to create multiple networks rather than having just one. Using multiple networks confines traffic to only the network that it needs to be on, which reduces overall network traffic levels. Multiple subnets also create more broadcast domains, which in turn reduces network wide broadcast traffic.

 Subnetting does not increase the number of IP addresses available. It increases the number of network IDs and, as a result, decreases the number of node IDs per network. It also creates more broadcast domains—broadcasts are not forwarded by routers, so they are limited to just the network on which they originate.

Identifying the Differences Between Public and Private Networks

IP addressing involves many considerations, not least important of which are public and private networks. A *public network* is a network to which anyone can connect. The best, and perhaps only pure, example of such a network is the Internet. A *private network* is any network to which access is restricted. A corporate network or a network in a school are examples of private networks.

The Internet Assigned Numbers Authority (IANA) is responsible for assigning IP addresses to public networks, however, because of the workload involved in maintaining the systems and processes to do this, they have delegated the assignment process to a number of regional authorities. For more information, visit http://www.iana.org/ipaddress/ip-addresses.htm.

The main difference between public and private networks, apart from the fact that access to a private network is tightly controlled and access to a public network is not, is that the addressing of devices on a public network must be considered carefully, whereas addressing on a private network has a little more latitude.

As already discussed, in order for hosts on a network to communicate by using TCP/IP, they must have unique addresses. This number defines the logical network each host belongs to and the host's address on that network. On a private network with, say, three logical networks and 100 nodes on each network, addressing is not a particularly complex task. On a network on the scale of the Internet, however, addressing is very complex.

If you are connecting a system to the Internet, you need to get a valid registered IP address. Most commonly, you would obtain this address from your ISP. Alternatively, for example, if you wanted a large number of addresses, you could contact the organization responsible for address assignment in your geographical area. You can determine who the regional numbers authority for your area is by visiting the IANA website.

Because of the nature of their business, ISPs have large blocks of IP addresses that they can assign to their clients. If you need a registered IP address, getting one from an ISP will almost certainly be a simpler process than going through a regional numbers authority. Some ISPs' plans actually include blocks of registered IP addresses, working on the principle that businesses are going to want some kind of permanent presence on the Internet. Of course, if you discontinue your service with the ISP, you will no longer be able to use the IP address they provided.

Private Address Ranges

To provide flexibility in addressing and to prevent an incorrectly configured network from polluting the Internet, certain address ranges are set aside for private use. These address ranges are called *private ranges* because they are designated for use only on private networks. These addresses are special because Internet routers are configured to ignore any packets they see that use these addresses. This means that if a private network "leaks" onto the Internet, it won't make it any farther than the first router it encounters.

Three ranges are defined in RFC 1918—one each from Classes A, B, and C. You can use whichever range you want, although the Class A and Class B address ranges offer more addressing options than does Class C. The address ranges are defined in Table 5.4.

Table 5.4	Private Address Ranges	
Class	Address Range	Default Subnet Mask
A	10.0.0.0–10.255.255.255	255.0.0.0
B	172.16.0.0–172.31.255.255	255.255.0.0
C	192.168.0.0–192.168.255.255	255.255.255.0

Assigning IP Addresses

Having established the need for each system on a TCP/IP based network to have a unique address, we can now go on to look at how those systems receive their addresses.

Static Addressing

Static addressing refers to the manual assignment of IP addresses to a system. There are two main problems with this approach. Statically configuring one system with the correct address is simple, but in the course of configuring, say, a few hundred systems, mistakes are likely to be made. If the IP addresses are entered incorrectly, the system will most likely not be capable of connecting to other systems on the network. Another drawback of static addressing is reconfiguration. If the IP addressing scheme for the organization changes, each system must again be manually reconfigured. In a large organization with hundreds or thousands of systems, such a reconfiguration could take a considerable amount of time. These drawbacks to static addressing are so significant that nearly all networks use dynamic IP addressing.

Dynamic Addressing

Dynamic addressing refers to the assignment of IP addresses automatically. On modern networks the mechanism used to do this is the Dynamic Host Configuration Protocol (DHCP). DHCP is a protocol, part of the TCP/IP protocol suite, which enables a central system to provide client systems with IP addresses. Assigning addresses automatically with DHCP alleviates the burden of address configuration and reconfiguration that occurs with static IP addressing.

The basic function of the DHCP service is to automatically assign IP addresses to client systems. To do this, ranges of IP addresses, known as *scopes*, are defined on a system that is running a DHCP server application. When another system configured as a DHCP client is initialized, it asks the server for an address. If all things are as they should be, the server assigns an address to the client for a predetermined amount of time, which is known as the *lease*, from the scope.

A DHCP server can typically be configured to assign more than just IP addresses; they are often used to assign the subnet mask, the default gateway, and Domain Name Service (DNS) information.

Using DHCP means that administrators do not have to manually configure each client system with a TCP/IP address. This removes the common problems associated with statically assigned addresses such as human error. The potential problem of assigning duplicate IP addresses is also eliminated. DHCP also removes the need to reconfigure systems if they move from one subnet to another, or if you decide to make a wholesale change of the IP addressing structure.

DHCP—Dependent and Independent

DHCP is a protocol-dependant service, not a platform dependent service. This means that you can use, for example, a Linux DHCP server for a network with Windows clients or a Novell DHCP server with Linux clients.

Like DHCP, BOOTP is a broadcast-based system. Therefore, routers must be configured to forward BOOTP broadcasts. Today, it is far more likely that DHCP, rather than BOOTP, is used.

APIPA

Automatic Private IP addressing (APIPA) is a feature introduced with Windows 98, and has been included in all subsequent Windows versions. The function of APIPA is that a system is capable of providing itself with an IP address in the event that it is incapable of receiving an address dynamically from a DHCP server. In such an event, APIPA assigns the system an address from the 169.254.0.0 address range and configures an appropriate subnet mask (255.255.0.0). However, it doesn't configure the system with a default gateway address. As a result, communication is limited to the local network.

If a system that does not support APIPA is unable to get an address from a DHCP server, it will typically assign itself an IP address of **0.0.0.0**. Keep this in mind when troubleshooting IP addressing problems on non-APIPA platforms.

The idea behind APIPA is that systems on a segment can communicate with each other in the event of DHCP server failure. In reality, the limited usability of APIPA makes it little more than a last resort measure. For example, imagine that a system is powered on while the DHCP server is operational and receives an IP address of 192.168.100.2. Then the DHCP server fails. Now, if the other systems on the segment are powered on and are unable to get an address from the DHCP server because it is down, they would self-assign addresses in the 169.254.0.0 address range via APIPA. The systems with APIPA addresses would be able to talk to each other, but they couldn't talk to a system that received an address from the DHCP server. Likewise, any system that received an IP address via DHCP would be unable to talk to systems with APIPA assigned addresses. This, and the absence of a default gateway, is why APIPA is of limited use in real-world environments.

TCP/IP Protocols

The TCP/IP protocol suite is made up of many different protocols, each of which performs a specific task or function. CompTIA identifies a number of these protocols in the objectives for the Network+ exam. The following sections look at the functions of these protocols and their purposes.

Internet Protocol (IP)

The IP protocol is a network layer protocol responsible for transporting data between network devices and for handling IP addressing. IP is a connectionless protocol, meaning that data delivery is not guaranteed; it takes the best-effort approach.

Transmission Control Protocol (TCP)

TCP functions at the transport layer of the OSI model and is a connection-oriented protocol that uses IP as its network protocol. Being connection-oriented means that TCP establishes a mutually acknowledged session between two hosts before communication takes place. TCP provides reliability to IP communications. Specifically, TCP adds features such as flow control, sequencing, and error detection and correction. For this reason, higher-level applications that need guaranteed delivery use TCP rather than its lightweight and connectionless brethren, the User Datagram Protocol (UDP).

User Datagram Protocol (UDP)

UDP operates at the transport layer of the OSI model and performs functions similar to that of TCP, with one notable difference; UDP is a connectionless protocol and does not guarantee data delivery. Both TCP and UDP use IP as its transport protocol.

Because UDP does not need to guarantee data delivery it is much more efficient than TCP, so for applications that don't need the added features of TCP, UDP is much more economical in terms of bandwidth and processing effort. A good example of UDP is an online radio station that sends data but does not confirm data delivery.

File Transfer Protocol (FTP)

The FTP protocol is an application layer protocol that provides a method for uploading and downloading files from a remote system running FTP server software. FTP uses the TCP transport protocol to guarantee the delivery of data packets.

FTP has some basic security capabilities, such as a capability to authenticate users. However, rather than create a user account for every user, you can configure FTP server software to accept anonymous logons. When you do this, the username is anonymous, and the password is normally the user's email address. Most FTP servers that offer files to the general public operate in this way.

FTP is popular for distributing files over the Internet but is also used within organizations that need to frequently exchange large files with other people or organizations that find it impractical to use regular email.

FTP Security Concerns

One significant issue with FTP is that usernames and passwords are communicated between client and host in clear text. This is a potential security concern. For this reason, secure methods of copying files such as SFTP, discussed later, are becoming more commonly used.

FTP is platform independent, meaning that all the common network operating systems offer FTP server capabilities. In addition, all commonly used client operating systems offer FTP client functionality. Alternatively, third-party utilities such as SmartFTP and CuteFTP are often used.

There are several commands that can be used with FTP; you are expected to understand these commands for the Network+ exam. Table 5.5 lists the commands that are used with the FTP protocol.

Table 5.5	FTP Commands
Command	**Purpose**
ls	Lists the files in the current directory on the remote system.
cd	Changes the working directory on the remote host.
lcd	Changes the working directory on the local host.
put	Uploads a single file to the remote host.
get	Downloads a single file from the remote host.
mput	Uploads multiple files to the remote host.
mget	Downloads multiple files from the remote host.
binary	Switches transfers into binary mode.
ascii	Switches transfers into ASCII mode (the default).

Secure File Transfer Protocol (SFTP)

One of the big problems associated with FTP is that it transmits data between sender and receiver in an unencrypted format. The solution is the Secure File Transfer Protocol, which is based on Secure Shell (SSH) technology. SSH provides robust authentication between sender and receiver, in addition to encryption capabilities.

SFTP is implemented through client and server software that is available for all commonly used computing platforms.

Trivial File Transfer Protocol (TFTP)

A variation on FTP is TFTP, which is also a file transfer mechanism. FTP and TFTP are both application layer protocols; however, TFTP does not have the rudimentary security capability or the level of functionality that FTP has. TFTP uses only UDP as a transport protocol, making it a *connectionless* protocol. As such, it has a lower overhead than FTP.

The biggest difference between TFTP and FTP is that TFTP is a connectionless protocol, using only the UDP transport protocol.

Another feature that TFTP does not offer is directory navigation. In FTP, commands can be executed to navigate around and manage the file system; TFTP offers no such capability. TFTP requires that you request not only exactly what you want, but also from what specific location.

Simple Mail Transfer Protocol (SMTP)

The SMTP protocol defines how mail messages are sent between hosts. SMTP is a connection-oriented protocol; it uses TCP connections to guarantee error-free delivery of messages. SMTP is not overly sophisticated and requires that the destination host always be available. For this reason, mail systems spool incoming mail so that users can read it at a later time. How the user then reads the mail depends on how the client accesses the SMTP server. SMTP is an application layer protocol. Today, SMTP is often used to send email between servers, whereas another protocol such as POP3 or IMAP4 is used to download the email from the server to a client system.

Hypertext Transfer Protocol (HTTP)

In practical uses, HTTP is the protocol that allows text, graphics, multimedia, and other material to be downloaded from an HTTP server (commonly called a Web server). HTTP defines which actions clients can request and how servers should answer those requests. HTTP uses TCP as a transport protocol, making it a connection-oriented protocol. However, it can also use UDP for certain functions.

HTTP uses a uniform resource locator (URL) to determine which page should be downloaded from the remote server. The URL contains the type of request (for example, http://), the name of the server being contacted (for example, www.novell.com), and optionally the page being requested (for example, /support). The result is the syntax that Internet-savvy people are familiar with: http://www.novell.com/support. HTTP functions at the application layer of the OSI model.

Hypertext Transfer Protocol Secure (HTTPS)

Normal HTTP requests are sent in clear text, and for some Internet transactions such as online banking or e-commerce, this poses a significant security problem. The solution for such applications is to use the HTTPS protocol. HTTPS uses a security technology known as *Secure Sockets Layer (SSL)*, which encrypts the information sent between the client and the host. You can tell when you are accessing a page with HTTPS because the URL will have an HTTPS:// address as opposed to 'plain' HTTP, which uses an address of HTTP://. An example of an HTTPS URL address is https://www.nationalonlinebank.com.

Like HTTP, HTTPS uses the TCP transport protocol and operates at the application layer of the OSI model.

Post Office Protocol version 3 (POP3) and Internet Message Access Protocol version 4 (IMAP4)

Both POP3 and IMAP4 are mechanisms for downloading, or pulling, email from a mail server. They are necessary because, although the mail is transported around the network via SMTP, users cannot always read it immediately so it must be stored in a central location. From this location, it must then be downloaded, which is what POP3 and IMAP4 allow you to do.

One of the problems with POP3 is that the password used to access a mailbox is transmitted across the network in clear text. That means if someone wanted to, he could determine your POP3 password with relative ease. This is an area in which IMAP4 offers an advantage over POP3. It uses a more sophisticated authentication system, which makes it harder for someone to determine a password.

Telnet

The function of Telnet is to allow the establishment of sessions on a remote host. A user can then execute commands on that remote host as if he were physically sitting at the system. Telnet is widely used to access UNIX and Linux systems, as well as to administer some managed networking equipment such as switches or routers. Telnet uses TCP as a transport layer protocol and functions at the application layer of the OSI model.

One of the problems with Telnet is that it is not secure. As a result, remote session functionality is now almost always achieved by using alternatives such as Secure Shell (SSH) .

Secure Shell (SSH)

Secure Shell (SSH) is a secure alternative to Telnet. SSH provides security by encrypting data as it travels between systems. It also provides more robust authentication systems than Telnet.

Although SSH, like Telnet, is primarily associated with UNIX and Linux systems, implementations of SSH are available for all commonly used computing platforms including Windows and Macintosh. As discussed earlier, SSH is the foundational technology for the Secure File Transfer Protocol (SFTP).

Internet Control Message Protocol (ICMP)

ICMP is a protocol that works with IP to provide error checking and reporting functionality. In effect, ICMP is a tool that IP uses in its quest to provide best-effort delivery. ICMP functions at the network layer of the OSI model.

ICMP can be used for a number of functions. Its most common is probably the widely used and incredibly useful `ping` utility. `ping` sends a stream of ICMP echo requests to a remote host. If the host is able to respond, it does so by sending echo reply messages back to the sending host. In that one simple process, ICMP enables the verification of the protocol suite configuration of both the sending and receiving nodes and any intermediate networking devices.

Address Resolution Protocol/Reverse Address Resolution Protocol (ARP/RARP)

The basic function of the ARP protocol is to resolve IP addresses to Media Access Control (MAC) addresses. When a system attempts to contact another host, IP first determines whether the other host is on the same network it is on by looking at the IP address. If IP determines that the destination is on the local network, it consults the ARP cache to determine whether it has a corresponding entry.

 The function of ARP is to resolve IP addresses to MAC addresses or layer 2 addresses.

If there is not an entry for the host in the ARP cache, IP sends a broadcast on the local network, asking the host with the target IP address to send back its MAC address. The communication is sent as a broadcast because without the target system's MAC address, the source system is unable to communicate directly with the target system.

The Reverse Address Resolution Protocol (RARP) performs the same function as ARP, but in reverse. In other words, it resolves MAC addresses to IP addresses. RARP makes it possible for applications or systems to learn their own IP address from a router or DNS server. Such a resolution comes in handy for tasks such as performing reverse lookups in DNS.

Network Time Protocol (NTP)

NTP uses the TCP transport protocol and is the protocol that facilitates the communication of time information between systems. The idea is that one system configured as a time provider transmits time information to other systems that can be both the time receivers and the time providers to other systems.

Network News Transport Protocol (NNTP)

The Network News Transfer Protocol (NNTP) is a protocol associated with posting and retrieving messages from newsgroups. A newsgroup is the name given to a discussion forum that is hosted on a remote system. By using NNTP client software, similar to that included with many common email clients, users can post, reply, and retrieve messages.

NNTP is an application layer protocol that uses TCP as its transport mechanism.

Secure Copy Protocol (SCP)

The Secure Copy Protocol (SCP) is another protocol based on Secure Shell (SSH) technology. SCP provides a secure means to copy files between systems on a network. By using SSH technology, it encrypts data as it travels across the network, thereby securing it from eavesdropping. It is intended as a more secure substitute for the Remote Copy Protocol (RCP). SCP is most commonly associated with UNIX or Linux platforms, though it is available as a command-line utility or as part of application software for most commonly used computing platforms. SCP operates at the application layer of the OSI model.

Lightweight Directory Access Protocol (LDAP)

The Lightweight Directory Access Protocol (LDAP) is a protocol that provides a mechanism to access and query directory services systems. In the context of the Network+ exam, these directory services systems are most likely to be Novell Directory Services (NDS) and Microsoft's Active Directory. Although LDAP supports command-line queries that are executed directly against the directory database, most LDAP interactions will be via utilities such as an authentication program (network logon) or locating a resource in the directory through a search utility. LDAP operates at the application layer of the OSI model.

Internet Group Management Protocol (IGMP)

The Internet Group Management Protocol (IGMP) protocol is associated with the process of multicasting. Multicasting is a mechanism by which groups of network devices can send and receive data between the members of the group at one time, rather than separately sending messages to each device in the group.

The IGMP protocol is used to register devices into a multicast group, as well as to discover what other devices on the network are members of the same multicast group. Common applications for multicasting include groups of routers on an internetwork and videoconferencing clients. IGMP operates at the network layer of the OSI model.

Line Printer Remote (LPR)

The Line Printer Remote (LPR) protocol provides a means to connect to print servers on a network. It is a generic printing protocol supported by all commonly used operating systems including UNIX, Windows, and Linux.

To make use of LPR, client software is installed on a system. When a file is sent to print, it is channeled over the network by LPR to a print server or printer. That server or printer runs a print server program, normally the Line Printer Daemon (LPD), which accepts the LPR information and adds that job to the print queue. LPR operates at the application layer of the OSI model.

TCP/IP Protocol Suite Summary

The details of each of the protocols discussed in the preceding sections are summarized in Table 5.6. You can use this table for review before you take the Network+ exam.

Table 5.6   TCP/IP Protocol Suite Summary

Protocol	Full Name	Description	OSI Layer
IP	Internet Protocol	Connectionless protocol used for moving data around a network.	Network
TCP	Transmission Control Protocol	Connection-oriented protocol that offers flow control, sequencing, and retransmission of dropped packets.	Transport
UDP	User Datagram Protocol	Connectionless alternative to TCP that is used for applications that do not require the functions offered by TCP.	Transport
FTP	File Transfer Protocol	Protocol for uploading and downloading files to and from a remote host; also accommodates basic file-management tasks.	Application
SFTP	Secure File Transfer Protocol	Protocol that performs a similar function to FTP, but provides more secure authentication and encryption mechanisms.	Application

(continued)

Table 5.6   TCP/IP Protocol Suite Summary *(continued)*

Protocol	Full Name	Description	OSI Layer
TFTP	Trivial File Transfer Protocol	File transfer protocol that does not have the security or error-checking capabilities of FTP; uses UDP as a transport protocol and is therefore connectionless.	Application
SMTP	Simple Mail Transfer Protocol	Mechanism for transporting email across networks.	Application
HTTP	Hypertext Transfer Protocol	Protocol for retrieving files from a Web server.	Application
HTTPS	Hypertext Transfer Protocol Secure	Secure protocol for retrieving files from a Web server.	Application
POP3/IMAP4	Post Office Protocol version 3/ Internet Message Access Protocol version 4	Used for retrieving email from a server on which the mail is stored.	Application
Telnet	Telnet	Allows sessions to be opened on a remote host.	Application
SSH	Secure Shell	Like Telnet, allows sessions to be opened on a remote host, but provides authentication and encryption capabilities.	Application
ICMP	Internet Control Message Protocol	Used for error reporting, flow control, and route testing.	Network
ARP	Address Resolution Protocol	Resolves IP addresses to MAC addresses, to enable communication between devices.	Network

(continued)

Protocol	Full Name	Description	OSI Layer
Table 5.6 **TCP/IP Protocol Suite Summary** *(continued)*			
RARP	Reverse Address Resolution Protocol	Resolves MAC addresses to IP addresses.	Network
NTP	Network Time Protocol	Used to communicate time synchronization information between devices.	Application
NNTP	Network News Transport Protocol	Protocol used for accessing and downloading messages from Internet-based newsgroups.	Application
SCP	Secure Copy Protocol	Protocol that uses Secure Shell (SSH) technology to provide a safe way to copy files between systems.	Application
LDAP	Lightweight Directory Access Protocol	Provides a mechanism to access directory services systems.	Application
IGMP	Internet Group Management Protocol	Protocol used for communication between devices in a multicast group.	Network
LPR	Line Printer Remote	Provides a mechanism to send printing tasks to a print server.	Application

TCP/UDP Port Functions

Each TCP/IP protocol or application has a port associated with it. When a communication is received, the target port number is checked to determine which protocol or service it is destined for. The request is then forwarded to that protocol or service. Take, for example, HTTP, whose assigned port number is 80. When a Web browser forms a request for a web page, the request is sent to port 80 on the target system. When the target system receives the request, it examines the port number and when it sees that the port is 80, it forwards the request to the Web server application.

TCP/IP has 65,535 ports available with 0 to 1023 being labeled as the well-known ports. Although a detailed understanding of the 65,535 ports is not necessary for the Network+ exam, it is important to understand the numbers of some of the well-known ports, as administration often requires you to specify port assignments when working with applications and configuring services. Table 5.7 shows some of the most common port assignments.

For the Network+ exam, you should concentrate on the information provided in this table, and you should be able to answer any port-related questions you might receive.

Table 5.7	TCP/IP Port Assignments for Commonly Used Protocols
Protocol	**Port Assignment**
FTP	20
FTP	21
SSH	22
Telnet	23
SMTP	25
DNS	53
TFTP	69
HTTP	80
POP3	110
NNTP	119
NTP	123
IMAP4	143
HTTPS	443

The term *well-known ports* identifies the ports ranging from **0** to **1023**. When CompTIA states "identify the well-known ports," this is what it is referring to.

You might have noticed in Table 5.7 that two ports are associated with FTP. Port **20** is considered the data port, whereas Port **21** is considered the control port. In practical use, FTP connections use port **21**. Port **20** is rarely used in modern implementations.

Network Services

Network services provide the ability to manage and administer TCP/IP-based networks. Today, it is quite likely that a network of any size will use a number of network services, making them an important component of network administration. The following sections discuss each of the network services covered on the CompTIA exam.

 For the Network+ exam, be prepared to identify the function of the network services discussed in this chapter.

Domain Name Service (DNS)

The function of the DNS service is to resolve hostnames, such as server1.examcram.com, to IP addresses. Such a resolution system makes it possible for people to remember the names of, and refer to frequently used hosts, using the easy-to-remember hostnames rather than the hard-to-remember IP addresses.

 When hostnames are expressed with the domain they belong to, and with any other domain identifiers, they are referred to as Fully Qualified Domain Names (FQDN). For example, if the hostname is **server1** and it resides in the domain **examcram.com**, the FQDN for the host would be **Server1.examcram.com**.

Similar to other TCP/IP-based services, DNS is a platform-independent protocol. Therefore, it can be used on Linux, UNIX, Windows, NetWare, and almost every other platform.

On networks where there is no DNS server, it is possible to resolve hostnames to IP address using the *HOSTS* file; however, such environments are becoming increasingly rare. All common network operating systems now include DNS server application software.

The HOSTS file is a text file, found on almost all PC operating systems, in which you can place hostname-to-IP-address resolution information. When HOSTS files are used, it's up to the administrator to manually make changes to the file if needed.

This factor alone is sufficient to make the installation of a DNS server an obvious choice.

 On the Network+ exam, you might be asked to identify the purpose and function of a HOSTS file and a DNS server. Both are responsible for resolving hostnames to IP addresses.

Network Address Translation (NAT) and Internet Connection Sharing (ICS)

NAT and ICS are two strategies that enable networks to access the Internet through a single connection. Having a single access point for the network enables an organization to have Internet access with a single IP address.

NAT

The basic principle of NAT is that many computers can "hide" behind a single registered IP address or a group of registered IP addresses. Using NAT means that, in its most basic implementation, only one registered IP address is needed on the external interface of the system that is acting as the gateway between an internal private network and an external public network such as the Internet.

A system performing the NAT service funnels the requests that are given to it to the external network. For instance, a client requests a website, and the request goes through the NAT server to the Internet. To the remote system, the request looks like it is originating from a single address, that of the NAT server, and not the individual client systems making the request. The system that is performing the NAT function keeps track of who asked for what and makes sure that when the data is returned, it is directed to the correct system.

Servers that provide NAT functionality do so in different ways. For example, it is possible to statically map a single internal IP address to a single external one so that outgoing requests are always tagged with the same IP address. Alternatively, if you have a group of public IP addresses, you can have the NAT system assign addresses to devices on a first-come, first-serve basis. Either way, the basic function of NAT is the same.

ICS

Although ICS is discussed separately from NAT, it is nothing more than an implementation of NAT on Windows platforms since Windows Me. ICS makes it very simple to share an Internet connection with multiple systems on the network.

Because ICS was intended as a simple mechanism for a small office network or a home network to share a single Internet connection, configuration is simple. However, simplicity is also the potential downfall of ICS. ICS provides no security, and the system providing the shared connection is not secure against outside attacks. For that reason, ICS should be used only when no other facilities are available or in conjunction with a firewall application, which later versions of Microsoft Windows, such as XP, now include.

Windows Internet Name Service (WINS)

On Windows networks, a system called WINS enables Network Basic Input/Output System (NetBIOS) names to be resolved to IP addresses. NetBIOS name resolution is necessary on Windows networks so that systems can locate and access each other by using the NetBIOS computer name rather than the IP address. It's a lot easier for a person to remember a computer called *secretary* than to remember its IP address, 192.168.2.34. The NetBIOS name needs to be resolved to an IP address and subsequently to a MAC address (by ARP).

NetBIOS name resolution can be performed three ways on a network. The simplest way is to use a WINS server on the network that will automatically perform the NetBIOS name resolution. If a WINS server is not available, the NetBIOS name resolution can be performed statically using a LMHOSTS file. Using a LMHOSTS file requires that you manually configure at least one text file with the entries. As you can imagine, this can be a time-consuming process, particularly if the systems on the network change frequently. The third method, and the default, is that systems will resolve NetBIOS names using broadcasts. There are two problems with this approach. First, the broadcasts create additional network traffic, and second, the broadcasts cannot traverse routers unless the router is configured to forward them. This means that resolutions between network segments are not possible.

Simple Network Management Protocol (SNMP)

SNMP is a management protocol that enables network devices to communicate information about their state to a central system. It also enables the central system to pass configuration parameters to the devices.

In an SNMP configuration, a system known as a *manager* acts as the central communication point for all the SNMP-enabled devices on the network. On each device that is to be managed and monitored via SNMP, software called an *SNMP agent* is set up and configured with the IP address of the manager. Depending on the configuration, the SNMP manager is then capable of communicating with and retrieving information from the devices running the SNMP agent software. In addition, the agent is able to communicate the occurrence of certain events to the SNMP manager as they happen. These messages are known as *traps*.

The messages sent by SNMP agents to an SNMP management system are called 'trap' messages.

An important part of SNMP is an *SNMP management system*, which is a computer running a special piece of software called a *Network Management System (NMS)*. These software applications can be free, or they can cost thousands of dollars. The difference between the free applications and those that cost a great deal of money normally boils down to functionality and support. All NMS systems, regardless of cost, offer the same basic functionality. Today, most NMS applications use graphical maps of the network to locate a device and then query it. The queries are built in to the application and are triggered by a point and click. You can actually issue SNMP requests from a command-line utility, but with so many tools available, it is simply not necessary.

An SNMP agent can be any device capable of running a small software component that facilitates communication with an SNMP manager. SNMP agent functionality is supported by almost any device designed to be connected to a network.

Network File System (NFS)

The Network File System (NFS) is a protocol and network service that allows you to access file systems on remote computers across the network. NFS is most commonly associated with UNIX and Linux operating system platforms, but versions of NFS are available for a wide range of server operating systems including Microsoft Windows. From a client perspective, UNIX and Linux implementations use NFS as the default file system access mechanism. However, versions of NFS client software are also available for most commonly deployed workstation operating systems.

NFS is the default file access and sharing protocol used on Linux and UNIX systems.

Zero Configuration (Zeroconf)

Zero Configuration (Zeroconf) provides a means of networking computer systems together without requiring specific network configuration. This approach is becoming increasingly necessary as we use a larger number and wider variety of computing devices in a networked scenario.

There are three basic requirements for a system to support Zeroconf. First, the system must be capable of assigning itself an IP address without the need for a DHCP server. Second, the system must be capable of resolving the hostname of another system to an IP address without the use of a DNS server. Finally, a system must be capable of locating or advertising services on the network without a directory services system such as Microsoft's Active Directory or Novell Directory Services. Currently, Zero Configuration is supported, with additional software, by Mac and Windows operating systems, as well as by Linux and UNIX.

For the exam, remember that the three requirements of Zeroconf are a capability to self-assign an IP address, a capability to independently resolve hostnames, and a mechanism for independently locating services on the network.

Server Message Block (SMB)

Server Message Block (SMB) is an application and presentation layer protocol that provides a mechanism to access shared network resources such as files or printers on network servers. SMB is the default file access method used on Windows networks. Today, SMB is more commonly referred to as the Common Internet File System (CIFS), though the functionality remains the same. On a network that uses Windows servers and clients, administrators access the functionality of SMB through Windows Explorer and the command line NET utility.

Samba enables UNIX and Linux servers to provide file and print services to Windows clients. No additional client configuration or software is required.

SMB is the default file access and sharing protocol for Windows-based systems.

Apple File Protocol (AFP)

The Apple File Protocol (AFP), more correctly called the AppleTalk Filing Protocol, is to Apple systems what NFS is to Linux/UNIX systems, and

SMB or CIFS is to Windows Systems. It is a protocol through which the file system on remote computers can be accessed. AFP is not widely used outside of Apple networks, and unless you are working on networks that use Apple Macintosh systems, you are unlikely to encounter AFP.

> AFP is the default file access and sharing protocol for Apple Macintosh systems.

Line Printer Daemon (LPD)

The Line Printer Daemon (LPD) protocol provides print services on both client and server systems. The most common use of LPD is as a print server and client on UNIX and Linux systems. As well as providing the basic print mechanisms, LPD supports a set of commands that enable the print queue to be controlled. It also provides commands for controlling print jobs once they have been placed in the print queue.

TCP/IP Service Summary

Table 5.8 helps you quickly identify the purpose and function of each of the TCP/IP services covered in the previous sections.

Table 5.8 Summary of TCP/IP Services	
Service	**Purpose/Function**
DNS	Resolves hostnames to IP addresses.
NAT	Translates private network addresses into public network addresses.
ICS	Enables a single Internet connection to be shared among multiple systems on the network.
WINS	Resolves NetBIOS names to IP addresses.
SNMP	Provides network management facilities on TCP/IP-based networks.
NFS	Service that provides file sharing between server and client. Typically associated with UNIX and Linux operating systems, but versions are available for most commonly deployed operating systems.
Zeroconf	Provides a system by which devices can communicate with no network configuration or setup.
SMB	Application and presentation layer protocol that provides access to file and print services on server platforms that provide SMB access.
AFP	Provides remote file system access on Apple networks.
LPD	Printing service that provides both server and client printing functions.

Review and Test Yourself

The following sections provide you with the opportunity to review what you learned in this chapter and to test yourself.

The Facts

For the exam, don't forget these important concepts:

➤ A Class A address uses only the first octet to represent the network portion, a Class B address uses two octets, and a Class C address uses three octets.

➤ Class A addresses span from 1 to 126 with a default subnet mask of 255.0.0.0.

➤ Class B addresses span from 128 to 191 with a default subnet mask of 255.255.0.0.

➤ Class C addresses span from 192 to 223 with a default subnet mask of 255.255.255.0.

➤ The 127 network ID is reserved for the local loopback.

➤ A valid IPv6 address is 42DE:7E55:63F2:21AA:CBD4:D773:CC21:554F.

➤ A public network is a network to which anyone can connect, such as the Internet.

➤ Subnetting enables bits from the node portion of an IP address to be used to create more network addresses.

➤ A private network is any network to which access is restricted. Reserved IP addresses are 10.0.0.0, 172.16.0.0 – 172.31.0.0, and 192.168.0.0.

➤ Without a default gateway, connectivity is limited to just the local network segment.

➤ IP addresses can be assigned dynamically, via DHCP, or statically. In addition, some platforms such as Windows support APIPA addressing.

➤ On a Windows platform, APIPA assigns addresses from the 169.254.x.x address range.

➤ DNS resolves hostnames to IP addresses.

➤ NAT/ICS translates private network addresses into public ones.

➤ WINS resolves NetBIOS names to IP addresses.

➤ SNMP provides network-management facilities on TCP/IP-based networks.

➤ SMB, NFS, and AFP are file access/sharing mechanisms used on Windows, UNIX/Linux and Apple Macintosh, respectively.

Exam Prep Questions

1. What is the function of ARP?

   ❑ A. It resolves IP addresses to MAC addresses.

   ❑ B. It resolves NetBIOS names to IP addresses.

   ❑ C. It resolves MAC addresses to IP addresses.

   ❑ D. It resolves hostnames to IP addresses.

2. As the network administrator, you decide to block port 80. Which of the following services will be unavailable for network users?

   ❑ A. DNS

   ❑ B. POP3

   ❑ C. FTP

   ❑ D. HTTP

3. Which of the following addresses is a Class B address?

   ❑ A. 129.16.12.200

   ❑ B. 126.15.16.122

   ❑ C. 211.244.212.5

   ❑ D. 193.17.101.27

4. You are the administrator for a network with 2 Windows Server 2003 systems and 65 Windows XP Professional systems. At 10 a.m., three users call to report that they are experiencing network connectivity problems. Upon investigation, you determine that the DHCP server has failed. How can you tell that the DHCP server failure is the cause of the connectivity problems experienced by the three users?

   ❑ A. When you check their systems, they have an IP address of 0.0.0.0.

   ❑ B. When you check their systems, they have an IP address in the 192.168.x.x address range.

   ❑ C. When you check their systems, they have a default gateway value of 255.255.255.255.

   ❑ D. When you check their systems, they have an IP address from the 169.254.x.x range.

5. You want to provide a mechanism by which users can securely copy files to and from a remote server. Which of the following are you most likely to use for this purpose? (Choose two.)

   ❑ A. SCP

   ❑ B. RCP

   ❑ C. TFTP

   ❑ D. SFTP

6. Which of the following IP addresses is not from a private address range?

☐ A. 192.168.200.117

☐ B. 172.16.3.204

☐ C. 127.45.112.16

☐ D. 10.27.100.143

7. You have been tasked with temporarily disabling Telnet access for external users. Which is the best way to accomplish this?

☐ A. Block port 53 on the corporate firewall.

☐ B. Block port 23 on the corporate firewall.

☐ C. Uninstall the Telnet service.

☐ D. Configure ICS to ignore client-initiated Telnet requests.

8. Which of the following layer 4 protocols is used to provide connectionless service?

☐ A. UDP

☐ B. TCP

☐ C. IP

☐ D. FTP

9. Which of the following protocols provides the security for HTTPS?

☐ A. HTTP

☐ B. SSL

☐ C. Telnet

☐ D. TCP

10. Which of the following best describes the function of the default gateway?

☐ A. Provides the route for destinations outside of the local network.

☐ B. Enables a single Internet connection to be used by several users.

☐ C. Identifies the local subnet and formulates a routing table.

☐ D. Used to communicate in a multiple-platform environment.

Answers to Exam Prep Questions

1. The correct answer is A. The function of ARP is to resolve IP addresses to MAC addresses. Answer B is incorrect; the responsibility for resolving NetBIOS names to IP addresses is a function of WINS or it can be achieved via broadcasts. Answer C describes the function of the RARP protocol. Resolving hostnames to IP addresses is a function of DNS; thus, answer D is incorrect.

2. The correct answer is D. This is correct because the HTTP service uses port 80, so blocking port 80 will prevent users from using the

HTTP service. Answer A is incorrect as DNS uses port 53; answer B is also incorrect, as POP3 uses port 110; and finally FTP (answer C) is incorrect, as it uses port 21.

3. The correct answer is A. Class B addresses fall into the range 128 to 191. Therefore, answer A is the only one of the addresses listed that falls into that range. Answer B is a Class A address, and answers C and D are both Class C IP addresses.

4. The correct answer is D. When a Windows XP Professional system that is configured to obtain an IP address via DHCP fails to obtain an address, it uses APIPA to assign itself an address from the 169.254.x.x address range. An address of 0.0.0.0 normally results from a system that does not support APIPA failing to get an address via DHCP. The 192.168.x.x address range is not used by APIPA. The IP address 255.255.255.255 is the broadcast address. A DHCP failure would not lead to a system assigning itself this address.

5. The correct answers are A and D. The Secure Copy Protocol (SCP) uses SSH technology to ensure that authentication information and data are kept secure. The Secure File Transfer Protocol (SFTP) can also be used for that purpose. The Remote Copy Protocol (RCP) and the Trivial File Transfer Protocol (TFTP) are both considered insecure, as they do not encrypt information as it travels across the network.

6. The correct answer is C. The 127.x.x.x network range is reserved for the loopback function. It is not one of the recognized private address ranges. The private address ranges as defined in RFC 1918 are 10.x.x.x, 172.16.x.x–172.31.x.x, and 192.168.x.x.

7. The correct answer is B. By blocking port 23, you can disable the Telnet service. Answer A is incorrect, as port 53 is used by DNS. Uninstalling the Telnet service (answer C) is not a practical solution, and D is an invalid answer.

8. The correct answer is A. UDP provides connectionless service and operates at layer 4 or the transport layer of the OSI model. TCP also operates at layer 4 but provides connection-oriented service. None of the other options function at the transport layer.

9. The correct answer is B. The Secure Socket Layer protocol is used to provide security for HTTPS. HTTP is a insecure version of HTTPS. Telnet is a protocol used to send or receive files from a remote system. It is not a security mechanism. TCP is a connection oriented transport protocol. It does not provide security for other protocols.

10. The correct answer is A. The default gateway enables systems on one local subnet to access those on another. Answer B describes Internet Connection Sharing (ICS). None of the other answers best describe the main function of a default gateway.

Need to Know More?

Bird, Drew and Harwood, Mike. *Network+ Exam Prep 2*. Que Publishing, 2005.

Habraken, Joe. *Absolute Beginner's Guide to Networking*, Fourth Edition. Que Publishing, 2003.

Sportack, Mark. *TCP/IP First-Step*. Cisco Press, 2004.

Mitch Tulloch, Ingrid Tulloch. *Microsoft Encyclopedia of Networking, Second Edition*. Microsoft Press. 2002.

Subnetting information—www.howtosubnet.com.

WAN Technologies Internet Access, and Security Protocols

Objectives

2.14 Identify the basic characteristics (for example, speed, capacity, and media) of the following WAN (wide area network) technologies:

- ✓ Packet switching
- ✓ Circuit switching
- ✓ ISDN (Integrated Services Digital Network)
- ✓ FDDI (Fiber Distributed Data Interface)

- ✓ T1 (T Carrier level 1)/E1/J1
- ✓ T3 (T Carrier level 3)/E3/J3
- ✓ OCx (Optical Carrier)
- ✓ X.25

2.15 Identify the basic characteristics of the following Internet access technologies:

- ✓ xDSL (Digital Subscriber Line)
- ✓ Broadband Cable (Cable modem)
- ✓ POTS/PSTN (Plain Old Telephone

Service/Public Switched Telephone Network)
- ✓ Satellite
- ✓ Wireless

2.16 Define the function of the following remote access protocols and services:

- ✓ RAS (Remote Access Service)
- ✓ PPP (Point-to-Point Protocol)
- ✓ SLIP (Serial Line Internet Protocol)
- ✓ PPPoE (Point-to-Point Protocol over Ethernet)

- ✓ PPTP (Point-to-Point Tunneling Protocol)
- ✓ VPN (Virtual Private Network)
- ✓ RDP (Remote Desktop Protocol)

2.17 Identify the following security protocols and describe their purpose and function:

- ✓ IPSec (Internet Protocol Security)
- ✓ L2TP (Layer 2 Tunneling Protocol)
- ✓ SSL (Secure Sockets Layer)

- ✓ WEP (Wired Equivalent Privacy)
- ✓ WPA (Wi-Fi Protected Access)
- ✓ 802.1x

2.18 Identify authentication protocols (for example, CHAP (Challenge Handshake Authentication Protocol), MS-CHAP (Microsoft Challenge Handshake Authentication Protocol), PAP (Password Authentication Protocol), RADIUS (Remote Authentication Dial-In User Service), Kerberos and EAP (Extensible Authentication Protocol)).

What you need to know

✓ Identify the various characteristics of WAN technologies.
✓ Identify the functions and characteristics of various remote access protocols.
✓ Identify the functions and characteristics of various security protocols.
✓ Identify the technologies needed to establish remote connectivity.

Introduction

Many technologies are used to create today's wide area networks (WANs). Each of these technologies has advantages and disadvantages, making some of them well suited for certain environments and completely impractical in others. Each of the technologies varies in terms of media, speed, availability, and cost. This chapter examines various WAN technologies and the protocols used to secure and establish the connections.

WAN Technologies

Many of today's network environments are not restricted to a single location or LAN. Instead, many of these networks span great distances, becoming wide area networks (WANs). When they do, hardware and software are needed to connect these networks. This section reviews the characteristics of various WAN technologies. Before we go on to discuss the specific WAN technologies, we must first look at an important element of the WAN technologies—switching methods.

Switching Methods

In order for systems to communicate on a network, there has to be a communication path or multiple paths between which the data can travel. To communicate with another entity, these paths move the information from one location to another and back. This is the function of *switching*. Switching provides communication pathways between two endpoints and manages how data is to flow between these endpoints. Two of the more common switching methods used today include:

➤ Packet switching

➤ Circuit switching

For the Network+ exam, you will be expected to identify the differences between switching methods.

Packet Switching

In packet switching, messages are broken down into smaller pieces called *packets*. Each packet is assigned source, destination, and intermediate node addresses. Packets are required to have this information because they do not always use the same path or route to get to their intended destination. Referred to as *independent routing*, this is one of the advantages of packet switching. Independent routing allows for a better use of available bandwidth by letting packets travel different routes to avoid high-traffic areas. Independent routing also allows packets to take an alternate route if a particular route is unavailable for some reason.

Packet switching is the most popular switching method for networks and is used on most LANs.

In a packet-switching system, when packets are sent onto the network, the sending device is responsible for choosing the best path for the packet. This path might change in transit, and it is possible for the receiving device to receive the packets in a random or nonsequential order. When this happens, the receiving device waits until all the data packets are received, and then it reconstructs them according to their built-in sequence numbers.

Two types of packet-switching methods are used on networks: *virtual-circuit packet switching* and *datagram packet switching*.

➤ **Virtual-Circuit Packet Switching**—When virtual-circuit switching is used, a logical connection is established between the source and the destination device. This logical connection is established when the sending device initiates a conversation with the receiving device. The logical communication path between the two devices can remain active for as long as the two devices are available or can be used to send packets once. After the sending process has completed, the line can be closed.

➤ **Datagram Packet Switching**—Unlike virtual-circuit packet switching, datagram packet switching does not establish a logical connection between the sending and transmitting devices. The packets in datagram packet switching are independently sent, meaning that they can take different paths through the network to reach their intended destination. To do this, each packet must be individually addressed to determine where its source and destination are. This method ensures that packets take the easiest possible routes to their destination and avoid high-traffic areas.

Circuit Switching

In contrast to the packet-switching method, *circuit switching* requires a dedicated physical connection between the sending and receiving devices. The most commonly used analogy to represent circuit switching is a telephone conversation in which the parties involved have a dedicated link between them for the duration of the conversation. When either party disconnects, the circuit is broken and the data path is lost. This is an accurate representation of how circuit switching works with network and data transmissions. The sending system establishes a physical connection, the data is transmitted between the two, and when the transmission is complete, the channel is closed.

Some clear advantages to the circuit-switching technology make it well suited for certain applications. The primary advantage is that after a connection is established, there is a consistent and reliable connection between the sending and receiving device. This allows for transmissions at a guaranteed rate of transfer.

Like all technologies, circuit switching has downsides. As you might imagine, a dedicated communication line can be very inefficient. After the physical connection is established, it is unavailable to any other sessions until the transmission is complete. Again, using the phone call analogy, this would be like a caller trying to reach another caller and getting a busy signal. Circuit switching can therefore be fraught with long connection delays.

Integrated Services Digital Network (ISDN)

ISDN has long been an alternative to the slower modem WAN connections but at a higher cost. ISDN allows the transmission of voice and data over the same physical connection.

ISDN connections are considerably faster than regular modem connections. To access ISDN, a special phone line is required, and this line is usually paid for through a monthly subscription. You can expect these monthly costs to be significantly higher than those for traditional dial-up modem connections.

To establish an ISDN connection, you dial the number associated with the receiving computer, much as you do with a conventional phone call or modem dial-up connection. A conversation between the sending and receiving devices is then established. The connection is dropped when one end disconnects or hangs up. The line pickup of ISDN is very fast, allowing a connection to be established, or brought up, much more quickly than a conventional phone line.

ISDN has two defined interface standards—Basic Rate Interface (BRI) and Primary Rate Interface (PRI).

BRI

BRI ISDN uses three separate channels—two bearer (B) channels of 64Kbps each and a delta (D) channel of 16Kbps. B channels can be divided into 4 D channels, which allows businesses to have 8 simultaneous Internet connections. The B channels carry the voice or data, and the D channels are used for signaling.

The two B channels can be used independently as 64Kbps carriers, or they can be combined to provide 128Kbps transfer speeds.

BRI ISDN channels can be used separately using 64Kbps transfer or combined to provide 128Kbps transfer rates.

PRI

PRI is a form of ISDN that is generally carried over a T1 line and can provide transmission rates of up to 1.544Mbps. PRI is composed of 23 B channels, each providing 64Kbps for data/voice capacity, and one 64Kbps D channel, which is used for signaling. Table 6.1 compares BRI and PRI ISDN.

ISDN is considered a *leased line* because access to ISDN is leased from a service provider.

Table 6.1   BRI and PRI ISDN Comparison

Characteristic	PRI	BRI
Speed	1.544Mbps	128Kbps
Channels	23B+D	2B+D
Transmission carrier	T1	ISDN

Be ready to answer questions about the characteristics of both BRI and PRI for the Network+ exam.

Fiber Distributed Data Interface (FDDI)

FDDI is an American National Standards Institute (ANSI) topology standard that uses fiber-optic cable and token-passing media access.

FDDI is implemented using both multimode and single-mode fiber cable and can reach transmissions speeds of up to 100Mbps at distances of more than 2 kilometers. FDDI combines the strengths of Token Ring, the speed of Fast Ethernet, and the security of fiber-optic cable. Such advantages make FDDI a strong candidate for creating network backbones and connecting private LANs to create MANs and WANs.

 The Copper Distributed Data Interface (CDDI) standard defines FDDI over copper cable rather than fiber-optic cable. However, the limitations of copper cable—such as increased EMI risk and attenuation—are in effect.

Unlike the regular 802.5 network standard, FDDI uses a dual-ring configuration. The first, or primary, ring is used to transfer the data around the network, and the secondary ring is used for redundancy and fault tolerance; the secondary ring waits to take over if the primary ring fails. If the primary ring fails, the secondary ring kicks in automatically, with no disruption to network users.

 Even though the second ring sits dormant, you can connect network devices to both rings. Network devices that attach to both rings are referred to as *Class A stations*, or dual attached stations (DASs). Network devices that connect to a single ring are called *Class B stations*, or single attached stations (SASs).

FDDI has a few significant advantages—some of which stem directly from the fact that it uses fiber-optic cable as its transmission media. These include a resistance to EMI, the security offered by fiber, and the longer distances available with fiber cable. In addition to the advantages provided by the fiber-optic cable, FDDI itself has a few strong points, including

➤ **Fault-tolerant design**—By using a dual-ring configuration, FDDI provides some fault tolerance. If one cable fails, the other can be used to transmit the data throughout the network.

➤ **Speed because of the use of multiple tokens**—Unlike the IEEE 802.5 standard, FDDI uses multiple tokens, which increase the overall network speed.

➤ **Beaconing**—FDDI uses beaconing as a built-in error-detection method, making finding faults, such as cable breaks, a lot easier.

Like every technology, there are always a few caveats:

➤ **High cost**—The costs associated with FDDI and the devices and cable needed to implement an FDDI solution are very costly; too costly for many small organizations.

➤ **Implementation difficulty**—FDDI setup and management can be very complex, requiring trained professionals with significant experience to manage and maintain the cable and infrastructure.

T-carrier Lines

T-carrier lines are high-speed dedicated digital lines that can be leased from telephone companies. This creates an always open, always available line between you and whomever you choose to connect to when you establish the service. T-carrier lines can support both voice and data transmissions and are often used to create point-to-point private networks. Because they are a dedicated link, they can be a costly WAN option. Four types of T-carrier lines are available:

➤ **T1**—T1 lines offer transmission speeds of 1.544Mbps, and they can create point-to-point dedicated digital communication paths. T1 lines have commonly been used for connecting LANs.

➤ **T2**—T2 leased lines offer transmission speeds of 6.312Mbps. They accomplish this by using 96 64Kbps B channels.

➤ **T3**—T3 lines offer transmission speeds of up to 44.736Mbps, using 672 64Kbps B channels.

➤ **T4**—T4 lines offer impressive transmission speeds of up to 274.176Mbps by using 4,032 64Kbps B channels

Of these T-carrier lines, the ones commonly associated with networks and the ones most likely to appear on the Network+ exam are the T1 and T3 lines.

NOTE | Because of the cost of a T-carrier solution, it is possible to lease portions of a T-carrier service. Known as *fractional T*, you can subscribe and pay for service based on 64Kbps channels.

It is important to point out that T-carrier is the designation to the technology used in the United States and Canada. In Europe, they are referred to as E-carriers and in Japan, J-carriers. Table 6.2 shows the T/E/J carriers.

Name	Transmission Speed
Table 6.2 Comparing T/E/J Carriers	
T-1	1.544Mbps
T-1C	3.152Mbps
T-2	6.312Mbps
T-3	44.736Mbps
T-4	274.176Mbps
J-0	64Kbps
J-1	1.544Mbps
J-1C	3.152Mbps
J-2	6.312Mbps
J-3	32.064Mbps
J-3C	97.728Mbps
J-4	397.200Mbps
E-0	64Kbps
E-1	2.048Mbps
E-2	8.448Mbps
E-3	34.368Mbps
E-4	139.264Mbps
E-5	565.148Mbps

Ensure that you review the speeds of the various T-carriers for the Network+ exam.

SONET/OC-x Levels

Bell Communications Research developed SONET, a fiber-optic WAN technology that delivers voice, data, and video at speeds in multiples of 51.84Mbps. Bell's main goals in creating SONET were to create a standardized access method for all carriers and to unify different standards around the world. SONET is capable of transmission speeds between 51.84Mbps and 2.488Gbps.

One of Bell's biggest accomplishments with SONET was to create a new system that defined data rates in terms of Optical Carrier (OC) levels, as shown in Table 6.3.

Table 6.3	OC Levels and Transmission Rates
OC Level	**Transmission Rate**
OC-1	51.84Mbps
OC-3	155.52Mbps
OC-12	622.08Mbps
OC-24	1.244Gbps
OC-48	2.488Gbps
OC-192	9.953Gbps

Synchronous Digital Hierarchy (SDH) is the International counterpart to SONET.

X.25

One of the older WAN technologies is X.25, which is a packet-switching technology. Today, X.25 is not as widely implemented as it once was. X.25's veteran status is both its greatest advantage and its greatest disadvantage. On the upside, X.25 is a global standard that can be found in many places. X.25 had an original maximum transfer speed of 56Kbps, which, when compared to other technologies in the mid-1970s, was fast but almost unusable for most applications on today's networks. In the 1980s a digital version of X.25 was released increasing throughput to a maximum 64kbps. This too is slow by today's standards.

Because X.25 is a packet-switching technology, it uses different routes to get the best possible connection between the sending and receiving device at a given time. As conditions on the network change, such as increased network traffic, so do the routes that the packets take. Consequently, each packet is likely to take a different route to reach its destination during a single communication session. The devices that make it possible to use X.25 service are called *packet assemblers/disassemblers* (PADs). A PAD is required at each end of the X.25 connection. Table 6.4 compares the various WAN technologies reviewed in this Chapter.

Table 6.4	Comparing WAN Technologies			
WAN Technology	**Speed**	**Supported Media**	**Switching Method Used**	**Key Characteristics**
ISDN	BRI: 64Kbps to 128Kbps PRI: 64Kbps to 1.5Mbps	Copper/ fiber-optic	Can be used for circuit-switching or packet-switching connections	ISDN can be used to transmit all types of traffic, including voice, video, and data. BRI uses 2B+D channels, PRI uses 23B+D channels. B channels are 64Kbps. ISDN uses the public network and requires dial-in access.
T-carrier (T1, T3)	T1: 1.544Mbps T3: 44.736Mbps	Copper/ fiber-optic	Circuit switching	T-carrier is used to create point-to-point network connections for private networks.
FDDI	100Mbps	Fiber-optic	N/A	Uses a dual-ring con-figuration for fault tolerance. Uses a token-passing media-access method. Uses beaconing for error detection.
X.25	56Kbps/ 64Kbps	Copper/ fiber-optic	Packet switching	X.25 is limited to 56Kbps. X.25 provides a packet-switching network over standard phone lines.
SONET/Ocx	51.8Mbps	Fiber-optic to 2.4Gbps	N/A	SONET defines synchronous data transfer over optical cable.

Internet Access Technologies

Internet access has become an integral part of modern business. There are several ways to obtain Internet access. The type chosen will often depend on the cost as well as what technologies are available in the area you are located. This section explores some of the more common methods of obtaining Internet access.

The term *broadband* is often used to refer to high-speed Internet access. Both DSL and cable modem are common broadband Internet technologies. Broadband routers and broadband modems are network devices that support both DSL and cable.

xDSL Internet Access

DSL is an Internet access method that uses a standard phone line to provide high-speed Internet access. DSL is most commonly associated with high-speed Internet access; because it is less expensive than technologies such as ISDN, it is often used in homes and small businesses. With DSL, a different frequency can be used for digital and analog signals, which means that you can talk on the phone while you're uploading data.

DSL arrived on the scene in the late 1990s, and it brought with it a staggering number of flavors. Together, all these variations are known as xDSL:

➤ **Asymmetric DSL (ADSL)**—Probably the most common of the DSL varieties is ADSL. ADSL uses different channels on the line: One channel is used for POTS and is responsible for analog traffic, the second channel is used to provide upload access, and the third channel is used for downloads. With ADSL, downloads are faster than uploads.

➤ **Symmetric DSL (SDSL)**—SDSL offers the same speeds for uploads and for downloads, making it most suitable for business applications such as Web hosting, intranets, and e-commerce. It is not widely implemented in the home/small business environment and cannot share a phone line.

➤ **ISDN DSL (IDSL)**—ISDN DSL is a symmetric type of DSL that is commonly used in environments where SDSL and ADSL are unavailable. IDSL does not support analog phones.

➤ **Rate Adaptive DSL (RADSL)**—RADSL is a variation on ADSL that can modify its transmission speeds based on the signal quality. RADSL supports line sharing.

➤ **Very High Bit Rate DSL (VHDSL)**—VHDSL is an asymmetric version of DSL and, as such, can share a telephone line.

➤ **High Bit Rate DSL (HDSL)**—HDSL is a symmetric technology that offers identical transmission rates in both directions. HDSL does not allow line sharing with analog phones.

Why are there are so many DSL variations? The answer is quite simply that each flavor of DSL is aimed at a different user, business, or application.

Businesses with high bandwidth needs are more likely to choose a symmetric form of DSL, whereas budget-conscious environments such as home offices are likely to opt for an option that allows phone line sharing at the expense of bandwidth. In addition, some of the DSL variants are simply older technologies. While the name persists, they have been replaced with newer DSL implementations. When you're working in a home/small office environment, you should expect to work with an ADSL system.

Table 6.5 summarizes the maximum speeds of the various DSL options. Keep in mind that maximum speeds are rarely obtained.

Table 6.5 DSL Speeds		
DSL Variation	Upload Speed	Download Speed
ADSL	1Mbps	8Mbps
SDSL	1.5Mbps	1.5Mbps
IDSL	144Kbps	144Kbps
RADSL	1Mbps	7Mbps
VHDSL	1.6Mbps	13Mbps
HDSL	768Kbps	768Kbps

Cable Internet Access

Cable Internet access is an always on Internet access method that is available in areas that have digital cable television. Cable Internet access is attractive to many small businesses and home office users because it is both inexpensive and reliable. Most cable providers do not restrict how much use is made of the access. Connectivity is achieved by using a device called a *cable modem*; it has a coaxial connection for connecting to the provider's outlet and an Unshielded Twisted Pair (UTP) connection for connecting directly to a system or to a hub or switch.

Cable providers often supply a cable modem free of charge, although of course you are paying for the rental of the modem in a monthly service fee. Many cable providers offer free or low-cost installation of cable Internet service, which includes installing a network card in a PC. Some providers also do not charge for the network card. Cable Internet costs are comparable to DSL subscription.

Most cable modems supply a 10Mbps Ethernet connection for the home LAN, although you wouldn't expect the actual Internet connection to reach these speeds. The actual speed of the connection can vary somewhat depending on the utilization of the shared cable line in your area. In day-to-day application, data rates range from 1.5Mbps to 3Mbps.

A cable modem is generally equipped with a medium-dependent interface crossed (MDI-X) port, so a straight through UTP cable can be used to connect the modem to a system.

One of the biggest disadvantages of cable access is cited (by DSL providers at least) as the fact that you share the available bandwidth with everyone else in your cable area. As a result, during peak times, performance of a cable link might be poorer than in low-use periods. In residential areas, busy times are evenings and weekends, and particularly right after school. In general, though, performance with cable systems is good, and in low-usage periods, it can be very fast.

Although the debate between cable and DSL goes on, for us regular users, it really won't make that much difference which one we choose. Although cable modem technology delivers *shared bandwidth* within the local neighborhood, its speeds are marginally higher but influenced by this shared bandwidth. DSL delivers *dedicated local bandwidth* but is sensitive to distance that impacts overall performance. With the monthly costs about the same, it really is too close to call.

Broadband Security Considerations

Whether using DSL or cable Internet access, there are a few things to keep in mind. Each of these technologies offers always on service. This means that even when you are away from your computer, it is still on the Internet. As you can imagine, this creates a security risk. The longer you are online, the more chance someone has of remotely accessing your system.

The operating systems we use today all have some security holes through which some people are waiting to exploit. These attacks often focus on technologies such as email or open TCP/UDP ports. Combining OS security holes with an always on Internet technology is certainly a dangerous mix.

Today, DSL and cable Internet connections have to be protected by mechanisms such as firewalls to protect the system. The firewall system will offer features such as packet filtering and network address translation (NAT). The firewall can be a third-party software application installed on the system, or it can be a hardware device.

In addition to a firewall, it is equally important to ensure that the operating system you are using is completely up-to-date in terms of service packs and security updates. Today's client systems typically offer automatic update features that will alert you when a new security update is available.

Following a few safety rules, both DSL and cable Internet can provide safe Internet access. We just have to be security diligent.

POTS/PSTN (Plain Old Telephone Service/Public Switched Telephone Network)

The most popular means of connecting to the Internet or a remote network might still be the good old telephone line and modem.

Internet access through a phone system requires two things: a modem and a dial-up access account through an ISP. *Modems* are devices that convert the digital signals generated by a computer system into analog signals that can travel across a phone line. A computer can have either an internal or external modem. External modems tend to be less problematic to install and troubleshoot because they don't require reconfiguration of the host system. Internal modems use one of the serial port assignments (that is, a COM port) and must therefore be configured not to conflict with other devices.

The second piece of the puzzle, the dial-up ISP account, can easily be obtained by contacting one of the many local, regional, or national ISPs. Most ISPs offer a range of plans that are normally priced based on the amount of time the user is allowed to spend online. Almost without exception, ISPs offer 56Kbps access, the maximum possible under current standards. Most ISPs also provide email accounts, access to newsgroup servers, and often small amounts of Web space.

It is a good idea to research an ISP choice carefully. Free services exist, but they generally restrict users to a certain number of online hours per month or use extensive banner advertising to pay for the services. Normally, you pay a monthly service fee for an ISP; doing so provides a degree of reassurance because the ISP can be held accountable. Paid-for service also tends to provide a higher level of support.

Another big consideration for dial-up Internet access is how many lines the ISP has. ISPs never have the same number of lines as subscribers; instead, they work on a first-come, first-serve basis for dial-up clients. This means that on occasion, users get busy signals when they try to connect. Before signing up for a dial-up Internet access account, you should ask the company what its ratio of lines to subscribers is and use that figure as part of your comparison criteria.

Satellite Internet Access

Many of us take DSL and cable Internet access for granted, but these technologies are not offered everywhere. For areas where cheaper broadband options are not available, there are a limited number Internet options. One of the primary ones is Internet via satellite.

Satellite access provides a viable Internet access solution for those who cannot get other methods of broadband. Satellite Internet offers an always on connection with theoretical speeds advertised anywhere from 512Kbps upload speeds to 2048Kbps download speeds, considerably faster than a 56k dial-up connection. One of the primary drawbacks to satellite Internet is the cost, and even with the high price tag, it is not as fast as DSL or cable modem.

Although satellite Internet is slower and more costly than DSL or cable, it offers some very attractive features—first of which has to be its portability. Quite literally, wherever you go, you can have Internet access. For business with remote users and clients, the benefit to this is clear. But the technology has far reaching impact; it is not uncommon to see RVs with a satellite dish on the roof. They have 24/7 unlimited access to the Internet as they travel.

There are many companies offering satellite Internet services, and a quick Internet search will reveal many. These Internet providers offer different Internet packages that vary greatly in terms of price, access speeds, and service. Some target business, whereas others are aiming for the private market.

Two different types of broadband Internet satellite services are deployed: one-way and two-way systems. A *one-way satellite system* requires a satellite card and a satellite dish installed at the end user's site; this system works by sending outgoing requests on one link using a phone line, with inbound traffic returning on the satellite link. A *two-way satellite system*, on the other hand, provides data paths for both upstream and downstream data. Like a one-way system, a two-way system also uses a satellite card and a satellite dish installed at the end user's site; bidirectional communication occurs directly between the end user's node and the satellite.

Home satellite systems are asymmetric; that is, download speeds are faster than upload speeds. In fact, a home satellite system is likely to use a modem for the upline traffic, with downloads coming over the satellite link. The exact speeds you can expect with satellite Internet depend on many factors. As with other wireless technologies, atmospheric conditions can significantly affect the performance of satellite Internet access. One additional consideration for satellite Internet is increased *propagation time*—the time it takes for the signal to travel back and forth from the satellite. In networking terms, this time is very high and an important consideration for business applications.

Wireless Internet Access

Not too long ago, it would have been inconceivable to walk into your local coffee shop with your laptop under your arm and surf the Web while drinking a latte. Putting aside the fact that beverages and laptops don't mix, wireless Internet access is everywhere and increasing.

Wireless Internet access is provided by a Wireless Internet Service Provider (WISP). The WISP provides public wireless Internet access known as *hotspots*. Hotspots provide Internet access for mobile network devices such as laptops, handheld computers, and cell phones in airports, coffee shops, conference rooms, and so on. A hotspot is created using one or many wireless access points near the hotspot location.

Client systems might need to install special application software for billing and security purposes; others require no configuration other than obtaining the network name (SSID). Hotspots do not always require a fee for service as companies use them as a marketing tool to lure Internet users to their businesses.

As of today, hotspots are not everywhere, but finding them is not difficult. Typically, airports, hotels, and coffee shops will advertise that they offer Internet access for customers or clients. In addition, WISP providers list their hotspot sites online so that they are easily found.

Establishing a connection to a wireless hotspot is a straightforward process. If not equipped with built-in wireless capability, laptops will require an external wireless adapter card. With the physical requirements of the wireless card taken care of, connect as follows:

1. When you arrive at the hotspot site, power up your laptop. In some instances, you might need to reboot your system if it was on standby to clear out old configuration settings.

2. The card might detect the network automatically. If this is the case, configuration settings, such as the SSID, will be automatically detected, and the wireless Internet will be available. If Internet access is free, there is little else to do; if it is a paid-for service, you will need to enter a method of payment. One thing to remember is to verify that you are using encryption for secure data transfer.

3. If for some reason the wireless settings are not automatically detected, you will need to open up your wireless NICs configuration utility and manually set the configurations. These settings can include setting the mode to infrastructure, inputting the correct SSID, and setting the level of encryption used.

In addition to using a WISP, some companies such as hotels and cafes will provide wireless Internet access by connecting a wireless router to a DSL or cable Internet connection. The router becomes the wireless access point to which the users connect, and it allows clients to connect to the Internet through the broadband connection. The technology is based on the 802.11 standards, typically 802.11b/g, and client systems require only an internal or external wireless adapter.

Remote Access Protocols and Services

Today, there are many ways to establish remote access into networks. Some of these include such things as virtual private networks (VPNs) or plain old modem dial-up access. Regardless of the technique used for remote access or the speed at which access is achieved, certain technologies need to be in place in order for the magic to happen. These technologies include the protocols to allow the access to the server and to secure the data transfer after the connection is established. Also necessary are methods of access control that make sure only authorized users are using the remote access features.

All the major operating systems include built-in support for remote access. They provide both the access methods and security protocols necessary to secure the connection and data transfers.

Remote Access Service (RAS)

RAS is a remote access solution included with Windows Server products. RAS is a feature-rich, easy-to-configure, and easy-to-use method of configuring remote access.

In Windows 2000, Microsoft renamed the RAS service Routing and Remote Access Service (RRAS). The basic RAS functionality, however, is the same as in previous versions of Windows.

Any system that supports the appropriate dial-in protocols, such as PPP, can connect to a RAS server. Most commonly, the clients are Windows systems that use the dial-up networking feature; but any operating system that supports dial-up client software will work. Connection to a RAS server can be made over a standard phone line, using a modem, over a network, or via an ISDN connection.

RAS supports remote connectivity from all the major client operating systems available today, including all newer Windows OSs:

➤ Windows 2000 Professional–based clients

➤ Windows XP Home–based clients

➤ Windows XP Professional–based clients

➤ UNIX-based\Linux clients

➤ Macintosh-based clients

Although the system is called RAS, the underlying technologies that enable the RAS process are dial-up protocols such as Serial Line Internet Protocol (SLIP) and Point-to-Point Protocol (PPP).

SLIP

SLIP was designed to allow data to be transmitted via Transmission Control Protocol/Internet Protocol (TCP/IP) over serial connections in a UNIX environment. SLIP did an excellent job, but time proved to be its enemy. SLIP was developed in an atmosphere in which security was not an overriding concern; consequently, SLIP does not support encryption or authentication. It transmits all the data used to establish a connection (username and password) in clear text, which is, of course, dangerous in today's insecure world.

 Clear text simply means that the information is sent unencrypted, and anyone can intercept with a packet capture program and read the data with his or her favorite word processor.

In addition to its inadequate security, SLIP also does not provide error checking or packet addressing, so it can be used only in serial communications. It supports only TCP/IP, and log in is accomplished through a terminal window.

Many operating systems still provide at least minimal SLIP support for backward capability to older environments, but SLIP has been replaced by a newer and more secure alternative: PPP. SLIP is still used by some government agencies and large corporations in UNIX remote access applications, so you might come across it from time to time.

PPP

PPP is the standard remote access protocol in use today. PPP is actually a family of protocols that work together to provide connection services.

Because PPP is an industry standard, it offers interoperability between different software vendors in various remote access implementations. PPP provides a number of security enhancements compared to regular SLIP—the most important being the encryption of usernames and passwords during the authentication process. PPP allows remote clients and servers to negotiate data encryption methods and authentication methods and support new technologies. PPP even gives administrators the ability to choose which particular local area network (LAN) protocol to use over a remote link. For example, administrators can choose among NetBIOS Extended User Interface (NetBEUI), NWLink (Internetwork Packet Exchange/Sequenced Packet Exchange (IPX/SPX)), AppleTalk, or TCP/IP.

PPP can use a variety of LAN protocols to establish a remote link.

During the establishment of a PPP connection between the remote system and the server, the remote server needs to authenticate the remote user and does so by using the PPP authentication protocols. PPP accommodates a number of authentication protocols, and it's possible on many systems to configure more than one authentication protocol. The protocol used in the authentication process depends on the security configurations established between the remote user and the server. PPP authentication protocols include CHAP, MS-CHAP (2), EAP, SPAP, and PAP. Each of these authentication methods is discussed later in this chapter in the section on authentication protocols.

Macintosh users can dial in to a Windows 2000 server by using PPP over AppleTalk Control Protocol (ATCP). ATCP is installed when the AppleTalk protocol is installed, or it can be installed separately.

If you are working on a network that uses SLIP and run into connectivity problems, try upgrading to PPP, as it is more flexible and secure.

PPPoE (Point-to-Point Protocol over Ethernet) is a protocol used for connecting multiple network users on an Ethernet local area network to a remote site through a common device. For example, using PPPoE it is possible to have all users on a network share the same link such as a DSL, cable modem, or a wireless connection to the Internet. PPPoE is a combination of PPP and the Ethernet protocol, which supports multiple users in a local area network. Hence the name. The PPP protocol information is encapsulated within an Ethernet frame.

With PPPoE, a number of different users can share the same physical connection to the Internet, and in the process, PPPoE provides a way to keep track of individual user Internet access times. Because PPPoE allows for individual authenticated access to high-speed data networks, it is an efficient way to create a separate connection to a remote server for each user. This strategy allows Internet access and billing on a per-user basis rather than a per-site basis.

Users accessing PPPoE connections require the same information as required with standard dial-up phone accounts, including a username and password combination. As with a dial-up PPP service, an Internet service provider (ISP) will most likely automatically assign configuration information such as the IP address, subnet mask, default gateway, and DNS server.

There are two distinct stages in the PPPoE communication process—the discover stage and the PPP session stage. The discovery stage has four steps to complete to establish the PPPoE connection: initiation, offer, request, and session confirmation. These steps represent back and forth communication between the client and the PPPoE server. Once these steps have been negotiated, the PPP session can be established using familiar PPP authentication protocols.

PPTP

The function of the Point-to-Point Tunneling Protocol (PPTP) is to create a secure transmission *tunnel* between two points on a network. The tunneling functionality that PPTP provides forms the basis for creating multi-protocol virtual private networks (VPNs), which allow users to access remote networks through a secure connection. PPTP works in conjunction with PPP and, as such, uses PPP authentication methods including PAP, CHAP, and MS-CHAP.

PPTP uses tunneling to provide secure data transmissions over a public network. In many cases, PPTP is used to create a VPN across the Internet.

To establish a PPTP session between a client and server, a TCP connection known as a *PPTP control connection* is required to create and maintain the communication tunnel. The PPTP control connection exists between the IP address of the PPTP client and the IP address of the PPTP server, using TCP port 1723 on the server and a dynamically assigned port on the client. It is the function of the PPTP control connection to pass the PPTP control and management messages used to maintain the PPTP communication tunnel between the remote system and the server. Once the PPTP connection is made, it provides a secure channel, or tunnel, using the original PPP connection between the devices.

Virtual Private Networks

VPNs are one of the most popular methods of remote access. Essentially, a VPN extends a LAN by establishing a remote connection, using a public network such as the Internet. A VPN provides a point-to-point dedicated link between two points over a public IP network.

VPN encapsulates encrypted data inside another datagram that contains routing information. The connection between two computers establishes a switched connection that is dedicated to the two computers. The encrypted data is encapsulated inside the PPP or IPSec protocols and that connection is used to deliver the data.

A VPN allows anyone with an Internet connection to use the infrastructure of the public network to dial in to the main network and access resources as if he or she were logged on to the network locally. It also allows two networks to be connected to each other securely. Once connected, data can be exchanged between networks. In this way, VPNs create a WAN.

Many elements are involved in establishing a VPN connection, including the following:

➤ **A VPN client**—The VPN client is the computer that initiates the connection to the VPN server.

➤ **A VPN server**—The VPN server authenticates connections from VPN clients.

➤ **An access method**—As mentioned, a VPN is most often established over a public network such as the Internet; however, some VPN implementations use a private intranet. The network that is used must be IP based.

➤ **VPN protocols**—Protocols are required to establish, manage, and secure the data over the VPN connection. PPTP and L2TP are commonly associated with VPN connections.

VPNs have become very popular because they allow the public Internet to be safely used as a wide area network (WAN) connectivity solution.

 VPNs support analog modems and ISDN, as well as dedicated broadband connections such as cable and DSL. You should remember this for the exam.

Remote Desktop Protocol

In a Windows environment, Terminal Services provides a way for a client system to connect to a server, such as Windows server 2000/2003, and by using the Remote Desktop Protocol (RDP) run programs on the server as if they were local client applications. Such a configuration is known as *thin client computing*, whereby client systems use the resources of the server instead of their local processing power.

Originally, Terminal Services was available in remote administration mode or application server mode. Today, in Windows Server 2003, Terminal Services remote administration mode is no more as it has been replaced with the Remote Desktop feature.

Windows Server 2003 and XP Professional have built-in support for Remote Desktop Connections. The underlying protocol used to manage the connection is RDP. RDP is a low bandwidth protocol used to send mouse movements, keystrokes, and bitmap images of the screen on the server to the client computer. RDP does not actually send data over the connection—only screenshots and client keystrokes.

Security Protocols

Any discussion of remote access is sure to include security, and for a good reason: Remote access opens your network to remote users. Although you'd like to think that only authorized users would try to connect from remote locations, the reality is that an equal number of illegitimate users will probably attempt to connect. Because many of the methods used to establish remote access are over public networks, securing the data you send and the points at which you connect at an important consideration. A significant element of this security is encryption.

Encryption is the process of encoding data so that it can be securely sent over remote connections. As well as encrypting the data itself, the usernames and passwords used to gain access to the remote network are also typically encrypted. In practical terms, *encryption* is the process of encoding data using a mathematical algorithm that makes it difficult for unauthorized users to read the data if they are able to intercept it. The algorithm used in the encryption is actually a mathematical value known as a *key*. The key is required in order to read the encrypted data. Encryption techniques use public and private keys; public keys can be shared, and private keys cannot.

IP Security (IPSec)

IPSec was created by the Internet Engineering Task Force (IETF) and can be used on both IPv4 and IPv6 networks. It is designed to encrypt data and authenticate users. IPSec encryption ensures that data on a network cannot be viewed, accessed, or modified by those who should not have access to it. IPSec provides security for both internal and external networks. It might seem that protection on an internal network is less necessary than on an external network; however, much of the data you send across networks has little or no protection, allowing unwanted eyes to access it.

IPSec provides several key security services:

➤ **Data verification and authentication**—It verifies that the data received is from the intended source.

➤ **Protection from data tampering**—It ensures that the data has not been tampered with and changed between the sending and receiving devices.

➤ **Private transactions**—It ensures that the data sent between the sending and receiving devices is unreadable by any other devices.

IPSec operates at the network layer of the Open Systems Interconnect (OSI) model and provides security for protocols that operate at higher layers of the OSI model. Thus, by using IPSec, you can secure practically all TCP/IP-related communications.

Layer 2 Tunneling Protocol (L2TP)

The *Layer 2 Tunneling Protocol (L2TP)* is a combination of PPTP and Cisco's L2F technology. L2TP utilizes tunneling to deliver data. It authenticates the client in a two-phase process: It first authenticates the computer and then the user. By authenticating the computer, it prevents the data from being intercepted, changed, and returned to the user in what is known as a *man-in-the-middle attack*. L2TP assures both parties that the data they are receiving is the data sent by the originator.

L2TP operates at the data-link layer, making it protocol independent. This means that an L2TP connection can support protocols such as IPX and AppleTalk.

L2TP and PPTP are both tunneling protocols, so you might be wondering which you should use. Here is a quick list of some of the advantages of each, starting with PPTP:

➤ PPTP has been around the longest; it offers more interoperability than L2TP.

➤ PPTP is easier to configure than L2TP because L2TP uses digital certificates.

➤ PPTP has less overhead than L2TP.

The following are some of the advantages of L2TP:

➤ L2TP offers greater security than PPTP.

➤ L2TP supports common public key infrastructure technology.

➤ L2TP provides support for header compression.

Secure Sockets Layer (SSL)

SSL is a security protocol that is used on the Internet. Originally developed by Netscape for use with its Navigator browser, SSL uses public key encryption to establish secure connections over the Internet. SSL provides three key services:

➤ **Server authentication**—SSL allows a user to confirm a server's identity. For example, you can use this ability when you are purchasing something online with a credit card but first want to verify the server's identity.

➤ **Client authentication**—SSL allows a server to confirm a user's identity. This functionality is often used when a server is sending sensitive information—such as banking information or sensitive documents—to a client system and wants to verify the client's identity.

➤ **Encrypted connections**—It is possible to configure SSL to require all information sent between a client and a server to be encrypted by the sending software and decrypted by the receiving software. Doing this establishes private and secure communication between two devices. In addition, SSL has a mechanism to determine whether the data sent has been tampered with or altered in transit.

You can see SSL security on the Web when you access a secure universal resource locator (URL). Secure websites begin with `https://` instead of the `http://`. Hypertext Transfer Protocol over SSL (HTTPS) connections require a browser with built-in security features to establish a secure connection.

WEP

WEP was the first attempt to keep wireless networks safe. WEP was designed to be easy to configure and implement. Originally, it was hoped that WEP would provide the same level of security to wireless networks as was available to wired. It was soon discovered that WEP had significant shortcomings.

WEP is an IEEE standard, introduced in 1997, designed for securing 802.11 networks. With WEP enabled, each data packet transmitted over the wireless connection would be encrypted. Originally, the data packet was combined with a secret 40-bit number key as it passed through an encryption algorithm known as RC4. The packet was scrambled and sent across the airwaves. On the receiving end, the data packet passed through the RC4 backward, and the host received the data as it was intended. WEP originally used a 40-bit number key, but later specified 128-bit encryption, making WEP that much more robust.

WEP was designed to provide security by encrypting data from the sending and receiving devices. In a short period of time, however, it was discovered that WEP encryption was not nearly as secure as hoped. Part of the problem was that when the 802.11 standards were being written, security was not the major concern it is today. As a result, WEP security was easy to crack with freely available hacking tools. From this point, wireless communication was regarded as a potentially insecure transmission media.

WPA

Security weaknesses associated with WEP provided administrators with a very valid reason to be concerned with wireless security. The need for increased wireless security was important for wireless networking to reach its potential and to bring a sense of confidence for those with sensitive data to use wireless communications. In response, the Wi-Fi Protected Access (WPA) was created. WPA was designed to improve on the security weaknesses of WEP and to be backward compatible with older devices using the WEP standard. WPA addressed two main security concerns:

> **Enhanced data encryption**—WPA uses a Temporal Key Integrity Protocol (TKIP), which scrambles encryption keys using a hashing algorithm. Then the keys are issued an integrity check to verify that they have not been modified or tampered with during transit.

> **Authentication**—WPA uses the Extensible Authentication Protocol (EAP). WEP regulates access to a wireless network based on a computer's hardware-specific MAC address, which is relatively simple to be sniffed out and stolen. EAP is built on a more secure public-key encryption system to ensure that only authorized network users can access the network.

802.1x

802.1x is an IEEE standard specifying port-based network access control. 802.1x was not specifically designed for wireless networks—rather, it provides authenticated access for both wired and wireless networks. Port-based network access control uses the physical characteristics of a switched local area network (LAN) infrastructure to authenticate devices that are attached to a LAN port and to prevent access to that port in cases in which the authentication process fails.

During a port-based network access control interaction, a LAN port adopts one of two roles: authenticator or supplicant. In the role of authenticator, a LAN port enforces authentication before it allows user access to the services that can be accessed through that port. In the role of supplicant, a LAN port requests access to the services that can be accessed through the authenticator's port. An authentication server, which can either be a separate entity or co-located with the authenticator, checks the supplicant's credentials on behalf of the authenticator. The authentication server then responds to the authenticator, indicating whether the supplicant is authorized to access the authenticator's services.

The authenticator's port-based network access control defines two logical access points to the LAN through one physical LAN port. The first logical access point, the uncontrolled port, allows data exchange between the authenticator and other computers on the LAN, regardless of the computer's authorization state. The second logical access point, the controlled port, allows data exchange between an authenticated LAN user and the authenticator.

Authentication Protocols

Two primary technologies are required for securing data transmissions: encryption and authentication. Encryption was discussed earlier; in this section, authentication protocols are reviewed.

When designing a remote connection strategy, it is critical to consider how remote users will be authenticated. Authentication defines the way in which a remote client and server will negotiate on a user's credentials when the user is trying to gain access to the network. Depending on the operating system used and the type of remote access involved, several different protocols are used to authenticate a user. The following authentication protocols are used with various technologies, including PPP:

➤ **Challenge Handshake Authentication Protocol (CHAP)**—CHAP is an authentication system that uses the MD5 encryption scheme to secure authentication responses. CHAP is a commonly used protocol, and as the name suggests, anyone trying to connect is challenged for authentication information. When the correct information is supplied, the systems "shake hands," and the connection is established.

➤ **Microsoft Challenge Handshake Authentication Protocol (MS-CHAP)**—MS-CHAP, based on CHAP, was developed to authenticate remote Windows-based workstations. There are two versions of MS-CHAP; the main difference between the two is that MS-CHAP version 2 offers mutual authentication. This means that both the client and the server must prove their identities in the authentication process. Doing so ensures that the client is connecting to the expected server.

➤ **Password Authentication Protocol (PAP)**—PAP is the least secure of the authentication methods because it uses unencrypted passwords. PAP is often not the first choice of protocols used; rather, it is used when more sophisticated types of authentication fail between a server and a workstation.

> **Extensible Authentication Protocol (EAP)**—EAP is an extension made to standard PPP. EAP has additional support for a variety of authentication schemes including smart cards. It is often used with VPNs to add security against brute-force or dictionary attacks.

> **Shiva Password Authentication Protocol (SPAP)**—SPAP is an encrypting authentication protocol used by Shiva remote access servers. SPAP offers a higher level of security than other authentication protocols such as PAP, but it is not as secure as CHAP.

Remote Authentication Dial-In User Service (RADIUS)

Among the potential issues network administrators face when implementing remote access are utilization and the load on the remote access server. As a network's remote access implementation grows, reliance on a single remote access server might be impossible, and additional servers might be required. RADIUS can help in this scenario.

RADIUS is a protocol that enables a single server to become responsible for all remote access authentication, authorization, and auditing (or accounting) services. The RADIUS protocol can be implemented as a vendor-specific product such as Microsoft's Internet Authentication Server (IAS).

RADIUS functions as a client/server system. The remote user dials in to the remote access server, which acts as a RADIUS client, or network access server (NAS), and connects to a RADIUS server. The RADIUS server performs authentication, authorization, and auditing (or accounting) functions and returns the information to the RADIUS client (which is a remote access server running RADIUS client software); the connection is either established or rejected based on the information received.

Kerberos

Seasoned administrators can tell you about the risks of sending clear-text, unencrypted passwords across any network. The Kerberos network authentication protocol is designed to ensure that the data sent across networks is safe from attack. Its purpose is to provide authentication for client/server applications.

Kerberos authentication works by assigning a unique key (called a *ticket*), to each client that successfully authenticates to a server. The ticket is encrypted and contains the password of the user, which is used to verify the user's identity when a particular network service is requested.

Kerberos was created at Massachusetts Institute of Technology to provide a solution to network security issues. With Kerberos, the client must prove its identity to the server, and the server must also prove its identity to the client. Kerberos provides a method to verify the identity of a computer system over an insecure network connection.

For the exam, you should know that the security tokens used in Kerberos are known as *tickets*.

Kerberos is distributed freely, as is its source code, allowing anyone interested to view the source code directly. Kerberos is also available from many different vendors that provide additional support for its use.

Review and Test Yourself

The following sections provide you with the opportunity to review what you learned in this chapter and to test yourself.

The Facts

For the exam, don't forget these important concepts:

➤ BRI ISDN uses 2 B channels of 64Kbps each.

➤ PRI ISDN uses 23 B channels offering up to 1.5Mbps transfer rates.

➤ T1 lines offer transmission speeds of up to 1.544Mbps, but are more costly than an ISDN solution.

➤ T3 lines offer transmission speeds of 44.736Mbps.

➤ T-carrier lines are used to create point-to-point network connections for private networks.

➤ FDDI can use a dual-ring configuration for fault tolerance.

➤ FDDI uses a token-passing media-access method.

➤ X-25 is restricted to transmission rates of 56Kbps or 64Kbps with digital implementations.

➤ SONET can transfer speeds of 51.8Mbps to 2.4Gbps.

➤ When a connection is made to the RAS server, the client is authenticated and the system that is dialing in becomes a part of the network.

➤ RAS supports remote connectivity from all the major client operating systems.

➤ Although the system is called RAS, the underlying technologies that enable the RAS process are dial-up protocols such as PPP and SLIP.

➤ SLIP also does not provide error checking or packet addressing, so it can be used only in serial communications.

➤ PPP provides a number of security enhancements compared to SLIP— the most important being the encryption of usernames and passwords during the authentication process.

➤ Windows 2000/XP clients natively support SLIP and PPP.

➤ The RDP protocol allows client systems to access and run applications on a server, using the resources of the server, with only the user interface, keystrokes, and mouse movement being transferred between the client and server computers.

➤ IPSec is designed to encrypt data during communication between two computers.

➤ IPSec operates at the network layer of the OSI model and provides security for protocols that operate at higher layers of the OSI model.

➤ L2TP operates at the data-link layer, making it protocol independent.

➤ SSL is a security protocol that is used on the Internet.

➤ Secure websites begin with `https://` instead of the `http://`. Hypertext Transfer Protocol over SSL (HTTPS) connections require a browser to establish a secure connection.

➤ Secure SSL connections for web pages are made through port `443` by default.

➤ WEP was the original wireless security standard. WEP encryption techniques were found to be weak, and commonly found utilities were capable of cracking the encryption.

➤ WPA was introduced to address the shortcomings of WEP and offered increased encryption strength and authentication.

➤ 802.1x is used by wireless networks to increase security using port controlled access.

➤ Kerberos provides a method to verify the identity of a computer system over an insecure network connection.

➤ The security tokens used in Kerberos are known as *tickets*.

Key Terms

- ➤ PSTN
- ➤ Modem
- ➤ ISDN
- ➤ BRI
- ➤ PRI
- ➤ T-carrier
- ➤ T1/E1
- ➤ T3/E3
- ➤ FDDI
- ➤ X.25
- ➤ SONET/OC-*x*
- ➤ RAS
- ➤ SLIP
- ➤ PPP
- ➤ CHAP
- ➤ MS-CHAP
- ➤ PAP
- ➤ EAP
- ➤ SPAP
- ➤ PPTP
- ➤ RDP
- ➤ Security protocol
- ➤ Encryption
- ➤ IPSec
- ➤ L2TP
- ➤ SSL
- ➤ Kerberos
- ➤ VPN
- ➤ Tickets

Exam Prep Questions

1. Which of the following dial-up protocols can use multiple LAN proto-
   cols over a link?
   - ❑ A. PPP
   - ❑ B. SLIP
   - ❑ C. IPX/SPX
   - ❑ D. UDP/TCP

2. Which of the following protocols is used with HTTPS?
   - ❑ A. SSH
   - ❑ B. SSL
   - ❑ C. Proxy
   - ❑ D. IPSec

3. What is the total bandwidth available when combining all BRI ISDN
   communication channels?
   - ❑ A. 128Kbps
   - ❑ B. 64Kbps
   - ❑ C. 96Kbps
   - ❑ D. 1,544Kbps

4. As a remote user, you need to access your company's private network
   through the Internet. Which of the following protocols can you use to
   establish a secure connection?
   - ❑ A. IPX/SPX
   - ❑ B. TCP/IP
   - ❑ C. PPP
   - ❑ D. PPTP

5. Which of the following is an advantage of ISDN over PSTN?
   - ❑ A. ISDN is more reliable.
   - ❑ B. ISDN is cheaper.
   - ❑ C. ISDN is faster.
   - ❑ D. ISDN uses fixed-length packets called cells.

6. Which of the following technologies is associated with dial-up access
   type?
   - ❑ A. FDDI
   - ❑ B. ISDN
   - ❑ C. Packet switching
   - ❑ D. OCx

7. Your company wants to create a secure tunnel between two networks over the Internet. Which of the following protocols would you use to do this?

   ❑ A. IPX

   ❑ B. CHAP

   ❑ C. PPTP

   ❑ D. SLIP

8. Which of the following protocols is used in thin-client computing?

   ❑ A. RDP

   ❑ B. PPP

   ❑ C. PPTP

   ❑ D. RAS

9. Which of the following URLs is using SSL?

   ❑ A. http:ssl//www.comptia.org

   ❑ B. http://www.comptia.org

   ❑ C. httpssl://www.comptia.org

   ❑ D. https://www.comptia.org

10. Which of the following statements best describes the function of a PPP?

   ❑ A. It is a secure technology that allows information to be securely downloaded from a website.

   ❑ B. It is a dial-up protocol used over serial links.

   ❑ C. It is a technology that allows a secure tunnel to be created through a public network.

   ❑ D. It provides a public key/private key exchange mechanism.

Answers to Exam Prep Questions

1. The correct answer is A. The PPP protocol can use multiple LAN protocols such as IPX/SPX, TCP/IP, or NetBEUI.

2. The correct answer is B. HTTPS uses SSL to create secure connections over the Internet. Answer A is incorrect as SSH provides a secure multiplatform replacement for Telnet. Answer C is not valid, and IPSec is designed to encrypt data during communication between two computers.

3. The correct answer is A. BRI ISDN uses two 64Kbps channels that, when combined, offer 128Mbps transfer speeds. None of the other options are valid.

4. The correct answer is D. PPTP is used to establish a secure transmission tunnel over an insecure public network such as the Internet. The other protocols mentioned do not provide secure transmissions over a public network.

5. The correct answer is C. One clear advantage that ISDN has over the PSTN is its speed. ISDN can combine 64Kbps channels for faster transmission speeds than the PSTN can provide. ISDN is no more or less reliable than the PSTN. ISDN is more expensive than the PSTN. Answer D describes ATM, not ISDN, thus it is not a valid answer.

6. The correct answer is B. ISDN establishes dial-up connections to initiate the communication session. The other answers are not valid.

7. The correct answer is C. To establish the VPN connection between the two networks, you can use PPTP. IPX is a part of the IPX/SPX protocol suite and associated with NetWare networks. CHAP is not used to create a point-to-point tunnel; it is a authentication protocol. SLIP is not a secure dial-up protocol.

8. The correct answer is A. The RDP protocol is used in thin-client networking, where only screen, keyboard, and mouse inputs are sent across the line. PPP is a dial-up protocol used over serial links. PPTP is a technology used in VPNs, and RAS is a remote access service.

9. The correct answer is D. You can identify when SSL is used by the s in the URL (in this case, https://www.comptia.org). Answer B is a valid HTTP URL, but it is not secure. None of the other answers are correct.

10. The correct answer is B. PPP is a protocol that can be used for dial-up connections over serial links. Answer A describes SSL; answer C describes a VPN, and answer D describes PKI.

Need to Know More?

 Bird, Drew and Harwood, Mike. *Network+ Exam Prep*. Que Publishing, 2004.

 Habraken, Joe. *Absolute Beginner's Guide to Networking*, Fourth Edition. Que Publishing, 2003.

Davis, Harold. *Absolute Beginner's Guide to Wi-Fi Wireless Networking*. Que Publishing, 2004.

Network Operating Systems and Client Connectivity

. . . .

Objectives

3.1 Identify the basic capabilities (for example, client support, interoperability, authentication, file and print services, application support, and security) of the following server operating systems to access network resources:

- ✓ UNIX/Linux/Mac OS X Server
- ✓ NetWare
- ✓ Windows
- ✓ Appleshare IP (Internet Protocol)

3.2 Identify the basic capabilities needed for client workstations to connect to and use network resources (for example, media, network protocols, and peer and server services)

3.3 Identify the appropriate tool for a given wiring task (for example, wire crimper, media tester/certifier, punch down tool, or tone generator)

3.4 Given a remote connectivity scenario composed of a protocol, an authentication scheme, and physical connectivity, configure the connection. Includes connection to the following servers:

- ✓ UNIX/Linux/MAC OS X Server
- ✓ NetWare
- ✓ Windows
- ✓ Appleshare IP (Internet Protocol)

What you need to know

- ✓ Identify the main features and characteristics of network operating systems
- ✓ Understand operating system interoperability and client support
- ✓ Configure client systems to access network resources
- ✓ Understand common wiring tools and what tasks can be achieved using them
- ✓ Configure remote connectivity to a network

Introduction

Network operating systems (NOS) are some of the most powerful and complex software products available today. This chapter looks at a number of operating systems that are widely used in today's network environments. Even though the Network+ exam does not require that you be an expert in the operating systems discussed in this chapter, a basic knowledge of each is required.

In this chapter, we will also look at the interoperability capabilities of each network operating system and at the range of client support it provides. However, the information described in this chapter is not intended to provide a complete tutorial in any of the operating systems discussed. Rather, this chapter provides an overview of each operating system, highlighting the areas you can expect to know for the Network+ exam.

Part of the job of a network administrator is to manage the network media. This chapter reviews some of the common tools used to manage network media.

Finally, configuring client systems to access a network is a common task for administrators. There are several steps that must be completed including establishing the physical connections and protocols. Similarly, this chapter explores the requirements to connect client systems outside the local network. Again, establishing the physical connections and configuring protocols is required.

Network Operating Systems

Early network operating systems provided just the basics in terms of network services, such as file and printer sharing. Today's network operating systems offer a far broader range of network services; some of these services are used in almost every network environment, and others are used in only a few.

Despite the complexity of operating systems, the basic function and purpose of a network operating system is straightforward: to provide services to the network. The following are some of the most common of these services:

➤ Authentication services

➤ File and print services

➤ Web server services

➤ Firewall and proxy services

➤ Dynamic Host Configuration Protocol (DHCP) and Domain Name System (DNS) services

These are just a few of a large number of services that a network operating system can provide.

The following sections discuss the major operating systems currently in use and how each of them deals with basic services such as authentication, security, and file and print services.

Linux/UNIX

Providing a summary of Linux in a few paragraphs is a difficult task. Unlike other operating systems, each of which has only a single variation, Linux is a freely distributable open source operating system that has many variants called distributions. Each of these distributions offers a slightly different approach to certain aspects of the operating system, such as installation and management utilities. Some of the most common Linux distributions include Red Hat, SuSE, Debian, and Caldera. In light of the many versions of Linux, if a command or an approach is listed in this section and is not available in the version of Linux you are using, you can look for an equivalent command or approach in your version, and you will very likely find one.

Linux Authentication

People who are used to working on a Windows-based system will no doubt discover that administration on a Linux system is very different. For instance, authentication information such as a list of users is kept in a text file. This file, /etc/passwd, controls who can and cannot log on to the system.

For a user to log on to the system, a valid username and password combination must be supplied. Both of these pieces of information are case sensitive.

Linux File and Print Services

Although it is not the most obvious choice for a file and print server platform, Linux can perform the role of a file and print server admirably. In a base configuration, the volumes on a Linux server are not available to network clients. To make them available, one of two file sharing services is commonly used:

➤ **NFS**—NFS is the original file-sharing system used with Linux. NFS makes it possible for areas of the hard disk on a Linux system to be shared with other clients on the network. Once the share has been established from the client side, the fact that the drive is on another system is transparent to the user.

> ➤ **Samba**—Samba provides Server Message Block functionality so that areas of the Linux server disks can be made available to Windows clients. In much the same way as on Windows servers, Samba facilitates the sharing of folders that can then be accessed by Windows client computers. Samba also makes it possible for Linux printer resources to be shared with Windows clients.

As with the other NOS discussed in this chapter, Linux has a file system permission structure that makes it possible to restrict access to files or directories. In Linux, each file or directory can be assigned a very basic set of file rights that dictates the actions that can be performed on the file. The basic rights are Read, Write, and Execute. The rights can be expressed in an alphabetic format (that is, RWX) or a numeric format (777). The rights to a file can be derived from the file ownership, from a group object, or from an "everyone" designator, which covers all users who are authenticated on the server. The Linux file permission structure might not be as sophisticated as those found in other network operating systems, but it is still more than sufficient in many environments.

Printing on a Linux system occurs through a service called the *Line Printer daemon*. The Line Printer functionality can be accessed by any user on the network who is properly authorized and connected. In later versions of Linux, some distributions have started to provide a more enhanced printing system called the *Common UNIX Printing System* (*CUPS*). Many people, however, still prefer to use the traditional Line Printer system because of its simplicity and efficiency.

Linux Application Support

If you can think of an application that you might need, chances are that it is available for Linux in some form. As well as highly sophisticated commercial applications produced by large software companies, you can find software for the Linux platform that is written by an equally enthusiastic army of small software development companies and individuals. This means that application support for Linux is on par with, if not greater than, that in other network operating systems, such as NetWare, even if it has not yet reached the levels achieved by Windows server platforms.

In a sense, all applications created for Linux are third-party applications in that Linux itself is only an operating system kernel. The applications that run on this kernel provide Linux with its functionality.

On the assumption that a network server will have a number of requirements, it is common practice for the Linux kernel to be bundled with various applications and provided to customers as a package, which, as discussed earlier, is called a *distribution*.

One aspect in which Linux certainly has the edge over other operating systems is that many Linux applications are free. Developed in the same spirit as Linux itself, and in many cases governed by the same licensing types, these free applications can seriously reduce the cost of maintaining a network server. Although it can be said that there are also free server-type applications for Windows and NetWare, there are certainly not as many of them as there are for Linux. (Note that we are referring to server applications, not applications targeted at workstation or end-user applications.)

Linux Security

Considerable effort has been put into making Linux a very secure network operating system, and those efforts are evident. When it is configured correctly, Linux is a very secure operating system; therefore, it is often used as a company's firewall server. The following are a few highlights of Linux security:

➤ **Resource access**—As in the other network operating systems, access to resources on a Linux network is controlled through permissions. Access control lists identifying systems and who can access what resources are held in text files such as hosts.deny and hosts.allow. Permissions for network resources and services can be assigned to an individual user or to a group of users.

➤ **User authentication**—To access the local system resources or any network resources, user authentication, in the form of a username and a password, is required. The user account information is kept in a text file known as the /etc/passwd file in the Linux system.

 To log on to a Linux server, the user must supply a valid username and password. Both of these values are case sensitive.

➤ **File and directory security**—The default file system used by Linux is the EXT2 file system. Like NTFS, which is used with Windows servers, EXT2 allows administrators to assign permissions to individual files and folders. These permissions are used to control who is allowed access to specific data on the server. A secure server should have permissions set on the important data in the system.

As Linux continues to grow in popularity, it will become an increasingly common sight in server rooms of organizations of all sizes. As a network administrator, you should prepare yourself for *when* you encounter a Linux system—not *if*.

Of the platforms discussed in this chapter, UNIX and Linux have the most simplistic approach to file system security, although for most environments, this approach is more than sufficient. File permissions can be assigned to either the creator of a file or directory, a group, or the entity "everyone," which includes any authenticated user.

UNIX and Linux have only three rights that can be assigned. These rights are listed in Table 7.1.

Table 7.1 File Permissions on UNIX/Linux	
Right	**Description**
Read	Allows files to be listed, opened, and read
Write	Allows files to be created, written to, or modified
Execute	Allows files to be executed (that is, run)

The file permissions are listed to the right of the file. The first value specifies whether the file is a file (-) or a directory (d). The next three values specify the file rights for the user, the next three for the group, and the next three for the "everyone" assignment.

Mac OS X Server

Mac OS is the operating system created for Apple Computer's line of personal computers. Mac OS has a long history, with the original version being released in 1984 to run on the original Macintosh computer. In 1999, Apple released its last major revision to its aging 'Classic' operating system, Mac OS 9.

The successor to the Classic Mac OS was Mac OS X, a UNIX-like operating system with a friendly and familiar user interface. Successive versions of Mac OS X have a decimal numeral—for example, Mac OS X.1, X.2, and so on.

Because Mac OS X uses Linux/UNIX technology, most of the previous section on Linux applies to a Mac OS X server.

To identify a version of an operating system installed on any Macintosh computer, click on the Apple menu, and choose About This Mac, or About This Computer. You will see a screen listing the version number of the operating system as well as the amount of RAM installed.

Mac OS X File Systems and File and Print Services

As you might expect, the file systems used on Windows-based PCs is different from those used in an Apple system. Instead of the FAT or FAT32 file system, the original Mac file system was Apple's Macintosh File System (MFS). MFS was used with earlier Mac versions including Mac OS 1–3.

Mac OS 4 introduced Apple's Hierarchical File System (HFS). HFS was the primary file system format used on the Macintosh Plus and later models, until Mac OS 8.1, when HFS was replaced by HFS Plus.

HFS+ is the file system most commonly associated with Mac OS X. Like NTFS, HFS+ includes many enhanced features. HFS+ supports disk quotas, byte-range locking, finder information in metadata, support for hiding file extensions on a per-file basis, and more. One of the more publicized features of HFS+ is journaling. In a journaled file system, the system keeps a log of the hard disk's main data activity. In case of a crash or other system failure, the file system can retrieve lost data by consulting the "journal" log, restoring the system to its previous state instead of having to go through the lengthy process of rebuilding the data.

 When installing the Mac OS on a computer, always choose an HFS+ or HFS+ (journaled) file system type. Other file systems do not properly support metadata and permissions used by the OS.

The following is a list of other file systems supported by Mac OS X:

➤ **ISO9660**—Mac supports the ISO9660 file system standard. This is a system-independent file system for read-only data CDs.

➤ **MS-DOS**—Mac OS X includes support for MS-DOS file system (FAT12, FAT16, and FAT32).

➤ **NTFS**—Mac OS X includes read-only support for NTFS.

➤ **UDF**—UDF (Universal Disk Format) is the filesystem used by DVD-ROM (including DVD-video and DVD-audio) discs and by many CD-R/RW packet-writing programs.

When working in a heterogeneous network environment (one that uses different OS platforms), Mac OS X offers a wide-range of support for network file and print services supporting various file sharing protocols. A file sharing protocol is a high-level network protocol that provides the structure and language for file requests between clients and servers. It provides the commands for opening, reading, writing, and closing files across the network. Each OS has a different protocol used as the file sharing protocol.

In order for a client to have access to multiple servers running different operating systems, either the client supports the file sharing protocol of each operating system or the server supports the file sharing protocol of each client. Software that adds this capability is very common and enables interoperability between Windows, Macintosh, NetWare, and UNIX platforms. The following is a list of file sharing protocols supported by Mac OS X:

➤ **Apple Filing Protocol (AFP)**—The Apple Filing Protocol (AFP) is an Apple proprietary protocol for file sharing over the network using TCP/IP. If you have a Windows NT or Windows 2000\2003 server, you can turn on Apple File Protocol (AFP). AFP is the native Macintosh file sharing protocol and when enabled, Macs will be able to see the server.

➤ **Server Message Blocks/ Common Internet File System (SMB/CIFS)**—Mac OS X includes cross-platform support for SMB/CFS, the protocols that enable file sharing between network nodes in a Windows environment. Using Mac OS X, Macintosh clients can connect directly to Windows servers thanks to the SMB client built in to the Mac OS. Support for SMB/CFS is supplied by the Samba software package, and installed on all versions of Mac OS X by default. Samba is a networking tool originally designed to integrate Windows file sharing protocol (SMB/CIFS) and UNIX systems on a network. Running on a UNIX system, it allows Windows to share files and printers on the UNIX host, and it also allows UNIX users to access resources shared by Windows systems. Whenever possible, use Mac OS X v10.2 or greater to ensure the best compatibility with Windows file servers. When using the SMB protocol to connect to a Windows 2000 or 2003 file server, make sure that SMB signing (packet signing) is disabled on that server.

➤ **Network Filing System (NFS)**—NFS is a file sharing protocol associated with UNIX/Linux systems. Clients using Mac OS X are able to connect to Linux/UNIX servers using NFS, just like the other UNIX stations on the network. NFS can be problematic because file permissions are applied to newly created files and folders on the server based on the user ID and group ID from the client computer, unless otherwise specified by the server administrator.

Mac OS X Security

As with any other OS, Mac OS X has been designed to meet the security needs of today's businesses. This includes security measures in the local network and security protocols to be used on remote networks.

The most fundamental level of security lies within the operating system itself. Any interaction with the system requires some form of authentication.

The first level is *user authentication*. Mac OS X implements role-based user accounts. Three account types are available on Mac OS X client machines (machines not a part of a Windows domain or Mac OS X Server infrastructure), whose options can be configured in the Accounts area in the System Preferences application.

➤ **Limited**—The most restricted type of account, limited users might only be able to see certain parts of the file system, and only run applications approved by an administrative user. As of Mac OS X v10.4, system administrators can also restrict network access to lists of approved websites and email addresses.

➤ **Standard**—Most users on a machine will fall into this category. Standard users are allowed to run any applications that are installed in directories they have access to, but can only write to their home directories and directories that have been set up for them by a system administrator. Standard users are also restricted from making any configuration changes that affect anything beyond their user account (such as network settings).

➤ **Administrator**—This account type allows the user to make systemwide changes to the machine, change permissions of files and directories they do not directly own, and manage accounts. Every Mac OS X computer must have at least one administrative account.

Being a UNIX-like operating system, Mac OS X naturally inherits a UNIX-style file system permission system. Every file and folder on the machine has three levels of access with three possible settings each. Persons familiar with UNIX, Linux, and BSD systems will feel right at home with this environment. Refer to Table 7.1 for details on Mac OS X permissions. Fortunately for those not familiar with the chmod and chown GNU commands, the MAC Finder provides an interface for managing permissions in the Get Info window. In the info window for any file or folder on the computer, there is an Ownership & Permissions area listing all possible permissions variables for the given object. The three levels of access for each file and folder are Owner, Group, and Everyone (or Other). The owner is usually the user who created the object on the system. Groups are logical collections of users on a machine. On Mac OS X Client machines, groups cannot be created or modified; however, two key groups are automatically created and maintained to assist with machine administration:

➤ All administrator level users automatically belong to the Admin group.

➤ All other users belong to the Staff group.

Novell NetWare

Once the network operating system of choice for all but a few networks, NetWare's popularity has declined significantly over recent years. However, NetWare is still widely used in many environments, including government and education. The latest version of NetWare, version 6.5, continues Novell's tradition of providing feature rich enterprise class network operating systems.

> The information this chapter provides on Novell NetWare is intended to apply to NetWare 6 and 6.5. If you find yourself working on an older version of NetWare, you might find that some of the commands and utilities are different from those discussed here.

One of the features that really put NetWare on the networking map was Novell Directory Services (NDS). Like Microsoft's Active Directory, NDS (which has been around since 1994) is a directory services system that enables network objects to be stored in a database. This database can then be divided and distributed among different servers on the network. These processes are known as *partitioning* (the dividing) and *replication* (the distribution among servers on the network). Although introduced as NDS with NetWare 4.x, Novell has now renamed the product eDirectory and made it platform independent.

> Although a detailed understanding of eDirectory is not required for the Network+ exam, working with a NetWare server will most certainly require a thorough knowledge of this product.

Like the other network operating systems, NetWare is a full-featured operating system that offers all the functions required by an organization, including file and print services, DNS and DHCP servers, and FTP and Web servers. NetWare also supports a wide range of third-party hardware and software.

NetWare Authentication

As with all the other network operating systems discussed in this chapter, by default NetWare authentication is performed by using a username and password combination. As well as supplying this information, users also need to tell client software which NDS tree to authenticate to and the location of the user object in the NDS tree. NetWare also supports numerous other authentication mechanisms such as smartcards and biometrics.

By default, passwords in NetWare are not case sensitive.

After a user has been validated to the eDirectory tree, an assortment of restrictions is evaluated, including allowed logon times and station restrictions. These prevent users from logging on during restricted times and from certain workstations.

In versions of NetWare up to and including 3.x, NetWare used a system called the *Bindery* to store user, group, and printing information. NDS was introduced with NetWare 4 to replace the Bindery and has been used on every NetWare version since then, though as mentioned, the product is now called eDirectory.

Information about the user account and what the user can and can't access is stored in the NDS. For this reason, a copy of the NDS must be available in order for the user to be able to log on. Also, each time a user attempts to access a resource, their authentication status is checked in the NDS to make sure that they are who they say they are, and that they are allowed to access the resource. One benefit of this system is that a user need only log on once in order to be permitted resources anywhere on the network.

NetWare File Services

For many years, NetWare was considered *the* operating system of choice for providing file and print services. Although that might no longer be the case, many people in the IT industry still see NetWare as primarily a file and print server platform.

NetWare uses a file sharing system in which all areas of the disk are available to all users who have permissions. There is no concept of share points as with Windows server operating systems, although it is possible for a user to connect to a specific folder on the server if necessary. Instead, users can map a drive to an area of a disk called a *volume*. Only the areas of the volume to which the user has been assigned permissions are available to that user.

In versions of NetWare since 5.1, Novell has offered a service called Novell Storage Services (NSS). NSS allows for larger volume sizes and improves the performance of file serving.

Novell offers compatibility with various client operating systems by using special software drivers known as *name spaces* to make drives available to clients. Most commonly, the driver that mimics the file properties of Windows clients, which is called "long," is used, though NFS is also enabled by default in NetWare 6.x.

File system security on NetWare is the most sophisticated of any of the popular network operating systems. In addition to a full set of file permissions, NetWare also accommodates file permission inheritance and filters to cancel out that inheritance. For those who are unfamiliar with the various features of NetWare file system security, it can all seem a bit bewildering. When you are used to it, though, you realize that it allows an extremely high level of control over files and directories.

The term *inheritance* is used to describe the process of rights flowing down the folder structure. For example, rights are assigned at the top of the folder structure, and unless they are blocked at a lower level, they flow to the bottom of the structure. All common network operating systems employ file inheritance in one way or another.

At the core of NetWare file system security are the basic permissions. These permissions can be assigned to individual files or, where appropriate, folders. The file system rights available on a NetWare server are listed in Table 7.2.

Table 7.2 File Permissions on a NetWare Server	
Right	**Description**
Supervisor	Supervisory—implies all rights
Read	Allows the file to be read
Write	Allows the file to be written to
Create	Allows new files to be created
Erase	Allows files to be deleted
Modify	Allows the attributes of the file to be changed
Filescan	Allows the file to be viewed
Access Control	Allows the file permissions to be manipulated

In addition to file permission rights, on a NetWare server, files can also be assigned a range of attributes. These attributes include options such as Rename Inhibit and Delete Inhibit.

NetWare Print Services

Printing with NetWare can be implemented in a variety of ways. Traditionally, printers were defined on the server, and print queues were associated with those printers. In NetWare 6, a feature called Novell Distributed Print Services was introduced, which enables a more dynamic printing environment to be created. NetWare 6 also introduced a new feature called iPrint, which allows users to see graphical maps of the network and point and click to access network devices.

To access a printer on NetWare, clients capture the output that would normally be directed to a local printer port and send it to the network printer. In early versions of NetWare, this was a process performed by using a command-line utility, called capture. Today, the process has been hidden behind the graphical interface of the client software and is largely unnoticed.

NetWare Application Support

Although application support will always be a topic of much debate, the reality is that third-party application support for NetWare is not nearly at the same level as it is for the Windows server platforms. NetWare would even have a hard time competing against Linux in this respect. However, many applications are available for NetWare, and you are likely to have a choice of applications for any given purpose.

 On a NetWare server, console utilities and drivers are implemented through pieces of software called NetWare Loadable Modules (NLMs). Most NLMs can be loaded and unloaded as needed.

Even though third-party support might be lacking, the applications included with the NetWare package provide many of the commonly desired network services. This includes a DHCP server, a DNS server, and a Web server application, as well as a range of other services.

NetWare Security

Similar to the other network operating systems, NetWare has many security features to help secure the server and the network. The key areas of NetWare security include the following:

➤ **Resource access**—Resource access in NetWare is controlled, as is everything else related to security, through directory services. For a user to gain access to a network resource—whether it be a file, directory, printer, or server—the appropriate permissions must be applied through the directory. Permissions can be granted to the user, to a group to which the user belongs, or to an eDirectory container object in which the user resides. Rights to objects can be inherited or gained from other user IDs through a process called *security equivalence*.

➤ **User authentication**—As with the other network operating systems, accessing a NetWare server and network resources requires a username and password combination. To log on to a NetWare server, the context of the user must also be specified and, in some instances, the name of the eDirectory or NDS tree must also be provided. *Context* is a term used to refer to the location of an object, in this case the user object, in the eDirectory tree. Without the correct context, the security subsystem is unable to identify the correct user ID and does not grant access to the server. Because the context can be quite complex and the tree name is generally not used except at the point of login, it's common practice to configure users' workstations to default to a certain tree and context rather than requiring them to provide this information. This way, a user needs to provide only a username and password.

To gain access to a NetWare server, or more accurately eDirectory or NDS, four pieces of information are normally required: a username, a password, a directory context, and the name of the tree to which the user wants to log in. In addition, you can specify a server name, although this is not required.

➤ **File and directory security**—NetWare provides a very comprehensive file and directory permissions system, which allows rights to be assigned to users, groups, and other directory services objects. Rights are inheritable, which means that rights assigned at one file system level flow down through the structure until they reach the end of the file system tree, unless they are countered by an inherited rights mask or by an explicit trustee assignment. Much the same process is used to manage and assign rights within the eDirectory tree, although the actual set of rights that can be assigned is different.

The NetWare console can and should be locked for security purposes. You can lock the NetWare console by using a utility called scrsaver, which you run from the server command line.

With the proliferation of Microsoft Windows server platforms, you might not actually get to work with a NetWare server. But if you do, you'll find that there is good reason why NetWare was king of the network operating system hill for so long.

Windows 2000 and Windows Server 2003

Windows 2000 was the follow-up to the popular Windows NT 4 network operating system, and it quickly established itself as a reliable and robust operating system. Windows 2000 built on the success of its predecessor and offered many improvements and advancements. In 2003, Microsoft released the latest version of its Windows server family of products—the aptly named Windows Server 2003. Microsoft still currently supports Windows 2000, and many organizations still have Windows 2000 Server systems deployed.

Three different versions of Windows 2000 are available for server platforms: Windows 2000 Server, Advanced Server, and Datacenter Server. Windows 2000 is also available as a workstation operating system: Windows 2000 Professional. Windows 2000 Professional has the majority of features, capabilities, and strengths of Windows 2000 Server products but omits the server-type network services and capabilities.

Like Windows 2000, there are also a number of versions of Windows Server 2003; Windows Server 2003 Standard Edition, Windows Server 2003 Enterprise Edition, and Windows Server 2003 Datacenter Edition. Additionally, Windows Server 2003 Web Edition is designed as a platform for Web-based applications and services. Microsoft fully expects that you will mix and match editions of Windows Server 2003 on a network, so interoperability between the editions is seamless.

 To make things easier, from this point on, we'll refer to both Windows 2000 Server and Windows Server 2003 simply as Windows servers, unless there is a need to identify differences between the two.

Microsoft Active Directory

Active Directory is a directory services system, similar in nature to Novell's eDirectory, which allows network objects such as users and groups to be placed into logical areas of a database. This database can then be distributed among various servers—all of which participate in the Active Directory structure. Because all the network object information is placed in a single database, albeit a distributed one, it can be used by any network application or subsystem, eliminating the need for duplicate information to be held on each server of the network. In the case of Microsoft server operating systems, Windows 2000 was the first network operating system to take this approach. Previous to this, user accounts on Windows servers were stored on each server, and special relationships called *trusts* had to be set up in order to allow users on one server to access resources in another. In Active Directory, trusts still exist, though their role is somewhat different.

Windows servers on a network can either be domain controllers or member servers. Domain controllers are servers that have Active Directory installed and hold a copy of the Active Directory database. The term *domain* is used to describe a logical section of the Active Directory database. Domain controllers store user account information, so they can provide network authentication. An Active Directory domain can have several domain controllers, with each one having a read/write copy of the Active Directory database. In fact, for fault-tolerant reasons, this is a good strategy to employ.

Active Directory is a complex subject, and much of the information in this section is not needed for the Network+ exam. For further information on Active Directory, refer to Microsoft's website (www.microsoft.com).

Member servers are not involved in the authentication of network users and do not take part in the Active Directory replication process. Member servers are commonly employed as file and print servers, or with additional software, as database servers, Web servers, firewalls, or servers for other important network services such as DHCP and DNS.

Windows Authentication

The authentication process facilitated by a Windows server allows users logging on to the network to identify themselves to the Active Directory, and subsequently to access all the network resources to which they have permissions. This means that it is necessary to log on only once to access all the resources on the network. The nature of directory services means that other applications, such as a Web server, can interface with the directory and use the same authentication information.

Microsoft Active Directory uses Kerberos as its native authentication protocol. For more information on Kerberos, refer to Chapter 6, "WAN Technologies, Remote Access, and Security Protocols."

Passwords on Windows server operating systems are case sensitive.

In addition to the standard authentication mechanism of usernames and passwords, Windows server platforms also support other authentication systems such as smartcards and biometrics. Implementation of these methods requires additional hardware and software.

Windows Server File and Print Services

The provision of file and print sharing services is a mainstay of any network operating systems, and Windows servers are no exception. Windows server systems use a principle called *shares* to make areas of a disk available to users. These shares can be secured by share permissions that can be used on any file system, along with file and folder permissions if they are resident on New Technology File System (NTFS) partitions.

In order to use file or folder level permissions on a Windows server system, the disk must be formatted with the NTFS file system. FAT or FAT32 partitions do not support file level permissions, and must rely solely on share permissions to provide security.

Both Windows 2000 Server and Windows Server 2003 use the same mechanisms to provide file system security. Rights can be assigned to users, groups, and some special entities, which include the "everyone" assignment. Table 7.3 describes the basic file permissions that can be used with NTFS on Windows Server platforms.

Table 7.3 Basic File Permissions with NTFS on Windows and Windows Server 2003	
Right	**Description**
Full Control	Provides all rights
Modify	Allows files to be modified
Read & Execute	Allows files to be read and executed (that is, run)
List Folder Contents	Allows the files in a folder to be listed
Read	Allows a file to be read
Write	Allows a file to be written to

An added complexity to file system security on Windows platforms is that the shares created to allow users to access folders across the network can also be assigned a set of permissions. Although these permissions are quite basic (Full Control, Change, and Read), they must be considered because, when assigned, they are combined with NTFS permissions. The rule in this situation is that the most restrictive permissions assignment applies. For example, if a user connects through a share with Read permission and then tries to access a file to which he has the NTFS Full Control right, the actual permissions would be Read. The most restrictive right (in this case, the Share Read permission) overrides the other permissions assignment.

In addition to the basic file sharing and permission systems, Windows server systems also include some advanced features to further enhance the file and server capabilities. These features include the following:

► **Disk quotas**—The amount of disk space available to a user can be restricted and managed through disk quotas. This is a useful element of control over disk usage.

► **Encrypting File System (EFS)**—EFS allows files to be encrypted while on the disk, preventing unauthorized access. The main advantage of EFS is that it keeps the files encrypted even if the user or organization loses physical control of the drives, such as with a laptop computer.

► **Distributed File System (DFS)**—DFS allows multiple directories on distributed servers to be represented through a single share point, simplifying access for users and administration.

Windows server systems support the FAT, FAT32, and NTFS file systems. However, if you are configuring a server, you are unlikely to use FAT or FAT32 as they do not offer any file level security. Also, you need NTFS if you want to take advantage of features such as disk quotas, DFS, EFS, file compression, or auditing. You also need NTFS to support Active Directory.

Client operating systems such as Windows 95, 98, and Me do not support NTFS. You can only create NTFS partitions on Windows XP, Windows NT 4, Windows 2000, and Windows Server 2003.

Windows client systems often use the FAT32 file system, but on a server, you should always use NTFS unless you have a very good reason not to. With FAT or FAT32, you can only use share level permissions; you cannot protect files or folders directly as you can with NTFS.

Although it is possible to convert a partition formatted with FAT or FAT32, it is recommended that you format a drive as NTFS when you are creating partitions rather than converting at a later date. Drives originally formatted with NTFS have less fragmentation and better performance than those converted from FAT. If you do need to convert a partition, you can use the CONVERT utility, but the process is one way. Once you have converted from FAT, you can never go back.

You can use the **Convert.exe** utility to convert from FAT or FAT32 to NTFS. The syntax is *Convert c:/fs:ntfs /v.*

It is recommended that, whenever possible, you format a drive as NTFS when you are creating partitions rather than convert from FAT to NTFS at a later date. Drives originally formatted with NTFS have less fragmentation and better performance than those converted from FAT.

Windows server provides comprehensive print server functionality. Clients are able to connect to printers across the network without the need for locally installed printer drivers. The drivers are stored on the server and downloaded when the user connects to the printer, making it easy to ensure that users are using the latest version of the correct driver.

Printing on a Windows server can be controlled through a permission mechanism similar to that used in file system security, though it is less complex. Preconfigured groups also allow you to delegate the management of printing functions, which can be a good idea in large environments.

All these features combine to make Windows a very solid choice as a file and print server.

Windows Application Support

Of all the network operating systems discussed in this chapter, Windows server platforms have the best overall level of support by third-party applications. In addition to having superb third-party application support, Windows server operating systems come with a complete set of tools and services that satisfy almost every need a company could have from a network operating system. These applications include DNS and DHCP server services, performance-monitoring tools, Web server applications, remote access capabilities, and network monitoring tools.

Windows Security

Windows server operating systems provide a full range of security features that make for very secure network operating systems. Windows Server 2003 is considered more secure than Windows 2000, as it employs a "secure by default" strategy through which unnecessary applications, services, and security configurations are disabled by default. Administrators can then enable applications and services on an as needed basis.

Watch the Caps Lock To log on to a Windows server system, a valid username and password are required. The password is case sensitive, but the username is not.

As with any other network operating system, you should make sure that Windows servers are updated with the latest operating systems service packs, patches, and security updates. Without them, your systems might be vulnerable to a range of threats and attacks that might compromise your network.

Authentication security is provided on Windows servers through Kerberos version 5. File system security and encryption are provided through NTFS permissions and EFS. Network communication can be protected by a range of security and authentication protocols, though IPSec (which is discussed in Chapter 6) is most commonly used on Windows server networks to provide both encryption and authentication for network data.

AppleShare IP

Mac OS–based computers usually can be counted on to rely on the AppleShare IP protocol (although, this is very much at the whim of a network administrator with a modern network, as both Mac OS clients and Mac OS servers support so many other protocols). When connecting Macintosh clients to a server of a different platform, it is often necessary to enable AppleShare services to provide backward compatibility to older workstations, or to provide effective security.

In the classic versions of the Mac OS, AppleShare functionality was provided by a suite of extensions and control panels providing configuration and core services for this networking protocol. As always, when integrating computers using older software onto a newer network, download and install the latest versions of the AppleShare software from Apple Computer's website, and make sure that the operating system is up-to-date. Download the latest version of AppleShare from Apple's support website at http://www.apple.com/support/. Mac OS X computers should be kept up-to-date with the Software Update utility accessible via System Preferences.

Although AppleShare IP provides a secure way for a user and server to exchange names and passwords, it is not an encrypted protocol. It is theoretically possible for an IP packet to be intercepted and its contents read by a third party. Therefore, care should be taken when exchanging sensitive data. Fortunately, AppleShare IP is a pure TCP/IP protocol, so it may be "tunneled" using any variety of encryption methods. The Mac OS itself supports L2TP over IPSec and PPTP, which are capable of encrypting network packets to prevent anyone from reading intercepted packets.

AppleShare Authentication

The most important task to be accomplished between the client and server using the AppleShare protocol is authentication. How is the server to know that the user can be trusted to perform operations on files and folders? What if the user is attempting to connect to a non-Apple file server that supports a unique authentication standard?

On connecting to any AppleShare service on any server, the first thing the client does is try to determine what method of authentication the server supports. Can an Apple protocol be used? What about Kerberos, or the Microsoft authentication protocol? If the server supports more than one authentication method, the user is asked to choose one. The exception is the plain-text method. If the server and client don't have compatible authentication software installed, a username and password can be exchanged via plain text, if the server has been allowed to support it. However, if any more secure method is available, the plain-text option won't be given.

Because various software vendors sell servers that support AppleShare IP, clients need to be able to add authentication methods. Recent versions of AppleShare support user authentication modules, which are simple plug-ins that add authentication methods to a client.

The most common plug-in is the Microsoft UAM, required to connect to Windows 2000 and 2003 servers. This software comes with the server and is also available for download from Microsoft's support website. This module allows AppleShare IP clients to use Microsoft's native Windows authentication protocol, allowing administrators to provide enhanced security by using SMB services with packet signing turned on, as well as providing secure access to Macintosh clients.

Operating System Interoperability

Rather than use the same network operating system on all servers, modern networks often work in multivendor environments, meaning that you might encounter more than one of the major network operating systems functioning on the same network. Although it is completely possible to use a single operating system for all the common network server tasks, in some situations, a more flexible approach is required.

To facilitate such environments, network operating system manufacturers build in features and services that enable their operating systems to coexist on networks with other vendors' operating systems.

The following sections take a brief look at how well some of the major network operating systems "play" with each other.

Using Windows with NetWare

In some environments, you might find that both Windows and NetWare servers are deployed. Unfortunately for Novell, an increasing number of these environments are in place to facilitate migration to a completely Windows-based network.

In some other environments, organizations leverage the power of eDirectory and NetWare for file and print services and use a Windows server product for application hosting. Because it realizes that there will be such environments, Microsoft supplies a range of tools, including the following, to help in the communication between Windows server products and NetWare:

➤ **Client Services for NetWare (CSNW)**—CSNW is designed to enable Windows client systems to access file and print services on a NetWare server. CSNW is installed on a client system and enables only that client to connect to the NetWare server. In effect, CSNW is a Microsoft-provided client for NetWare.

➤ **Gateway Services for NetWare (GSNW)**—GSNW is used on Windows 2000 systems to enable Windows client systems to access resources on a NetWare server. GSNW is installed on the Windows server and enables clients to connect to the NetWare server through it. As the name suggests, the service enables a Windows server to act as a gateway to the NetWare server. GSNW is not included with Windows Server 2003. Clients do not need to authenticate against the Novell server directly. Authentication is performed on behalf of all users through the GSNW software.

For Windows Server 2003, Microsoft provides Windows Services for NetWare. This free download is geared more toward facilitating the migration from a NetWare/eDirectory environment to Active Directory than as a tool for providing long-term integration.

You should understand the functions of CSNW and GSNW for the Network+ exam. You should also understand where they are installed.

Using Windows and Linux Servers

In today's environments, Linux and Windows servers are commonly used together, and therefore, the servers themselves must be capable of communicating. That said, most of that communication is likely to take place with industry standard protocols such as FTP and HTTP, so no additional client software is necessary to communicate between servers under these conditions.

Microsoft provides some degree of integration for UNIX systems via a special add-on pack called Windows Services for UNIX. This add-on pack provides compatibility with the UNIX NFS and a variety of UNIX utilities. The add-on pack can also be used on Linux servers. However, Microsoft states clearly that Windows Services for UNIX has only been tested on a limited number of versions of UNIX and only one version of Linux—Red Hat 8.

Using NetWare and Linux Servers

NetWare and Linux servers are fully interoperable and are often found together in network environments. For instance, a NetWare file and print server might coexist with a Linux firewall and proxy server. In addition, it is possible, by using eDirectory, to integrate the management of Linux servers into the directory services system in order to streamline administration.

To make these scenarios possible, Linux supports both IPX/SPX, which is required for NetWare 3.x and 4.x, and TCP/IP, which is used in the later NetWare versions. However, many of the Linux distributions do not natively support IPX/SPX. If you use one of those distributions, you need to download extra software and perform additional configuration.

Operating System Client Support

Because many different client operating systems—including Linux, Windows, and Macintosh—are used in today's networks, network operating systems need to provide support for these clients to connect to the network. Of the three client systems mentioned, Microsoft Windows is by far the most popular. However, in recent years, other platforms have experienced a surge in popularity.

Windows Server Client Support

Windows-based servers support all the client software that is used on networks today. Microsoft provides client software for all previous versions of

Windows, allowing for easy client connectivity. In the latest client operating systems such as Windows 2000 Professional and Windows XP Professional, network functionality is tightly integrated into the operating system. On older versions of Windows, additional software might have to be installed to gain the full benefits of network connectivity.

 Although you can use a system running Windows XP Home Edition to connect to network resources, you cannot join a domain or log on to Active Directory.

To support Macintosh clients, Windows server platforms include a File Services for Macintosh service, as well as a Print Services for Macintosh service. These allow Macintosh clients to access shared resources on a Windows server. The aforementioned Windows Services for UNIX provides some client functionality for UNIX and Linux clients connecting to Windows client platforms.

NetWare Server Client Support

To connect a Windows client system to a Novell network, you can use Novell-supplied client software or Microsoft's own client—CSNW. Novell makes its client software available for download from the company's website. The client software for current versions of Windows operating systems is called Novell Client for Windows XP/2000.

To connect Windows desktop systems to a NetWare 3.x or 4.x network, Microsoft NWLink is required on the workstation, as is CSNW or the Novell client software. NetWare 5.x does not specifically require that clients use NWLink as it also supports TCP/IP. NetWare 6 does not necessarily require client-side software.

Linux Server Client Support

Because a Linux workstation uses the same operating system that is running on the server, client support is both integrated and seamless. Linux client systems can access all the resources offered by a Linux server with ease. The most common resources are file sharing, which is normally facilitated through NFS, and printing, which is made available through the Line Printer daemon (LPD).

One of the programs used to increase interoperability between Linux and Windows clients is Samba. Samba is a software application that enables Linux servers to easily share resources with Windows workstations. Samba is available free of charge and is commonly installed by default during a Linux installation. Connection to a Samba server requires the use of the Microsoft network client, which is installed by default with most Windows client operating systems.

You might be asked about Samba on the Network+ exam. As discussed in Chapter 5, TCP/IP, Samba is an implementation of the Server Message Block (SMB)/Common Internet File System (CIFS) file sharing and access protocols.

Configuring a Client to Access and Use Network Resources

Part of the role of the network administrator is to expand the network to include new client systems. Many factors are required to connect a client to the network including media, protocols, and services. This section explores the requirements to connect a client system to an existing network.

Choosing a NIC

A client system cannot access the network if it does not have a network card installed. There are several factors to consider when selecting a network card:

➤ **Bus compatibility**—Some older systems have only Industry Standard Architecture (ISA) slots, but most modern systems have either Peripheral Component Interconnect (PCI) slots or both PCI and ISA slots. Either way, you should verify that there is an expansion slot of the correct type available. Wireless NICs can be installed using a USB adapter.

➤ **Type of network**—As mentioned in the discussion on NICs in Chapter 3, "Networking Devices," unless you are using a networking system other than Ethernet, you should not need to specify another type of NIC. The exception here is if the client system is being attached using a wireless connection. A Wireless NIC would then be required.

➤ **Media compatibility**—Modern LANs use NICs that support UTP cable. There are some out there, however, that still require coaxial connectors and more modern ones might have fiber connectors.

Besides these criteria, which dictate to a certain extent which NICs you can use, the choice then depends on manufacturer, cost, and requirements. The NIC might come preinstalled in the system or, as in an increasing number of cases, the NIC might be built on to the system board. In either of these situations, you do not have to install a NIC.

Media

With the NIC installed and functioning, the next step is to connect the PC to the network via network media. This can be simple or complicated, depending on the type of network you are using. The following are some of the factors you should consider when connecting a new system to an existing network:

> **Connecting to a coaxial network**—The biggest considerationwhen connecting to a coaxial network is that it might be necessary to break the coaxial segment to insert a *Bayonet Neill Concelman (BNC)* T-connector to physically connect the PC. Unfortunately, breaking a coaxial cable segment prevents any device connected to it from working. This means that if you are adding a computer to a coaxial segment and you need to add a length of cable and a connector, you need to either arrange with network users for a few minutes when the network will be unavailable or add the cable and connector before or after working hours. The good news is that you can leave spare BNC T-connectors in the coaxial cable segment as a just-in-case precaution. Doing so can mean that you can add a system to the coaxial segment without affecting users other than the one whose system you are connecting.

> **Connecting to a twisted-pair network**—Twisted pair is the easiest of all the network types to connect to. All you need to connect is a cable (referred to as a *patch cable*) that connects the system to a hub or switch. In environments that use a structured cable system, the cable can be connected to a wall jack or a jack in a floor box. In a less structured environment, the cable can be run directly between the system and the hub or switch. One item worthy of note is that if you are using a Token Ring network, you must configure the NIC to work at the correct speed. Twisted-pair Ethernet networks can accommodate different speeds if the networking hardware supports a speed higher than the base 10Mbps. Token Ring networks do not offer this function; all devices on the ring must operate at the same speed (4Mbps or 16Mbps). Connecting a system to the network with a NIC configured for the wrong speed prevents the system from communicating on the network, and it might even cause problems with other devices on the segment.

➤ **Connecting to a wireless network**—Wireless network connections use radio frequency instead of traditional wire. Connecting a wireless client requires a wireless access point, which provides a bridge between a wired network and the wireless network segment. Wireless standards use RF frequencies of 2.4GHz for 802.11b/g and 5GHz for 802.11a. The wireless client also requires the SSID of the wireless access point and the security settings to connect. Once connected, the wireless client can access the wired network through the AP.

After the physical connection to the network has been established, you need to consider the network protocols to use.

Choosing LAN Protocols

Choosing the correct protocol is an important consideration when configuring a network or adding systems to an existing network. The client and the server must use the same protocol in order for communication to take place. This section provides a brief summary of the commonly used protocols. For a complete description of the various protocols, refer to Chapter 4, "OSI Model and Network Protocols."

➤ **TCP/IP**—By far the most prevalent of network protocol suites, TCP/IP is available for almost every computing platform and has widespread industry support. The majority of LANs now use TCP/IP as the default protocol. Configuring TCP/IP connectivity requires the use of an IP address, a subnet mask, a default gateway, and possibly Domain Name Service (DNS) server information and Windows Internet Naming System (WINS) information.

➤ **IPX/SPX**—Novell invented and implemented IPX/SPX when it introduced NetWare in the 1980s. At that time, TCP/IP was for the most part an academic/military/government protocol, and Novell realized the need for a robust, routable protocol. IPX/SPX is one of the main reasons that Novell owned the networking market through the 1980s and most of the 1990s. IPX/SPX was also easy to install and configure. Today, TCP/IP has largely displaced IPX. One of the advantages of IPX is that workstation configuration is very simple. Generally speaking, the only item that might need to be configured is the frame type, which determines the format in which data is grouped into the frames that are placed on the network. Older versions of NetWare use a frame type called 802.3, whereas newer versions use a frame type called 802.2. Fortunately, most client software is capable of detecting the frame type automatically.

➤ **AppleTalk**—AppleTalk is aprotocol associated with Apple networks. The AppleTalk protocol is an established protocol suite having been introduced in the early 1980s, it soon became a viable internetworking protocol. Similar to the IPX/SPX and TCP/IP protocol suites, the AppleTalk protocol suite is composed of several protocols.

➤ **NWLink**—When Microsoft began working on adding support for interoperability with NetWare, it opted to develop its own fully compatible version of Novell's proprietary IPX/SPX. This development was necessary because earlier versions of NetWare did not support authentication over TCP/IP.

 On the Network+ exam, be careful when determining whether connectivity to a NetWare server is required from a Microsoft client. NWLink is the required protocol because Microsoft does not directly support IPX/SPX. Watch for this same situation in reverse as well: NetWare uses IPX/SPX to communicate with a Windows Server running NWLink.

➤**NetBEUI**—Microsoft chose IBM's NetBEUI as the protocol for its first networking implementation in the mid-1980s. One of the reasons Microsoft chose to base its early networking efforts on NetBEUI was the protocol's simplicity and speed. Microsoft wanted to offer a very simple, easy workgroup configuration. Name resolutions and network addressing, or more accurately naming, are both handled automatically with NetBEUI. There are no configuration issues, other than setting up the NIC and installing NetBEUI as the protocol. Because of NetBEUI's simplicity, administrators sometimes use it to troubleshoot hard-to-find communication problems between two machines. The simplicity of NetBEUI also created problems for Microsoft as the 1980s progressed. NetBEUI is a non-routable protocol, and as networks began to interconnect, Microsoft found its clients stranded within the confines of small LANs.

As mentioned earlier, TCP/IP is by far the most common of the networking protocols in use today. For that reason, the next section takes a more in-depth look at configuring client systems to use TCP/IP.

Configuring Client Systems for TCP/IP

In a TCP/IP network, there are several settings to configure to enable a client system to access peer and server services. Configuring a client system for TCP/IP can be a relatively complex task, or it can be simple. Any complexity involved is related to the possible need to configure TCP/IP manually. The simplicity is related to the fact that TCP/IP configuration can occur automatically via DHCP. Brief explanations of the IP related settings used to connect to a TCP/IP network follow:

➤ **IP address**—Each system must be assigned a unique IP address so that it can communicate on the network.

➤ **Subnet mask**—The subnet mask enables the system to determine which portion of the IP address represents the network address and which portion represents the node address.

➤ **Default gateway**—The default gateway enables the system to communicate with systems on a remote network, without the need for explicit routes to be defined.

➤ **DNS server addresses**—DNS servers enable dynamic hostname resolution to be performed. It is common practice to have two DNS server addresses defined so that if one server becomes unavailable, the other can be used.

➤ **WINS server addresses**—A WINS server enables Network Basic Input/Output System (NetBIOS) names to be resolved to IP addresses. As with DNS servers, it is common practice to enter two WINS server addresses to provide a degree of fault tolerance.

 At the very minimum, an IP address and a subnet mask are required to connect to a TCP/IP network. With just this minimum configuration, connectivity is limited to the local segment, and DNS and WINS resolution are not be possible.

Using Network Tools

There are a number of tools a network administrator might be required to use. Some of these tools (such as the tone generator and locator) can be used for troubleshooting media connections, and others (such as *wire crimpers* and *punchdown* tools) are used to create network cables and connections. In either case, for the Network+ exam, you will be expected to identify the function of various networking tools.

Wire Crimpers

Wire crimpers are tools that most network administrators will find themselves using at some point. Basically, a wire crimper is a tool that you use to attach media connectors to the ends of cables. For instance, you use one type of wire crimper to attach RJ-45 connectors on Unshielded Twisted Pair (UTP) cable, and you use a different type of wire crimper to attach *Bayonet Neill Concelman (BNCs)* to coaxial cabling.

In a sense, you can think of a wire crimper as a pair of special pliers. You insert the cable and connector separately into the crimper, making sure that the wires in the cable align with the appropriate connectors. Then, by squeezing the crimper's handles, you force metal connectors through the wires of the cable, making the connection between the wire and the connector.

If you do need to make your own cables instead of buying them, it is a good idea to test them before putting them on the network. It only takes a momentary lapse to make a mistake when creating a cable, and you can waste time later trying to isolate a problem in a faulty cable. If you do choose to make your own cables, you should test them with an electronic 'patch tester' before installing them on your network.

Punchdown Tools

If you have ever looked in a network closet, you have probably seen a distribution block, more commonly called a patch panel. A *patch panel* is a free-standing or wall-mounted unit with a number of port connections on the front. In a way, it looks like a wall-mounted hub without the light-emitting diodes (LEDs). The patch panel provides a connection point between network equipment such as hubs and switches and the ports to which PCs are connected, which are normally distributed throughout a building.

Behind each of the individual RJ-45 jacks on the patch panel are connectors to which are attached the eight wires from a piece of twisted-pair cable. These wires are commonly attached to the patch panel by using a tool called a *punchdown tool*. To use the punchdown tool, you place the wires from the cable into the appropriate slots in the back of the patch panel, and then use the tool push the wires firmly down into the slots. The insulation is stripped, and the wire becomes firmly embedded into the connector. Because the connector strips the insulation on the wire, it is known rather grandiosely as an insulation displacement connector (IDC).

Tone Generators (and Tone Locators)

A *tone generator* is a device that can save a network installer many hours of frustration. Strangely, the tone generator has a partner that goes wherever it goes but is seldom mentioned: the tone locator. You might hear the tone generator and the tone locator referred to as the *fox and hound*.

As you might expect, the purpose of the tone generator is to generate a signal that is transmitted on the wire you are attempting to locate. At the other end, you press the tone locator against individual wires. When it makes contact with the wire that has the signal on it, the locator emits an audible signal or tone.

The tone locator is a useful device, but it does have some drawbacks. First, it often takes two people to operate—one at each end of the cable. Of course, one person could just keep running back and forth; but if the cable is run over great distances, this could be a problem. Second, using the tone generator is a time-consuming process because it must be attached to each cable independently.

Media Testers

A *media tester*, also called a cable tester, is used to test whether a cable is working properly. Any tool that facilitates the testing of a cable can be deemed a cable tester. One of the simplest cable-testing devices is a *multimeter*. By using the continuity setting, you can test for shorts in a length of coaxial cable; or, if you know the correct cable pinouts and have needlepoint probes, you can test twisted-pair cable. Various other single-purpose and multipurpose devices allow you to test cables. Some of these devices tell you if the cable is working correctly and, if it's not, give you some idea why it's not.

Because the majority of network cabling is copper based, most of the tools designed to test cabling are designed for copper-based cabling. However, when you test fiber-optic cable, you need an optical tester.

An *optical cable tester* performs the same basic function as a wire media tester, but on optical media. Unlike wire cables, the most common problem with an optical cable is a break in the cable that prevents the signal from reaching the other end. Because of the extended distances that can be covered with fiber-optic cables, degradation is rarely an issue in a fiber-optic LAN environment.

Ascertaining whether a signal reaches the other end of a fiber-optic cable is a relatively easy task, but when you determine that there is a break, the problem becomes locating the break. That's when you need a tool called an *optical time-domain reflectometer (OTDR)*. By using an OTDR, you can locate how far along in the cable the break occurs. The connection on the other end of the cable might be the source of the problem, or perhaps there is a break halfway along the cable. Either way, an OTDR can pinpoint the problem.

Unless you work extensively with fiber-optic cable, you're unlikely to have an OTDR or even a fiber-optic cable tester in your toolbox. Specialized cabling contractors will have them, though, so knowing that they exist is important.

Hardware Loopback Connectors

Hardware loopback connectors are simple devices that redirect outgoing transmissions from a system directly back into it. Hardware loopback connectors are used in conjunction with diagnostic software for diagnosing transmission problems. Loopback connectors are available for a number of ports, including RJ-45, serial, and parallel ports.

Specifically, a hardware loopback connector loops the outgoing data signal wires back into the system on the incoming data signal line. In effect, it tricks the system into thinking that the PC is sending and receiving data on the network, when in fact the data being sent is just being rerouted back in. Note that in some cases, a hardware loopback connector is referred to as an adapter or a plug.

The hardware loopback adapter checks the electrical signals sent out from the NIC.

Configuring Remote Connectivity

The capability to remotely access networks has become an important part of the modern IT infrastructure. All organizations, from the smallest business to the largest corporation, are taking advantage of the potential that remote network access provides. Therefore, today's network administrators are as likely to be responsible for managing remote network access as they are for LAN access. Configuring and managing remote access requires knowledge of the protocols and procedures involved in establishing a remote connection.

The following sections explore some of the common considerations in configuring a remote connection, including a discussion of physical connections, protocols (which facilitate the connection), software (which establishes the connection), the dial-up connection method, and security issues.

Despite the network operating system used, they all have remote connection technologies in common. Authentication protocols, physical connections, and such are common to popular OSs.

Physical Connections

There are many ways to connect to a remote network. Some, such as the Plain Old Telephone Service (POTS), offer a direct connection between you and the remote host. Others, such as cable and Digital Subscriber Lines (DSL), allow you to connect, but the connection occurs over a public network (the Internet), which can bring additional considerations such as authentication and security problems. The methods that can be used to establish a remote connection are discussed in Chapter 6. A summary is provided here:

➤ **Public switched telephone network (PSTN)**—The PSTN offers by far the most popular method of remote connectivity. A modem and a POTS line allow for inexpensive and somewhat reliable, if not fast, remote access.

➤ **Integrated Services Digital Network (ISDN)**—ISDN is a dial-up technology that works much like the PSTN, but instead of using analog signals to carry the data, ISDN uses digital signals. This makes it faster than the PSTN.

➤ **Cable**—In an effort to take advantage of the increasing demand for high-speed Internet access, cable TV providers now offer broadband Internet access over the same connection that is used to carry cable TV signals.

➤ **DSL**—DSL services are the telecom companies' broadband offering. *x*DSL (that is, the family of DSL services) comes in many varieties, and as with cable, you need a special modem in order to use it.

➤ **Satellite**—Perhaps the least popular of the connection methods discussed here, satellite provides wireless Internet access; although in some scenarios, a PSTN connection is also required for upstream access. Of the technologies discussed in this section, satellite is the least suitable for remote access.

➤ **Wireless Internet**—Wireless Internet access is provided by a Wireless Internet Service Provider (WISP). The WISP provides public wireless Internet access known as hotspots. Hotspots provide Internet access for mobile network devices such as laptops, handheld computers, and cell phones in airports, coffee shops, conference rooms, and so on. A hotspot is created using one or many wireless access points near the hotspot location. A hotspot typically requires a WAP at each location connected to a high speed broadband connection such as DSL, cable Internet, or even T1 connections. The technology is based on the 802.11 standards; typically, 802.11b/g and client systems require only an internal or external wireless adapter.

More information on remote access technologies and Internet technologies can be found in Chapter 6.

Protocols

When you have decided on the physical aspect of the connection, the next consideration is the protocols that allow you to make a connection to the remote server.

To facilitate a connection between a remote system and a remote access server, common protocols must be used between the systems. Two types of protocols are required to establish a remote connection. You first need to have the protocols that communicate at the data-link layer, including the following:

➤ **Point-to-Point Protocol (PPP)**—PPP is actually a family of protocols that work together to provide connection services. PPP enables remote clients and servers to negotiate authentication between devices. PPP can employ a variety of encryption methods to secure transmissions.

➤ **Serial Line Internet Protocol (SLIP)**—SLIP is an older connection protocol than PPP, and it was originally designed to enable data to be transmitted via Transmission Control Protocol/Internet Protocol (TCP/IP) over serial connections in a UNIX environment. Unfortunately, SLIP does not support encryption or authentication and therefore has largely fallen out of favor. If you have users that employ SLIP to connect from remote systems, you should move them to PPP connections as soon as possible.

➤ **Point-to-Point Protocol over Ethernet (PPPoE)**—PPPoE is a method of using PPP connections over Ethernet. Using PPPoE and a broadband connection such as xDSL or cable Internet access, it is possible for individual users to have authenticated access to high-speed data networks, which provides an efficient way to create a separate connection to a remote server for each user. This strategy allows Internet access and billing on a per-user basis rather than a per-site basis. Users accessing PPPoE connections require the same information as required with standard dial-up phone accounts, including a username and password combination. As with a dial-up PPP service, an Internet service provider (ISP) will most likely automatically assign configuration information such as the IP address, subnet mask, default gateway, and DNS server information.

After a data link has established the connection between the devices, LAN protocols are used. This includes TCP/IP, AppleTalk, and IPX/SPX.

Each of these remote access protocols require authentication protocols to complete the connection. Common authentication protocols include MS-CHAP, MS-CHAP v2, CHAP, PAP, or EAP. Each of these protocols is discussed in Chapter 6.

Many remote access products are available; however, Windows RAS is the most likely of these products to appear on the Network+ exam. RAS is reviewed in Chapter 6.

Review and Test Yourself

The following sections provide you with the opportunity to review what you learned in this chapter and to test yourself.

The Facts

For the exam, don't forget these important concepts:

➤ To log on to a Netware server, you might need a username, password, tree, and context.

➤ The following list summarizes the file permissions on Windows server platforms that use the NTFS file system:

Right	Description
Full Control	Provides all rights
Modify	Allows files to be modified
Read & Execute	Allows files to be read and executed (that is, run)
List Folder Contents	Allows the files in a folder to be listed
Read	Allows a file to be read
Write	Allows a file to be written to

➤ Valid file permissions on a UNIX/Linux system include Read, Write, and Execute.

➤ On Windows server platforms, you can convert from FAT partitions to NTFS partitions with the convert command.

➤ Valid permissions for NetWare systems include Supervisor, Read, Write, Create, Erase, Modify, Filescan, and Access Control.

➤ The usernames and passwords are case sensitive when logging on to a Linux system.

➤ CSNW enables Windows-based clients to access file and print services on a NetWare server.

➤ GSNW enables Windows client systems to access resources on a NetWare server through a Windows server that is acting as a gateway.

➤ Samba enables Linux servers to share resources with Windows workstations.

Key Terms

➤ Authentication

➤ File and print services

➤ Web server services

➤ Novell NetWare

➤ UNIX

➤ Linux

➤ Macintosh

➤ Active Directory

➤ FAT

➤ FAT32

➤ NTFS

➤ NDS

➤ NLMs

➤ NFS

➤ Samba

➤ CSNW

➤ GSNW

Exam Prep Questions

1. You have been instructed to install a Novell NetWare server on your network. All the other servers are Windows 2000 systems. You want Windows XP Professional clients to be able to access both the Windows 2000 servers and the NetWare server. Which of the following strategies could you adopt? (Choose the two best answers.)

   ❑   A. Install the Novell Client for Windows XP/2000 on each workstation.

   ❑   B. Install GSNW on the NetWare server.

   ❑   C. Install GSNW on the Windows XP Professional clients.

   ❑   D. Install GSNW on one of the Windows 2000 servers.

2. Which of the following is NOT a valid file permission on a UNIX or Linux system?

   ❑   A. Read

   ❑   B. Change

   ❑   C. Write

   ❑   D. Execute

3. A user calls to report that he is having problems saving changes to a file held on an NTFS partition of a Windows Server 2003 system. The user is accessing the file through a share called NEWDATA. He has accessed the file before, but has never made any changes to it. Which of the following is NOT a valid reason for the issue the user is experiencing?

   ❑   A. An inheritance filter is blocking permissions.

   ❑   B. The user might not have the necessary permissions, but doesn't realize that.

   ❑   C. The share permissions might be overriding the NTFS permissions.

   ❑   D. The NTFS permissions might be overriding the share permissions.

4. Which of the following versions of NetWare use eDirectory or NDS for storing and managing network objects such as user accounts? (Choose two.)

   ❑   A. NetWare 3.11

   ❑   B. NetWare 3.12

   ❑   C. NetWare 4.11

   ❑   D. NetWare 6.5

5. A tone generator and locator are commonly referred to as what?

 □ A. Fox and rabbit
 □ B. Fox and hare
 □ C. Fox and hound
 □ D. Fox and dog

6. Which of the following services is required to make the file and print resources of a Linux server available to Windows clients?

 □ A. Squid
 □ B. GSFL
 □ C. FP4Linux
 □ D. Samba

7. Which of the following represent the minimum requirement to access a TCP/IP network? (Choose two.)

 □ A. WINS information
 □ B. Subnet mask
 □ C. DNS information
 □ D. IP address
 □ E. Default gateway

8. What tool would you use when working with an IDC?

 □ A. Wire crimper
 □ B. Media tester
 □ C. OTDR
 □ D. Punchdown tool

9. Which of the following technologies enable individual files on a Windows server system to be secured against unauthorized access or viewing? (Choose two.)

 □ A. EFS
 □ B. HPFS
 □ C. WINS
 □ D. NTFS

10. As a network administrator, you find yourself working in a wiring closet in which none of the cables have been labeled. Which of the following tools are you most likely to use to locate the physical ends of the cable?

 □ A. Tone generator
 □ B. Wire crimper
 □ C. Punchdown tool
 □ D. ping

Answers to Exam Prep Questions

1. The correct answers are A and D. To facilitate connection to a NetWare server from Windows clients, you can install the Novell Client for Windows XP/2000 on each workstation or install Gateway Services for NetWare on a Windows 2000 server. Alternatively, Microsoft supplies a client for NetWare that can be used in place of the Novell provided client. GSNW is a server-based service and would not be installed on the client. Answer B is not valid. GSNW is a Windows server-based service. You cannot run it on a NetWare server. For more information, see the section "Operating System Interoperability," in this chapter.

2. The correct answer is B. Change is not a permission used on UNIX or Linux. Read, Write, and Execute are supported.

3. The correct answer is A. NTFS does not provide an inheritance filter system. Therefore, an inheritance filter cannot be the issue. It might be that the user does not have the necessary permissions to edit the file, or it could be that the NTFS or share permissions are preventing the user from accessing the file. When a user accesses a file with NTFS permission on it through a share, the more restrictive of the two permission sets applies. Therefore, either one can override the other.

4. The correct answers are C and D. NDS was introduced with Netware 4.x and has been used on all subsequent versions, although it has since been renamed eDirectory. NetWare 3.x and prior versions of NetWare used a system called the Bindery to store user and account information.

5. The correct answer is C. A tone generator and locator are commonly referred to the fox and hound. None of the other answers are valid.

6. The correct answer is D. Samba is used to provide Windows clients with file and print services from a Linux server. None of the other options are valid.

7. The correct answers are B and D. To log on to a TCP/IP network, you need both the subnet mask and the IP address. Without entering the DNS and WINS configurations, these services will be unavailable, but you would still be able to log on to the network. Without the gateway configured, the client system would be restricted to the local segment.

8. The correct answer is D. You use a punchdown tool when working with an IDC. All the other tools are associated with making and troubleshooting cables, but they are not associated with IDCs.

9. The correct answers are A and D. Both EFS and NTFS are mechanisms that are used to secure individual files or folders from unauthorized viewing or access. HPFS is the High Performance File System used with the OS/2 operating system. WINS resolves NetBIOS names to the IP address.

10. The correct answer is A. The tone generator tool, along with the tone locator, can be used to trace cables. Crimpers and punchdown tools are not used for locating a cable. The ping utility would be of no help in this situation.

Need to Know More?

 Bird, Drew and Harwood, Mike. *Network+ Exam Prep 2*. Que Publishing, 2005.

Nemeth, Evi, Garth Snyder, Trent Hein. *Linux Administration Handbook*. Prentice Hall, 2002.

Williams, G Robert, Mark Walla. *The Ultimate Windows 2000 Systems Administrators Guide*. Addison-Wesley, 2000.

Morimoto, Rand, et al. *Microsoft Windows Server 2003 Unleashed, Second Edition*. Sams Publishing, 2004.

Frisch, Aleen. *Essential System Administration, Third Edition*. O'Reilly & Associates, 2002.

Ness, Robyn, Ray, John. *Sams Teach Yourself Mac OS X Panther All In One*. Sams Publishing, 2004.

Harris, Jeffrey. *Novell NetWare 6.5 Administrator's Guide*. Novell Press, 2003.

Network Security

Objectives

3.5 Identify the purpose, benefits, and characteristics of using a firewall

3.6 Identify the purpose, benefits, and characteristics of using a proxy service

3.7 Given a connectivity scenario, determine the impact on network functionality of a particular security implementation (for example, port blocking/filtering, authentication, and encryption)

3.9 Identify the main characteristics and purpose of extranets and intranets

What you need to know

✓ Understand the function of a firewall in a networked environment
✓ Understand the function of a proxy server in a networked environment
✓ Identify the effects of port blocking
✓ Identify encryption methods
✓ Understand how to create a secure password policy
✓ Identify the purpose of extranets and intranets

Introduction

Two important elements of a network security strategy are the use of proxy servers and firewall systems. A firewall system acts as a protective layer to network access by controlling the traffic that passes between the interfaces on a system. Proxy servers allow you to centralize access to the Internet and therefore provide a way to control and monitor network access.

In this chapter, we will also examine how other security measures—such as port blocking, password policies, and encryption—fit into network security strategy. We also take a quick look at the purpose and characteristics of extranets and intranets.

The topics in this chapter focus on some of the logical aspects of network security, in contrast to the physical aspects. Although CompTIA does not specifically mention physical security in the Network+ objectives, you should still be aware of basic physical security measures such as controlling access to equipment and safeguarding backup tapes. You might not get asked directly about these things in the exam, but knowing the difference between physical and logical security measures might help you to better answer or interpret a question.

Firewalls

In today's network environments, firewalls are being used to protect systems from external as well as internal threats. Although firewalls initially became popular in corporate environments, many home networks with a broadband Internet connection now also implement a firewall to protect against Internet borne threats.

Essentially, a firewall is an application, device, system, or group of systems that controls the flow of traffic between two networks. The most common use of a firewall is to protect a private network from a public network such as the Internet. However, firewalls are also increasingly being used as a means to separate a sensitive area of a private network from less-sensitive areas.

At its most basic, a *firewall* is a device (it could be a computer system or a dedicated hardware device) that has more than one network interface and manages the flow of network traffic between those interfaces. How it manages the flow and what it does with certain types of traffic depends on its configuration. Figure 8.1 shows the most basic firewall configuration.

Strictly speaking, a firewall performs no action on the packets it receives besides the basic functions just described. However, in a real-world implementation, a firewall is likely to offer other functionality, such as *Network Address Translation* (*NAT*) and proxy server services. Without NAT, any host on the internal network that needs to send or receive data through the firewall needs a registered IP address. Although there are such environments, most people have to settle for using a private address range on the internal network and therefore rely on the firewall system to translate the outgoing request into an acceptable public network address.

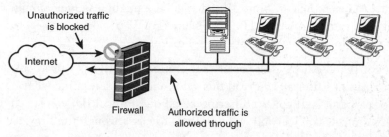

Figure 8.1   A basic firewall implementation.

Although the fundamental purpose of a firewall is to protect one network from another, you need to configure the firewall to allow some traffic through. If you don't need to allow traffic to pass through a firewall, you can dispense with it entirely and completely separate your network from others.

A firewall can employ a variety of methods to ensure security. A firewall can use just one of these methods, or it can combine different methods to produce the most appropriate and robust configuration. The following sections discuss the various firewall methods that are commonly used: packet-filtering firewalls, circuit-level firewalls, and application gateway firewalls.

Packet-filtering Firewalls

Of the firewall methods discussed in this chapter, *packet filtering* is the most commonly implemented. Packet filtering enables the firewall to examine each packet that passes through it and determine what to do with it, based on the configuration. A packet-filtering firewall deals with packets at the data-link and network layers of the *Open Systems Interconnect (OSI)* model. The following are some of the criteria by which packet filtering can be implemented:

➤ **IP address**—By using the IP address as a parameter, the firewall can allow or deny traffic, based on the source or destination IP address. For example, you can configure the firewall so that only certain hosts on the internal network are able to access hosts on the Internet. Alternatively, you can configure it so that only certain hosts on the Internet are able to gain access to a system on the internal network.

> ➤ **Port number**—As discussed in Chapter 5, "TCP/IP (Transmission Control Protocol/Internet Protocol)," the TCP/IP suite uses port numbers to identify which service a certain packet is destined for. By configuring the firewall to allow certain types of traffic, you can control the flow. You might, for example, open port 80 on the firewall to allow Hypertext Transfer Protocol (HTTP) requests from users on the Internet to reach the corporate Web server. You might also, depending on the application, open the HTTP Secure (HTTPS) port, port 443, to allow access to a secure Web server application.

> ➤ **Protocol ID**—Because each packet transmitted with IP has a protocol identifier in it, a firewall can read this value and then determine what kind of packet it is. If you are filtering based on protocol ID, you specify which protocols you will and will not allow to pass through the firewall.

> ➤ **MAC address**—This is perhaps the least used of the packet-filtering methods discussed, but it is possible to configure a firewall to use the hardware-configured MAC address as the determining factor in whether access to the network is granted. This is not a particularly flexible method, and it is therefore suitable only in environments in which you can closely control who uses which MAC address. The Internet is not such an environment.

Circuit-level Firewalls

Circuit-level firewalls are similar in operation to packet-filtering firewalls, but they operate at the transport and session layers of the OSI model. The biggest difference between a packet-filtering firewall and a circuit-level firewall is that a circuit-level firewall validates TCP and UDP sessions before opening a connection, or circuit, through the firewall. When the session is established, the firewall maintains a table of valid connections and lets data pass through when session information matches an entry in the table. The table entry is removed, and the circuit is closed when the session is terminated.

Application Gateway Firewalls

The *application gateway firewall* is the most functional of all the firewall types. As its name suggests, the application gateway firewall functionality is implemented through an application. Application gateway firewall systems can implement sophisticated rules and closely control traffic that passes through. Features of these firewalls can include user authentication systems and the capability to control which systems an outside user can access on the internal network. Some also provide bandwidth control mechanisms. Because application gateway firewalls operate above the Session layer of the OSI model, they can provide protection against any software-based network traffic that attempts to pass through them.

 The three firewall methods described in this chapter are often combined into a single firewall application. Packet filtering is the basic firewall function. Circuit-level functionality provides NAT, and an application gateway firewall provides proxy functionality. This is a good point to remember for the Network+ exam.

Firewalls are now a common sight in businesses and homes alike. As the Internet becomes an ever more hostile place, firewalls and the individuals who understand them are likely to become an essential part of the IT landscape.

Proxy Servers

A proxy service provides management and control over what is now an essential feature of any modern network—Internet access. A *proxy server*, which can be a computer or a dedicated hardware device running proxy service software, acts as an intermediary between a user on the internal network and a service on the external network (normally the Internet). The proxy server takes requests from a user and then performs those requests on behalf of the user. To the external system, the request looks as if it originated from the proxy server, not from the user on the internal network. Figure 8.2 shows how a proxy server fits into a network configuration.

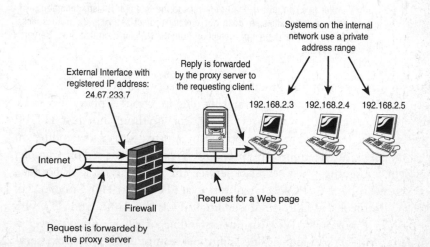

Figure 8.2 A proxy server in a typical network configuration.

A proxy server enables a network to appear to external networks as a single IP address—that of the external network interface of the proxy server.

There are a couple of excellent reasons to implement a proxy server:

➤ **To perform NAT functions**—A proxy server can process and execute commands on behalf of clients that have *private* IP addresses. This enables an organization with only one registered IP address to provide Internet access to a large number of computers. This process is known as IP proxy.

➤ **To allow Internet access to be controlled**—Having a centralized point of access allows for a great deal of control over the use of the Internet. By using the functionality of a proxy server application or by using an add-on feature, proxy servers can filter requests made by clients and either allow or disallow them. You can, for example, implement *uniform resource locator (URL)* filtering, which allows or denies users access to certain sites. More sophisticated products can also perform tests on retrieved material, to see if it fits acceptable criteria. Such measures are intended to prevent users from accessing inappropriate Internet web pages. As an "after the event" feature, proxy server applications also normally provide logging capabilities so that Internet usage can be monitored.

The function of a proxy server should not be confused with the function of a firewall, even though some applications integrate the functionality of both. In basic terms, a proxy server is a centralized point of access to the Internet. It also, generally, provides caching capabilities. It does not directly protect the network from attack, though there is some degree of protection from the NAT function that proxy servers typically provide.

Although the most common function of a proxy server is to provide access to the Web for internal clients, that is not its only function. A proxy server, by definition, can be used as an intermediary for anything, not just HTTP requests. Other services can be supported by a proxy server, depending on the proxy server application being used and its configuration. For example, you might configure a proxy server to service HTTP requests (TCP port 80), Post Office Protocol 3 (POP3) email retrieval (TCP port 110), Simple Mail Transfer Protocol (SMTP) mail sending (TCP port 25), and HTTPS requests (TCP port 443). With an understanding of what a proxy server is designed to do, you can look at one additional feature built in to proxy server functionality, *caching*.

Caching Proxy Servers

An additional feature offered by many proxy server applications is caching; such a server is known as a *caching proxy server*. Caching enables the proxy server to store pages that it retrieves as files on disk. Consequently, if the same pages are requested again, they can be provided more quickly from the cache than if the proxy server had to continue going back to the Web server from which the pages were originally retrieved. This approach has two benefits:

 Proxy servers are sometimes referred to as *HTTP proxies* or *HTTP proxy servers*. In reality, most proxy servers provide proxy services for multiple protocols, not just HTTP.

► **Significantly improves performance**—Performance is improved particularly in environments such as a school, where there is a great likelihood that more than one user might retrieve the same page.

► **Reduces demands on Internet connections**—Because there are fewer requests to the Internet when a caching proxy server is in use, there is a reduced demand on the Internet connection. In some cases, this results in a general speed improvement. In extreme cases, it might even be possible to adopt a less expensive Internet connectivity method because of the lower level of demand.

As with any technology, with caching proxy servers, there are issues to be considered. Sometimes a sizable amount of hard disk space is required to store the cached pages. With the significant decline in the cost of hard disk space over recent years, this is not likely to be much of a problem, but it still needs to be considered.

Another factor is that it's possible for pages held in the cache to become stale. As a result, a user might retrieve a page and believe that it is the latest version when, in fact, it has since changed, but the new page has not been updated in the proxy server cache. To prevent this problem, caching proxy servers can implement measures such as aging of cached information so that it is removed from the cache after a certain amount of time. Some proxy applications can also make sure that the page stored in the cache is the same as the page currently available on the Internet. If the page in the cache is the same as the one on the Internet, it is served to the client from the cache. If the page is not the same, the newer page is retrieved, cached, and supplied to the client.

Using a Proxy Server

Before clients can use a proxy server, it is sometimes necessary to configure the client applications to use it, and in other cases, additional client software is needed. In the case of Web browsers, it is sometimes necessary to manually tell the application that it needs to use a proxy server. Figure 8.3 shows Proxy Settings configuration screen in Microsoft Internet Explorer.

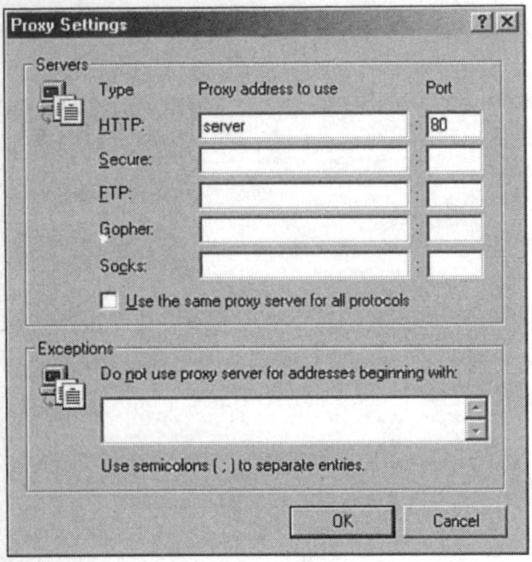

Figure 8.3   The Proxy Settings configuration screen in Internet Explorer.

Other applications besides Web browsers might need to use the proxy server functionality. In some cases, you might need to actually load client software. In essence, this client software modifies elements of the TCP/IP software on the system, to either make it aware of or enable it to cope with the existence of a proxy server. The good news is that the use of proxy servers is now so widespread that applications requiring special client software are becoming increasingly rare.

When Two Become One

By now, you might have realized that both firewalls and proxy servers play an important part in the network infrastructure. For that reason, many applications are now available that combine the functionality of both roles. These *firewalling proxy servers* provide a convenient means for an organization to control and secure the access of its network, and at the same time provide the benefits of Internet access to users.

Understanding How Security Affects a Network

Implementing security measures can have a significant impact on the network. How much of an impact it has depends on which security measures are implemented and the habits of the network users. Several security measures are used on networks including port blocking, authentication schemes, encryption, and so on. While in today's world we may have no choice but to implement these measures, as a network administrator, you'll need to be aware how they impact the overall network. The following sections help you prepare for this part of the exam.

Blocking Port Numbers

Port blocking is one of the most widely used security methods on networks. Port blocking is associated with firewalls and proxy servers, although it can be implemented on any system that provides a means to manage network data flow, according to data type.

Essentially, when you block a port, you disable the ability for traffic to pass through that port, thereby filtering the traffic. Port blocking is typically implemented to prevent users on a public network from accessing systems on a private network, although it is equally possible to block internal users from external services, and internal users from other internal users, by using the same procedure.

Depending on the type of firewall system in use on a network, you might find that all the ports are disabled (blocked) and that the ones you need traffic to flow through must be opened. The benefit of this strategy is that it forces the administrator to choose the ports that should be unblocked rather than specify those that need to be blocked. This ensures that you allow only those services that are absolutely necessary into the network.

What ports remain open largely depends on the needs of the organization. For example, the ports associated with the services listed in Table 8.1 are commonly left open.

Table 8.1	Commonly Opened Port Numbers and Their Associated Uses	
Port Number	**Protocol**	**Purpose**
21	FTP	File transfers
22	SSH	Secure remote sessions

(continued)

Table 8.1 Commonly Opened Port Numbers and Their Associated Uses *(continued)*		
Port Number	**Protocol**	**Purpose**
25	SMTP	Email sending
53	DNS	Hostname resolution
80	HTTP	Web browsing
110	POP3	Email retrieval
123	NTP	Time information
161	SNMP	Network Management
443	HTTPS	Secure Web transactions
3389	RDP	Windows Terminal Services or Windows Remote Desktop

These are, of course, only a few of the services you might need on a network, and allowing traffic from other services to traverse a firewall is as easy as opening the port. Keep in mind, though, that the more ports that are open, the more vulnerable you become to outside attacks. You should never open a port on a firewall unless you are absolutely sure that you need to.

You can obtain a complete list of port numbers and their associated protocols from the Internet Assigned Numbers Authority (IANA), at www.iana.org/assignments/port-numbers.

Port Blocking and Network Users

Before you implement port blocking, you should have a very good idea of what the port is used for. Although it is true that blocking unused ports does not have any impact on internal network users, if the wrong port is blocked, you can create connectivity issues for users on the network.

For instance, imagine that a network administrator was given the task of reducing the amount of spam emails received by his company. He decided to block port 25, the port used by the Simple Mail Transfer Protocol (SMTP). He may have succeeded in blocking the spam email, but in the process, he also prevented users from sending email.

Authentication

As a security mechanism, authentication is provided by every major network operating system and is implemented in all but the most insecure networks. Its 'impact on network functionality,' as stated in item 3.7 of the Network+

objectives, is that it will require users to identify themselves to the network. This process provides two benefits. It secures the network from unauthorized access and provides a degree of accountability for users once they are logged on.

There are three basic categories of authentication used on modern networks:

➤ **Passwords**— The 'traditional' authentication method, passwords do a good job of providing security, but users who choose passwords that are too simple to guess can negate their effectiveness. Additionally, passwords can be passed from one person to another, diminishing their role as an accountability mechanism. Although network users will likely be very comfortable with using passwords, you should make them aware of the rules governing password use in your organization. You should also ensure that they understand the electronic policies that will dictate conditions such as password length and expiration times.

➤ **Smartcards**—Smartcards, which are normally used in conjunction with a password or personal identification number (PIN), provide a higher level of accountability and access control than passwords. This is because the user has to be in possession of a physical item (the smartcard), as well as information (the password or PIN) in order to gain access.

➤ **Biometrics**—Biometrics, which can mean the scanning or verification of some part of your person, is the ultimate 'proof of person' authentication technique. As it is almost impossible to fake biometric mediums such as fingerprints or retinal patterns, you can be very sure that someone gaining access to the system biometrically is who they say they are. Even so, biometric systems typically also use passwords or PIN numbers as an additional measure of security.

Passwords and Password Policies

Although biometrics and smartcards are becoming more common, they still have a very long way to go before they attain the level of popularity that username and password combinations enjoy. Apart from the fact that usernames and passwords do not require any additional equipment, which practically every other method of authentication does, the username and password process is familiar to users, easy to implement, and relatively secure. For that reason, they are worthy of more detailed coverage than the other authentication systems already discussed.

Passwords are a relatively simple form of authentication in that only a string of characters can be used to authenticate the user. However, how the string of characters is used and which policies you can put in place to govern them make usernames and passwords an excellent form of authentication.

Password Policies

All popular network operating systems include password policy systems that allow the network administrator to control how passwords are used on the system. The exact capabilities vary between network operating systems. However, generally they allow the following:

➤ **Minimum length of password**—Shorter passwords are easier to guess than longer ones. Setting a minimum password length does not prevent a user from creating a longer password than the minimum, although each network operating system has a limit on how long a password can be.

➤ **Password expiration**—Also known as the *maximum password age*, password expiration defines how long the user can use the same password before having to change it. A general practice is that a password is changed every month or every 30 days. In high-security environments, you might want to make this value shorter, but you should generally not make it any longer. Having passwords expire periodically is an important feature because it means that if a password is compromised, the unauthorized user will not have access indefinitely.

➤ **Prevention of password reuse**—Although a system might be able to cause a password to expire and prompt the user to change it, many users are tempted to simply use the same password again. A process by which the system remembers the last, say, 10 passwords is most secure because it forces the user to create completely new passwords. This feature is sometimes called *enforcing password history*.

➤ **Prevention of easy-to-guess passwords**—Some systems have the capability to evaluate the password provided by a user to determine whether it meets a required level of complexity. This prevents users from having passwords such as *password* or *12345678*.

 On the Network+ exam, you will need to identify an effective password policy. For example, a robust password policy would include forcing users to change their passwords on a regular basis.

Password Strength

No matter how good a company's password policy, it is only as effective as the passwords that are created within it. A password that is hard to guess, or *strong*, is more likely to protect the data on a system than one that is easy to guess, or *weak*.

To understand the difference between a strong password and a weak one, consider this: A password of six characters that uses only numbers and letters and is not case sensitive has 10,314,424,798,490,535,546,171,949,056 possible combinations. That might seem like a lot, but to a password-cracking program, it's really not much security. A password that uses eight case-sensitive characters, with letters, numbers, and special characters has so many possible combinations that a standard calculator is not capable of displaying the actual number.

There has always been debate over how long a password should be. It should be sufficiently long that it is hard to break but sufficiently short that the user is able to easily remember it (and type it). In a normal working environment, passwords of 8 characters are sufficient. Certainly, they should be no fewer than 6 characters. In environments where security is a concern, passwords should be 10 characters or more.

Users should be encouraged to use a password that is considered strong. A strong password has at least eight characters; has a combination of letters, numbers, and special characters; uses mixed case; and does not form a proper word. Examples might include 3Ecc5T0h and e1oXPn3r. Such passwords might be secure, but users are likely to have problems remembering them. For that reason, a popular strategy is to use a combination of letters and numbers to form phrases or long words. Examples include d1eTc0La and tAb1eT0p. These passwords might not be quite as secure as the preceding examples, but they are still very strong and a whole lot better than the name of the user's household pet.

Passwords—The Last Word

One last password-related topic is worth mentioning. A password is effective only if just the intended users have it. As soon as a password is given to someone else, its effectiveness as an authentication mechanism is diminished. As a tool for accountability, the password is almost useless. Passwords are a means of accessing a system and the data on it. Passwords that are known by anyone other than the intended user(s) might as well not be set at all.

Encryption

Encryption is the process of encoding data so that, without the appropriate unlocking code, the encrypted data can't be read. Encryption is used as a means of protecting data from being viewed by unauthorized users. If you have ever used a secure website, you have used encryption.

On private networks, encryption is generally not a very big issue. Modern network operating systems often invisibly implement encryption so that passwords are not transmitted openly throughout the network. On the other hand, normal network transmissions are not usually encrypted, although they can be if the need arises. A far more common use for encryption is for data that is sent across a public network such as the Internet or across wireless networks where outside users might be able to gain access to the data. In both of these cases, there is plenty of opportunity for someone to take the data from the network and then read the contents of the packets. This process is often referred to as *packet sniffing*.

By sniffing packets from the network and reading their contents, unauthorized users can gain access to private information. They can also alter the information in the packet. Therefore, the stronger the encryption method that is used, the better protected the data is.

A number of encryption methods are commonly used, including

➤ IP Security (IPSec)

➤ Secure Sockets Layer (SSL)

➤ Triple Data Encryption Standard (3DES)

➤ Pretty Good Privacy (PGP)

For more information on the characteristics of common encryption protocols, refer to Chapter 6, "WAN Technologies, Internet Access, and Security Protocols."

Implementing Encryption

Irrespective of which encryption method or protocol is used, network administrators must be aware that providing encryption for network traffic is not without its considerations. These include

➤ **Network traffic overhead**—Encrypting data on a network increases the volume of traffic. Even if, as it is with some encryption methods, the size of the data packets that traverse the network do not increase in size, there is often traffic associated with the setup and breakdown of encrypted communication sessions.

➤ **Processor Overhead**—While modern encryption protocols are designed to be as lightweight as possible, there is still always an overhead associated with encrypting or decrypting data. In a small environment with just a few computers, this overhead might be negligible, and server or workstation performance might not be affected. In larger environments, however, or with servers that handle very large amounts of network traffic, the overhead associated with encryption must be considered more carefully.

➤ **Supported Operating Systems**—Not all operating systems support all encryption mechanisms. For example, Microsoft Windows Server 2003 relies on IPSec as the primary means of encryption, and Windows XP Professional Edition also supports IPSec, as does Windows 2000 Professional. Earlier versions of Windows, such as Windows 98 and Windows Me, however, do not support IPSec without additional client software.

Another key consideration when using encryption, particularly from a connectivity perspective, is that some operating systems can be configured to deny requests from clients that are not using encryption. This configuration should be implemented only after it has been confirmed that all the client systems can also use encryption. Otherwise, they will not be able to connect to the server.

Public Key Infrastructure (PKI)—No discussion of encryption would be complete without the inclusion of Public Key Infrastructure, or PKI. PKI provides a mutually accessible certification authority from which encryption protocols such as IPSec and SSL can obtain, exchange, and transmit keys, in the form of certificates. These certificates then provide a common mechanism by which data can be encrypted and decrypted.

Extranets and Intranet

Over recent years, the terms intranet and extranct have established themselves firmly in the IT vocabulary. Even so, many people are still unsure about what exactly defines, or is defined by, either an intranet or an extranet.

Intranets

The term intranet is commonly used to describe a web-based application or system that provides tools for groups of people to work together collaboratively. The key element of an intranet is that only people within an organization can access it. Intranets are typically hosted, maintained, and operated completely independently from an organization's external Web presence, even though some of the information provided through both mechanisms might be the same. An example of an intranet is shown in Figure 8.4

Intranet—Technically speaking, any privately operated network to which external access is restricted could be considered an intranet. In common use terms, though, the description provided in this section is the most common interpretation of the term intranet.

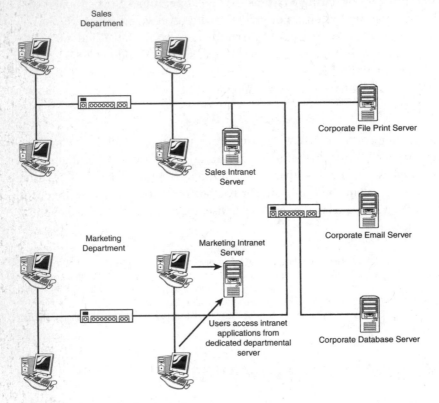

Figure 8.4 An example of an intranet.

 Because they are typically accessed using Web browsers, and hosted by Web server applications, intranets rely on protocols such as the Hypertext Transfer Protocol (HTTP) and File Transfer Protocol (FTP).

Intranets are commonly identified by the following characteristics:

➤ **Limited access**—Access to an intranet is normally limited to users, or a sub-group of users, within the organization.

➤ **Browser based**—Most intranets operate as Web server–based applications, and so are accessed through a Web browser.

➤ **Types of application**—Although no specific rules define what applications an intranet can host, the most common are collaborative, 'groupware' applications.

Extranets

Any network or application that is accessible from outside the physical and logical boundaries of an organization can be called an *extranet*. This means that any network on which remote access services are provided could, technically, be considered an extranet. Commonly, though, the term extranet is used to describe a system or application, hosted within an organization, which is securely made available to selected individuals or entire organizations outside of the hosting organization.

The key consideration to this model is that the company providing the system controls access to the extranet. In other words, only selected clients and associates are provided with access, and they might even be required to access the extranet over secure virtual private networking (VPN) links. Contrast this with the model used by, for example, online bookstores, where anyone can access the site, even though a username and password is subsequently required to place or track orders. Although the bookstore could decide to prevent a certain user from accessing the site, they are unlikely to do so. Figure 8.5 shows an example of an extranet.

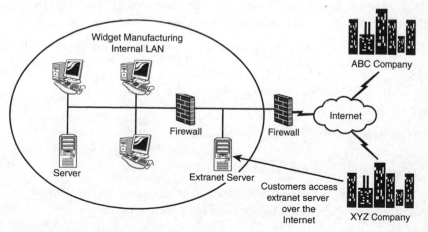

Figure 8.5   An example of an extranet.

Extranets are commonly identified by the following characteristics:

➤ **Users are outside of the hosting organization**—Access to the extranet system is made available to individuals and organizations that are not directly affiliated with the host organization.

➤ **Only the owner of the system grants access**—Access to the extranet is normally granted and controlled by the operating organization.

➤ **Secure**—Extranets are typically secure, and connection to the extranet might require the use of secure communication channels such as a VPN.

Typically, though not exclusively, extranet applications, like intranet applications, are hosted on a Web server and accessed through a Web browser.

Review and Test Yourself

The following sections provide you with the opportunity to review what you learned in this chapter and to test yourself.

The Facts

For the exam, don't forget these important concepts:

➤ Common password policies typically include a minimum length of password, password expiration, prevention of password reuse, and prevention of easy-to-guess passwords.

➤ A password that uses eight case-sensitive characters, with letters, numbers, and special characters, is considered hard to crack, or *strong*.

➤ A firewall is a system or group of systems that controls the flow of traffic between two networks.

➤ A firewall often provides such services as NAT, proxy, and packet filtering.

➤ TCP/IP protocol suite uses port numbers to identify which service a certain packet is destined for. By configuring the firewall to allow certain types of traffic, you can control the flow.

➤ A proxy server acts as an intermediary between a user on the internal network and a service on the external network such as the Internet.

➤ A proxy server enables a network to appear to external networks as a single IP address—that of the external network interface of the proxy server.

➤ A proxy server allows Internet access to be controlled; having a centralized point of access allows for a great deal of control over the use of the Internet.

➤ Port blocking is one of the most widely used security methods on networks. Port blocking is associated with firewalls and proxy servers, although in fact it can be implemented on any system that provides a means to manage network data flow, according to data type.

➤ An intranet is a web-based application that is commonly used to provide groupware and collaboration applications to users within an organization.

➤ An application, normally Web server based, that is made available to external users is classed as an extranet. Because extranets very often use the Internet as an access mechanism, security is of a major concern.

Key Terms

➤ Authentication

➤ Password policy

➤ Firewalls

➤ Packet filtering

➤ Port number

➤ MAC address

➤ Circuit-level firewall

➤ Application gateway firewall

➤ Personal firewalls

➤ Proxy server

➤ NAT

➤ Caching proxy server

➤ Encryption

➤ IPSec

➤ SSL

➤ 3DES

➤ PGP

➤ Intranet

➤ Extranet

Exam Prep Questions

1. After noticing that there have been several attempts to access your network from the Internet, you decide to block port 53. Which of the following services is associated with port 53?

   ❑ A. WINS

   ❑ B. DNS

   ❑ C. SMTP

   ❑ D. POP3

2. Which of the following statements would you associate with an extranet? (Choose the two best answers.)

   ❑ A. It is typically hosted by a Web server application and accessed through a Web browser.

   ❑ B. It is only available to users within an organization.

   ❑ C. It is used to provide application access to users outside of an organization.

   ❑ D. Security is generally not a priority.

3. What is the basic reason for implementing a firewall?

   ❑ A. It reduces the costs associated with Internet access.

   ❑ B. It provides NAT functionality.

   ❑ C. It provides a mechanism to protect one network from another.

   ❑ D. It allows Internet access to be centralized.

4. Which of the following are benefits of using a proxy server? (Choose the three best answers.)

   ❑ A. It allows costs associated with Internet access to be reduced.

   ❑ B. It provides a central point of Internet access.

   ❑ C. It allows Internet access to be controlled.

   ❑ D. It allows hostnames to be resolved to IP addresses.

5. While on vacation, another system administrator decides to use the firewall to filter out all ports between 50 and 100. Which of the following services will now be unavailable to network users?

   ❑ A. HTTP

   ❑ B. HTTPS

   ❑ C. POP3

   ❑ D. DNS

6. You are the network administrator for a large company. You have recently been tasked with supplying Internet access to all network users. Which of the following could you do to accomplish this?

   ❏ A. Implement a firewall
   ❏ B. Implement a proxy server
   ❏ C. Enable port 80 on all workstations
   ❏ D. Disable port 80 on all workstations

7. Which of the following is the strongest password?

   ❏ A. password
   ❏ B. WE300GO
   ❏ C. 100Ka1ivE
   ❏ D. lovethemusic

8. As system administrator, you have been asked to prevent users from using Web-based email during work. Which of the following might you do to accomplish this?

   ❏ A. Set a password policy on the Web-based email
   ❏ B. Block port 123
   ❏ C. Block port 80
   ❏ D. Configure the proxy server to filter out Web-based email requests

9. Your manager has asked you to look at the feasibility of implementing encryption on your network. Which of the following factors will you NOT consider as part of your evaluation?

   ❏ A. Whether to use password or smartcard authentication
   ❏ B. Network traffic overhead
   ❏ C. Processor overhead
   ❏ D. Operating system support

10. You have installed a proxy server on your network and have configured it to allow all the hosts on your internal network to access the Internet through it. None of the users on the internal network can access the Internet, although they could before. What is the most likely cause of the problem?

   ❏ A. The proxy server is not configured correctly.
   ❏ B. The Internet connection is not working.
   ❏ C. The Web browser on the client system needs to be reconfigured to use a proxy server.
   ❏ D. The HTTP proxy service is not enabled on the system.

Answers to Exam Prep Questions

1. The correct answer is B. DNS uses port 53. WINS uses TCP/IP port 42. SMTP uses TCP/IP port 25. POP3 uses TCP/IP port 110.

2. The correct answers are A and C. Extranets are typically Web server–based applications that are accessed through a Web browser. Applications on an extranet are made available to users outside the organization. Because they are accessed by outside users, security is a major concern.

3. The correct answer is C. Implementing a firewall allows you to have protection between networks, typically from the Internet to a private network. All the other answers describe functions offered by a proxy server. Note that some firewall systems do offer NAT functionality, but NAT is not a firewall feature; it is an added benefit of these systems.

4. The correct answers are A, B, and C. A proxy server enables the costs associated with Internet access to be reduced, provides a central point of Internet access, and allows Internet access to be controlled. Answer D describes the function of a DNS server.

5. The correct answers are A and D. HTTP uses port 80, and DNS uses port 53; both of these services would be affected by the filtering. HTTPS uses port 443, and POP3 uses port 110; therefore, these services would be unaffected.

6. The correct answer is B. A proxy server allows a central point through which all network users can access the Internet. A firewall typically does not provide this functionality. Enabling or disabling port 80 on the workstations is not a valid answer.

7. The correct answer is C. Strong passwords include a combination of letters and numbers and upper- and lowercase letters. In this question, answer C is by far the strongest password. Answer A is not a strong password because it is a standard word, contains no numbers, and is all in lowercase. Answer B mixes letters and numbers, and it is not a recognized word, so it is a strong password, although it is not as strong as answer C. Answer D is too easy to guess and contains no numbers.

8. The correct answer is C. Blocking port 80 would prevent users from accessing Web-based email; it would however also block Web access altogether. Setting a password policy would have little effect. TCP/IP port 123 is associated with the Network Time Protocol (NTP). Blocking port 123 would likely have no effect on a user's ability to access Web-based email. A proxy server is not used to filter Web-based

email. Filtering of this nature would be performed by a firewall.

9. The correct answer is A. The authentication mechanism used on a network does not affect the implementation of encryption. Network traffic overhead, processor overhead, and operating system support are all considerations when implementing encryption.

10. The correct answer is C. In order for Web browsers to access the Internet through a Web browser, they must often be configured to do so. The Web browsers on client systems must be configured to use the proxy server.

Need to Know More?

Bird, Drew and Harwood, Mike. *Network+ Exam Prep*. Que Publishing, 2005.

Habraken, Joe. *Absolute Beginner's Guide to Networking, Fourth Edition*. Que Publishing, 2003.

Maiwald, Eric. *Network Security: A Beginner's Guide, Second Edition*. McGraw-Hill Osborne Media, 2003.

9

VLANs, Antivirus, Fault Tolerance, and Disaster Recovery

Objectives

3.8 Identify the main characteristics of VLANs (virtual local area networks)

3.10 Identify the purpose, benefits, and characteristics of using antivirus software

3.11 Identify the purpose and characteristics of fault tolerance:

✓ Power
✓ Link redundancy
✓ Storage
✓ Services

3.12 Identify the purpose and characteristics of disaster recovery:

✓ Backup/restore
✓ Offsite storage
✓ Hot and cold spares
✓ Hot, warm, and cold sites

What you need to know

✓ Understand the importance of data redundancy
✓ Explain how the various RAID levels function
✓ Understand the difference between fault tolerance and disaster recovery
✓ Understand the various backup strategies
✓ Identify tape rotation strategies
✓ Understand the function of VLANs
✓ Review the function of using antivirus software

Introduction

As far as network administration goes, nothing is more important than *fault tolerance* and *disaster recovery*. First and foremost, it is the responsibility of the network administrator to safeguard the data held on the servers and to ensure that when requested, this data is ready to go.

Because both fault tolerance and disaster recovery are such an important part of network administration, they are well represented in the CompTIA Network+ exam. In that light, this chapter is important both in terms of real-world application as well as the exam itself.

Before diving into the fault tolerant and disaster recovery objectives, we will start this chapter by reviewing the function of virtual LANs (VLANS).

Virtual LANs

To understand VLANs, it is first necessary to have a basic understanding of how a traditional LAN operates. A standard local area network (LAN) uses hardware such as hubs, bridges, and switches in the same physical segment to provide a connection point for all end node devices. All network nodes are capable of communicating with each other without the need for a router; however, communications with devices on other LAN segments does require the use of a router.

As a network grows, routers are used to expand the network. The routers provide the capability to connect separate LANs and to isolate users into broadcast and collision domains. Using routers to route data around the network and between segments increases *latency*. Latency refers to delays in transmission caused by the routing process.

Virtual LANs (VLANs) provide an alternate method to segment a network and in the process, significantly increase the performance capability of the network, and remove potential performance bottlenecks. A VLAN is a group of computers that are connected and act as if they are on their own physical network segments, even though they might not be. For instance, suppose that you work in a three-story building in which the advertising employees are spread over all three floors. A VLAN can let all the advertising personnel use the network resources as if they were connected on the same segment. This virtual segment can be isolated from other network segments. In effect, it would appear to the advertising group that they were on a network by themselves.

VLANs allow you to create multiple broadcast domains on a single switch. In essence, this is the same as creating separate networks for each VLAN.

VLANs offer some clear advantages. Being able to create logical segmentation of a network gives administrators flexibility beyond the restrictions of the physical network design and cable infrastructure. VLANs allow for easier administration because the network can be divided into well-organized sections. Further, you can increase security by isolating certain network segments from others. For instance, you can segment the marketing personnel from finance or the administrators from the students. VLANs can ease the burden on overworked routers and reduce broadcast storms. Table 9.1 summarizes the benefits of VLANs.

802.1q is the Institute of Electrical and Electronics Engineers (IEEE) specification developed to ensure interoperability of VLAN technologies from the various vendors.

Table 9.1   Benefits of VLANs

Advantages	Description
Increased security	By creating logical (virtual) boundaries, network segments can be isolated.
Increased performance	By reducing broadcast traffic throughout the network, VLANs free up bandwidth.
Organization	Network users and resources that are linked and communicate frequently can be grouped together in a VLAN.
Simplified administration	With a VLAN, the network administrator's job is easier when moving users between LAN segments, recabling, addressing new stations, and reconfiguring hubs and routers.

VLAN Membership

You can use several methods to determine VLAN membership or how devices are assigned to a specific VLAN. The following sections describe the common methods of determining how VLAN membership is assigned.

Protocol-based VLANs

With *protocol-based VLAN* membership, computers are assigned to VLANs by using the protocol that is in use and the Layer 3 address. For example, this method enables an Internetwork Packet Exchange (IPX) network or a particular Internet Protocol (IP) subnet to have its own VLAN.

It is important to note that although VLAN membership might be based on Layer 3 information, this has nothing to do with routing or routing functions. The IP numbers are used only to determine the membership in a particular VLAN—not to determine routing.

Port-based VLANs

Port-based VLANs require that specific ports on a network switch be assigned to a VLAN. For example, ports 1 through 8 might be assigned to marketing, ports 9 through 18 might be assigned to sales, and so on. Using this method, a switch determines VLAN membership by taking note of the port used by a particular packet. Figure 9.1 shows an example of a port-based VLAN.

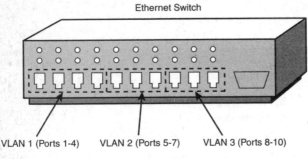

Figure 9.1 Port-based VLAN configuration.

MAC Address–based VLANs

As you might have guessed, the *Media Access Control (MAC)* address type of VLAN assigns membership according to the MAC address of the workstation. To do this, the switch must keep track of the MAC addresses that belong to each VLAN. The advantage of this method is that a workstation computer can be moved anywhere in an office without needing to be reconfigured; because the MAC address does not change, the workstation remains a member of a particular VLAN. Table 9.2 provides examples of MAC address–based VLANs.

Table 9.2 MAC Address–based VLANs		
MAC Address	**VLAN**	**Description**
44-45-53-54-00-00	1	Sales
44-45-53-54-13-12	2	Marketing
44-45-53-54-D3-01	3	Administration
44-45-53-54-F5-17	1	Sales

Although the acceptance and implementation of VLANs has been slow, the ability to logically segment a LAN provides a new level of administrative flexibility, organization, and security.

Viruses, Virus Solutions, and Malicious Software

Viruses, spyware, worms, and other malicious code are an unfortunate part of modern computing. In today's world, an unprotected computer is at high risk of having some form of malicious software installed on the system: A protected system is still at risk; the risk is just lower.

By definition, a *virus* is a program that is self-replicating and operates on a computer system without the user's knowledge. These viruses will either attach to or replace system files, system executables, and data files. Once in, the virus can perform many different functions. It might completely consume system resources making the system basically too slow to use, it might completely corrupt and down a computer, or it might compromise data integrity and availability.

In order to be considered a virus, the malicious code must meet two criteria: It must be self-replicating, and it must be capable of executing itself. Three common virus types are listed below:

➤ **Boot sector virus**—Boot sector viruses target the boot record of hard disks or floppy disks. In order to boot, floppy disks or hard drives contain an initial set of instructions that start the boot process. Boot sector viruses infect this program and activate when the system boots. This enables the virus to stay hidden in memory and operate in the background.

➤ **File viruses**—Very common are the file viruses. File viruses attack applications and program files. This type of virus often targets the .exe, .com, and .bat by either destroying them, preventing applications to run, or by modifying them and using them to propagate the virus.

Viruses are not necessarily a file virus or a boot sector virus; they can be both. One virus can be designed to both attack the boot sector and the applications.

➤ **Macro viruses**—The actual data—such as documents, spreadsheets, and so on—represents the most important and irreplaceable elements on a computer system. Macro viruses are designed to attack documents and files and therefore are particularly nasty.

Trojans, Worms, Spyware, and Hoaxes

There are other forms of malicious programs, which by definition are not a virus but still threaten our computer systems.

Trojan horse is a program that appears harmless or even helpful, but after being executed performs an undesirable and malicious action. For instance, a Trojan horse can be a program advertised to be a patch, harmless application such as a calculator or a product upgrade or enhancement. The trick is to fool the user to download and install the program. Once executed, the Trojan horse can perform the function it was actually designed to do. This might include crashing a system, stealing data, and corrupting data.

Trojan horses are not viruses, as they do not replicate; they are installed by the user mistakenly. Trojan horses are often delivered through email or by downloading applications from the Internet.

Worms are similar to viruses in that they replicate, but they do not require a host file to spread from system to system. The difference between viruses and worms is that a worm does not attach itself to an executable program as do viruses: A worm is self-contained and does not need to be part of another program to propagate itself. This makes a worm capable of replicating at incredible speeds. This can cause significant network slowdowns as the worm spreads.

A worm can do any number of malicious actions, including deleting files and sending documents via email without the user knowing. A worm can also carry another program designed to open a backdoor in the system used by spam senders to send junk mail and notices to a computer. Once this backdoor access is open to the computer, your system, it is vulnerable and open to data theft, modification, or worse.

Spyware is a new threat that can be very hidden and easy to get. Spyware is designed to monitor activity on a computer, such as Web surfing activity, and send that information to a remote source. It is commonly installed along with a free program that might have been downloaded.

Spyware detection software is becoming increasingly popular and given the information that can be stolen, should be considered an important part of a secure system.

One final consideration is that of virus hoaxes. The threat of virus activity is very real, and, as such, we are alerted to it. Some take advantage of this to create elaborate virus hoaxes. Hoaxes will often pop up on the computer screen or arrive in the email warning of a virus or claiming that your system has contracted a virus. These are more annoying than dangerous but serve to confuse and complicate the virus issue.

 Malicious code varies by the type of virus and also how they operate. For instance, polymorphic viruses change themselves each time they infect a system. This makes them very difficult to scan for as they are always changing their look. Stealth viruses become part of a program and make it appear as if the program is operating normally when in fact there is a virus at work. This too makes them difficult to scan for.

Protecting Computers from Viruses

The threat from malicious code is a very real concern. We need to take the steps to protect our systems, and although it might not be possible to eliminate the threat, it is possible to significantly reduce the threat.

One of the primary tools used in the fight against malicious software is antivirus software. Antivirus software is available from a number of companies, and each offers similar features and capabilities. The following is a list of the common features and characteristics of antivirus software.

➤ **Real-time protection**—An installed antivirus program should continuously monitor the system looking for viruses. If a program is downloaded, an application opened, or a suspicious email received, the real-time virus monitor will detect and remove the threat. The virus application will sit in the background and will be largely unnoticed by the user.

➤ **Virus scanning**—An antivirus program must be capable of scanning selected drives and disk either locally or remotely. Scans can either be run manually, or they can be scheduled to run at a particular time.

➤ **Scheduling**—It is a best practice to schedule virus scanning to occur automatically at a predetermined time. In a network environment, this would typically occur off hours when the overhead of the scanning process won't impact users.

➤ **Live updates**—New viruses and malicious software are released with alarming frequency. It is recommended that the antivirus software be configured to receive virus updates regularly.

➤ **Email vetting**—Emails represent one of the primary sources for virus delivery. It is essential to use antivirus software that provides email scanning for both inbound and outbound email.

➤ **Centralized management**—If used in a network environment, it is a good idea to use software that supports centralized management of the virus program from the server. Virus updates and configurations only need to be made on the server and not on each individual client station.

Software is only part of the solution in a proactive virus solution. A complete virus protection strategy requires many aspects to help limit the risk of viruses and includes the following:

➤ **Develop in-house policies and rules**—In a corporate environment or even a small office, it is important to establish what information can be placed onto a system. For example, should users be able to download programs from the Internet? Can users bring in their own floppy disks or other storage media?

➤ **Monitoring virus threats**—With new viruses coming out all the time, it is important to check to see if new viruses have been released and what they are designed to do.

➤ **Educate users**—One of the keys to a complete antivirus solution is to train users in virus prevention and recognition techniques. If users know what they are looking for, it can prevent a virus from entering the system or the network.

➤ **Back up copies of important documents**—It should be mentioned that no solution is absolute and care should be taken to ensure that the data is backed up. In the event of a malicious attack, redundant information is available in a secure location.

➤ **Automate virus scanning and updates**—Today's antivirus software can be configured to scan and update itself automatically. Because such tasks can be forgotten and overlooked, it is recommended to have these processes scheduled to run at predetermined times.

➤ **Email vetting**—Email is one of the commonly used virus delivery mechanisms. Antivirus software can be used to check inbound and outbound emails for virus activity.

Fault Tolerance

As far as computers are concerned, *fault tolerance* refers to the capability of the computer system or network to provide continued data availability in the event of hardware failure. Every component within a server, from CPU fan to power supply, has a chance of failure. Some components such as processors rarely fail, whereas hard disk failures are well documented.

Almost every component has fault-tolerant measures. These measures typically require redundant hardware components that can easily or automatically take over when there is a hardware failure.

Of all the components inside computer systems, the one that requires the most redundancy are the hard disks. Not only are hard disk failures more common than any other component but they also maintain the data, without which there would be little need for a network.

Hard Disks Are Half the Problem

In fact, according to recent research, hard disks are responsible for one of every two server hardware failures. This is an interesting statistic to think about.

Disk-level Fault Tolerance

Making the decision to have *hard disk fault tolerance* on the server is the first step; the second is deciding which fault-tolerant strategy to use. Hard disk fault tolerance is implemented according to different *RAID* (redundant array of inexpensive disks) levels. Each RAID level offers differing amounts of data protection and performance. The RAID level appropriate for a given situation depends on the importance placed on the data, the difficulty of replacing that data, and the associated costs of a respective RAID implementation. Oftentimes, the cost of data loss and replacement outweigh the costs associated with implementing a strong RAID fault-tolerant solution.

RAID 0: Stripe Set Without Parity

Although it's given RAID status, *RAID 0* does not actually provide any fault tolerance; in fact, using RAID 0 might even be less fault tolerant than storing all of your data on a single hard disk.

RAID 0 combines unused disk space on two or more hard drives into a single logical volume with data being written to equally sized stripes across all the disks. By using multiple disks, reads and writes are performed simultaneously across all drives. This means that disk access is faster, making the performance of RAID 0 better than other RAID solutions and significantly better than a single hard disk. The downside of RAID 0 is that if any disk in the array fails, the data is lost and must be restored from backup.

Because of its lack of fault tolerance, RAID 0 is rarely implemented. Figure 9.2 shows an example of RAID 0 striping across three hard disks.

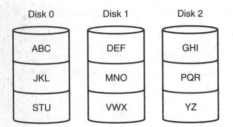

Figure 9.2 RAID 0 striping without parity.

RAID 1

One of the more common RAID implementations is *RAID 1*. RAID 1 requires two hard disks and uses *disk mirroring* to provide fault tolerance. When information is written to the hard disk, it is automatically and simultaneously written to the second hard disk. Both of the hard disks in the mirrored configuration use the same hard disk controller; the partitions used on the hard disk need to be approximately the same size to establish the mirror. In the mirrored configuration, if the primary disk were to fail, the second mirrored disk would contain all the required information and there would be little disruption to data availability. RAID 1 ensures that the server will continue operating in the case of the primary disk failure.

There are some key advantages to a RAID 1 solution. First, it is cheap, as only two hard disks are required to provide fault tolerance. Second, no additional software is required for establishing RAID 1, as modern network operating systems have built-in support for it. RAID levels using striping are often incapable of including a boot or system partition in fault-tolerant solutions. Finally, RAID 1 offers load balancing over multiple disks, which increases read performance over that of a single disk. Write performance however is not improved.

Because of its advantages, RAID 1 is well suited as an entry-level RAID solution, but it has a few significant shortcomings that exclude its use in many environments. It has limited storage capacity—two 100GB hard drives only provide 100GB of storage space. Organizations with large data storage needs can exceed a mirrored solutions capacity in very short order. RAID 1 also has a single point of failure, the hard disk controller. If it were to fail, the data would be inaccessible on either drive. Figure 9.3 shows an example of RAID 1 disk mirroring.

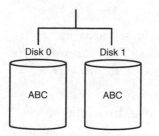

Figure 9.3   RAID 1 disk mirroring.

An extension of RAID 1 is *disk duplexing*. Disk duplexing is the same as mirroring with the exception of one key detail: It places the hard disks on separate hard disk controllers, eliminating the single point of failure.

 Be aware of the differences between disk duplexing and mirroring for the exam.

RAID 5

RAID 5, also known as *disk striping with parity*, uses *distributed parity* to write information across all disks in the array. Unlike the striping used in RAID 0, RAID 5 includes parity information in the striping, which provides fault tolerance. This parity information is used to re-create the data in the event of a failure. RAID 5 requires a minimum of three disks with the equivalent of a single disk being used for the parity information. This means that if you have three 40GB hard disks, you have 80GB of storage space with the other 40GB used for parity. To increase storage space in a RAID 5 array, you need only add another disk to the array. Depending on the sophistication of the RAID setup you are using, the RAID controller will be able to incorporate the new drive into the array automatically, or you will need to rebuild the array and restore the data from backup.

Many factors have made RAID 5 a very popular fault-tolerant design. RAID 5 can continue to function in the event of a single drive failure. If a hard disk were to fail in the array, the parity would re-create the missing data and continue to function with the remaining drives. The read performance of RAID 5 is improved over a single disk.

There are only a few drawbacks for the RAID 5 solution. These are as follows:

▶ The costs of implementing RAID 5 are initially higher than other fault-tolerant measures requiring a minimum of three hard disks. Given the costs of hard disks today, this is a minor concern.

▶ RAID 5 suffers from poor write performance because the parity has to be calculated and then written across several disks. The performance lag is minimal and won't have a noticeable difference on the network.

▶ When a new disk is placed in a failed RAID 5 array, there is a regeneration time when the data is being rebuilt on the new drive. This process requires extensive resources from the server.

Figure 9.4 shows an example of RAID 5 striping with parity.

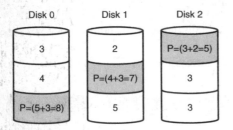

Figure 9.4 RAID 5 striping with parity.

RAID 10

Sometimes RAID levels are combined to take advantage of the best of each. One such strategy is *RAID 10*, which combines RAID levels 1 and 0. In this configuration, four disks are required. As you might expect, the configuration consists of a *mirrored stripe set*. To some extent, RAID 10 takes advantage of the performance capability of a stripe set while offering the fault tolerance of a mirrored solution. As well as having the benefits of each though, RAID 10 also inherits the shortcomings of each strategy. In this case, the high overhead and the decreased write performance are the disadvantages. Figure 9.5 shows an example of a RAID 10 configuration. Table 9.3 provides a summary of the various RAID levels.

RAID levels 2, 3, and 4 are omitted from this discussion as they are infrequently used and will rarely, if at all, be seen in modern network environments.

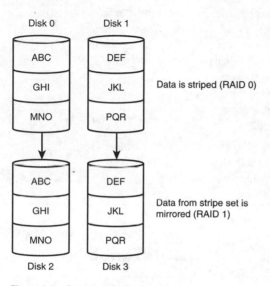

Figure 9.5 Disks in a RAID 10 configuration.

Table 9.3	Summary of RAID Levels			
RAID Level	**Description**	**Advantages**	**Disadvantages**	**Required Disks**
RAID 0	Disk striping	Increased read and write performance. RAID 0 can be implemented with only two disks.	Does not offer any fault tolerance.	Two or more
RAID 1	Disk mirroring	Provides fault tolerance. Can also be used with separate disk controllers, reducing the single point of failure (called *disk duplexing*).	RAID 1 has a 50% overhead and suffers from poor write performance.	Two

(continued)

Table 9.3	Summary of RAID Levels *(continued)*			
RAID Level	**Description**	**Advantages**	**Disadvantages**	**Required Disks**
RAID 5	Disk striping with distributed parity	Can recover from a single disk failure; increased read performance over a poor write single disk. Disks can be added to the array to increase storage capacity.	May slow down network during regeneration time, and may suffer from performance	Minimum of three
RAID 10	Striping with mirrored volumes striping;	Increased performance with striping; offers mirrored fault tolerance.	High overhead as with mirroring.	Four

Server and Services Fault Tolerance

In addition to providing fault tolerance for individual hardware components, some organizations go the extra mile to include the entire server in the fault-tolerant design. Such a design keeps servers and the services they provide up and running. When it comes to server fault tolerance, two key strategies are commonly employed: stand-by servers and server clustering.

Stand-by Servers

Stand-by servers are a fault-tolerant measure in which a second server is configured identically to the first one. The second server can be stored remotely or locally and set up in a *failover configuration*. In a failover configuration, the secondary server is connected to the primary and ready to take over the server functions at a heartbeat's notice. If the secondary server detects that the primary has failed, it will automatically cut in. Network users will not notice the transition, as there will be little or no disruption in data availability.

The primary server communicates with the secondary server by issuing special notification notices referred to as *heartbeats*. If the secondary server stops receiving the heartbeat messages, it assume that the primary has died and so assumes the *primary server configuration*.

Server Clustering

Those companies wanting maximum data availability that have the funds to pay for it can choose to use *server clustering*. As the name suggests, server clustering involves grouping servers together for the purposes of fault tolerance and load balancing. In this configuration, other servers in the cluster can compensate for the failure of a single server. The failed server will have no impact on the network, and the end users will have no idea that a server has failed.

The clear advantage of server clusters is that they offer the highest level of fault tolerance and data availability. The disadvantages are equally clear—cost. The cost of buying a single server can be a huge investment for many organizations; having to buy duplicate servers is far too costly.

Link Redundancy

Although a failed network card might not actually stop the server or a system, it might as well. A network server that cannot be used on the network makes for server downtime. Although the chances of a failed network card are relatively low, our attempts to reduce the occurrence of downtime have led to the development of a strategy that provides fault tolerance for network connections.

Through a process called *adapter teaming*, groups of network cards are configured to act as a single unit. The teaming capability is achieved through software, either as a function of the network card driver or through specific application software. The process of adapter teaming is not widely implemented; though the benefits it offers are many, so it's likely to become a more common sight. The result of adapter teaming is increased bandwidth, fault tolerance, and the ability to manage network traffic more effectively. These features are broken down into three sections:

➤ **Adapter fault tolerance**—The basic configuration enables one network card to be configured as the primary device and others as secondary. If the primary adapter fails, one of the other cards can take its place without the need for intervention. When the original card is replaced, it resumes the role of primary controller.

➤ **Adapter load balancing**—Because software controls the network adapters, workloads can be distributed evenly among the cards so that each link is used to a similar degree. This distribution allows for a more responsive server because one card is not overworked while another is under worked.

➤ **Link aggregation**—This provides vastly improved performance by allowing more than one network card's bandwidth to be *aggregated*—combined into a single connection. For example, through link aggregation, four 100MBps network cards can provide a total of 400MBps bandwidth. Link aggregation requires that both the network adapters and the switch being used support it. In 1999, the IEEE ratified the 802.3ad standard for link aggregation, allowing compatible products to be produced.

Using Uninterruptible Power Supplies

No discussion of fault tolerance can be complete without a look at power-related issues and the mechanisms used to combat them. When you're designing a fault-tolerant system, your planning should definitely include UPSs (Uninterruptible Power Supplies). A *UPS* serves many functions and is a major part of server consideration and implementation.

On a basic level, a UPS is a box that holds a battery and a built-in charging circuit. During times of good power, the battery is recharged; when the UPS is needed, it's ready to provide power to the server. Most often, the UPS is required to provide enough power to give the administrator time to shut down the server in an orderly fashion, preventing any potential data loss from a dirty shutdown.

Why Use a UPS?

Organizations of all shapes and sizes need UPSs as part of their fault-tolerance strategies. A UPS is as important as any other fault-tolerance measure. Three key reasons make a UPS necessary:

➤ **Data availability**—The goal of any fault-tolerance measure is data availability. A UPS ensures access to the server in the event of a power failure—or at least as long as it takes to save a file.

➤ **Protection from data loss**—Fluctuations in power or a sudden power down can damage the data on the server system. In addition, many servers take full advantage of caching, and a sudden loss of power could cause the loss of all information held in cache.

➤ **Protection from hardware damage**—Constant power fluctuations or sudden power downs can damage hardware components within a computer. Damaged hardware can lead to reduced data availability while the hardware is being repaired.

Power Threats

In addition to keeping a server functioning long enough to safely shut it down, a UPS also safeguards a server from inconsistent power. This inconsistent power can take many forms. A UPS protects a system from the following power-related threats:

➤ **Blackout**—A total failure of the power supplied to the server.

➤ **Spike**—A spike is a very short (usually less than a second) but very intense increase in voltage. Spikes can do irreparable damage to any kind of equipment, especially computers.

➤ **Surge**—Compared to a spike, a surge is a considerably longer (sometimes many seconds) but usually less intense increase in power. Surges can also damage your computer equipment.

➤ **Sag**—A sag is a short-term voltage drop (the opposite of a spike). This type of voltage drop can cause a server to reboot.

➤ **Brownout**—A brownout is a drop in voltage that usually lasts more than a few minutes.

Many of these power-related threats can occur without your knowledge; if you don't have a UPS, you cannot prepare for them. For the cost, it is worth buying a UPS, if for no other reason than to sleep better at night.

Disaster Recovery

Even the most fault-tolerant networks will fail, which is an unfortunate fact. When those costly and carefully implemented fault-tolerant strategies do fail, you are left with *disaster recovery*.

Disaster recovery can take on many forms. In addition to real disaster, fire, flood, theft, and the like, many other potential business disruptions can fall under the banner of disaster recovery. For example, the failure of the electrical supply to your city block might interrupt the business function. Such an event, although not a disaster per se, might invoke the disaster recovery methods.

The cornerstone of every disaster recovery strategy is the preservation and recoverability of data. When talking about preservation and recoverability, we are talking about backups. When we are talking about backups, we are likely talking about tape backups. Implementing a regular backup schedule can save you a lot of grief when fault tolerance fails or when you need to recover a file that has been accidentally deleted. When it comes time to design a backup schedule, there are three key types of backups that are used—full, differential, and incremental.

Full Backup

The preferred method of backup is the *full backup* method, which copies all files and directories from the hard disk to the backup media. There are a few reasons why doing a full backup is not always possible. First among them is likely the time involved in performing a full backup.

A full backup is the fastest way to restore all of the methods discussed here because only one tape, or set of tapes, is required for a full restore.

Depending on the amount of data to be backed up, full backups can take an extremely long time and can use extensive system resources. Depending on the configuration of the backup hardware, this can slow down the network considerably. In addition, some environments have more data than can fit on a single tape. This makes taking a full backup awkward, as someone may need to be there to manually change the tapes.

The main advantage of full backups is that a single tape or tape set holds all the data you need backed up. In the event of a failure, a single tape might be all that is needed to get all data and system information back. The upshot of all this is that any disruption to the network is greatly reduced.

Unfortunately, its strength can also be its weakness. A single tape holding an organization's data can be a security risk. If the tape were to fall into the wrong hands, all the data can be restored on another computer. Using passwords on tape backups and using a secure offsite and onsite location can minimize the security risk.

Differential Backup

For those companies that just don't quite have enough time to complete a full backup daily, there is the *differential backup*. Differential backups are faster than a full backup, as they back up only the data that has changed since the last full backup. This means that if you do a full backup on a Saturday and a differential backup on the following Wednesday, only the data that has changed since Saturday is backed up. Restoring the differential backup will require the last full backup and the latest differential backup.

Differential backups know what files have changed since the last full backup by using a setting known as the *archive bit*. The archive bit flags files that have changed or been created and identifies them as ones that need to be backed up. Full backups do not concern themselves with the archive bit, as all files are backed up regardless of date. A full backup, however, will clear the archive bit after data has been backed up to avoid future confusion. Differential backups take notice of the archive bit and use it to determine which files have changed. The differential backup does not reset the archive bit information.

If you experience trouble with any type of backup, you should clean the tape drive and then try the backup again. Also visually inspect the tape for physical damage.

Incremental Backup

Some companies have a very finite amount of time they can allocate to backup procedures. Such organizations are likely to use *incremental backups* in their backup strategy. Incremental backups save only the files that have changed since the last full or incremental backup. Like differential backups, incremental backups use the archive bit to determine the files that have changed since the last full or incremental backup. Unlike differentials, however, incremental backups clear the archive bit, so files that have not changed are not backed up.

Full and incremental backups clear the archive bit after files have been backed up.

The faster backup times of incremental backups comes at a price—the amount of time required to restore. Recovering from a failure with incremental backups requires numerous tapes—all the incremental tapes and the most recent full backup. For example, if you had a full backup from Sunday and an incremental for Monday, Tuesday, and Wednesday, you would need four tapes to restore the data. Keep in mind: Each tape in the rotation is an additional step in the restore process and an additional failure point. One damaged incremental tape and you will be unable to restore the data. Table 9.4 summarizes the various backup strategies.

Table 9.4 Backup Strategies

Backup Type	Advantages	Disadvantages	Data Backed Up	Archive Bit
Full	Backs up all data on a single tape or tape set. Restoring data requires the least amount of tapes.	Depending on the amount of data, full backups can take a long time.	All files and directories are backed up.	Does not use the archive bit, but resets it after data has been backed up.
Differential	Faster backups than a full.	Uses more tapes than a full backup. Restore process takes longer than a full backup.	All files and directories that have changed since the last full or differential backup.	Uses the archive bit to determine the files that have changed, but does not reset the archive bit.
Incremental	Faster backup times.	Requires multiple disks; restoring data takes more time than the other backup methods.	The files and directories that have changed since the last full or incremental backup.	Uses the archive bit to determine the files that have changed, and resets the archive bit.

Tape Rotations

After you have decided on the backup type you will use, you are ready to choose a *backup rotation*. Several backup rotation strategies are in use—some good, some bad, and some really bad. The most common, and perhaps the best, rotation strategy is the Grandfather, Father, Son rotation (GFS).

The *GFS* backup rotation is the most widely used and for good reason. An example GFS rotation may require 12 tapes: four tapes for daily backups (son), five tapes for weekly backups (father), and three tapes for monthly backups (grandfather).

Using this rotation schedule, it is possible to recover data from days, weeks, or months previous. Some network administrators choose to add tapes to the monthly rotation to be able to retrieve data even further back, sometimes up to a year. In most organizations, however, data that is a week old is out of date, let alone six months or a year.

Backup Best Practices

Many details go into making a backup strategy a success. The following list contains issues to consider as part of your backup plan.

➤ **Offsite storage**—Consider having backup tapes stored offsite so that in the event of a disaster in a building, a current set of tapes is still available offsite. The offsite tapes should be as current as any onsite and should be secure.

➤ **Label tapes**—The goal is to restore the data as quickly as possible, and trying to find the tape you need can be difficult if not marked. Further, it can prevent you from recording over a tape you need.

➤ **New tapes**—Like old cassette tapes, the tape cartridges used for the backups wear out over time. One strategy used to prevent this from becoming a problem is to introduce new tapes periodically into the rotation schedule.

➤ **Verify backups**—Never assume that the backup was successful. Seasoned administrators know that checking backup logs and performing periodic test restores are parts of the backup process.

➤ **Cleaning**—From time to time, it is necessary to clean the tape drive. If the inside gets dirty, backups can fail.

 A backup strategy must include offsite storage to account for theft, fire, flood, or other disasters.

Hot and Cold Spares

The impact that a failed component has on a system or network depends largely on the pre-disaster preparation and on the recovery strategies used. Hot and cold spares represent a strategy for recovering from failed components.

Hot Spare and Hot Swapping

Hot spares gives system administrators the ability to quickly recover from component failure—another mechanism to deal with component failure. In a common use, a hot spare enables a RAID system to automatically failover to a spare hard drive should one of the other drives in the RAID array fail. A hot spare does not require any manual intervention—rather, a redundant drive resides in the system at all times, just waiting to take over if another drive fails. The hot spare drive will take over automatically, leaving the failed drive to be removed at a later time. Even though hot-spare technology adds an extra level of protection to your system, after a drive has failed and the hot spare has been used, the situation should be remedied as soon as possible.

Hot swapping is the ability to replace a failed component while the system is running. Perhaps the most commonly identified hot-swap component is the hard drive. In certain RAID configurations, when a hard drive crashes, hot swapping allows you simply to take the failed drive out of the server and install a new one.

The benefits of hot swapping are very clear in that it allows a failed component to be recognized and replaced without compromising system availability. Depending on the system's configuration, the new hardware will normally be recognized automatically by both the current hardware and the operating system. Nowadays, most internal and external RAID subsystems support the hot-swapping feature. Some hot-swappable components include power supplies and hard disks.

Cold Spare and Cold Swapping

The term *cold spare* refers to a component, such as a hard disk, that resides within a computer system but requires manual intervention in case of component failure. A hot spare will engage automatically, but a cold spare might require configuration settings or some other action to engage it. A cold spare configuration will typically require a reboot of the system.

The term cold spare has also been used to refer to a redundant component that is stored outside the actual system but is kept in case of component failure. To replace the failed component with a cold spare, the system would need to be powered down.

Cold swapping refers to replacing components only after the system is completely powered off. This strategy is by far the least attractive for servers because the services provided by the server will be unavailable for the duration of the cold-swap procedure. Modern systems have come a long way to ensure that cold swapping is a rare occurrence. For some situations and for some components, however, cold swapping is the only method to replace a failed component. The only real defense against having to shut down the server is to have redundant components residing in the system.

The term "warm swap" is applied to a device that can be replaced while the system is still running but that requires some kind of manual intervention to disable the device before it can be removed. Using a PCI hot plug is technically a warm-swap strategy because it requires that the individual PCI slot be powered down before the PCI card is replaced. Of course, a warm swap is not as efficient as a hot swap, but it is far and away better than a cold swap.

Hot, Warm, and Cold Sites

A disaster recovery plan might include the provision for a recovery site that can be brought quickly into play. These sites fall into three categories: hot, warm, and cold. The need for each of these types of sites depends largely on the business you are in and the funds available. Disaster recovery sites represent the ultimate in precautions for organizations that really need it. As a result, they don't come cheap.

The basic concept of a disaster recovery site is that it can provide a base from which the company can be operated during a disaster. The disaster recovery site is not normally intended to provide a desk for every employee, but is intended more as a means to allow key personnel to continue the core business function.

In general, a cold recovery site is a site that can be up and operational in a relatively short time span, such as a day or two. Provision of services, such as telephone lines and power, is taken care of, and the basic office furniture might be in place, but there is unlikely to be any computer equipment, even though the building might well have a network infrastructure and a room ready to act as a server room. In most cases, cold sites provide the physical location and basic services.

Cold sites are useful if there is some forewarning of a potential problem. Generally speaking, cold sites are used by organizations that can weather the storm for a day or two before they get back up and running. If you are the regional office of a major company, it might be possible to have one of the other divisions take care of business until you are ready to go; but if you are the one and only office in the company, you might need something a little hotter.

For organizations with the dollars and the desire, hot recovery sites represent the ultimate in fault-tolerance strategies. Like cold recovery sites, hot sites are designed to provide only enough facilities to continue the core business function, but hot recovery sites are set up to be ready to go at a moment's notice.

A hot recovery site will include phone systems with the phone lines already connected. Data networks will also be in place, with any necessary routers and switches plugged in and turned on. Desks will have desktop PCs installed and waiting, and server areas will be replete with the necessary hardware to support business-critical functions. In other words, within a few hours, the hot site can become a fully functioning element of an organization.

The issue that confronts potential hot-recovery site users is simply that of cost. Office space is expensive at the best of times, but having space sitting idle 99.9 percent of the time can seem like a tremendously poor use of money. A very popular strategy to get around this problem is to use space provided in a disaster recovery facility, which is basically a building, maintained by a third-party company, in which various businesses rent space. Space is apportioned, usually, on how much each company pays.

Sitting in between the hot and cold recovery sites is the warm site. A warm site will typically have computers but not configured ready to go. This means that data might need to be upgraded or other manual interventions might need to be performed before the network is again operational. The time it takes to get a warm site operational lands right in the middle of the other two options, as does the cost.

 A hot site that mirrors the organization's production network will be capable of assuming network operations in a moment's notice. Warm sites have the equipment needed to bring the network to an operational state but require configuration and potential database updates. A cold site has the space available with basic service but typically requires equipment delivery.

Review and Test Yourself

The following sections provide you with the opportunity to review what you learned in this chapter and to test yourself.

The Facts

For the exam, don't forget these important concepts:

➤ RAID 0 uses disk striping over two or more disks but offers no fault tolerance.

➤ RAID 1 uses two disks in a mirrored configuration.

➤ Disk duplexing is a RAID 1 implementation using separate hard disk controllers.

➤ RAID 5 is disk striping with parity, requiring three disks at a minimum.

➤ With a full backup, all data is backed up and data can be restored from a single tape set. Full backups do not use the archive bit but clear it after files have been copied to tape.

➤ With incremental backups, all data changed since the last full or incremental is backed up. The restore procedure requires several tapes: the latest full backup and all incremental tapes since the last full backup. Incremental uses the archive bit and clears it after a file is saved to disk.

➤ With a differential backup, all data changed since the last full backup is backed up. The restore procedure requires the latest full backup tape and the latest differential backup tape. Differential uses the archive bit to determine which files need to be backed up, but does not clear it.

➤ You should use an offsite tape rotation scheme to store current copies of backups in a secure offsite location. A commonly used rotation is the Grandfather, Father, Son (GFS) rotation.

➤ You should periodically introduce new tapes into the tape rotation and destroy the old tapes.

➤ Two key strategies are commonly employed for server fault tolerance: stand-by servers and server clustering.

➤ VLANs are used to segment networks.

➤ Antivirus software is an essential component in an overall virus prevention strategy.

➤ Hot, warm, and cold spares are designed to replace failed system components.

➤ Hot, warm, and cold sites are designed to provide alternate locations for network operations in the event of a disaster.

Key Terms

➤ RAID

➤ Disk mirroring

➤ Disk duplexing

➤ Disk striping

➤ Full backup

➤ Incremental backup

➤ Differential backup

➤ VLANs

➤ Antivirus

➤ Hot site

➤ Cold site

➤ Warm site

➤ Hot Spare

➤ Cold spare

Exam Prep Questions

1. During your lunch break, you rummage around the company's storage closet and discover two 20GB IDE hard disks and two hard disk controllers. You decide to use the equipment to provide a fault-tolerant solution in one of your company's existing servers. Which of the following fault-tolerant RAID levels could you implement using this equipment. (Choose two answers.)

   ❑ A. RAID 0
   ❑ B. RAID 1
   ❑ C. Disk duplexing
   ❑ D. RAID 5

2. Which two types of tape backup methods clear the archive bit after the backup has been completed?

   ❑ A. Full
   ❑ B. Differential
   ❑ C. Incremental
   ❑ D. GFS

3. You come in to work on Thursday morning to find that the server has failed and you need to restore the data from backup. You had finished a full backup on Sunday and incremental backups on Monday, Tuesday, and Wednesday. How many tapes are required to restore the backup?

   ❑ A. 4
   ❑ B. 2
   ❑ C. 3
   ❑ D. 5

4. In the server room you find a box with five 15GB hard disks. If you were to implement a RAID 5 solution using all five disks, how much storage space would you have for the actual data?

   ❑ A. 75GB
   ❑ B. 60GB
   ❑ C. 30GB
   ❑ D. 45GB

5. Which of the following RAID levels offers the greatest read and write performance?

   ❑ A. RAID 0
   ❑ B. RAID 1
   ❑ C. Disk duplexing
   ❑ D. RAID 5
   ❑ E. RAID 10

6. Which of the following recovery sites might require the delivery of computer equipment and an update of all network data?

   ❑ A. Cold site

   ❑ B. Warm site

   ❑ C. Hot site

   ❑ D. None of the above

7. As part of your network administrative responsibilities, you have completed your monthly backups. As part of backup best practices, where should the tapes be stored?

   ❑ A. In a secure location in the server room

   ❑ B. In a secure onsite location in the building

   ❑ C. In an offsite location

   ❑ D. In a secure offsite location

8. As network administrator, you have been tasked with designing a disaster recovery plan for your network. Which of the following might you include in a disaster recovery plan?

   ❑ A. RAID 5

   ❑ B. Offsite tape backup

   ❑ C. Mirrored hard disks

   ❑ D. UPS

9. Which of the following power-related problems is associated with a short-term voltage drop?

   ❑ A. Surge

   ❑ B. Brownout

   ❑ C. Sag

   ❑ D. Spike

10. As a network administrator, you have been asked to implement a RAID solution that offers high performance. Fault tolerance is not a concern. Which RAID level are you likely to use?

   ❑ A. RAID 0

   ❑ B. RAID 1

   ❑ C. RAID 2

   ❑ D. RAID 5

   ❑ E. RAID 10

Answers to Exam Prep Questions

1. The correct answers are B and C. Using the equipment that you found, it would be possible to implement RAID 1, as there are two hard disks for the mirror configuration. You could also implement disk duplexing, as there was an additional hard disk controller. Answer A is incorrect as RAID 0 is not a fault-tolerant RAID level. Answer D is incorrect because RAID 5 requires a minimum of three disks.

2. The correct answers are A and C. The archive bit is reset after a full backup and an incremental backup. Answer B is incorrect as the differential backup does not reset the archive bit and answer D is wrong because GFS is a rotation strategy, not a backup method.

3. The correct answer is A. Incremental backups save all files and directories that have changed since the last full or incremental backup. To restore, you need the latest full backup and all incremental tapes. In this case, you need four tapes to complete the restore process.

4. The correct answer is B. RAID 5 uses distributed parity. The parity information is spread across all disks and requires the equivalent space of a single hard disk. In this example, there are five 15GB disks, giving a total of 75GB of storage. 15GB is required for the parity information, leaving 60GB for saving actual data.

5. The correct answer is A. Although not a fault-tolerant RAID level, RAID 0 offers the best performance of any RAID level. Other RAID levels do offer some performance improvements over a single disk; their fault-tolerant considerations inhibit the write operations.

6. The correct answer is A. A cold site provides an alternate location but typically not much more. A cold site will often require the delivery of computer equipment and other services.

7. The correct answer is D. Although not always done, it is a best practice to store tape backups in a secure offsite location in case of fire or theft. Answer A is incorrect because if the server room is damaged by fire or flood, the tapes and the data on the server can be compromised by the same disaster. Similarly, answer B is incorrect because storing the backups onsite does not eliminate the threat of a single disaster destroying the data on the server and tapes. Answer C is incorrect for security reasons. The offsite tapes must be secured.

8. The correct answer is B. Offsite tape storage is part of a disaster recovery plan. The other answers listed are considered fault tolerance measures as they are implemented to ensure data availability.

9. The correct answer is C. A sag is a short-term voltage drop. A brownout is also a voltage drop, but it lasts longer than a sag. A surge is an increase in power that lasts a few seconds. A spike is a power increase that lasts a few milliseconds.

10. The correct answer is A. RAID 0 offers the highest level of performance but does not offer any fault tolerance. If the performance of RAID 0 is required and so is fault tolerance, RAID 10 is a better choice. RAID 1 offers fault tolerance but no increase in performance.

Need to Know More?

 Bird, Drew and Harwood, Mike. *Network+ Prep*. Que Publishing, 2004.

 Habraken, Joe. *Absolute Beginner's Guide to Networking, Fourth Edition*. Que Publishing, 2003.

Troubleshooting Connectivity

Objectives

4.1 Given a troubleshooting scenario, select the appropriate network utility from the following:

- ✓ tracert/traceroute
- ✓ ping
- ✓ arp
- ✓ netstat
- ✓ nbtstat
- ✓ ipconfig/ifconfig
- ✓ winipcfg
- ✓ nslookup/dig

4.2 Given output from a network diagnostic utility (for example, those utilities listed in objective 4.1), identify the utility and interpret the output

4.3 Given a network scenario, interpret visual indicators (for example, link LEDs [Light Emitting Diode] and collision LEDs [Light Emitting Diode]) to determine the nature of a stated problem

4.4 Given a troubleshooting scenario involving a client accessing remote network services, identify the cause of the problem (for example, file services, print services, authentication failure, protocol configuration, physical connectivity, and SOHO [Small Office/Home Office] router)

4.5 Given a troubleshooting scenario between a client and the following server environments, identify the cause of a stated problem:

- ✓ UNIX/Linux/Mac OS X Server
- ✓ Netware
- ✓ Windows
- ✓ Appleshare IP (Internet Protocol)

What you need to know

- ✓ Use various TCP/IP troubleshooting tools including **ping**, **tracert**, **traceroute**, **arp**, **netstat**, **nbtstat**, **ipconfig**, **ifconfig**, **winipcfg**, **nslookup**, and **dig**. Interpret the output from these tools.
- ✓ Interpret visual indicators such as LEDs on network devices to help troubleshoot connectivity problems.
- ✓ Understand the most common causes of remote connectivity issues, including troubleshooting of Internet access mechanisms such as Cable, DSL, and Dial-Up.
- ✓ Identify the cause and remedy for common network client connectivity issues such as authentication failure, permissions issues, and incorrect protocol configurations.

Introduction

For anyone working with TCP/IP networks, troubleshooting connectivity is something that is simply going to have to be done. This chapter identifies the tools that are used in the troubleshooting process and identifies scenarios in which these tools can be used.

In addition, the chapter covers troubleshooting in remote connectivity scenarios and troubleshooting client connectivity on networks.

Troubleshooting with Diagnostic Utilities

Many utilities can be used when troubleshooting TCP/IP. Although the actual utilities available vary from platform to platform, the functionality between platforms is quite similar. Table 10.1 lists the TCP/IP troubleshooting tools covered in the Network+ exam along with their purpose.

Table 10.1 Common TCP/IP Troubleshooting Tools and Their Purpose	
Tool	**Purpose**
tracert/ traceroute	Used to track the path a packet takes as it travels across a network. **tracert** is used on Windows systems, **traceroute** is used on UNIX, Linux, and Macintosh systems.
ping	Used to test connectivity between two devices on a network.
arp	Used to view and work with the IP address to MAC address resolution cache.
netstat	Used to view the current TCP/IP connections on a system.
nbtstat	Used to view statistics related to NetBIOS name resolutions, and to see information about current NetBIOS over TCP/IP connections.
ipconfig	Used to view and renew TCP/IP configuration on a Windows system.
ifconfig	Used to view TCP/IP configuration on a UNIX, Linux or Macintosh system.
winipcfg	Graphical tool used to view TCP/IP configuration on Windows 95, 98, and Me.
nslookup/dig	Used to perform manual DNS lookups. **nslookup** can be used on Windows, UNIX, Macintosh, and Linux systems. **dig** can only be used on UNIX, Linux, and Macintosh systems.

The following sections look in more detail at these utilities and the output they produce.

Many of the utilities discussed in this chapter have a help facility that can be accessed by typing the command followed by a /?or a -?. On a Windows system, for example, you can get help on the **netstat** utility by typing the command **netstat /?** Sometimes, using a utility with an invalid switch will also bring up the help screen.

For the exam, be prepared to identify what tool to use in a given scenario. Remember, there might be more than one tool that could be used—you will be expected to pick the best one for the situation described.

On the Network+ exam, you will be asked to identify the output from a command, and you should be able to interpret the information provided by the command.

The Trace Route Utility (tracert/traceroute)

The trace route utility does exactly what its name implies—it traces the route between two hosts. It does this by using Internet Control Message Protocol (ICMP) echo packets to report information back at every step in the journey. Each of the common network operating systems provides a trace route utility, but the name of the command and the output vary slightly on each. However, for the purposes of the NetWork+ exam, you should not concern yourself with the minor differences in the output format. Table 10.2 shows the trace route command syntax used in various operating systems

The phrase trace route utility is used in this section to refer generically to the various route tracing applications available on common operating systems. In a live environment, you should make yourself familiar with the version of the tool used on the operating systems you are working with.

Table 10.2 Trace Route Utility Commands	
Operating System	**Trace Route Command Syntax**
Windows Server 2000/2003	**tracert** *<IP address>*
Novell NetWare	**iptrace**
Linux/UNIX	**traceroute** *<IP address>*
Macintosh	**traceroute** *<IP address>*

Trace route provides a lot of useful information, including the IP address of every router connection it passes through and, in many cases, the name of the router (although this depends on the router's configuration). Trace route also reports the length, in milliseconds, of the round-trip the packet made from the source location to the router and back. This information can help identify where network bottlenecks or breakdowns might be. The following is an example of a successful `tracert` command on a Windows 2000 system:

```
C:\>tracert 24.7.70.37
Tracing route to c1-p4.sttlwa1.home.net [24.7.70.37]
 over a maximum of 30 hops:
  1    30 ms    20 ms    20 ms  24.67.184.1
  2    20 ms    20 ms    30 ms  rd1ht-ge3-0.ok.shawcable.net [24.67.224.7]
  3    50 ms    30 ms    30 ms  rc1wh-atm0-2-1.vc.shawcable.net
      [204.209.214.193]
  4    50 ms    30 ms    30 ms  rc2wh-pos15-0.vc.shawcable.net
      [204.209.214.90]
  5    30 ms    40 ms    30 ms  rc2wt-pos2-0.wa.shawcable.net [66.163.76.37]
  6    30 ms    40 ms    30 ms  c1-pos6-3.sttlwa1.home.net [24.7.70.37]
Trace complete.
```

Similar to the other common operating systems covered by the Network+ exam, the `tracert` display on a Windows-based system includes several columns of information. The first column represents the hop number. You may recall that 'hop' is the term used to describe a step in the path a packet takes as it crosses the network. The next three columns indicate the round-trip time, in milliseconds, that a packet takes in its attempts to reach the destination. The last column is the hostname and the IP address of the responding device.

Of course, not all trace route attempts are successful. The following is the output from a `tracert` command on a Windows Server 2003 system that doesn't manage to get to the remote host:

```
C:\>tracert comptia.org

Tracing route to comptia.org [216.119.103.72]
over a maximum of 30 hops:
  1    27 ms    28 ms    14 ms  24.67.179.1
  2    55 ms    13 ms    14 ms  rd1ht-ge3-0.ok.shawcable.net [24.67.224.7]
  3    27 ms    27 ms    28 ms  rc1wh-atm0-2-1.shawcable.net
      [204.209.214.19]
  4    28 ms    41 ms    27 ms  rc1wt-pos2-0.wa.shawcable.net
      [66.163.76.65]
  5    28 ms    41 ms    27 ms  rc2wt-pos1-0.wa.shawcable.net [66.163.68.2]
  6    41 ms    55 ms    41 ms  c1-pos6-3.sttlwa1.home.net [24.7.70.37]
  7    54 ms    42 ms    27 ms  home-gw.st6wa.ip.att.net [192.205.32.249]
  8     *         *         *    Request timed out.
  9     *         *         *    Request timed out.
 10     *         *         *    Request timed out.
 11     *         *         *    Request timed out.
 12     *         *         *    Request timed out.
 13     *         *         *    Request timed out.
 14     *         *         *    Request timed out.
 15     *         *         *    Request timed out.
```

In this example, the trace route request only gets to the seventh hop, at which point it fails; this failure indicates that the problem lies on the far side of the device in step 7 or on the near side of the device in step 8. In other words, the device at step 7 is functioning but might not be able to make the next hop. The cause of the problem could be a range of things, such as an error in the routing table or a faulty connection. Alternatively, the seventh device might be operating 100%, but device 8 might not be functioning at all. In any case, you can isolate the problem to just one or two devices.

It should be noted that in some cases the owner of a router may configure it to not return ICMP traffic like that generated by ping or trace route. If this is the case, the ping or trace route will fail just as if the router did not exist or was not operating.

Although we have used the Windows **tracert** command to provide sample output in these sections, the output from **traceroute** on a UNIX, Linux, or Macintosh system is extremely similar.

The trace route utility can also help you isolate a heavily congested network. In the following example, the trace route packets fail in the midst of the tracert from a Windows Server 2003 system, but subsequently are able to continue. This behavior can be an indicator of network congestion:

```
C:\>tracert comptia.org

Tracing route to comptia.org [216.119.103.72]over a maximum of 30 hops:
  1     96 ms     96 ms     55 ms   24.67.179.1
  2     14 ms     13 ms     28 ms   rd1ht-ge3-0.ok.shawcable.net [24.67.224.7]
  3     28 ms     27 ms     41 ms   rc1wh-atm0-2-1.shawcable.net
➡  [204.209.214.19]
  4     28 ms     41 ms     27 ms   rc1wt-pos2-0.wa.shawcable.net
➡  [66.163.76.65]
  5     41 ms     27 ms     27 ms   rc2wt-pos1-0.wa.shawcable.net [66.163.68.2]
  6     55 ms     41 ms     27 ms   c1-pos6-3.sttlwa1.home.net [24.7.70.37]
  7     54 ms     42 ms     27 ms   home-gw.st6wa.ip.att.net [192.205.32.249]
  8     55 ms     41 ms     28 ms   gbr3-p40.st6wa.ip.att.net [12.123.44.130]
  9      *         *         *      Request timed out.
 10      *         *         *      Request timed out.
 11      *         *         *      Request timed out.
 12      *         *         *      Request timed out.
 13     69 ms     68 ms     69 ms   gbr2-p20.sd2ca.ip.att.net [12.122.11.254]
 14     55 ms     68 ms     69 ms   gbr1-p60.sd2ca.ip.att.net [12.122.1.109]
 15     82 ms     69 ms     82 ms   gbr1-p30.phmaz.ip.att.net [12.122.2.142]
 16     68 ms     69 ms     82 ms   gar2-p360.phmaz.ip.att.net [12.123.142.45]
 17    110 ms     96 ms     96 ms   12.125.99.70
 18    124 ms     96 ms     96 ms   light.crystaltech.com [216.119.107.1]
 19     82 ms     96 ms     96 ms   216.119.103.72
Trace complete.
```

Generally speaking, trace route utilities allow you to identify the location of a problem in the connectivity between two devices. After you have determined this location, you might need to use a utility such as ping to continue troubleshooting. In many cases, as in the examples provided in this chapter, the routers might be on a network such as the Internet and therefore not within your control. In that case, there is little you can do except inform your ISP of the problem.

ping

Most network administrators are very familiar with the ping utility and are likely to use it on an almost daily basis. The basic function of the ping command is to test the connectivity between the two devices on a network. All the command is designed to do is determine whether the two computers can see each other and to notify you of how long the round-trip takes to complete.

Although ping is most often used on its own, a number of switches can be used to assist in the troubleshooting process. Table 10.3 shows some of the commonly used switches with ping on a Windows system.

Table 10.3   ping Command Switches

Option	Description
ping -t	Pings a device on the network until stopped
ping -a	Resolves addresses to hostnames
ping -n count	Specifies the number of echo requests to send
ping -r count	Records route for count hops
ping -s count	Timestamp for count hops
ping -w timeout	Timeout in milliseconds to wait for each reply

ping works by sending ICMP echo request messages to another device on the network. If the other device on the network hears the ping request, it automatically responds with an ICMP echo reply. By default, the ping command on a Windows-based system sends four data packets; however, using the -t switch, a continuous stream of ping requests can be sent.

ping is perhaps the most widely used of all network tools; it is primarily used to verify connectivity between two network devices. On a good day, the results from the ping command will be successful, and the sending device will receive a reply from the remote device. Not all ping results are that successful, and to be able to effectively use ping, you must be able to interpret the results of a failed ping command.

The Destination Host Unreachable Message

The *Destination Host Unreachable* error message means that a route to the destination computer system cannot be found. To remedy this problem, you might need to examine the routing information on the local host to confirm that the local host is correctly configured, or you might need to make sure that the default gateway information is correct. The following is an example of a ping failure that gives the Destination host unreachable message:

```
Pinging 24.67.54.233 with 32 bytes of data:
Destination host unreachable.
Destination host unreachable.
Destination host unreachable.
Destination host unreachable.
Ping statistics for 24.67.54.233:
    Packets: Sent = 4, Received = 0, Lost = 4 (100% loss),
Approximate round trip times in milli-seconds:
    Minimum = 0ms, Maximum =  0ms, Average =  0ms
```

The Request Timed Out Message

The *Request Timed Out* error message is very common when you use the ping command. Essentially, this error message indicates that your host did not receive the ping message back from the destination device within the designated time period. Assuming that the network connectivity is okay on your system, this is typically an indicator that the destination device is not connected to the network, is powered off, or is not configured correctly. It could also mean that some intermediate device is not operating correctly. In some rare cases, it can also indicate that there is so much congestion on the network that timely delivery of the ping message could not be completed. It might also mean that the ping is being sent to an invalid IP address or that the system is not on the same network as the remote host, and an intermediary device is not configured correctly. In any of these cases, the failed ping should initiate a troubleshooting process that might involve other tools, manual inspection, and possibly reconfiguration. The following example shows the output from a ping to an invalid IP address:

```
C:\>ping 169.76.54.3
Pinging 169.76.54.3 with 32 bytes of data:

Request timed out.
Request timed out.
Request timed out.
Request timed out.

Ping statistics for 169.76.54.3:
    Packets: Sent = 4, Received = 0, Lost = 4 (100%
Approximate round trip times in milli-seconds:
    Minimum = 0ms, Maximum =  0ms, Average =  0ms
```

During the `ping` request, you might receive some replies from the remote host that are intermixed with `Request timed out` errors. This is often a result of a congested network. An example follows; notice that this example, which was run on a Windows Me system, uses the `-t` switch to generate continuous pings:

```
C:\>ping -t 24.67.184.65
Pinging 24.67.184.65 with 32 bytes of data:

Reply from 24.67.184.65: bytes=32 time=55ms TTL=127
Reply from 24.67.184.65: bytes=32 time=54ms TTL=127
Reply from 24.67.184.65: bytes=32 time=27ms TTL=127
Request timed out.
Request timed out.
Request timed out.
Reply from 24.67.184.65: bytes=32 time=69ms TTL=127
Reply from 24.67.184.65: bytes=32 time=28ms TTL=127
Reply from 24.67.184.65: bytes=32 time=28ms TTL=127
Reply from 24.67.184.65: bytes=32 time=68ms TTL=127
Reply from 24.67.184.65: bytes=32 time=41ms TTL=127

Ping statistics for 24.67.184.65:
    Packets: Sent = 11, Received = 8, Lost = 3 (27% loss),
Approximate round trip times in milli-seconds:
    Minimum = 27ms, Maximum =  69ms, Average =  33ms
```

In this example, three packets were lost. If this continued on your network, you would need to troubleshoot to find out why packets were being dropped.

The Unknown Host Message

The *Unknown Host* error message is generated when the hostname of the destination computer cannot be resolved. This error usually occurs when you `ping` an incorrect hostname, as shown in the following example, or try to use `ping` with a hostname when hostname resolution (via DNS or a HOSTS text file) is not configured:

```
C:\>ping www.comptia.ca
Unknown host www.comptia.ca
```

If the `ping` fails, you need to verify that the `ping` is being sent to the correct remote host. If it is, and if name resolution is configured, you have to dig a little more to find the problem. This error might indicate a problem with the name resolution process, and you might need to verify that the DNS or WINS server is available. Other commands, such as `nslookup` or `dig`, can help in this process.

The Expired TTL Message

The *Time to Live (TTL)* is an important consideration in understanding the `ping` command. The function of the TTL is to prevent circular routing, which occurs when a `ping` request keeps looping through a series of hosts.

The TTL counts each hop along the way toward its destination device. Each time it counts one hop, the hop is subtracted from the TTL. If the TTL reaches 0, the TTL has expired, and you get a message like the following:

```
Reply from 24.67.180.1: TTL expired in transit
```

If the TTL is exceeded with `ping`, you might have a routing problem on the network. You can modify the TTL for `ping` on a Windows system by using the `ping -i` command.

Troubleshooting with `ping`

Although `ping` does not completely isolate problems, you can use it to help identify where a problem lies. When troubleshooting with `ping`, take the following steps:

1. `ping` the IP address of your local loopback, using the command `ping 127.0.0.1`. If this command is successful, you know that the TCP/IP protocol suite is installed correctly on your system and functioning. If you are unable to `ping` the local loopback adapter, TCP/IP might need to be reloaded or reconfigured on the machine you are using.

The Loopback Address

The *loopback* is a special function within the protocol stack that is supplied for troubleshooting purposes. The Class A IP address 127.X.X.X is reserved for the loopback; although convention dictates that you use 127.0.0.1, you can use any address in the 127.X.X.X range, except for the network number itself (127.0.0.0) and the broadcast address (127.255.255.255). You can also `ping` by using the default hostname for the local system, which is called `localhost` (for example, `ping localhost`).

---

2. `ping` the assigned IP address of your local network interface card (NIC). If the `ping` is successful, you know that your NIC is functioning on the network and has TCP/IP correctly installed. If you are unable to `ping` the local NIC, TCP/IP might not be bound correctly to the NIC or the NIC drivers might be improperly installed.

3. `ping` the IP address of another known good system on your local network. By doing so, you can determine whether the computer you are using can see other computers on the network. If you can `ping` other devices on your local network, you have network connectivity.

If you cannot `ping` other devices on your local network and you were able to `ping` the IP address of your system, you might not be connected to the network correctly.

4. After you've confirmed that you have network connectivity for the local network, you can verify connectivity to a remote network by sending a ping to the IP address of the default gateway.

5. If you are able to ping the default gateway, you can verify remote connectivity by sending a ping to the IP address of a system on a remote network.

On the Network+ exam, you might be asked to relate the correct procedure for using **ping** for a connectivity problem.

Using just the ping command in these steps, you can confirm network connectivity on not only the local network, but also on a remote network. The whole process requires as much time as it takes to type in the command, and you can do it all from a single location.

If you are an optimistic person, you can perform step 5 first. If that works, all the other steps will also work, saving you the need to test them. If your step 5 trial fails, you can go back to step 1 and start the troubleshooting process from the beginning.

All but one of the **ping** examples used in this section show the **ping** command using the IP address of the remote host. It is also possible to **ping** the Domain Name Service (DNS) name of the remote host (for example, **ping www.comptia.org**, **ping server1**); this, of course, can be done only if your network uses a DNS server. On a Windows-based network, you can also **ping** by using the Network Basic Input/Output System (NetBIOS) computer name.

ARP

The *Address Resolution Protocol* (*ARP*) is used to resolve IP addresses to MAC addresses. This is important because on a network, devices find each other using the IP address, but communication between devices requires the MAC address.

For the Network+ exam, remember that the function of the ARP command is to resolve IP addresses to Layer 2 or MAC addresses.

When a computer wants to send data to another computer on the network, it must know the MAC address of the destination system. To discover this information, ARP sends out a discovery packet to obtain the MAC address. When the destination computer is found, it sends its MAC address to the sending computer. The ARP-resolved MAC addresses are stored temporarily on a computer system in the ARP cache. Inside this ARP cache is a list of matching MAC and IP addresses. This ARP cache is checked before a discovery packet is sent on to the network to determine if there is an existing entry.

Entries in the ARP cache are periodically flushed so that the cache doesn't fill up with unused entries. The following code shows an example of the ARP command with the output from a Windows 2000 system:

```
C:\>arp -a
Interface: 24.67.179.22 on Interface 0x3
  Internet Address      Physical Address      Type
  24.67.179.1           00-00-77-93-d8-3d      dynamic
```

As you might notice in the previous code, the type is listed as dynamic. Entries in the ARP cache can be added statically or dynamically. Static entries are added manually and do not expire. The dynamic entries are added automatically when the system accesses another on the network.

As with other command-line utilities, there are several switches available for the arp command. Table 10.4 shows the available switches for Windows-based systems.

Table 10.4 ARP Switches	
Switch	Description
-a or -g	Displays both the IP and MAC addresses and whether they are dynamic or static entries
inet_addr	Specifies a specific internet address
-N if_addr	Displays the ARP entries for a specified network interface
eth_addr	Specifies a MAC address
if_addr	Specifies an Internet address
-d	Deletes an entry from the ARP cache
-s	Adds a static permanent address to the ARP cache

The netstat Command

The netstat command displays the protocol statistics and current TCP/IP connections on the local system. Used without any switches, the netstat command shows the active connections for all outbound TCP/IP connections. In addition, several switches are available that change the type of information netstat displays. Table 10.5 shows the various switches available for the netstat utility.

Table 10.5	netstat Switches
Switch	**Description**
-a	Displays the current connections and listening ports
-e	Displays Ethernet statistics
-n	Lists addresses and port numbers in numerical form
-p	Shows connections for the specified protocol
-r	Shows the routing table
-s	Lists per-protocol statistics
interval	Specifies the length of time to wait before redisplaying statistics

The **netstat** and the **route print** commands can be used to show the routing table.

The netstat utility is used to show the port activity for both TCP and UDP connections, showing the inbound and outbound connections. When used without switches, the netstat utility has four information headings.

➤ **Proto**—Lists the protocol being used, either UDP or TCP.

➤ **Local address**—Specifies the local address and port being used.

➤ **Foreign address**—Identifies the destination address and the port being used.

➤ **State**—Specifies whether the connection is established.

In its default usage, the netstat command shows outbound connections that have been established by TCP. The following shows a sample output from a netstat command without using any switches:

```
C:\>netstat
Active Connections
  Proto  Local Address          Foreign Address        State
  TCP    laptop:2848            MEDIASERVICES1:1755    ESTABLISHED
  TCP    laptop:1833            www.dollarhost.com:80  ESTABLISHED
  TCP    laptop:2858            194.70.58.241:80       ESTABLISHED
  TCP    laptop:2860            194.70.58.241:80       ESTABLISHED
  TCP    laptop:2354            www.dollarhost.com:80  ESTABLISHED
  TCP    laptop:2361            www.dollarhost.com:80  ESTABLISHED
  TCP    laptop:1114            www.dollarhost.com:80  ESTABLISHED
```

```
TCP     laptop:1959          www.dollarhost.com:80   ESTABLISHED
TCP     laptop:1960          www.dollarhost.com:80   ESTABLISHED
TCP     laptop:1963          www.dollarhost.com:80   ESTABLISHED
TCP     laptop:2870          localhost:8431          TIME_WAIT
TCP     laptop:8431          localhost:2862          TIME_WAIT
TCP     laptop:8431          localhost:2863          TIME_WAIT
TCP     laptop:8431          localhost:2867          TIME_WAIT
TCP     laptop:8431          localhost:2872          TIME_WAIT
```

Like any other command-line utility, they are often used with switches. The following sections provide a brief explanation of the switches and a sample output from each.

netstat –e

The `netstat -e` command shows the activity for the NIC and displays the number of packets that have been both sent and received. An example of the `netstat -e` command is shown here:

```
C:\WINDOWS\Desktop>netstat -e
Interface Statistics

                       Received            Sent

Bytes                   17412385         40237510
Unicast packets            79129            85055
Non-unicast packets          693              254
Discards                       0                0
Errors                         0                0
Unknown protocols            306
```

As you can see, the `netstat -e` command shows more than just the packets that have been sent and received:

➤ **Bytes**—The number of bytes that have been sent or received by the NIC since the computer was turned on.

➤ **Unicast packets**—Packets sent and received directly to this interface.

➤ **Non-unicast packets**—Broadcast or multicast packets that were picked up by the NIC.

➤ **Discards**—The number of packets rejected by the NIC, perhaps because they were damaged.

➤ **Errors**—The errors that occurred during either the sending or receiving process. As you would expect, this column should be a low number. If it is not, it could indicate a problem with the NIC.

➤ **Unknown protocols**—The number of packets that were not recognizable by the system.

netstat -a

The `netstat -a` command displays statistics for both TCP and User Datagram Protocol (UDP). Here is an example of the `netstat -a` command:

```
C:\WINDOWS\Desktop>netstat -a

Active Connections

  Proto  Local Address        Foreign Address          State
  TCP    laptop:1027          LAPTOP:0                 LISTENING
  TCP    laptop:1030          LAPTOP:0                 LISTENING
  TCP    laptop:1035          LAPTOP:0                 LISTENING
  TCP    laptop:50000         LAPTOP:0                 LISTENING
  TCP    laptop:5000          LAPTOP:0                 LISTENING
  TCP    laptop:1035          msgr-ns41.msgr.hotmail.com:1863 ESTABLISHED
  TCP    laptop:nbsession     LAPTOP:0                 LISTENING
  TCP    laptop:1027          localhost:50000          ESTABLISHED
  TCP    laptop:50000         localhost:1027           ESTABLISHED
  UDP    laptop:1900          *:*
  UDP    laptop:nbname        *:*
  UDP    laptop:nbdatagram    *:*
  UDP    laptop:1547          *:*
  UDP    laptop:1038          *:*
  UDP    laptop:1828          *:*
  UDP    laptop:3366          *:*
```

As you can see, the output includes four columns, which show the protocol, the local address, the foreign address, and the state of the port. The *TCP* connections show the local and foreign destination addresses and the current state of the connection. *UDP*, however, is a little different; it does not list a state status because as mentioned throughout this book, UDP is a connectionless protocol and does not establish connections. The following list briefly explains the information provided by the `netstat -a` command:

➤ **Proto**—The protocol used by the connection.

➤ **Local Address**—The IP address of the local computer system and the port number it is using. If the entry in the local address field is an asterisk (*), it indicates that the port has not yet been established.

➤ **Foreign Address**—The IP address of a remote computer system and the associated port. When a port has not been established, as with the UDP connections, `*:*` appears in the column.

➤ **State**—The current state of the TCP connection. Possible states include established, listening, closed, and waiting.

netstat -r

The `netstat -r` command is often used to view the routing table for a system. A system uses a routing table to determine routing information for TCP/IP traffic. The following is an example of the `netstat -r` command from a Windows Me system:

NOTE The **netstat -r** command output shows the same information as the output from the **route print** command.

```
C:\WINDOWS\Desktop>netstat -r
Route table

==============================================================================
==============================================================================
Active Routes:
Network Destination        Netmask          Gateway       Interface  Metric
          0.0.0.0          0.0.0.0      24.67.179.1    24.67.179.22       1
     24.67.179.0    255.255.255.0     24.67.179.22    24.67.179.22       1
    24.67.179.22  255.255.255.255        127.0.0.1       127.0.0.1       1
  24.255.255.255  255.255.255.255     24.67.179.22    24.67.179.22       1
       127.0.0.0        255.0.0.0        127.0.0.1       127.0.0.1       1
       224.0.0.0        224.0.0.0     24.67.179.22    24.67.179.22       1
 255.255.255.255  255.255.255.255     24.67.179.22               2       1
Default Gateway:       24.67.179.1
==============================================================================
Persistent Routes:
  None
```

netstat –s

The `netstat -s` command displays a number of statistics related to the TCP/IP protocol suite. Understanding the purpose of every field in the output is beyond the scope of the Network+ exam, but for your reference, sample output from the `netstat -s` command is shown here:

```
C:\>netstat -s

IP Statistics

  Packets Received                    = 389938
  Received Header Errors              = 0
  Received Address Errors             = 1876
  Datagrams Forwarded                 = 498
  Unknown Protocols Received          = 0
  Received Packets Discarded          = 0
  Received Packets Delivered          = 387566
  Output Requests                     = 397334
  Routing Discards                    = 0
  Discarded Output Packets            = 0
  Output Packet No Route              = 916
  Reassembly Required                 = 0
  Reassembly Successful               = 0
  Reassembly Failures                 = 0
  Datagrams Successfully Fragmented   = 0
  Datagrams Failing Fragmentation     = 0
  Fragments Created                   = 0
```

```
ICMP Statistics

                              Received    Sent
    Messages                  40641       41111
    Errors                    0           0
    Destination Unreachable   223         680
    Time Exceeded             24          0
    Parameter Problems        0           0
    Source Quenches           0           0
    Redirects                 0           38
    Echos                     20245       20148
    Echo Replies              20149       20245
    Timestamps                0           0
    Timestamp Replies         0           0
    Address Masks             0           0
    Address Mask Replies      0           0

TCP Statistics

    Active Opens                  = 13538
    Passive Opens                 = 23132
    Failed Connection Attempts    = 9259
    Reset Connections             = 254
    Current Connections           = 15
    Segments Received             = 330242
    Segments Sent                 = 326935
    Segments Retransmitted        = 18851

UDP Statistics

    Datagrams Received    = 20402
    No Ports              = 20594
    Receive Errors        = 0
    Datagrams Sent        = 10217
```

nbtstat

The nbtstat utility is used to view protocol statistics and information for NetBIOS over TCP/IP connections. nbtstat is commonly used to troubleshoot NetBIOS name resolution problems. Because nbtstat provides the resolution of NetBIOS names, it's available only on Windows systems.

A number of case-sensitive switches are available for the nbtstat command. Table 10.6 summarizes these switches.

Table 10.6 nbtstat Switches	
Switch	**Description**
nbtstat -a	(Adapter status) Outputs the NetBIOS name table and MAC addresses of the card for the specified computer
nbtstat -A (IP address)	(Adapter status) Lists the remote machine's name table given its IP address

(continued)

Table 10.6 nbtstat Switches *(continued)*	
Switch	**Description**
nbtstat -c (cache)	Provides a list of the contents of the NetBIOS name cache
nbtstat -n (names)	Lists local NetBIOS names
nbtstat -r (resolved)	Lists names resolved by broadcast or WINS
nbtstat -R (Reload)	Purges and reloads the remote cache name table
nbtstat -S (Sessions)	Summarizes the current NetBIOS sessions and their status
nbtstat -s (sessions)	Lists sessions table converting destination IP addresses to computer NetBIOS names
nbtstat -RR (ReleaseRefresh)	Sends Name Release packets to WINS, and then starts Refresh
nbtstat RemoteName	Remote host machine name
nbtstat IP address	Dotted decimal representation of the IP address
nbtstat interval	Redisplays selected statistics, pausing interval seconds between each display. Press Ctrl+C to stop redisplaying statistics

As an example, the following is the output from the nbtstat -n command:

```
C:\>nbtstat -n
Lana # 0:
Node IpAddress: [169.254.196.192] Scope Id: []

            NetBIOS Local Name Table

     Name              Type         Status
    -------------------------------------------
    LAPTOP        <00>  UNIQUE     Registered
    KCS           <00>  GROUP      Registered
    LAPTOP        <03>  UNIQUE     Registered
```

The ipconfig Command

The ipconfig command is a technician's best friend when it comes to viewing the TCP/IP configuration of a Windows system. Used on its own, the ipconfig command shows basic information such as the name of the network interface, the IP address, the subnet mask, and the default gateway. Combined with the /all switch, it shows a detailed set of information, as you can see in the following example:

```
C:\>ipconfig /all
Windows 2000 IP Configuration
   Host Name . . . . . . . . . . . . : server
```

```
Primary DNS Suffix  . . . . . . . : write
Node Type . . . . . . . . . . . . : Broadcast
IP Routing Enabled. . . . . . . . : Yes
WINS Proxy Enabled. . . . . . . . : No
DNS Suffix Search List. . . . . . : write
                                    ok.anyotherhost.net
Ethernet adapter Local Area Connection:

Connection-specific DNS Suffix  . : ok.anyotherhost.net
Description . . . . . . . . . . . : D-Link DFE-530TX PCI Fast Ethernet
Physical Address. . . . . . . . . : 00-80-C8-E3-4C-BD
DHCP Enabled. . . . . . . . . . . : Yes
Autoconfiguration Enabled . . . . : Yes
IP Address. . . . . . . . . . . . : 24.67.184.65
Subnet Mask . . . . . . . . . . . : 255.255.254.0
Default Gateway . . . . . . . . . : 24.67.184.1
DHCP Server . . . . . . . . . . . : 24.67.253.195
DNS Servers . . . . . . . . . . . : 24.67.253.195
                                    24.67.253.212
Lease Obtained.. . . . : Thursday, February 07, 2002 3:42:00 AM
Lease Expires .. . . . : Saturday, February 09, 2002 3:42:00 AM
```

As you can imagine, you can use the output from an `ipconfig /all` command in a massive range of troubleshooting scenarios. Table 10.7 lists some of the most common troubleshooting symptoms, along with where to look for clues about solving them in the `ipconfig /all` output.

When looking at **ipconfig** information, you should be sure that all information is present and correct. For example, a missing or incorrect default gateway parameter limits communication to the local segment.

Table 10.7 Common Troubleshooting Symptoms That ipconfig Can Help Solve	
Symptom	Field to Check in **ipconfig** Output
User is unable to connect to any other system.	Make sure the TCP/IP address and subnet mask are correct. If the network uses DHCP, make sure DHCP is enabled.
User is able to connect to another system on the same subnet but is not not able to connect to a remote system.	Make sure the default gateway is correctly configured.
User is unable to browse the Internet.	Make sure the DNS server parameters are configured correctly.
User is unable to browse across remote subnets.	Make sure the WINS or DNS server parameters are configured correctly, if applicable.

You should be prepared to identify the output from an **ipconfig** command in relationship to a troubleshooting scenario for the Network+ exam.

Using the /all switch might be far and away the most popular, but there are a few others. These include the switches listed in Table 10.8.

The **ipconfig** and its associated switches are widely used by network administrators and therefore should be expected to make an appearance on the exam.

Table 10.8 Ipconfig Switches	
Switch	**Description**
?	Displays the **ipconfig** help screen
/all	Displays additional IP configuration information
/release	Releases the IP address of the specified adapter
/renew	Renews the IP address of a specified adapter

The **ipconfig /renew** and **ipconfig /release** commands work only when your system is using DHCP.

The **ipconfig** command on Windows 2000, Windows XP and Windows Server 2003 provides additional switches and functionality geared toward Active Directory and Dynamic DNS. You do not need to be concerned with these switches for the Network+ exam, but you can view information on them by using the **ipconfig /?** command.

ifconfig

ifconfig performs the same function as ipconfig, but on a Linux, UNIX, or Macintosh system. Because Linux relies more heavily on command-line utilities than Windows, the Linux and UNIX version of ifconfig provides much more functionality than ipconfig. On a Linux or UNIX system, you can get information about the usage of the ifconfig command by using ifconfig --help. The following output provides an example of the basic ifconfig command run on a Linux system:

```
eth0      Link encap:Ethernet  HWaddr 00:60:08:17:63:A0
          inet addr:192.168.1.101  Bcast:192.168.1.255
➡   Mask:255.255.255.0
          UP BROADCAST RUNNING  MTU:1500  Metric:1
          RX packets:911 errors:0 dropped:0 overruns:0 frame:0
          TX packets:804 errors:0 dropped:0 overruns:0 carrier:0
          collisions:0 txqueuelen:100
          Interrupt:5 Base address:0xe400

lo        Link encap:Local Loopback
          inet addr:127.0.0.1  Mask:255.0.0.0
          UP LOOPBACK RUNNING  MTU:3924  Metric:1
          RX packets:18 errors:0 dropped:0 overruns:0 frame:0
          TX packets:18 errors:0 dropped:0 overruns:0 carrier:0
          collisions:0 txqueuelen:0
```

Although the ifconfig command displays the IP address, subnet mask and default gateway information for both the installed network adapter and the local loopback adapter, it does not report DCHP lease information. Instead, you can use the pump -s command to view detailed information on the DHCP lease including the assigned IP address, the address of the DHCP server, and the time remaining on the lease. The pump command can also be used to release and renew IP addresses assigned via DHCP and to view DNS server information.

The **winipcfg** Command

On a Windows 98 Second Edition and Windows Me systems, the winipcfg command is used in addition to the ipconfig command. The difference between the two utilities is that winipcfg is a graphical utility.

In basic mode, winipcfg shows information including the Media Access Control (MAC) address and IP address of the interface, the subnet mask, and the default gateway. For detailed information, similar to that produced with ipconfig /all, a More Info button allows you to switch into a much more detailed screen.

The same troubleshooting scenarios, with the same solutions, apply to winipcfg as to ipconfig. Table 10.9 lists some solutions to common problems.

Table 10.9 Common Troubleshooting Problems That **winipcfg** Can Help Solve	
Symptom	Field to Check in **winipcfg** Output
User is unable to connect to any other system.	Check that the TCP/IP address and subnet mask are correct. If using DHCP, make sure DHCP is enabled.

(continued)

Table 10.9 Common Troubleshooting Problems That **winipcfg** Can Help Solve *(continued)*	
Symptom	**Field to Check in winipcfg Output**
User is able to connect to other system on the same subnet, but is not able to connect to a remote system.	Check that the default gateway is correctly configured.
User is unable to browse the Internet.	Make sure the DNS server paramenters are configured correctly.
User is unable to browse across remote subnets.	Make sure the WINS or DNS server parameters are configured correctly (if applicable).

nslookup

nslookup is a utility used to troubleshoot DNS-related problems. Using nslookup, you can, for example, run manual name resolution queries against DNS servers, get information about the DNS configuration of your system or specify what kind of DNS record should be resolved.

When nslookup is started, it displays the current hostname and the IP address of the locally configured DNS server. You will then see a command prompt which allows you to specify further queries. This is known as 'interactive' mode. The commands you can enter in interactive mode are listed in Table 10.10.

Table 10.10 **nslookup** Switches	
Switch	**Description**
all	Prints options, as well as current server and host information
[no]debug	Prints debugging information
[no]d2	Prints exhaustive debugging information
[no]defname	Appends the domain name to each query
[no]recurse	Asks for recursive answer to query
[no]search	Uses domain search list
[no]vc	Always uses a virtual circuit
domain=NAME	Sets default domain name to **NAME**
srchlist=N1[/N2/.../N6]	Sets domain to N1 and search list to N1, N2, and so on
root=NAME	Sets root server to **NAME**
retry=X	Sets number of retries to **X**
timeout=X	Sets initial timeout interval to **X** seconds

(continued)

Table 10.10	nslookup Switches *(continued)*
Switch	**Description**
type=X	Sets query type (for example, A, ANY, CNAME, MX, NS, PTR, SOA, or SRV)
querytype=X	Same as type
class=X	Sets query class (for example, **IN** [Internet], **ANY**)
[no]msxfr	Uses MS fast zone transfer
ixfrver=X	Current version to use in IXFR transfer request
server NAME	Sets default server to **NAME**, using current default server
exit	Exits the program

Instead of using interactive mode, you can also execute nslookup requests directly at the command prompt. The following listing shows the output from nslookup when a domain name is specified to be resolved.

```
C:\>nslookup comptia.org
Server:  nsc1.ht.ok.shawcable.net
Address:  64.59.168.13

Non-authoritative answer:
Name:    comptia.org
Address:  208.252.144.4
```

As you can see from the output, nslookup shows the hostname and IP address of the DNS server against which the resolution was performed, along with the hostname and IP address of the resolved host.

dig

dig is used on Linux, UNIX or Macintosh system to perform manual DNS lookups. dig performs the same basic task as nslookup, but with one major distinction: The dig command does not have an interactive mode and instead uses only command-line switches to customize results.

dig is generally considered a more powerful tool than nslookup, but in the course of a typical network administrator's day, the minor limitations of nslookup are unlikely to be too much of a factor. Instead, dig is often simply the tool of choice for DNS information and troubleshooting on UNIX, Linux, or Macintosh systems. Like nslookup, dig can be used to perform simple name resolution requests. The output from this process can be seen in the following listing:

```
; <<>> DiG 8.2 <<>> examcram.com
;; res options: init recurs defnam dnsrch
;; got answer:
;; ->>HEADER<<- opcode: QUERY, status: NOERROR, id: 4
;; flags: qr rd ra; QUERY: 1, ANSWER: 1, AUTHORITY: 2, ADDITIONAL: 0
```

```
;; QUERY SECTION:
;;    examcram.com, type = A, class = IN

;; ANSWER SECTION:
examcram.com.         7h33m IN A    63.240.93.157

;; AUTHORITY SECTION:
examcram.com.         7h33m IN NS    usrxdns1.pearsontc.com.
examcram.com.         7h33m IN NS    oldtxdns2.pearsontc.com.

;; Total query time: 78 msec
;; FROM: localhost.localdomain to SERVER: default -- 209.53.4.130
;; WHEN: Sat Oct 16 20:21:24 2004
;; MSG SIZE  sent: 30  rcvd: 103
```

As you can see, `dig` provides a number of pieces of information in the basic output—more so than `nslookup`. There are three key areas of the output from which network administrators can gain information. These are the 'Answer Section,' the 'Authority Section,' and the last four lines of the output.

The Answer Section of the output provides the name of the domain or host being resolved, along with its IP address. The A in the results line indicates the record type that is being resolved.

The Authority Section provides information on the authoritative DNS servers for the domain against which the resolution request was performed. This information can be useful in determining whether the correct DNS servers are considered authoritative for a domain.

The last four lines of the output show how long the name resolution request took to process and the IP address of the DNS server that performed the resolution. It also shows the date and time of the request, as well as the size of the packets sent and received.

Interpreting Visual Indicators

One of the easiest ways to spot signs of trouble on a network or with a network component is to look at the devices' LEDs. Many of the devices used in modern networks—such as hubs, routers, switches, and even NICs—have these small indicator lights that let you know what, if anything, is going wrong. The following sections examine some of the common networking devices and what you can learn from their LEDs.

LEDs on Networking Devices

If you have seen a hub or a switch, you have no doubt noticed the LEDs on the front of the device. Each RJ-45 connector has one or two dedicated

LEDs. These LEDs are designed to provide the network administrator with a quick idea of the status of a connection or a potential problem. Table 10.11 provides some examples of link-light indicators functioning on a typical hub or switch.

Note that the LEDs' sequencing and meanings vary among the different hub manufacturers and therefore might be different from those listed in Table 10.11.

Table 10.11 Example Link-Light Indicator LED States for a Network Hub or Switch	
LED State	**Meaning**
Solid green	A device is connected to the port, but there is no activity on the device.
Blinking green	There is activity on the port. The connected system is sending or receiving data.
No LED lit	There is no detectable link. Either there's a problem with the connection between the device and the hub (such as an unplugged cable), or the remote system is powered down.
Fast continuous blinking for extended periods	This often indicates a fault with the connection, which can commonly be attributed to a faulty NIC.
Blinking amber	There are collisions on the network. A few orange LEDs flashing intermittently are okay, but continuously blinking amber LEDs indicate a problem.

In addition to link-light indicators, some hubs and switches have port-speed LEDs that, when lit, indicate the speed at which the connected device is functioning. Some also have LEDs that indicate whether the link is operating in full-duplex mode.

If a connection LED on a hub is not lit, all the physical connections are correct, and the connected system is powered on, you might have a faulty patch cable.

By understanding the function of the lights on networking devices, you can tell at a glance the status of a device and the systems connected to it. You should take the time to familiarize yourself with the indicator lights on the network devices you work with and with their various states.

LEDs on NICs and Other Devices

In addition to hubs and switches, most other networking devices have LEDs that provide a variety of information. Most NICs have at least one LED that indicates whether there is a link between the system and the network into which it is plugged. The link light operates at a physical level; in other words, it should be lit when the PC is on, regardless of whether the networking software is loaded, the network configuration is correct, or the user is logged on to the network. In addition to the link light LED, many NICs have additional lights to indicate the speed at which the network connection is established and/or when there is network activity on the link.

LEDs are also included on cable modems and DSL modems, which are commonly used in small or home office implementations for Internet connectivity. The number of LEDs and their functionality depends on the device. For example, one cable modem might have four LEDs: one indicating that the modem is online, a Send indicator, a Receive indicator, and one labeled Message. In contrast, a DSL modem might have six LEDs. One shows that the device is powered, and one flashes to indicate that the device is operating normally. Then there is a link light for both the local network and the DSL connection, and another LED for each interface that flashes to indicate activity on those links.

The usefulness of LEDs in troubleshooting scenarios cannot be overstated. LEDs provide an instant, visual indicator about the state of a network link. In some cases, as with collision lights, they can even alert you to problems on the network. Understanding how to interpret information provided by LEDs is important for the real world and for the Network+ exam.

Imagine a scenario in which a user who is working at workstation A calls and tells you she is unable to access the Internet. The Internet connection could be down, but by connecting to the Internet yourself, you determine that it is working correctly; therefore, it is safe to assume that the problem is at the user's end rather than with the Internet connectivity. Next, you decide to visit the user's workstation to see whether you can ping the Internet router. Before you begin the ping test, you look at the back of the system and see that the link LED on the NIC is not lit. At this point, you can be fairly sure that the ping test will not work because without the link light, there is no connectivity between the NIC and the switch.

Now you have narrowed the problem to one of a few sources. Either the NIC or the cable is faulty, the switch to which the user is connected is not functioning, or the port on the switch to which the user is connected is faulty.

The easiest way to test whether the cable is the problem is to borrow a known working cable from workstation B or C and swap it with the cable connecting workstation A to the hub, switch, or wall port. When you try this, if the link light does not come on, you can deduce that the NIC is faulty. If the light does come on, you can deduce that either the port on the switch or a cable is faulty. The next step is to swap the cable out or try the original cable in another switch port.

Expect to be asked to identify the purposes of link lights on the Network+ exam. You might be presented with diagrams and asked how you would use LEDs in the troubleshooting process.

Whatever the actual problem, link lights play an important role in the troubleshooting process. They give you an easy method of seeing what steps do and don't work.

Troubleshooting Remote Connectivity

Remote connectivity errors are bugs that prevent you from connecting to the office network, from remotely dialing in to your home computer, or from logging on to your ISP and subsequently the Internet.

Although many means and methods are available for establishing remote connectivity, network administrators can focus their attention on some common hot spots when troubleshooting errors, including authentication failure, protocol configuration problems, and physical connectivity.

Troubleshooting Physical Connectivity

When you're troubleshooting remote connectivity errors, it is often easy to forget the most basic troubleshooting practices. By this, we mean ensuring that all the physical connections are in place. When you suspect a physical connectivity problem, here are a few key places to look:

➤ Faulty cable

➤ Improperly connected cable

➤ Incorrect cable

➤ Faulty interface

➤ Faulty networking devices

Now that we have looked at some of the more generalized considerations of remote connectivity troubleshooting from a physical perspective, we'll focus specifically on some of the commonly used remote access technologies.

DSL

Troubleshooting DSL is similar to troubleshooting any other Internet connection. The following are a few things to check when users are experiencing problems with a DSL connection:

➤ Physical connections

➤ The NIC installed in the computer system

➤ Network card drivers

➤ Protocol configuration

➤ LEDs on the DSL modem

When troubleshooting remote connectivity on a cable or DSL modem, use the LEDs that are always present on these devices to aid in your troubleshooting process.

Cable Troubleshooting Procedures

In general, cable Internet access is a low-maintenance system with very few problems. When problems do occur, you can try various troubleshooting measures:

➤ Check the physical connections.

➤ Ensure that the protocol configuration on the system is valid.

➤ Check the indicator lights on the cable modem.

➤ Cycle the power on the cable modem, and on the system.

If you are sure that the connectors are all in place and the configuration of the system is correct, the next step is to call the technical support line of the cable provider.

Home Satellite Troubleshooting Procedures

Your ability to troubleshoot satellite Internet connections might be very limited. The hardware associated with home satellite remote access installations are very specialized, and equipment providers often prefer that you let them do the hardware troubleshooting. Given this limitation, calls to technical support occur very early in the troubleshooting process.

Wireless Internet Access Troubleshooting Procedures

Troubleshooting wireless access is normally confined to ensuring that the adapter is functioning correctly and configured properly.

The main factors that can affect wireless access are environmental conditions and outside interference. Many people who live in areas that often have fog or other damp conditions experience poor performance (or none at all) from wireless Internet service.

Here are some specific things you should check when troubleshooting a wireless connection:

➤ Check the configuration of the wireless interface.

➤ Move the computer around to find out if it's in a dead spot.

➤ Check with other people to see if there is a problem with the service, rather than just your system.

If you are sure that everything is configured correctly, you might have to contact the wireless provider to see if anything is amiss.

POTS Troubleshooting Procedures

Troubleshooting a dial-up connection problem can be tricky and time-consuming because you must consider many variables. In fact, of the remote connectivity mechanisms discussed in this chapter, you are far more likely to have problems with a POTS connection than any of the others. The following are some places to start your troubleshooting under various conditions.

If the user is unable to dial out, try the following:

➤ Check physical connections.

➤ Check that there is a dial tone on the line.

If the user can dial out but can't get a connection, try the following:

➤ Make sure that the user is dialing the correct number.

➤ Call the ISP to determine whether it is having problems.

➤ Determine if Call Waiting is enabled on the line, or there is some other telephone provider service interfering with communications.

If the user can dial out and can get a connection but is then disconnected, try the following:

➤ Ensure that the modem connection is configured correctly.

➤ Check that the username and password are correct.

➤ Verify that the connection settings are correct.

Modem-Specific Troubleshooting

If you are confident that a modem is installed and configured correctly, but it's still not working properly, you can test and configure it by using special commands from the *AT command set*. Table 10.12 lists some of the most commonly used AT commands.

Table 10.12 Commonly Used AT Commands	
AT Command	Result
ATA	Sets the modem to auto-answer
ATH	Hangs up an active connection
ATD	Dials a number
ATZ	Resets the modem
ATI3	Displays the name and model of the modem

In general, getting the modem to respond to an ATZ command is a good enough indicator that the modem is functioning.

You should be prepared to identify the function of basic AT commands for the Network+ exam.

Troubleshooting Authentication Failure

All forms of remote connectivity should require some form of authentication to confirm that those trying to access the remote resources have permission to do so. As a network administrator, you can expect to become very familiar with authentication troubleshooting. Quite often, authentication errors result from users incorrectly entering usernames and/or passwords.

If you're troubleshooting authentication failure, you should ensure that Caps Lock is turned off on the keyboard.

Authentication issues can also arise as a result of permissions changes in users' accounts. If you're troubleshooting remote connectivity and you have confirmed that the correct username and password are used, you should confirm that the user has the appropriate permissions to access the network.

The third and perhaps least likely cause for authentication failure is a downed authentication server. In such a circumstance, you are likely to receive numerous calls regarding authentication difficulty—not just one or two.

Troubleshooting Protocol Configuration Problems

Many, but not all, of the problems you encounter with remote connectivity can be addressed with the measures listed previously. However, you might encounter a problem when you have confirmed that the network user is using the correct username and password combination, that no changes have been made to the user's account information, that all physical connections are in place, and that the user still cannot establish a remote connection.

The next most likely cause of a client connectivity problem is protocol configuration. Protocol configuration issues are usually on the client side of the network. On a TCP/IP network, each client computer must have a unique address in order to participate on the network. Failure to obtain addressing information automatically could indicate a problem with a DHCP server. You should check the DHCP server to make sure that it is functioning and that addresses are available for assignment.

Beyond basic protocol issues such as addressing, remote connectivity troubleshooting also brings with it the additional considerations of authentication protocols. There is one basic rule that applies to all such issues. If a client in a remote connectivity solution is configured to use one type of authentication protocol, and the server to which he is connecting does not support that protocol, the connection will be refused.

If a client is attempting to connect to a remote system using one authentication protocol, and the remote access server does not support that protocol, the connection will be refused.

Troubleshooting Small Office/Home Office Router

As more people choose to use broadband Internet connectivity methods such as cable and DSL, the use of compact hub/router and switch/router combinations has become commonplace.

Most SOHO routers are, in fact, more than routers. Most are also Ethernet hubs or switches, making it possible to share an Internet connection with other systems on the network. They also typically provide basic firewalling capabilities and, in many cases, DHCP server functionality.

Configuration

The most common configuration method for SOHO routers is through a browser interface, though some models also use a custom application for this purpose. Configuration is generally straightforward, as SOHO routers are designed to be home user friendly.

Troubleshooting

Because a SOHO router is a network device, the rules and procedures that apply to other troubleshooting scenarios are valid. If you are experiencing Internet connectivity issues on a network with a SOHO router, the first step is to ensure that the SOHO router is powered on and that all the network connections are complete and secure. Also, familiarize yourself with the diagnostic LEDs on your SOHO router so that you can interpret the information they provide accordingly.

 SOHO routers typically function for long periods of time without a problem. If your SOHO router *hangs*, try powering it down, waiting a few moments, and then powering it back up again.

One of the easiest ways to test whether the SOHO router is the cause of a problem is to remove it from the communications chain and plug a PC directly in to the broadband interface (be that cable or DSL). If the PC is configured to obtain an IP address automatically, it should be able to get an IP address from the ISP just as easily as it would from the SOHO router. If the system subsequently works fine and can access the Internet, you know that the problem lies with the SOHO router and not the configuration of the system.

 When you remove a SOHO router from the communications chain, you need to be very aware that unless the PC itself is running a firewall, it is very exposed to Internet borne threats. You should install a software firewall on the system before you connect directly to the Internet.

Identifying and Troubleshooting Client Connectivity Problems

Client connectivity errors are one of the most common sources of network-related problems. Issues range from plain old user error to more complex protocol and cabling issues. Sometimes, even administrators make mistakes that can impact users! With so many possibilities, it is no wonder that client connectivity persists as one of the biggest network troubleshooting hotspots.

Protocol Errors

The client system must have a protocol assigned or bound to its NIC in order to access resources. You can use various tools to verify that a protocol is being used by the system—for example, on Windows 2000/XP/2003 systems, you use the `ipconfig` command; on older Windows client systems, you use the `winipcfg` command; and on Linux, UNIX, and Macintosh systems, you can use the `ifconfig` command.

Protocol-Specific Issues

You need to consider a number of factors related to network protocols when you troubleshoot a client connectivity. The following list describes some of the protocol-specific issues you should consider in such a situation:

➤ **Transmission Control Protocol/Internet Protocol (TCP/IP)**—For a system to operate on a TCP/IP-based network, it must have at the very least a unique IP address, the correct subnet mask for the network to which it is connected, and (for cross-network connectivity) a default gateway entry. In addition, Domain Name Service (DNS) server addresses might be required.

➤ **Internetwork Packet Exchange/Sequenced Packet Exchange (IPX/SPX)**—Each system on an IPX/SPX network must have a unique address, although the addresses are generated and assigned automatically. On older networks, care must be taken to ensure that the correct frame type is being used, although systems are usually able to autodetect the frame type that is in use.

➤ **Network BIOS Extended User Interface (NetBEUI)**—Each system on a network that uses NetBEUI must have a unique name to identify the computer on the network. For name resolution between network segments, a network needs either a Windows Internet Naming System (WINS) server or manual name resolution through an LMHOSTS file.

➤ **AppleTalk**—Each system on an AppleTalk network must have a unique address. If AppleTalk over TCP/IP is being used, ensure that the system is configured with a valid IP address, subnet mask, and (if needed) a default gateway.

 Remember that Windows systems use APIPA. If they are configured to use DHCP but cannot obtain an address from a server, they will self-assign an IP address from the **169.254.x.x** range. Non-APIPA systems that cannot obtain an IP address from a DHCP server will typically self assign an IP address of **0.0.0.0**.

When protocol settings are correctly configured, protocol problems are infrequent. Unless settings are manually changed, very little can go wrong.

Authentication

Before users can log on to any system, their identities must be verified. By far the most common type of authentication used is the standard username and password combination. When a user account is created, it is good practice for the administrator to set a password. The user should change that password immediately so that the administrator no longer knows it.

 With the exception of Novell NetWare, all the operating systems covered in the Network+ exam use case-sensitive passwords.

Most user password problems can be traced to users entering an incorrect password or entering the correct password incorrectly. All common operating systems offer the ability for the administrator to change a user's password, but none offer the capability to determine the user's existing password.

Therefore, if a user does forget his or her password, a new one has to be created and issued.

Permissions Errors

Access to applications and data across the network is controlled by permissions. Permissions are responsible for protecting the data on the network and ensuring that only those who should have access to it do.

The first rule of permissions troubleshooting is to remember that permissions do not change themselves. If a user cannot access a file, the first question to the user should always be, "Could you ever access the file?" If the user says, "Yes, but now I can't access the file," you should check server change logs or documentation to see if any changes have been made in the permissions structure.

If no changes have been made, you should verify that the user is in fact allowed access to that file or directory. In large environments, trying to keep track of who should have access to what can be a tricky business—one that is best left to defined policies and documentation.

The following are some other items you should consider when troubleshooting permissions problems:

➤ On some operating systems, rights and permissions can be inherited from parent directories or other directories that are higher in the directory structure. A change in the permissions assignments at one level might have an effect on a lower level in the directory tree.

➤ File permissions can be gained from objects other than the user's account. Depending on the operating system being used, rights can also be gained from group membership, other network objects, or security equivalence. When you are troubleshooting a permissions problem, be sure that you understand where rights are supposed to originate.

➤ File attributes can override file permissions, and they can prevent actions from being performed on certain files. To the uninitiated, this might seem like a file permissions problem, but in fact it is correct operation.

As with many other IT troubleshooting scenarios, you can solve most permissions problems effectively if you fully understand what you are troubleshooting and the factors that affect the situation. Also in common with other troubleshooting scenarios, you need to approach the problem methodically.

Physical Connectivity Errors

Although many of the problems associated with client connectivity can be traced to software-based problems such as configuration, authentication, and permissions issues, physical connectivity is often the root of the problem.

When you are troubleshooting physical connectivity errors, the first place to look is at the network cables. Although it is rare, cables can become loose or disconnected from NICs or from the ports on a hub or switch. Oftentimes, this is the result of other cables being plugged in or unplugged, or of other activity on the connections around the one that is having the problem. Other cable considerations include exceeded maximum lengths, cable breaks, and improperly terminated or made cables, although these are only a consideration in exceptional cases.

Physical connectivity errors also involve the devices used to establish the physical client/server connectivity. This can include hubs, switches, MSAUs, NICs, routers, and connectivity hardware. Although it is possible to have a problem with a single port on one of the aforementioned devices, it is more likely that the entire unit will malfunction. Thankfully, networking devices are very resilient devices that provide many years of service with few or no problems.

Troubleshooting Checklists

In a real-world networking environment, you will be expected to be able to troubleshoot client connectivity in many different areas. As a result, you can expect to be tested on them on the CompTIA exam. The following sections provide some troubleshooting checklists that can help you review some of the various troubleshooting areas in preparation for the exam.

Troubleshooting Cabling Problems

Cable accounts for a great many of the problems on a network. There are many places to look when you suspect a cable-related problem. If you suspect that cable is at the bottom of your network troubles, consider the following areas:

➤ **Loose connections**—You need to verify that cables are securely attached and that they are attached to the correct ports.

➤ **Poorly crimped or bent cable**—Sometimes a chair running over a cable or a cable that has a poor crimp can cause problems.

> ➤ **Incorrect cable length**—Recall from Chapter 2, "Cabling and Connectors," that cables cannot exceed a specified maximum length.

> ➤ **Cable placement**—Care must be taken when cables are run too closely to strong electrical devices. If cables are run too closely to electrical devices, you need to ensure that they are designed for the task.

Troubleshooting Operating System Connectivity

If you are struggling with operating system connectivity issues, consider the following:

> ➤ **Username/password**—Make sure that users are logging on to the network with the correct username/password combination.

> ➤ **Configuration**—It might be necessary to confirm that the network settings on the client computer have not changed.

> ➤ **Account activity**—You need to verify that the user has an active account on the network and that it has the correct permissions set. Log on with a known working account from the client's system, which will allow you to isolate the problem to the computer or the user account.

> ➤ **Physical connections**—You should check to see if a cable has come unplugged from the client's system.

> ➤ **NIC**—To confirm that a card is working, you might need to swap out the card with one that is known to be working.

Troubleshooting Network Printing

Printing is one of the services that network users expect to be working, and it is the administrator's job to make sure that it is available. When trying to get printing back up and running on the network, confirm the following:

> ➤ **Printer online status**—You should confirm that the printer is online and ready to go. If there is a problem with the printer itself, the printer might display error messages on an LCD panel or use LEDs to indicate a problem.

> ➤ **Printer functioning**—Nearly all printers have a test print feature. You can use it to make sure that the printer itself is functioning correctly.

➤ **Printer connectivity**—Verify that the printer is visible to the network. If the printer is connected directly to the network using TCP/IP, for instance, you can `ping` the printer to test for connectivity.

➤ **Client configuration**—Ensure that the computers that are trying to access the printer are configured correctly to use that printer.

➤ **Permissions**—On many operating systems, it is possible to set permissions to allow or deny users access to a printer. You need to verify that the correct permissions have been set.

➤ **Check logs**—Network operating systems log printer activity. Monitoring printer logs can often provide clues as to the source of a problem.

➤ **Driver software**—If you are having problems isolating a printing issue, consider reinstalling or replacing the printer driver.

Troubleshooting Data Access

The inability to access data is not always a result of connectivity errors. If a user is unable to access data, there are a few key areas to verify:

➤ **Proper network login**—Sometimes people use a shortcut or try to access data without being properly logged on to the network. You should verify that users are correctly logged on to the network and that any necessary network drives are connected.

➤ **Permissions**—When you are troubleshooting data access, ensure that the permissions are set correctly.

➤ **Connectivity**—You need to verify that the system that maintains the data is available. You need to confirm that the server is available. What can seem like a problem accessing a file can mask a potentially larger problem such as a disk or server failure.

➤ **Data integrity**—Sometimes data itself can be corrupt. This is the worst-case scenario, and the robust nature of today's file systems ensures that it occurs rarely. This is when you need backups.

➤ **Viruses**—In some cases, viruses might be your problem. You can use a virus-checking program to determine if indeed this is the problem.

Troubleshooting NICs

When NICs are configured correctly and verified to be working, very little goes wrong with them. When you are troubleshooting a NIC, you should consider the following:

➤ **Resource settings**—NICs require specific computer resources in order to operate. After you install a card or add new devices, you should check for device conflicts.

➤ **Speed settings**—If you are not getting the expected speed from the NIC, you should confirm the speed settings and, if applicable, the duplex settings.

➤ **Protocols**—In order for the NIC to work on the network, it must have a valid protocol assigned to it, and all addressing information needs to be in place.

➤ **Faulty card**—Some NICs are faulty when they ship from the manufacturer, and some are damaged through poor handling. To test for this, you can swap the card with one that is known to be working.

Review and Test Yourself

The following sections provide you with the opportunity to review what you learned in this chapter and to test yourself.

The Facts

For the exam, don't forget these important concepts:

➤ `ping` is a command-line utility designed to test connectivity between systems on a TCP/IP-based network.

➤ `ping` the IP address of your local loopback, using the command `ping 127.0.0.1`. If this command is successful, you know that the TCP/IP protocol suite is installed correctly on your system and functioning.

➤ If you cannot `ping` other devices on your local network and you were able to `ping` your local NIC, you might not be connected to the network correctly, or there might be a cable problem on the computer.

➤ Trace route is a TCP/IP utility that is used to track the path a packet takes to reach a remote host and isolate where network problems may be. Trace route functionality can be used on Windows platforms with the `tracert` command, and on Linux, UNIX, and Macintosh platforms with the `traceroute` command.

➤ Trace route reports the amount of time it takes to reach each host in the path. It is a useful tool for isolating bottlenecks in a network.

➤ `arp` is the part of the TCP/IP suite whose function is to resolve IP addresses to MAC addresses.

➤ `arp` operates at the Network layer of the Open Systems Interconnect (OSI) model.

➤ `netstat` is used to view both inbound and outbound TCP/IP network connections.

➤ The `netstat -r` command can be used to display the routing table of the system.

➤ `nbtstat` is used to display protocol and statistical information for NetBIOS over TCP/IP connections.

➤ The `ipconfig` command shows the IP configuration information for all NICs installed within a system.

➤ The `ipconfig/all` command is used to display detailed TCP/IP configuration information.

➤ The `ipconfig /renew` command is used to renew DHCP assigned IP address configurations.

➤ When looking for client connectivity problems using `ipconfig`, ensure that the gateway is correctly set.

➤ The `ifconfig` command is the Linux, Mac and UNIX equivalent of the `ipconfig` command.

➤ `winipcfg` is the Windows 95, Windows 98, and Windows Me equivalent of the `ipconfig` command.

➤ The `nslookup` command is a TCP/IP diagnostic tool that is used to troubleshoot DNS problems. On Linux, UNIX, and Macintosh systems, you can also use the `dig` command for the same purpose.

➤ Visual indicators such as link lights are often the first sign that something is not functioning correctly.

➤ By interpreting the LEDs on network devices, you can isolate and identify a range of connectivity issues.

➤ Troubleshooting remote connectivity involves a range of authentication, protocol configuration, and physical connectivity considerations.

➤ Most client connectivity issues can be solved by a methodical approach to troubleshooting and using commonly available tools and indicators.

➤ Client systems on a network can experience many problems including authentication issues, permission problems, and physical connectivity.

Key Terms

➤ tracert

➤ ping

➤ arp

➤ netstat

➤ nbtstat

➤ ipconfig

➤ ifconfig

➤ winipcfg

➤ nslookup

➤ dig

➤ POTS

➤ DSL

➤ Cable

➤ Wireless

➤ Troubleshooting

➤ Protocols

➤ Authentication

➤ Permissions

Exam Prep Questions

1. Which of these commands would produce the following output?

```
0 Ethernet adapter :
        IP Address. . . . . . . . . : 169.254.196.192
        Subnet Mask . . . . . . . . : 255.255.0.0
        Default Gateway . . . . . . :
1 Ethernet adapter :
        IP Address. . . . . . . . . : 0.0.0.0
        Subnet Mask . . . . . . . . : 0.0.0.0
        Default Gateway . . . . . . :
```

  ❑ A. `ping`
  ❑ B. `tracert`
  ❑ C. `ipconfig /all`
  ❑ D. `ipconfig`

2. You are working as a network administrator for a small organization. You receive a call from one of the company's remote users complaining that he is unable to log on to the network. You decide that you would like him to try and renew the IP configuration information. Which of the following commands would you ask him to use?

  ❑ A. `nbtstat -renew`
  ❑ B. `nbtstat /renew`
  ❑ C. `ipconfig -renew`
  ❑ D. `ipconfig /renew`

3. Which of the following `ping` switches is used to perform a continuous ping?

  ❑ A. `-c`
  ❑ B. `-t`
  ❑ C. `-o`
  ❑ D. `-w`

4. Which of the following commands can be used to show the systems routing table on a Windows Server 2003 system?

  ❑ A. `ping -R`
  ❑ B. `nbtstat -r`
  ❑ C. `netstat -r`
  ❑ D. `tracert -R`

5. You are working to provide telephone support for a local ISP. One of the residential users calls you complaining that he is no longer able to access the Internet. Upon further questioning, you determine that he recently moved the computer within his house. Which of the following connectivity problems might you suspect first?

   ❑ A. Protocol configuration
   ❑ B. DNS settings
   ❑ C. Gateway settings
   ❑ D. Physical cabling

6. When troubleshooting a network connectivity problem, you are able to ping your local loopback, the IP address of your system, and the IP address of another system on your network. However, you cannot ping the default gateway. Which of the following is *not* a valid reason for this problem?

   ❑ A. The default gateway is not operational.
   ❑ B. The IP address of the default gateway is not configured correctly.
   ❑ C. Routing is disabled on your workstation.
   ❑ D. There is no default gateway present.

7. Which of the following commands can be used to purge and reload the remote cache name table on a Windows 2000 Server system?

   ❑ A. nbtstat -R
   ❑ B. nbtstat -n
   ❑ C. nbtstat -r
   ❑ D. nbtstat -S

8. Which utility would produce the following output?

```
6 55 ms 27 ms 42 ms so-1-0-0.XL1.VAN1.NET [152.63.137.130]
7 55 ms 41 ms 28 ms 0.so-7-0-0.TL1.VAN1.NET [152.63.138.74]
8 55 ms 55 ms 55 ms 0.so-2-0-0.TL1.SAC1.NET [152.63.8.1]
9 83 ms 55 ms 55 ms 0.so-7-0-0.XL1.SAC1.NET [152.63.53.249]
10 82 ms 41 ms 55 ms POS6-0.BR5.SAC1.NET [152.63.52.225]
11 55 ms 68 ms 55 ms uu-gw.ip.att.net [192.205.32.125]
12 55 ms 68 ms 69 ms tbr2-p013802.ip.att.net [12.122.11.229]
13 96 ms 69 ms 82 ms tbr1-p012801.ip.att.net [12.122.11.225]
14 82 ms 82 ms 69 ms tbr2-p012402.ip.att.net [12.122.11.221]
```

   ❑ A. nbtstat -R
   ❑ B. netstat -R
   ❑ C. arp -s
   ❑ D. tracert

9. You are trying to access a workstation located on another LAN. The LANs are connected via a router. You are able to access other computers on your own LAN. Which of the following would best help you isolate where the failure is located?

   ❑   A.   `ping` the far side of the router

   ❑   B.   `ping` the near side of the router

   ❑   C.   `tracert` to the workstation on the other side of the router

   ❑   D.   `tracert` to a workstation on your local LAN

10. Which of the following utilities might you use on a Linux system to troubleshoot a name resolution problem? (Choose two.)

   ❑   A.   `dig`

   ❑   B.   `arp`

   ❑   C.   `traceroute`

   ❑   D.   `ipconfig`

Answers to Exam Prep Questions

1. The correct answer is D. Without using any switches, the `ipconfig` command shows the IP address, subnet mask, and default gateway for available adapters. Answer A is incorrect; `ping` is used to test the connectivity between devices and does not produce this output. Answer B is incorrect; `tracert` displays routing information. Answer C is incorrect; the `ipconfig /all` command shows much more of the IP configuration information than the output listed in the question.

2. The correct answer is D. In addition to viewing IP configuration information, `ipconfig` allows you to release and renew the IP configuration. The correct syntax for renewing IP configuration is `ipconfig /renew`. Answers A and B are incorrect. The `nbtstat` command cannot be used to renew the IP configuration from a DHCP server.

3. The correct answer is B. The `ping` command used with the `-t` switch will send out continuous `ping` requests. This is used when troubleshooting and the default four pings are not enough. Answer A and C are incorrect. These switches are not valid for pinging on a Windows system. Answer D is incorrect. The `-w` switch allows you to specify, in milliseconds, the amount of time the system should wait for a reply from the remote host.

4. The correct answer is C. The `netstat -r` command is commonly used by network administrators to show the system's routing table. The `route print` command can also be used to see the current routing table. Answer A is incorrect; the `ping` command is used to test network connectivity, not view TCP/IP configuration information. Answer B is incorrect; the `nbtstat` command displays NetBIOS over TCP/IP-related information. Answer D is incorrect because the `tracert` command is used to track the path between two devices on the network.

5. The correct answer is D. It is not unusual to get support calls after users have attempted to move their systems. When hearing that a system has recently been moved, one of the first places to explore is the physical cabling, verifying that all cables have been securely and correctly attached. Although it might be necessary to confirm settings, such as protocol information, you will likely start with the cabling moving to settings only after verifying correct cabling.

6. The correct answer is C. The routing functionality of the workstation is irrelevant in this scenario. All the other answers are valid reasons for the problem.

7. The correct answer is A. The `nbtstat -R` command purges and reloads the remote cache name table. The `-n` switch displays the local name table, `-r` provides resolution information, and `-s` shows the NetBIOS session table.

8. The correct answer is D. The output is from the Windows 2000 `tracert` command. All the other utilities listed provide different output.

9. The correct answer is C. The `tracert` command is used to trace how far a data packet travels before it cannot go further. By running a `tracert` to a workstation on the other side, you will be able to tell from the output where the transmission failed. Pinging is not as useful in determining where the failure occurred as its output only identifies whether the packet delivery was successful but does not indicate where the failure occurred. Using the `tracert` command on a workstation on the local LAN would not help isolate the problem on the far side of the router.

10. The correct answers are A and C. The `dig` command can be used on a Linux server to perform manual DNS lookups. The `traceroute` command can be used to test connectivity between the client and the DNS server. The `arp` command is used to view the IP address to MAC address resolutions performed by a system. It would not likely be used to troubleshoot a name resolution issue. `ipconfig` is a command associated with Windows operating systems.

Need to Know More?

Bird, Drew and Harwood, Mike. *Network+ Exam Prep 2*. Que Publishing, 2005.

Sloan, Joseph D. *Network Troubleshooting Tools*. O'Reilly System Administration. O'Reilly & Associates, 2001.

Sugano, Alan. *The Real-world Network Troubleshooting Manual: Tools, Techniques, and Scenarios*. Administrator's Advantage Series. Charles River Media, 2004.

Hunt, Craig. *TCP/IP Network Administration, Third Edition*. O'Reilly & Associates, 2002.

Troubleshooting and Supporting the Network

Objectives

4.6 Given a scenario, determine the impact of modifying, adding, or removing network services, for example, DHCP (Dynamic Host Configuration Protocol), DNS (Domain Name Service), and WINS (Windows Internet Name Server) for network resources and users

4.7 Given a troubleshooting scenario involving a network with a particular physical topology (for example, bus, star, mesh, or ring) and including a network diagram, identify the network area affected and the cause of the stated failure

4.8 Given a network troubleshooting scenario involving an infrastructure (for example, wired or wireless) problem, identify the cause of a stated problem (for example, bad media, interference, network hardware, or environment)

4.9 Given a network problem scenario, select an appropriate course of action based on a logical troubleshooting strategy. This strategy can include the following steps:

✓ 1. Identify the symptoms and potential causes.
✓ 2. Identify the affected area.
✓ 3. Establish what has changed.
✓ 4. Select the most probable cause.
✓ 5. Implement an action plan and solution including potential effects.
✓ 6. Test the result.
✓ 7. Identify the results and effects of the solution.
✓ 8. Document the solution and process.

What you need to know

✓ Use troubleshooting steps to isolate and correct a problem
✓ Identify and troubleshoot topology-specific errors
✓ Use troubleshooting techniques to identify and isolate client connectivity errors
✓ Use troubleshooting techniques to identify and isolate network wiring/infrastructure problems
✓ Identify the impact on the network of adding or removing network services

Introduction

Many duties and responsibilities fall under the umbrella of network administration. Of all these, one of the most practiced is that of troubleshooting. No matter how well a network is designed and how many preventative maintenance schedules are in place, troubleshooting will always be necessary. Because of this, network administrators have to develop those troubleshooting skills.

This chapter focuses on all areas of troubleshooting, including troubleshooting best practices and some of the tools and utilities you'll use to assist in the troubleshooting process. To start, we'll look at the impact of modifying network services.

Predicting the Impact of Modifying, Adding, or Removing Network Services

All network services require a certain amount of network resources in order to function. The amount of resources required depends on the exact service being used. Before implementing or removing any service on a network, it is very important to understand the impact that these services can have on the entire network. To provide some idea of the demands various services place on the network, this section outlines some of the most common network services and the impact their addition, modification, or removal might have on the network and clients.

Adding, Modifying, or Removing DHCP

DHCP automatically assigns TCP/IP addressing to computers when they join the network and automatically renews the addresses before they expire. The advantage of using DHCP is the reduced number of addressing errors, which makes network maintenance much easier.

One of the biggest benefits of using DHCP is that the reconfiguration of IP addressing can be performed from a central location, with little or no effect on the clients. In fact, you can reconfigure an entire IP addressing system without the users noticing. As always, a cost is associated with everything good, and with DHCP, the cost is increased network traffic.

You know what the function of DHCP is and the service it provides to the network, but what impact does the DHCP service have on the network itself? Some network services can consume huge amounts of network bandwidth, but DHCP is not one of them. The traffic generated between the DHCP server and the DHCP client is minimal during normal usage periods.

The bulk of the network traffic generated by DHCP occurs during two phases of the DHCP communication process: when the lease of the IP address is initially granted to the client system and when that lease is renewed. The entire DHCP communication process takes less than a second, but if there are a very large number of client systems, the communication process can slow down the network.

For most network environments, the traffic generated by the DHCP service is negligible. For environments in which DHCP traffic is a concern, you can reduce this traffic by increasing the lease duration for the client systems, thereby reducing communication between the DHCP client and the server.

If the DHCP service has to be removed, it can have a significant impact on network users. All client systems require a valid IP address to get onto the network. If DHCP is unavailable, each client system would need to be configured with a static IP address. Because DHCP IP addressing is automatic and does not assign duplicate IP addresses, as sometimes happens with manual entries, DHCP is the preferred method of network IP assignment.

If DHCP is added to a network, all client systems will need to be configured to use DHCP. In a Windows environment, this is as easy as selecting a radio button to use DHCP. If client systems are not configured to use the DHCP server, they will not be able to access the network.

Adding, Modifying, or Removing WINS

WINS is used on Microsoft networks to facilitate communications between computers by resolving NetBIOS names to IP addresses. Each time a computer starts, it registers itself with a WINS server by contacting that server over the network. If that system then needs to contact another device on the network, it can contact the WINS server to get the NetBIOS name resolved to an IP address. If you are thinking about not using WINS, you should know that the alternative is for computers to identify themselves and resolve NetBIOS names to IP addresses via broadcasts. Broadcasts are inefficient because all data is transmitted to every device on the network segment. Broadcasts can be a significant problem for large network segments. Also, if a network has more than one segment, you cannot browse to remote segments because broadcasts are not typically forwarded by routers, which will eliminate this method of resolution.

Because WINS actually replaces the broadcast communication on a network, it has a positive impact on network resources and bandwidth usage. This does not mean that WINS does not generate any network traffic—just that the traffic is more organized and efficient. The amount of network traffic generated by WINS clients to a WINS server is minimal and should not have a negative impact in most network environments.

WINS server information can be entered manually into the TCP/IP configuration on a system, or it can be supplied via DHCP. If the WINS server addresses change and the client configuration is being performed manually, each system needs to be reconfigured with the new WINS server addresses. If you are using DHCP, you need to update only the DHCP scope with the new information.

Removing WINS from a network increases the amount of broadcast traffic and can potentially limit browsing to a single segment unless another method of resolution (such as the use of the statically maintained LMHOSTS file) is in place.

Adding, Modifying, or Removing DNS

The function of DNS is to resolve hostnames to IP addresses. Without such a service, network users would have to identify a remote system by its IP address rather than by its easy-to-remember hostname.

Name resolution can be provided dynamically by a DNS server, or it can be accomplished statically, using the HOSTS file on the client system. If you are using a DNS server, the IP address of the DNS server is required. DNS server addresses can be entered manually, or they can be supplied through a DHCP server.

Identify and Troubleshoot Errors with a Particular Physical Topology

Each of the physical network topologies requires its own troubleshooting strategies and methods. When troubleshooting a network, it is important to know which topology is used as it can greatly impact the procedures used to resolve any problems. This section lists each of the respective physical network topologies and some common troubleshooting strategies.

In one form or another, you can expect to be asked questions regarding troubleshooting the different topologies.

Star Topology

The most common topology used today is the *star topology*. The star topology uses a central connection point such as a hub in which all devices on the network connect. Each device on the network uses its own length of cable, thus allowing devices to be added or removed from the network without disruption to current network users. When troubleshooting a physical star network, consider the following:

➤ The central device, hubs or switches, provides a single point of failure. When troubleshooting a loss of connectivity for several users, it might be a faulty hub. Try placing the cables in a known working hub to confirm.

➤ Hubs and switches provide *light-emitting diodes (LEDs)* that provide information regarding the port status. For instance, by using the LEDs, you can determine whether there is a jabbering network card, whether there is a proper connection to the network device, and whether there are too many collisions on the network.

➤ Each device, printer, or computer connects to a central device using its own length of cable. When troubleshooting a connectivity error in a star network, it might be necessary to verify that the cable works. This can be done by swapping the cable with a known working one or using a cable tester.

➤ Ensure that the patch cables and cables have the correct specifications.

Figure 11.1 shows how a single cable break would affect other client systems on the network.

Ring Topology

Although not as commonly used as it once was, you might find yourself troubleshooting a *ring network*. Most ring networks are *logical rings*, meaning that each computer is logically connected to each other. A *physical ring topology* is a rare find but a *Fiber Distributed Data Interface (FDDI)* is often configured in a physical ring topology. A logical ring topology uses a central connecting device as with a star network called a *multistation access unit (MSAU)*. When troubleshooting either a logical or physical ring topology, consider the following:

➤ A physical ring topology uses a single length of cable interconnecting all computers and forming a loop. If there is a break in the cable, all systems on the network will be unable to access the network.

➤ The MSAU on a logical ring topology represents a single point of failure. If all devices are unable to access the network, it might be that the MSAU is faulty.

➤ Verify that the cabling and connectors have the correct specifications.

➤ All Network Interface Cards (NICs) on the ring network must operate at the same speed.

➤ When connecting MSAUs in a ring network, ensure that the ring in and ring out configuration is properly set.

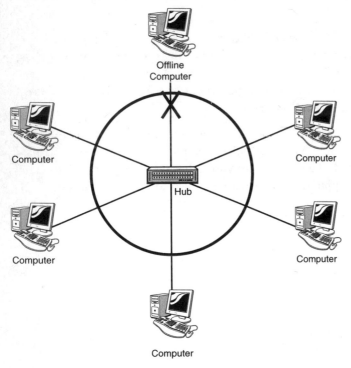

Figure 11.1   Identifying cable breaks in a star network.

Figure 11.2 shows how a single cable break would affect other client systems on a physical ring network.

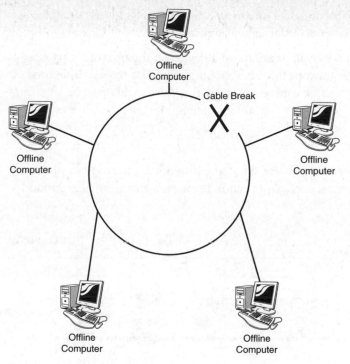

Figure 11.2   Identifying cable breaks in a physical ring network.

Bus Network Errors

Although the bus topology is rarely implemented anymore, enough of them are out there for it to be included in the CompTIA Network+ exam objectives. So if you do not encounter a bus network in the real world, you will most certainly be faced with one on the exam.

Troubleshooting a bus network can be a difficult and frustrating task. The following list contains a few hotspots to be aware of when troubleshooting a bus network:

➤ A bus topology must be continuous. A break in the cable at any point will render the entire segment unusable. If the location of the break in the cable is not apparent, you can check each length of cable systematically from one end to the other to identify the location of the break, or you can use a tool such as a time domain reflectometer, which can be used to locate a break in a cable.

➤ The cable used on a bus network has two distinct physical endpoints. Each of these cable ends requires a *terminator*. Terminators are used to absorb electronic signals so that they are not reflected back on the media, compromising data integrity. A failed or missing terminator will render the entire network segment unusable.

➤ The addition, removal, or failure of a device on the network might prevent the entire network from functioning. Also, the coaxial cable used in a bus network can be damaged very easily. Moving cables in order to add or remove devices can cause cable problems. The T connectors used on bus networks do allow devices to be added and removed without necessarily affecting the network, but care must be taken when doing this.

➤ One end of the bus network should be grounded. Intermittent problems or a high occurrence of errors can indicate poor or insufficient grounding.

Figure 11.3 shows how a single cable break would affect other client systems on a bus network.

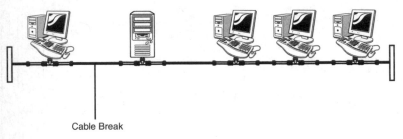

Cable Break

Figure 11.3 Identifying cable breaks in a bus network.

Mesh Network Errors

A *mesh topology* offers high redundancy by providing several paths for data to reach its destination. In a true mesh network, each device on the network is connected to every other device, and if one cable fails, there is another to provide an alternative data path. Although a mesh topology is resilient to failure, the number of connections involved can make a mesh network somewhat tricky to troubleshoot.

When troubleshooting a mesh network, consider the following points:

➤ A mesh topology interconnects all devices on the network, offering the highest level of redundancy of all the topologies. In a pure mesh environment, all devices are directly connected to all other devices. In a hybrid mesh environment, some devices are connected only to certain others in the topology.

➤ Although a mesh topology can accommodate failed links, mechanisms should still be in place so that failed links are detected and reported.

➤ Design and implementation of a true mesh network can be complex and often requires specialized hardware devices.

Mesh networks are so rare that it's unlikely you will be faced with troubleshooting one, but there will likely be questions on the Network+ Exam that focus on mesh networks.

 Most mesh networks are used to connect multiple networks, such as in a WAN scenario, rather than to connect computers in a LAN.

Infrastructure Troubleshooting

No doubt, you will find yourself troubleshooting wiring and infrastructure problems less frequently than you'll troubleshoot client connectivity problems—and thankfully so. Wiring- and infrastructure-related problems can be very difficult to trace, and sometimes a very costly solution is needed to remedy the situation. When troubleshooting these problems, a methodical approach is likely to pay off.

A network infrastructure refers to the physical components that are used to create the network. This includes the media used, switches, routers, bridges, patch panels, hubs and so on.

When troubleshooting the infrastructure it is important to know where these devices are on the network and what they are designed to do. In this section we explore two essential infrastructure components, media and hardware components.

Troubleshooting Network Media

The physical connections used to create the networks are sometimes at the root of a network connectivity error. Troubleshooting wiring involves knowing what wiring your network uses and where it is being used. When troubleshooting network media consider:

Media range (attenuation)—All cables used in networking have certain limitations, in terms of distance. It might be that the network problems are a result of trying to use a cable in an environment or a way for which it was not designed. For example, you might find that a network is connecting two workstations that are 130 meters apart with Category 5 UTP cabling. Category 5 UTP is specified for distances up to 100 meters, so exceeding the maximum cable length can be a potential cause of the problem. The first step in determining the allowable cable distance is to identify the type of cable used. Determining the cable type is often as easy as reading the cable. The cable should be stamped with its type—whether it is, for example, UTP Category 5, RG-58, or something else. Refer to Chapter 2 for more information on network media characteristics.

EMI and crosstalk interference—Copper-based media is subject to the effects of EMI and crosstalk interference. UTP cables are particularly susceptible to EMI caused by devices such as power lines, electric motors, fluorescent lighting and so on. Consider using plenum rated cable in environments where cables are run through areas where EMI may occur. This includes heating ducts, elevator shafts and through ceilings around lighting fixtures. Crosstalk occurs when cables are run in close proximity and the signals from one interfere with the signals on the other. This can be hard to troubleshoot and isolate, so when designing a network ensure that crosstalk preventative measures are taken.

Throughout limitations—A problem with a particular media may be simply that it cannot accommodate the throughout required by the network. This would create network-wide bottlenecks. It may be necessary to update the network media to correct the problem, for instance, upgrading the network backbone to fiber optic media.

Media connectors—Troubleshooting media requires verifying that the connectors are correctly attached. In the case of UTP or coaxial, sometimes it may be necessary to swap out a cable with a known working one to test. For fiber, different types of connectors are used in fiber optic cabling. Before implementing a fiber solution, ensure that the switches and routers used match with the connectors used with the fiber optic cable.

For more information on cabling characteristics and connectors, refer to Chapter 2 "Cabling and Connectors."

Before running a particular type of media, place identification tags at both ends of each cable, which will be helpful while troubleshooting a failed cable.

Troubleshooting Infrastructure Hardware

If you are looking for a challenge, troubleshooting hardware infrastructure problems is for you. It is often not an easy task and usually involves many processes, including baselining and performance monitoring. One of the keys to identifying the failure of a hardware network device is to know what devices are used on a particular network and what each device is designed to do. Some of the common hardware components used in a network infrastructure are shown in Table 11.1.

Table 11.1   Common network hardware components, their function and troubleshooting strategies.

Networking Device Signs	Function	Troubleshooting and Failure
Hubs	Hubs are used with a star network topology and UTP cable to connect multiple systems to a centralized physical device.	Because hubs connect multiple network devices, if many devices are unable to access the network, the hub may have failed. When a hub fails, all devices connected to it will be unavailable to access the network. Additionally, hubs use broadcasts and forward data to all the connected ports increasing network traffic. When network traffic is high and the network is operating slowly, it may be necessary to replace slow hubs.
Switches	Like hubs, switches are used with a star topology to create a central connectivity device.	The inability of several network devices to access the network may indicate a failed switch. If the switch fails, all devices connected to the switch will be unable to access the network. Switches forward data only to the intended recipient allowing them to better manage data than hubs.

(continued)

Table 11.1	Common network hardware components, their function and troubleshooting strategies. *(continued)*	
Networking Device Signs	**Function**	**Troubleshooting and Failure**
Routers	Routers are used to separate broadcast domains and to connect different networks.	If a router fails, network clients will be unable to access remote networks connected by the router. For example, if clients access a remote office through a network router and the router fails, the remote office would be unavailable. Testing router connectivity can be done using utilities such as ping and tracert.
Bridges	Bridges are commonly used to connect network segments within the same network. Bridges manage the flow of traffect between these network segments.	A failed bridge would prevent the flow of traffic between network segments. If communication between network segments has failed, it may be due to a failed bridge.
Wireless Access Points	Wireless access points provide the bridge between the wired and wireless network.	If wireless clients are unable to access the wired network, the WAP may have failed. However, there are many configuration settings to verify first.

For more information on network hardware devices and their function, refer to Chapter 3 "Network Devices."

Troubleshooting a Wireless Infrastructure

Wireless networks do not require physical cable to connect computers; rather, they use wireless media. The benefits of such a configuration are clear—users have remote access to files and resources without the need for physical connections. Wireless networking eliminates cable faults and cable breaks. It does, however, introduce its own considerations such as signal interference and security.

Wireless Signal Quality

Because wireless signals travel through the atmosphere, they are subjected to environmental factors that can weaken data signals. Everything from electrical devices, storms, RF interference, and obstacles such as trees can weaken wireless data signals. Just how weakened the signal becomes depends on many factors; however, all of these elements serve to decrease the power of the wireless signal.

NOTE Wireless signals degrade depending on the construction material used. Signals passing through concrete and steel are particularly weakened.

If you are troubleshooting a wireless connection that has a particularly weak signal, there are a few infrastructure changes that can be done to help increase the power of a signal.

➤ **Antenna**—Perhaps the first and most obvious thing to check is to ensure that the antenna on the wireless access point is positioned for best reception; this will often take a little trial and error to get the placement right. Today's wireless access cards commonly ship with diagnostic software that displays signal strength.

➤ **Device Placement**—One of the factors that can degrade wireless signals is RF interference. Because of this, it is important to try and keep wireless devices away from appliances that output RF noise. This includes devices such as microwaves, certain cordless devices using the same frequency, and electrical devices.

➤ **Network Location**—Although there might be limited choice, as much as possible, it is important to try to reduce the number of obstructions that the signal must pass through. Every obstacle strips a little more power from the signal. The type of material a signal must pass through also can have a significant impact on the signal integrity.

➤ **Boost Signal**—If all else fails, it is possible to purchase devices such as wireless repeaters that can amplify the wireless signal. The device takes the signal and amplifies it so that the signal has greater strength. This will also increase the distance that the client system can be placed from the WAP.

In order to successfully manage the wireless signals, you will need to know the wireless standard that you are using. The standards that are used today specify range distances, RF ranges, and speeds. It might be that the wireless standard is not capable of doing what you need. Table 11.2 highlights the characteristics of common wireless standards.

Table 11.2	Comparing Wireless Standards			
Standard	**Speed**	**Range**	**Frequency**	**Concerns**
802.11a	Up to 54Mbps	25–75 feet	5GHz	Not compatible with 802.11g or 802.11b
802.11b	Up to 11Mbps	Up to 150 feet	2.4GHz	Might conflict with other devices using the 2.4GHz range
802.11g	Up to 54Mbps	Up to 150 feet	2.4GHz	Might conflict with other devices using the 2.4GHz range
Bluetooth	720Kbps	33 feet	2.4GHz	Might conflict with other devices using the 2.4GHz range

As you can see in Table 11.2, the speeds are listed with the "Up to" disclaimer. This is because each standard will decrease the data rate if there is interference. 802.11b wireless link offers speeds up to 11Mbps, but it will automatically back down from 11Mbps to 5.5, 2, and 1Mbps when the radio signal is weak or when interference is detected. 802.11g auto sensing rates are 1, 2, 5.5, 6, 9, 12, 18, 24, 36, 48, and 54 Mbps. Finally, 802.11a provides rates up to 54Mbps, but will automatically back down to rates 48, 36, 24, 18, 12, 9, and 6Mbps.

 Be prepared to answer questions on the specific characteristics of wireless standards on the Network+ exam.

Wireless Channels

RF channels are important parts of wireless communications. A channel is the frequency band used for the wireless communication. Each standard specifies the channels that can be used. The 802.11a standards specifies radio frequencies ranging between 5.15 and 5.875GHz. In contrast, 802.11b and 802.11g standards operate between the 2.4 to 2.497GHz range. As far as channels are concerned, 802.11a has a wider frequency band, allowing more channels and therefore more data throughput. As a result of the wider band,

802.11a supports up to eight nonoverlapping channels. 802.11b/g standards use the smaller band and support only up to three nonoverlapping channels.

It is recommended that the nonoverlapping channels be used for communication. In the United States, 802.11b/g uses 11 channels for data communication as mentioned—three of these, channels 1, 6, and 11, are nonoverlapping channels. Most manufacturers set their default channel to one of the nonoverlapping channels to avoid transmission conflicts. With wireless devices, you have the option of selecting which channel your WLAN operates on in order to avoid interference from other wireless devices that operate in the 2.4GHz frequency range.

When troubleshooting a wireless network, be aware that overlapping channels can disrupt the wireless communications. For example, in many environments, APs are inadvertently placed closely together. Perhaps two access points in separate offices are located next door to each other or between floors. Signal disruption will result if there is channel overlap between the access points. The solution here is to try and move the access point to avoid the problem with the overlap or change channels to one of the other nonoverlapping channels. For example, switch from channel 6 to channel 11.

As far as troubleshooting is concerned, you would typically only change the channel of a wireless device if there is a channel overlap with another device. If a channel must be changed, it must be changed to another nonoverlapping channel.

SSIDs

The Service Set Identifier (SSID) is a configurable client identification that allows clients to communicate to a particular base station. In application, only clients that are configured with the same SSID can communicate with base stations having the same SSID. SSID provides a simple password arrangement between base stations and clients.

As far as troubleshooting is concerned, if a client is not able to access a base station, ensure that both are using the same SSID. Incompatible SSIDs are sometimes found when clients move computers, such as laptops, between different wireless networks. They obtain an SSID from one network and then if the system is not rebooted, the old SSID won't allow communication to a different base station.

WEP Settings

The Wired Equivalent Privacy (WEP) is a security protocol for wireless networks that encrypts transmitted data . WEP is easy to configure with only three possible security options—Off (no security), 64-bit (basic security), and

128-bit (stronger security). WEP is not difficult to crack, and using it reduces performance slightly.

If your network operates with WEP turned off, your system is very open for someone to access your data. Depending on the sensitivity of your data, you can choose between the 64-bit and 128-bit encryption. Although the 128-bit WEP encryption provides greater security, it does so at a performance cost. 64-bit offers less impact on system performance and less security.

As far as troubleshooting is concerned, in order for wireless communication to take place, wireless devices must all use the same WEP setting. Most devices are set to Off by default; if changed, all clients must use the same settings.

Wireless AP Coverage

Like any other network media, APs have a limited transmission distance. This limitation is an important consideration when deciding where an AP should be placed on the network. When troubleshooting a wireless network, pay close attention to the distance that client systems are away from the AP.

When faced with a problem in which client systems cannot consistently access the AP, you could try moving the AP to better cover the area, but then you might disrupt access for users in other areas. So what can be done to troubleshoot AP coverage?

Depending on the network environment, the quick solution might be to throw money at the solution and purchase another access point, cabling, and other hardware, and expand the transmission area through increased hardware. However, there are a few things to try before installing another wireless access point. The following list starts with the least expensive solution to the most expensive.

➤ **Increase transmission power**—Some access points have a setting to adjust the transmission power output. By default, most of these settings will be set to the maximum output; however, it is worth verifying just in case. As a side note, the transmission power can be decreased if trying to reduce the dispersion of radio waves beyond the immediate network. Increasing the power would provide clients stronger data signals and greater transmission distances.

➤ **Relocate the AP**—When wireless client systems suffer from connectivity problems, the solution might be as simple as relocating the WAP to another location. It might be that it is relocated across the room, a few feet, or across the hall. Finding the right location will likely take a little trial and error.

➤ **Adjust or replace antennas**—If the access point distance is not sufficient for some network clients, it might be necessary to replace the default antenna used with both the AP and the client with higher end antennas. Upgrading an antenna can make a big difference in terms of transmission range. Unfortunately, not all WAPs have replaceable antennas.

➤ **Signal amplification**—RF amplifiers add significant distance to wireless signals. An RF amplifier increases the strength and readability of the data transmission. The amplifier provides improvement of both the received and transmitted signals, resulting in an increase in wireless network performance.

➤ **Use a repeater**—Before installing a new AP, you might want to first think about a wireless repeater. When set to the same channel as the AP, the repeater will take the transmission and repeat it. So, the WAP transmission gets to the repeater, and then the repeater duplicates the signal and passes it forward. It is an effective strategy to increase wireless transmission distances.

Troubleshooting Steps and Procedures

Regardless of the problem, effective network troubleshooting follows some specific troubleshooting steps. These steps provide a framework in which to perform the troubleshooting process and, when followed, can reduce the time it takes to isolate and fix a problem. The following sections discuss the common troubleshooting steps and procedures as identified by the CompTIA Network+ objectives. CompTIA lists the troubleshooting steps as follows:

1. Identify the symptoms and potential causes.

2. Identify the affected area.

3. Establish what has changed.

4. Select the most probable cause.

5. Implement an action plan and solution including potential effects.

6. Test the result.

7. Identify the results and effects of the solution.

8. Document the solution and process.

Identify the Symptoms and Potential Causes

The first step in the troubleshooting process is to establish exactly what the symptoms of the problem are. This stage of the troubleshooting process is all about information gathering. To get this information, we need a knowledge of the operating system used, good communication skills, and a little patience. It is very important to get as much information as possible about the problem. You can glean information from three key sources: the computer (in the form of logs and error messages), the computer user experiencing the problem, and your own observation.

Once you have identified the symptoms, you can begin to formulate some of the potential causes of those symptoms.

For the Network+ exam, you do not need to know where error messages are stored on the respective operating systems; you only need to know that the troubleshooting process requires you to read system-generated log errors.

Identifying the Affected Area

Some computer problems are isolated to a single user in a single location; others affect several thousand users spanning multiple locations. Establishing the affected area is an important part of the troubleshooting process, and it will often dictate the strategies you use in resolving the problem.

On the Network+ exam, you might be provided with either a description of a scenario or a description augmented by a network diagram. In either case, you should read the description of the problem carefully, step by step. In most cases, the correct answer is fairly logical and the wrong answers can be identified easily.

Problems that affect many users are often connectivity issues that disable access for many users. Such problems can often be isolated to wiring closets, network devices, and server rooms. The troubleshooting process for problems that are isolated to a single user will often begin and end at that user's workstation. The trail might indeed lead you to the wiring closet or server, but that is not likely where the troubleshooting process would begin. Understanding who is affected by a problem can provide you with the first clues about where the problem exists.

Establishing What Has Changed

Whether there is a problem with a workstation's access to a database or an entire network, keep in mind that they were working at some point. Although many claim that the "computer just stopped working," it is unlikely. Far more likely is that there have been changes to the system or the network that caused the problem. Look for newly installed applications, applied patches or updates, new hardware, a physical move of the computer, or a new username and password. Establishing any recent changes to a system will often lead you in the right direction to isolate and troubleshoot a problem.

In the Network+ exam, avoid discounting a possible answer because it seems too easy. Many of the troubleshooting questions are based on possible real-world scenarios; some of which do have very easy or obvious solutions.

Selecting the Most Probable Cause of the Problem

There can be many different causes for a single problem on a network, but with appropriate information gathering, it is possible to eliminate many of them. When looking for a probable cause, it is often best to look at the easiest solution first and then work from there. Even in the most complex of network designs, the easiest solution is often the right one. For instance, if a single user cannot log on to a network, it is best to confirm network settings before replacing the NIC. Remember, though, that at this point, you are only trying to determine the most probable cause, and your first guess might, in fact, be incorrect. It might take a few tries to determine the correct cause of the problem.

Implement an Action Plan and Solution Including Potential Effects

After identifying a cause, but before implementing a solution, you should develop a plan for the solution. This is particularly a concern for server systems in which taking the server offline is a difficult and undesirable prospect. After identifying the cause of a problem on the server, it is absolutely necessary to plan for the solution. The plan must include details around when the server or network should be taken offline and for how long, what support services are in place, and who will be involved in correcting the problem.

Planning is a very important part of the whole troubleshooting process and can involve formal or informal written procedures. Those who do not have experience troubleshooting servers might be wondering about all the formality, but this attention to detail ensures the least amount of network or server downtime and the maximum data availability.

With the plan in place, you should be ready to implement a solution—that is, apply the patch, replace the hardware, plug in a cable, or implement some other solution. In an ideal world, your first solution would fix the problem, although unfortunately this is not always the case. If your first solution does not fix the problem, you will need to retrace your steps and start again.

It is important that you attempt only one solution at a time. Trying several solutions at once can make it very unclear which one actually corrected the problem.

You are likely to have questions on the Network+ exam that require you to identify the order in which the troubleshooting steps should be performed.

Testing the Results

After the corrective change has been made to the server, network, or workstation, it is necessary to test the results—never assume. This is when you find out if you were right and the remedy you applied actually worked. Don't forget that first impressions can be deceiving, and a fix that *seems* to work on first inspection might not actually have corrected the problem.

The testing process is not always as easy as it sounds. If you are testing a connectivity problem, it is not difficult to ascertain whether your solution was successful. However, changes made to an application or to databases you are unfamiliar with are much more difficult to test. It might be necessary to have people who are familiar with the database or application run the tests with you in attendance.

Identify the Results and Effects of the Solution

Sometimes, you will apply a fix that corrects one problem but creates another problem. Many such circumstances are hard to predict—but not always. For instance, you might add a new network application, but the application requires more bandwidth than your current network infrastructure can support. The result would be that overall network performance would be compromised.

Everything done to a network can have a ripple effect and negatively affect another area of the network. Actions such as adding clients, replacing hubs, and adding applications can all have unforeseen results. It is very difficult to always know how the changes you make to a network are going to affect the network's functioning. The safest thing to do is assume that the changes you make are going to affect the network in some way and realize that you just have to figure out how. This is when you might need to think outside the box and try to predict possible outcomes.

Documenting the Solution

Although it is often neglected in the troubleshooting process, documentation is as important as any of the other troubleshooting procedures. Documenting a solution involves keeping a record of all the steps taken during the fix—not necessarily just the solution.

For the documentation to be of use to other network administrators in the future, it must include several key pieces of information. When documenting a procedure, you should include the following information:

➤ **Date**—When was the solution implemented? It is important to know the date because if problems occur after your changes, knowing the date of your fix makes it easier to determine whether your changes caused the problems.

➤ **Why**—Although it is obvious when a problem is being fixed why it is being done, a few weeks later, it might become less clear why that solution was needed. Documenting why the fix was made is important because if the same problem appears on another system, you can use this information to reduce time finding the solution.

➤ **What**—The successful fix should be detailed, along with information about any changes to the configuration of the system or network that were made to achieve the fix. Additional information should include version numbers for software patches or firmware, as appropriate.

➤ **Results**—Many administrators choose to include information on both successes and failures. The documentation of failures might prevent you from going down the same road twice, and the documentation of successful solutions can reduce the time it takes to get a system or network up and running.

➤ **Who**—It might be that information is left out of the documentation or someone simply wants to ask a few questions about a solution. In both cases, if the name of the person who made a fix is in the documentation, he or she can easily be tracked down. Of course, this is more of a concern in environments in which there are a number of IT staff or if system repairs are performed by contractors instead of actual company employees.

Review and Test Yourself

The following sections provide you with the opportunity to review what you learned in this chapter and to test yourself.

The Facts

For the exam, don't forget these important concepts:

➤ When presented with a troubleshooting scenario, consider the following procedure:

1. Identify the symptoms and potential causes.

2. Identify the affected area.

3. Establish what has changed.

4. Select the most probable cause.

5. Implement an action plan and solution including potential effects.

6. Test the result.

7. Identify the results and effects of the solution.

8. Document the solution and process.

➤ The central device, hubs or switches, provides a single point of failure.

➤ Hubs and switches provide LEDs that provide information regarding the port status.

➤ A physical ring topology uses a single length of cable interconnecting all computers and forming a loop. If there is a break in the cable, all systems on the network will be unable to access the network.

➤ The MSAU on a logical ring topology represents a single point of failure. If all devices are unable to access the network, it might be that the MSAU is faulty.

➤ Verify that the cabling and connectors meet the correct specifications.

➤ All NICs on the ring network must operate at the same speed.

➤ When connecting MSAUs in a ring network, ensure that the ring in and ring out configuration is properly set.

➤ A bus topology must be continuous. A break in the cable at any point will render the entire segment unusable.

➤ The cable used on a bus network has two distinct physical endpoints.

➤ The addition, removal, or failure of a device on the network might prevent the entire network from functioning.

➤ Some types of wireless communications require a point-to-point direct line-of-sight connection. If something is blocking this line of sight such as a building, the transmissions might fail.

Key Terms

➤ Topology

➤ Bus

➤ Star

➤ Ring

➤ Mesh

➤ Wireless

➤ Protocol

➤ Authentication

➤ Media

➤ Interference

➤ Attenuation

➤ EMI

➤ Segment

➤ NetBEUI

➤ Hub

➤ Switch

➤ MSAU

➤ Termination

➤ SSID

➤ WEP

➤ AP

Exam Prep Questions

1. Which of the following should you consider when troubleshooting wiring problems? (Choose the three best answers.)

   ❏ A. The distance between devices
   ❏ B. Interference
   ❏ C. Atmospheric conditions
   ❏ D. Connectors

2. A user calls you complaining that he is unable to access an application that he uses for accounting. The application runs on the local computer, but the data files are stored on a remote Windows 2000 file server. The network uses TCP/IP and a DHCP server. What is your next step in the troubleshooting process?

   ❏ A. Check the server logs.
   ❏ B. Verify that the user is logged on correctly.
   ❏ C. Log on to the system using the administration account.
   ❏ D. Gather more information from the user.

3. You have just configured a wireless connection using the Bluetooth standard. At what speed does Bluetooth operate?

   ❏ A. 350Mbps
   ❏ B. 720Kbps
   ❏ C. 200Kbps
   ❏ D. 11Mbps

4. You are troubleshooting a problem with a bus topology network. Users are reporting that they are sometimes unable to access the network, but it is fine at other times. Which of the following might you consider? (Choose the two best answers.)

   ❏ A. Faulty hubs or switch
   ❏ B. Improper or faulty termination
   ❏ C. Improper grounding
   ❏ D. Cable lengths in excess of 100 meters

5. Which of the following technologies provides simple password arrangement between wireless base stations and clients.

   ❏ A. WEP
   ❏ B. SSID
   ❏ C. PPP
   ❏ D. PPTP

6. You have just purchased a new wireless access point that uses no WEP security by default. You change the security settings to use 128-bit encryption. How must the client systems be configured?

   ❑ A. All client systems must be set to 128-bit encryption.

   ❑ B. The client system will inherit security settings from the WEP.

   ❑ C. WEP does not support 128-bit encryption.

   ❑ D. The client WEP settings have to be set to 'auto detect.'

7. You are troubleshooting a network problem. The network is a star topology. There are four segments on the network: sales, marketing, admin, and research. Several users from the admin department call you reporting problems accessing the server. Where are you most likely to look for the source of the problem?

   ❑ A. The users' workstations

   ❑ B. The server

   ❑ C. The switch that services the admin segment

   ❑ D. The switch that services the sales segment

8. You are adding a new system to a network that uses a physical ring topology. Which of the following statements is true?

   ❑ A. All network users will not be affected by the addition of the new system.

   ❑ B. The network will be unavailable while the new system is added.

   ❑ C. As long as there is a port available in the MSAU, network users will not be disrupted.

   ❑ D. The MSAU will need to be powered down during the installation, affecting only the users connected to that particular MSAU.

9. A user calls to inform you that she is unable to print. Upon questioning her, you determine that the user has just been moved from the second floor to the third floor. The user connects to the printer via a wireless router on the first floor. You need to allow the user to print but do not want to purchase another WAP or disrupt other wireless users. Which of the following might you do?

   ❑ A. Move the WAP to allow the client system to access the network and therefore the printer.

   ❑ B. Search for RF interference on the 2.4GHz range.

   ❑ C. Change the channel.

   ❑ D. Configure an RF repeater to forward the wireless communications.

10. Which of the following wireless standards specifies an RF of 5Ghz?

   ❑ A. 802.11a

   ❑ B. 802.11b

   ❑ C. 802.11g

   ❑ D. 802.11t

Answers to Exam Prep Questions

1. The correct answers are A, B, and D. When you're troubleshooting a wiring problem, you should consider the distance between devices, interference such as crosstalk and EMI, and the connection points. Answer C is not correct because bound media (that is, cables) are not affected by atmospheric conditions.

2. The correct answer is D. Before implementing a solution to a problem, it is a troubleshooting best practice to first identify what has changed. In this scenario, the administrator would need to gather more information from the user to help isolate the problem and determine why he cannot access the accounting program. Although all of the answers provided can also be performed, they would typically be done after gathering more information from the user.

3. The correct answer is B. Bluetooth is a wireless standard commonly used to interconnect peripheral devices to the computer system. Bluetooth operates at 720Kbps.

4. The correct answers are B and C. A bus network must have a terminator at each physical end of the bus. It must also be grounded at one end. Improper grounding or faulty termination can lead to random network problems such as those described. Answer A is not correct because 10BASE-2 networks do not use hubs or switches. 10BASE-2 has a maximum cable length of 185 meters; therefore, answer D is not valid either.

5. The correct answer is B. The Service Set Identifier is a name assigned to a wireless Wi-Fi network. All devices connected to an AP must use the same SSID name, which is a text string up to 32 bytes long, in order to communicate.

6. The correct answer is A. On a wireless connection between an access point and the client, they must be configured to use the same WEP security settings. In this case, they must both be configured to use 128-bit encryption.

7. The correct answer is C. In this scenario, the common denominator is that all of the users reporting a problem are connected to the same network switch. Therefore, this would be the first place to look for a problem. Because there is more than one user with a problem, looking at their workstations is not the best troubleshooting step. Because you have not received any other calls from other departments, it is unlikely

that there is a problem with the server. Because no users from the sales dept. have reported a problem, there is unlikely to be a problem with the sales section of the network.

8. The correct answer is B. A physical ring topology uses a length of cable to form the ring function. A single break in this cable will take the entire network offline. To add a new system to a physical ring network, the ring must be broken. Therefore, the addition of the new client system will affect all network users.

9. The correct answer is D. By the description, it sounds like the client has moved beyond the reach of the WAP. To try to accommodate the client, an RF repeater could be used to duplicate and forward the wireless signal. It would not be wise to move the wireless access point, as the move might put it out of reach for other network users.

10. The correct answer is A. The 802.11a wireless standard uses the 5GHz frequency range. 802.11b/g uses the 2.4GHz range.

Need to Know More?

Bird, Drew and Harwood, Mike. *Network+ Prep.* Que Publishing, 2004.

Habraken, Joe. *Absolute Beginner's Guide to Networking, Fourth Edition.* Que Publishing, 2003.

Davis, Harold. *Absolute Beginner's Guide to Wi-Fi Wireless Networking.* Que Publishing, 2004.

12

Practice Exam 1

This exam consists of 72 questions that reflect the material covered in this book. The questions are representative of the types of questions you should expect to see on the Network+ exam; however, they are not intended to match exactly what is on the exam.

Some of the questions require that you deduce the best possible answer. Often, you are asked to identify the best course of action to take in a given situation. You must read the questions carefully and thoroughly before you attempt to answer them. It is strongly recommended that you treat this exam as if it were the actual exam. When you take it, time yourself, read carefully, and answer all the questions to the best of your ability.

The answers to all the questions appear in Chapter 13, "Answers to Practice Exam 1." Check your letter answers against those in Chapter 13, and then read the explanations provided. You might also want to return to the chapters in the book to review the material associated with any incorrect answers.

1. Which of the following devices operates at the Network layer of the OSI model?

   ⊖ A. WAP
   ○ B. Switch
   ○ C. Hub
   ○ D. Router

2. A client on your network has had no problem accessing the wireless network, but recently the client moved to a new office. Since the move, she has only intermittent network access. Which of the following is most likely the cause of the problem?

   ○ A. SSID on the client is misconfigured.
   ○ B. The client system has moved too far from the AP.
   ○ C. WEP settings are incorrect.
   ○ D. The AP is using an omni-directional antenna.

3. You are a network administrator managing a midsized network that uses a NetWare print server, a Windows application server, and a Linux firewall server. One of your servers loses network connectivity; you type `ifconfig` at the command line to determine whether the server has a valid IP address. Which server has lost connectivity?

   ○ A. The firewall server.
   ○ B. The print server.
   ○ C. The application server.
   ○ D. `ifconfig` is not a valid command on any of these platforms.

4. You are managing a network that uses both a UNIX server and a Windows 2000 server. Which of the following protocols can you use to transfer files between the two servers?

   ○ A. Telnet
   ○ B. PPP
   ○ C. FTP
   ○ D. PPTP

5. You have been called by a user who complains that access to a web page is very slow. What utility can you use to find the bottleneck?

   ○ A. `ping`
   ○ B. Telnet
   ○ C. `tracert`
   ○ D. `nbtstat`

6. During a busy administrative week, you install a new virus suite in your network of 55 computers, a new RAID array in one of the servers, and a new office suite on 25 of the computer systems. After all the updates, you are experiencing system errors throughout the entire network. Which of the following would you do to help isolate the problem?

   ○ A. Disable the RAID array
   ○ B. Uninstall the office suite
   ○ C. Check the virus suite vendor's website for system patches or service packs
   ○ D. Reinstall the virus software

7. What utility would you use to check the IP configuration on a Windows XP system?

   ○ A. netstat
   ○ B. winipcfg
   ○ C. ping
   ○ D. ipconfig

8. Which of the following services or protocols use SSH technology to provide additional security to communications? (Choose two).

   ○ A. SCP
   ○ B. SFTP
   ○ C. SNMP
   ○ D. SMTP

9. Which of the following backup methods clear the archive bit? (Choose the two best answers.)

   ○ A. Differential
   ○ B. Sequential
   ○ C. Full
   ○ D. Incremental

10. You are troubleshooting a server connectivity problem on your network—a Windows XP Professional system is having trouble connecting to a Windows 2000 Server. Which of the following commands would you use to display per-protocol statistics on the workstation system?

    ○ A. arp -a
    ○ B. arp -A
    ○ C. nbtstat -s
    ○ D. nbtstat -S
    ○ E. netstat -s

11. You are working as a network administrator on a UNIX system. The system uses dynamic name resolution. What is used to dynamically resolve a hostname on a UNIX server?

○ A. IPX

○ B. ARP

○ C. DNS

○ D. LMHOSTS

12. During the night, one of your servers powers down. Upon reboot, print services do not load. Which of the following would be the first step in the troubleshooting process?

○ A. Examine the server log files

○ B. Reboot the server

○ C. Reinstall the printer

○ D. Reinstall the printer software

13. Which of the following standards uses UTP cable?

○ A. 100BaseTX

○ B. 10BaseFL

○ C. 100BaseUX

○ D. 10Base2

14. Which of the following utilities can be used to view the current protocol connections on a Windows system?

○ A. `ping`

○ B. `netstat`

○ C. Telnet

○ D. `tracert`

15. Which of the following statements about the 10Mbps 802.3 network standards is incorrect?

○ A. There are 10Mbps networking standards for both UTP and fiber-optic cable.

○ B. The 802.3 10Mbps network standards use a logical bus topology.

○ C. Irrespective of the type of cable, the maximum length of a 10Mbps network segment is 185 meters.

○ D. 10Mbps networking standards use a CSMA/CD media access method.

16. Which of the following are connectionless protocols? (Choose the two best answers.)

○ A. TCP

○ B. SPX

○ C. IPX

○ D. UDP

17. Which of the following networking standards specifies a maximum segment length of 100 meters?

   ○ A. 10Base2
   ○ B. 10BaseFL
   ○ C. 10BaseYX
   ○ D. 10BaseT

18. After several passwords have been compromised in your organization, you have been asked to implement a network-wide password policy. Which of the following represents the most practical and secure password policy?

   ○ A. Daily password changes
   ○ B. Weekly password changes
   ○ C. Monthly password changes
   ○ D. Password changes only after an account has been compromised

19. You are experiencing a problem with a workstation and want to `ping` the local loopback. Which of the following are valid ways to check your local TCP/IP configuration? (Choose the two best answers.)

   ○ A. `ping host`
   ○ B. `ping localhost`
   ○ C. `ping 127.0.0.1`
   ○ D. `ping 127.0.0.0`

20. Which of the following network devices operates at the physical layer of the OSI model?

   ○ A. Router
   ○ B. Hub
   ○ C. Bridge
   ○ D. NIC

21. You have been asked to implement a RAID solution on one of your company's servers. You have two hard disks and two hard disk controllers. Which of the following RAID levels could you implement? (Choose the three best answers.)

   ○ A. RAID 0
   ○ B. RAID 1
   ○ C. Disk duplexing
   ○ D. RAID 10
   ○ E. RAID 5

22. Which of the following represents a Class B IP address?

   ○ A. `191.23.21.54`
   ○ B. `125.123.123.2`
   ○ C. `24.67.118.67`
   ○ D. `255.255.255.0`

23. What utility would produce the following output?

```
Proto  Local Address        Foreign Address              State
TCP    laptop:1028          LAPTOP:0                     LISTENING
TCP    laptop:1031          LAPTOP:0                     LISTENING
TCP    laptop:1093          LAPTOP:0                     LISTENING
TCP    laptop:50000         LAPTOP:0                     LISTENING
TCP    laptop:5000          LAPTOP:0                     LISTENING
TCP    laptop:1031          n218.audiogalaxy.com:ftp  ESTABLISHED
TCP    laptop:1319          h24-67-184-65.ok.shawcable.net:nbsess
```

   ○ A. netstat
   ○ B. nbtstat
   ○ C. ping
   ○ D. tracert -R

24. You have been called in to troubleshoot a problem with a newly installed email application. Internal users are able to communicate with each other via email, but neither incoming nor outgoing Internet email is working. You suspect a problem with the port-blocking configuration of the firewall system that protects the Internet connection. Which of the following ports would you allow to cure the problems with the email? (Choose the two best answers.)

   ○ A. 20
   ○ B. 25
   ○ C. 80
   ○ D. 110
   ○ E. 443

25. What is the default subnet mask for a Class B network?

   ○ A. 255.255.255.224
   ○ B. 255.255.255.0
   ○ C. 127.0.0.1
   ○ D. 255.255.0.0

26. At which OSI layer does TCP operate?

   ○ A. Network
   ○ B. Transport
   ○ C. Session
   ○ D. Presentation

27. What is the basic purpose of a firewall system?

   ○ A. It provides a single point of access to the Internet.
   ○ B. It caches commonly used web pages, thereby reducing the bandwidth demands on an Internet connection.
   ○ C. It allows hostnames to be resolved to IP addresses.
   ○ D. It protects one network from another by acting as an intermediary system.

28. Email and FTP work at which layer of the OSI model?

    ○ A. Application
    ○ B. Session
    ○ C. Presentation
    ○ D. User

29. You are the administrator for a small network with a single server. A user calls to report that he is experiencing problems logging on to the network. He is sure that the tree name and context are correct, but is not sure that he has the correct password. Which of the following operating systems could the server on your network be running? (Choose all that apply.)

    ○ A. Novell Netware 5
    ○ B. Novell Netware 3.11
    ○ C. Novell Netware 6
    ○ D. Novell Netware 4.1

30. While reviewing the security logs for your server, you notice that a user on the Internet has attempted to access your internal mail server. Although it appears that the user's attempts were unsuccessful, you are very concerned about the possibility that your systems might be compromised. Which of the following solutions are you most likely to implement?

    ○ A. A more secure password policy
    ○ B. A firewall system at the connection point to the Internet
    ○ C. File-level encryption
    ○ D. Kerberos authentication

31. Which of the following pieces of information is not likely to be supplied via DHCP?

    ○ A. IP address
    ○ B. NetBIOS computer name
    ○ C. Subnet mask
    ○ D. Default gateway

32. While troubleshooting a network connectivity problem, you notice that the network card in your system is operating at 10Mbps in half-duplex mode. At what speed is the network link operating?

    ○ A. 2.5Mbps
    ○ B. 5Mbps
    ○ C. 10Mbps
    ○ D. 11Mbps

33. Which of the following is a valid IPv6 address?

   ○ A. `42DE:7E55:63F2:21AA:CBD4:D773`

   ○ B. `42CD:7E55:63F2:21GA:CBD4:D773:CC21:554F`

   ○ C. `42DE:7E55:63F2:21AA`

   ○ D. `42DE:7E55:63F2:21AA:CBD4:D773:CC21:554F`

34. While troubleshooting a network connectivity problem on a Windows Server 2003 system, you need to view a list of the IP addresses that have been resolved to MAC addresses. Which of the following commands would you use to do this?

   ○ A. `arp -a`

   ○ B. `nbtstat -a`

   ○ C. `arp -d`

   ○ D. `arp -s`

35. Which of the following statements best describes RAID 5?

   ○ A. A RAID 5 array consists of at least two drives. Parity information is written across both drives to provide fault tolerance.

   ○ B. A RAID 5 array consists of at least three drives and distributes parity information across all the drives in the array.

   ○ C. A RAID 5 array consists of at least three drives and stores the parity information on a single drive.

   ○ D. A RAID 5 array consists of at least four drives. The first and last drives in the array are used to store parity information.

36. Which of the following IEEE specifications does CSMA/CD relate to?

   ○ A. 802.11b

   ○ B. 802.2

   ○ C. 802.5

   ○ D. 802.3

37. While you are troubleshooting a sporadic network connectivity problem on a Windows XP Professional system, a fellow technician suggests that you run the `ping -t` command. What is the purpose of this command?

   ○ A. It shows the route taken by a packet to reach the destination host.

   ○ B. It shows the time, in seconds, that the packet takes to reach the destination.

   ○ C. It allows the number of `ping` messages to be specific.

   ○ D. It `ping`s the remote host continually until it is stopped.

38. Which of the following IEEE wireless standards uses the 5GHz RF range?

   ○ A. 802.11g

   ○ B. Infrared

   ○ C. 802.11a

   ○ D. 802.11b

39. What type of physical topology is shown in the following diagram?

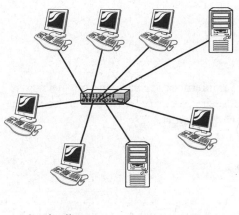

- ○ A. Star
- ○ B. Ring
- ○ C. Bus
- ○ D. Mesh

40. A remote user calls you to report a problem she is having connecting to the corporate network over her DSL connection. The user is able to connect to the Internet and browse web pages, but she can't connect to the corporate remote access gateway. Which of the following troubleshooting steps would you perform first?

- ○ A. Check the corporate remote access gateway to see if it is running and operating correctly
- ○ B. Have the user reboot her system
- ○ C. Have the user reconfigure the IP address on her system to one of the address ranges used on the internal corporate network, and then try again
- ○ D. Have the user power cycle the DSL modem and try again

41. You have installed a Web-based database system on your PC so that you can enter troubleshooting information and retrieve it from any location on the network. The IP address of your system is 192.168.1.164. You are not overly concerned about security, but as a basic measure, you allocate the Web server application a port number of 9191 rather than the default port of 80. Assuming that you are working from another system on the network, what would you type into the address bar of a Web browser to access the database?

- ○ A. http://192.168.1.164.9191
- ○ B. http://192.168.1.164/9191
- ○ C. http://192.168.1.164//9191
- ○ D. http://192.168.1.164:9191

42. Which of the following IEEE standards has the highest maximum transmissions speeds?

   ○ A. 802.3ae
   ○ B. 802.3xr
   ○ C. 802.3z
   ○ D. 802.3u

43. Your manager has asked you to implement security on your peer-to-peer network. Which of the following security models offers the highest level of security for this type of network?

   ○ A. Share level
   ○ B. User level
   ○ C. Password level
   ○ D. Layered

44. You are working on a Linux system and are having problems pinging a remote system by its hostname. DNS resolution is not configured for the system. What file might you look in to begin troubleshooting the resolution problem?

   ○ A. RESOLV
   ○ B. STATICDNS
   ○ C. PASSWD
   ○ D. HOSTS

45. You are tasked with specifying a way to connect two buildings across a parking lot. The distance between the two buildings is 78 meters. An underground wiring duct exists between the two buildings, although there are concerns about using it because it also houses high-voltage electrical cables. The budget for the project is very tight, but your manager still wants you to specify the most suitable solution. Which of the following cable types would you recommend?

   ○ A. Fiber-optic
   ○ B. UTP
   ○ C. Thin coax
   ○ D. STP

46. While installing a new Windows XP Professional system, you are offered a choice of file system with which to format the disk. If you want to use both file and share level permissions for data security, which of the file systems should you choose?

   ○ A. FAT
   ○ B. FAT32
   ○ C. NTFS
   ○ D. EXT2

47. A user calls to inform you that she can't access the Internet from her system. When you visit the user, you run the `ipconfig /all` utility and see the following information. What is the most likely reason the user is having problems accessing the Internet?

```
C:\>ipconfig /all

Windows 2000 IP Configuration
        Host Name . . . . . . . . . . . . : LAPTOP
        Primary DNS Suffix  . . . . . . . :
        Node Type . . . . . . . . . . . . : Broadcast
        IP Routing Enabled. . . . . . . . : No
        WINS Proxy Enabled. . . . . . . . : No

Ethernet adapter Local Area Connection:
        Connection-specific DNS Suffix  . :
        Description . . . . . . . . . . . : Intel 8255x-based PCI
Ethernet
        Physical Address. . . . . . . . . : 00 D0 59 09 07 51
        DHCP Enabled. . . . . . . . . . . : No
        IP Address. . . . . . . . . . . . : 192.168.2.1
        Subnet Mask . . . . . . . . . . . : 255.255.255.0
        Default Gateway . . . . . . . . . :
        DNS Servers . . . . . . . . . . . : 192.168.2.10
                                            192.168.2.20
```

   ○ A. The system is on a different subnet from the DNS servers.
   ○ B. DHCP is not enabled.
   ○ C. The subnet mask is incorrect.
   ○ D. The default gateway setting is not configured.

48. Your ISP account manager suggests that it might be appropriate for you to install a DNS server internally. Which of the following functions does the DNS server provide?

   ○ A. It performs network address translation services.
   ○ B. It streamlines the resolution of NetBIOS names to IP addresses.
   ○ C. It allows some hostname-to-IP address resolutions to occur internally.
   ○ D. It allows users to retrieve Internet web pages more quickly.

49. Which of the following is not one of the private address ranges?

   ○ A. 192.168.x.x
   ○ B. 10.x.x.x
   ○ C. 172.16.x.x
   ○ D. 224.181.x.x

50. You are the administrator for a network with two Windows Server 2003 systems, one Linux server, and 245 Windows XP Professional systems. Under what circumstances are you most likely to install Samba on the Linux server?

   ○ A. If one or two users with Windows XP Professional systems want to copy files to and from the Linux server

   ○ B. If a large number of users with Windows XP Professional systems want to use the Linux server as a file or print server

   ○ C. If you want to implement a network management system that will allow the Linux server to receive trap messages from the Windows servers

   ○ D. If you want to automate the allocation of IP addresses to all of the Windows XP Professional systems on the network

51. If you contacted IANA, what would you most likely be trying to do?

   ○ A. Get a new telephone number
   ○ B. Get an IP address to connect a system to a public network
   ○ C. Get an Internet domain name reassigned
   ○ D. Get an IP address to connect a system to a private network

52. Which of the following technologies can be implemented on a switch to create multiple separate logical networks?

   ○ A. Proxy
   ○ B. Subnet masking
   ○ C. NAS
   ○ D. VLAN

53. Which of the following protocols are responsible for network addressing? (Choose the two best answers.)

   ○ A. IP
   ○ B. SPX
   ○ C. IPX
   ○ D. TCP

54. You are upgrading the antenna on your wireless network. You need to purchase an antenna that provides a 360-degree dispersed wave pattern. Which of the following antenna types would you select?

   ○ A. Omni-dispersed antenna
   ○ B. Directional-dispersed antenna
   ○ C. Directional antenna
   ○ D. Omni-directional antenna

55. What protocol is used by systems within a multicast group to communicate registration information with each other?

   ○ A. ICMP
   ○ B. IGMP
   ○ C. NNTP
   ○ D. LDAP

56. Which of the following connectors would you use when working with fiber-optic cable? (Choose the two best answers.)

   ○ A. RJ-11
   ○ B. SC
   ○ C. RJ-45
   ○ D. ST
   ○ E. BNC

57. You are instructed by your manager to procure a cable with a Type A connector on one end, and a Type B connector on the other. What kind of interface are you most likely to be dealing with?

   ○ A. FireWire
   ○ B. USB
   ○ C. RJ-11
   ○ D. Fiber Optic

58. You are the network administrator for a Token Ring network. A NIC in a system fails, and you replace it with a new one. However, the system is still unable to connect to the network. What is the most likely cause of the problem?

   ○ A. The NIC is set to the wrong ring speed.
   ○ B. The NIC is a 100Mbps card, and the ring is configured for only 10Mbps.
   ○ C. The NIC is set to full-duplex, and the ring is running at only half-duplex.
   ○ D. The NIC is faulty.

59. You have enabled HTTPS because of concerns about the security of your Web server application, which runs on a Web server system in the DMZ of your corporate network. However, remote users are now unable to connect to the application. Which of the following is the most likely reason for the problem?

   ○ A. Port 80 is being blocked on the corporate firewall.
   ○ B. Port 443 is being blocked on the corporate firewall.
   ○ C. Remote users need to enable HTTPS support in their Web browsers.
   ○ D. Port 110 is being blocked on the corporate firewall.

60. Which of the following is a valid Class A IP address?

   ○ A. 124.254.254.254
   ○ B. 127.0.0.1
   ○ C. 128.16.200.12
   ○ D. 131.17.25.200

61. Which of the following wireless technologies provides limited transmission distance and is used primarily for personal area networking and cable replacement? (Select two.)

   ○ A. IrDA
   ○ B. 802.11a
   ○ C. Bluetooth
   ○ D. Ethernet wireless

62. You are the administrator for a network with two Windows 2000 server systems and 40 Windows XP Professional systems. One morning, three users call to report that they are having problems accessing either of the Windows servers. Upon investigation, you determine that the DHCP server application running on one of the servers has crashed and that the three systems are using addresses assigned via APIPA. All other systems, which were started before the DHCP server application crashed, are functioning correctly. Which of the following statements about the situation is correct? (Choose two.)

   ○ A. Systems with an APIPA assigned address will be able to communicate with each other.
   ○ B. Systems with an APIPA assigned address will be able to talk to other systems that have an IP address from the DHCP server.
   ○ C. Systems with an APIPA assigned address will not be able to access the Internet.
   ○ D. Each system with an APIPA assigned address will not be able to communicate with any other systems on the network.

63. Which of the following protocols are parts of the TCP/IP protocol suite? (Choose the three best answers.)

   ○ A. AFP
   ○ B. FTP
   ○ C. DHCP
   ○ D. HTTP
   ○ E. NCP

64. You are attempting to configure a client's email program. The user can receive mail but is unable to send any. In the mail server configuration screen of the mail application, you notice that the Type of Outgoing Mail Server field is blank. This explains why the client is unable to send mail. Which of the following protocols are you most likely to enter as a value in the Type of Outgoing Mail Server field?

   O A. NMP
   O B. POP3
   O C. SMTP
   O D. IMAP

65. Which of the following is a configurable client identification setting used to differentiate one WLAN from another?

   O A. SID
   O B. WEP
   O C. SSID
   O D. Wireless channel

66. Which of the following is a valid MAC address?

   O A. `00:D0:59:09:07:51`
   O B. `00:D0:59`
   O C. `192.168.2.1`
   O D. `00FE:56FE:230F:CDA2:00EB:32EC`
   O E. `00:DG:59:09:07:51`

67. Which of the following protocols allows you to execute queries against a directory services database such as Microsoft Active Directory or Novell Directory Services?

   O A. NNTP
   O B. ICMP
   O C. LDAP
   O D. SFTP

68. Which of the following is not a commonly implemented feature of a firewall system?

   O A. NAT
   O B. Packet filtering
   O C. Proxy
   O D. NAS

69. Which command produced the following output?

```
;; global options:  printcmd
;; Got answer:
;; ->>HEADER<<- opcode: QUERY, status: NOERROR, id: 17273
;; flags: qr rd ra; QUERY: 1, ANSWER: 3, AUTHORITY: 2, ADDITIONAL: 0

;; QUESTION SECTION:
;examcram.com.                IN    ANY

;; ANSWER SECTION:
examcram.com.          86191   IN    A     63.240.93.157
examcram.com.          86191   IN    NS    oldtxdns2.pearsontc.com.
examcram.com.          86191   IN    NS    usrxdns1.pearsontc.com.

;; AUTHORITY SECTION:
examcram.com.          86191   IN    NS    oldtxdns2.pearsontc.com.
examcram.com.          86191   IN    NS    usrxdns1.pearsontc.com.

;; Query time: 24 msec
;; SERVER: 127.0.0.1#53(127.0.0.1)
;; WHEN: Tue Sep  18 09:07:29 2004
;; MSG SIZE  rcvd: 131
```

- ○ A. nslookup
- ○ B. nbtstat
- ○ C. dig
- ○ D. netstat

70. When a system running TCP/IP receives a data packet, which of the following does it use to determine which service to forward the packet to?

- ○ A. Port number
- ○ B. Packet ID number
- ○ C. Data IP number
- ○ D. IP protocol service type

71. What command would generate the following output?

```
7    60 ms   30 ms   40 ms  home-gw.st6wa.ip.att.net [192.205.32.249]
8    30 ms   40 ms   30 ms  gbr3-p40.st6wa.ip.att.net [12.123.44.130]
9    50 ms   50 ms   60 ms  gbr4-p10.sffca.ip.att.net [12.122.2.61]
10   60 ms   60 ms   60 ms  gbr3-p10.la2ca.ip.att.net [12.122.2.169]
11   90 ms   60 ms   70 ms  gbr6-p60.la2ca.ip.att.net [12.122.5.97]
```

- ○ A. ipconfig
- ○ B. netstat
- ○ C. ping
- ○ D. tracert

72. Which layer of the OSI model is responsible for placing the signal on the network media?

- ○ A. Physical
- ○ B. Data-link
- ○ C. MAC
- ○ D. LLC

Answer Key to Practice Exam I

Answers to Exam Questions

1. D	16. C, D	31. B	46. C	61. A, C
2. B	17. D	32. C	47. D	62. A, C
3. A	18. C	33. D	48. C	63. B, C, D
4. C	19. B, C	34. A	49. D	64. C
5. C	20. B	35. B	50. B	65. C
6. C	21. A, B, C	36. D	51. B	66. A
7. D	22. A	37. D	52. D	67. C
8. A, B	23. A	38. C	53. A, C	68. D
9. C, D	24. B, D	39. A	54. D	69. C
10. E	25. D	40. A	55. B	70. A
11. C	26. B	41. D	56. B, D	71. D
12. A	27. D	42. A	57. B	72. A
13. A	28. A	43. B	58. A	
14. B	29. A, C, D	44. D	59. B	
15. C	30. B	45. A	60. A	

Answers and Explanations to Practice Exam I

1. **D.** Of the devices listed, only a router operates at the Network layer of the OSI model. A WAP and a switch are both considered data-link layer devices. A hub is considered a physical layer device.

2. **B.** A wireless AP has a limited range of which it can send and receive data signals. Once a client system moves out of this range, client network access will either fail completely or be inconsistent. An incorrect SSID or incompatible WEP settings would completely prevent communication between the wireless AP and client.

3. **A.** The ifconfig command is used on a Linux system to determine the IP configuration of the system. With NetWare, you use the config command to obtain information about network addresses. On a Windows 2000 system, the ipconfig command is used to view the networking configuration including the IP address. ifconfig can be used on UNIX/Linux platforms to view the networking configuration.

4. **C.** FTP can be used to transfer files between Windows and UNIX systems. FTP is part of the TCP/IP protocol suite and is platform independent. The telnet utility is used to open a virtual terminal session on a remote host (answer A). PPP is used to establish communications over a serial link; thus, answer B is incorrect. PPTP is used to establish a secure link over a public network such as the Internet (answer D).

5. **C.** tracert is a Windows command that can be used to display the full path between two systems, including the number of hops between the systems. The ping utility (answer A) can be used to test connectivity between two devices, but it only reports the time taken for the round-trip; it does not give information about the time it takes to complete each hop in the route. The telnet utility (answer B) is used to open a virtual terminal session on a remote host. The nbtstat command (answer D) is used to view statistical information about the NetBIOS status of a system.

6. **C.** Because the system errors are over the entire network, it is likely that the cause of the problem in this scenario lies with the virus suite because it is installed on all computers. To troubleshoot such a problem, it would be a good idea to check for patches or updates on the vendor's website. A problem with a RAID array (answer A) would affect only the server in which it is installed, not the entire network.

Since the office suite (answer B) was installed on only some of the systems, it can be eliminated as a problem because all the systems are affected. The virus software (answer D) appears to be the cause of the problem, but reinstalling it is unlikely to help.

7. **D.** The `ipconfig` utility can be used to view the TCP/IP configuration on a Windows 2000, Windows XP, or Windows Server 2003 system. None of these operating systems support the graphical `winipcfg` utility (answer B). The `netstat` utility (answer A) is used to view protocol statistics information. The `ping` utility (answer C) is used to test the connectivity between two systems on a TCP/IP network.

8. **A** and **B.** Secure Shell (SSH) technology is used by both the Secure Copy Protocol (SCP) and the Secure File Transfer Protocol (SFTP). The Simple Network Management Protocol (SNMP), and the Simple Mail Transfer Protocol (SMTP) do not use SSH technology for additional security.

9. **C** and **D.** Both the full and incremental backup methods clear the archive bit to indicate which data does and does not need to be backed up. In a differential backup (answer A), the archive bit is not cleared. Sequential (answer B) is not a type of backup.

10. **E.** The `netstat -s` command can be used to display per-protocol statistics. The `arp` command (answers A and B) is used to view a list of the IP address-to-MAC address resolutions performed by the system. The `nbtstat` utility (answers C and D) is used to view protocol statistics for the NetBIOS protocol.

11. **C.** DNS is used on UNIX-based systems to resolve hostnames. IPX (answer A) is a network-layer connectionless protocol. ARP (answer B) resolves IP addresses to MAC addresses. The `LMHOSTS` file (answer D) is used on Windows systems to resolve NetBIOS names to IP addresses.

12. **A.** In this scenario, your first step is to gather information by examining the server log files. When you have that information, you can proceed with the rest of the troubleshooting process. Rebooting the server (answer B) is unlikely to cure the problem. Before you reinstall the printer (answer C) or printer software (answer D), you should examine the log files to see if any problems are reported in the server log files.

13. **A.** 100BaseTX uses Category 5 cable. 10BaseFL uses fiber-optic cable. There is no standard called 100BaseUX 10Base2 is an Ethernet networking standard that uses thin coaxial cable.

14. **B.** The `netstat -a` command can be used to display the current connections and listening ports. The `ping` utility (answer A) is used to test connectivity between two devices on a TCP/IP network. Telnet (answer C) is an application-level protocol that allows a virtual terminal session on a remote host. The `tracert` utility (answer D) allows a path to be traced between two hosts.

15. **C.** The various 10Mbps 802.3 networking standards have different maximum cable lengths. With 10Base-FL, a segment can be up to 2,000 meters. Using thin coaxial cabling, the 10Base2 standard specifies a maximum segment length of 185 meters. 10Mbps implementations of Ethernet on UTP are limited to 100 meters. All Ethernet standards use a Collision Sense Multiple Access/Collision detect media access method. The 10Mbps 802.3 standards use a logical bus topology, though they can use physical star or physical bus topology.

16. **C** and **D.** UDP and IPXareboth connectionless protocols. SPX and TCP (answers A and B) are connection-oriented protocols.

17. **D.** 10BASET has a maximum segment length of 100 meters. The maximum length of a 10BASE2 segment is 185 meters. The maximum length of a 10BASEFL segment (answer B) is 2,000 meters. Answer C is not a valid networking standard.

18. **C.** Changing passwords too frequently is not practical, and changing them too infrequently represents a security risk. Monthly password changing is adequate for most environments. Changing passwords too frequently (answers A and B) can cause problems because users might have problems remembering passwords, so they use passwords that are too similar to one another. Although passwords should be changed if they are compromised, they should also be changed periodically, making answer D incorrect.

19. **B** and **C.** To verify the local IP configurationyou can either `ping` the 'localhost' or use the IP address `127.0.0.1`. The default hostname for a system is `localhost`, not `host`, which means that answer A is incorrect. Answer D is not correct as this is the network address for the Class A loopback address, not a valid node loopback address.

20. **B.** A network hub operates at the physical layer of the OSI model. A router (answer A) operates at the network layer of the OSI model. A bridge (answer C) operates at the data-link layer of the OSI model. An NIC (answer D) operates at the data-link layer of the OSI model.

21. **A, B** and **C.** With two hard disks and two controllers, you can implement RAID 0, RAID 1, and disk duplexing. RAID 5 (disk striping with parity; answer E) requires a minimum of three disks to be implemented. RAID 10 (answer D) is a combination of RAID 1 (disk mirroring) and RAID 0 (disk striping). RAID 10 requires a minimum of four disks.

22. **A.** The first octet of a Class B address must be in the range 128 to 191. Answers A and B represent Class A addresses. Class A addresses run from 1 to 126. Answer D is not a valid IP address.

23. **A.** The netstat utility can be used to display protocol statistics and TCP/IP network connections. The nbtstat utility (answer B) shows statistical information about the NetBIOS over TCP/IP connections. The ping utility (answer C) is used to test the connectivity between two devices on a TCP/IP network. The tracert utility (answer D) traces the path between two hosts on a TCP/IP network.

24. **B** and **D.** TCP/IP port 25 is used by SMTP. TCP/IP port 110 is used by POP3. Because SMTP is used to send mail and POP3 is used to retrieve mail, port 25 and port 110 are the two ports that would need to be allowed for incoming and outgoing Internet email. TCP/IP port 21 (answer A) is used by FTP. TCP/IP port 80 (answer C) is used by HTTP. TCP/IP port 443 (answer E) is used by HTTPS.

25. **D.** The default subnet mask for a Class B network is 255.255.0.0. Answer A is incorrect because it is not the default subnet mask for a Class B network. Answer B is not the default subnet mask for a Class B network. Answer C is the local loopback address.

26. **B.** TCP operates at the transport layer of the OSI model. Answers A, C, and D are all incorrect; TCP does not operate at the network layer.

27. **D.** The purpose of the firewall system is to protect one network from another. One of the most common places to use a firewall is to protect a private network from a public one such as the Internet. Answer A is incorrect because although a firewall can provide a single point of access, that is not its primary purpose. Answer B more accurately describes the function of a proxy server. Answer C describes the function of a DNS server.

28. **A.** Both email and FTP work at the application layer of the OSI model. Email and FTP are application-layer protocols, not session-layer protocols. User (answer D) is not a layer of the OSI model.

29. **A, C** and **D.** Since Netware 4, Novell has included a directory services system with NetWare that provides a centralized repository for network information including users, groups, printers and servers. Before NetWare 4, Novell used a system called Bindery, which worked on a single server, single database principle.

30. **B.** To prevent unauthorized access to a private network from the Internet, you can use a firewall server to restrict outside access. Implementing a more secure password policy (answer A) is a good idea, but it is not the best choice of those available. Implementing a file-level encryption system (answer C) is a good idea, but it is not the best choice of those available. Kerberos (answer D) is an authentication system, not a method to prevent unauthorized access to the system.

31. **B.** The NetBIOS computer name is not supplied to client systems by a DHCP server. The IP address (answer A) is one of the pieces of information provided by DHCP. The subnet mask (answer C) is one of the pieces of information provided by DHCP. The default gateway (answer D) is one of the pieces of information supplied by DHCP.

32. **C.** Because the NIC is functioning at half-duplex 10Mbps, the transfer rate is 10Mbps. None of the other answers are correct.

33. **D.** IPv6 uses a 128-bit address, which is expressed as eight octet pairs in hexadecimal format, separated by colons. Because it is hexadecimal, only numbers and the letters A through F can be used. An IPv6 address is composed of eight hexadecimal octets. Only numbers and the letters A through F can be used.

34. **A.** The `arp -a` command is used to display the IP addresses that have been resolved to MAC addresses. The `nbtstat` command (answer B) is used to view protocol statistics for NetBIOS connections. `arp -d` (answer C) is not a valid command. The `arp -s` command (answer D) allows you to add static entries to the ARP cache.

35. **B.** A RAID 5 array consists of at least three hard disks and stripes parity information across all disks in the array. RAID 5 (disk striping with parity; answer A) requires at least three drives. The parity information is stored in a stripe across all three drives in the array (answer B). RAID 5 requires only three drives, which makes answer D incorrect.

36. **D.** CSMA/CD relates to the IEEE specification 802.3. The 802.11b (answer A) standard describes wireless LAN networking. The 802.2 (answer B) standard defines the media access methods for various networking standards. The 802.5 (answer C) standard defines Token Ring networking.

37. **D.** The `ping -t` command is used to send continuous `ping` requests to a remote system. The `ping` request will continue until it is manually stopped. The `traceroute` utility (answer A) performs this task. The `ping` command (answer B) shows the amount of time a packet takes to complete the round-trip from the host to the destination. Answer C is incorrect because the `ping` command with the `-n` switch performs this task.

38. **C.** The IEEE 802.11a wireless standard specifies 5GHz as the RF transmissions range. IEEE wireless standards 802.11b/g both use the 2.4GHz RF range. Infrared wireless transmissions use the 2.4GHz RF.

39. **A.** The diagram in the question shows a star topology. Answers B, C, and D are all incorrect. The figure does not represent any of these network types.

40. **A.** In this scenario, you would first check the remote access gateway to see if it is running and operating correctly. Because the user can browse web pages, this is not a connectivity problem. Answer B is incorrect because although rebooting the system might help, the system appears to be working correctly, and rebooting it is unlikely to cure the problem. The IP address configuration appears to be working because the user is able to access web pages, so answer C is incorrect. The Internet connection appears to be working, so cycling the power on the DSL modem, as described in answer D, is unlikely to help.

41. **D.** To specify a TCP/IP port other than the default of 80, simply append the port number to the end of the address, using a colon (:) to separate the two. All of the other answers are incorrect.

42. **A.** The IEEE 802.3ae standard defines 10Gbps networking standards such as 10Gbase-LR and 10Gbase-SR. There is no IEEE 802.3xr standard. 802.3z defines gigabit Ethernet standards such as 1000Base-LX and 1000Base-SX. 802.3u defines fast Ethernet standards such as 100Base-TX and 100Base-FX.

43. **B.** User-level security is more secure than share-level security and requires a user to provide a login ID, usually a username and password combination to access network resources. Answer A is incorrect because share-level security is not as secure as user-level security. Answers C and D are not accepted terms for describing levels of security.

44. **D.** The HOSTS file is used to manually configure hostname resolution, and if there is a problem with hostname resolution, entries in this file must be checked. Answers A and B are incorrect because files are not used on a Linux system. Answer C is incorrect because the PASSWD file is used to store user account information.

45. **A.** Fiber-optic cable provides the most resistance to EMI and therefore is often used in environments in which there is a risk of interference. Although it is inexpensive, UTP (answer B) cable has very low resistance to EMI; therefore, it should not be run near high-voltage electric cables. Thin coax (answer C) has low resistance to EMI; therefore, it should not be run near high-voltage electric cables. STP (answer D) has a good level of resistance to EMI, but it is still not as resistant as fiber-optic. Not factoring in the cost, fiber-optic is the most suitable solution.

46. **C.** The New Technology File System (NTFS) provides both file and share-level security. FAT and FAT32 can be used with Windows to provide share-level security, but they do not provide file-level security. EXT2 is a file system associated with Linux. It cannot be used with Windows XP Professional.

47. **D.** The most likely cause of the problem is that the default gateway is not configured. Answer A is incorrect because from the output it appears that the DNS servers are on the same subnet as this system. Answer B does not apply because addressing is configured statically, so there is no DHCP service. This is not a problem, however. Answer C is incorrect because the subnet mask is the correct default subnet mask for a Class C network.

48. **C.** DNS allows hostname resolutions to occur internally. In most cases, companies use a DNS server provided by the ISP. In some cases, however, it might be appropriate to have a DNS server on the internal network. Answer A is incorrect as NAT is normally a function of firewall or proxy servers. Answer B describes the purpose of a WINS server. Answer D describes the function of a proxy server.

49. **D.** Private address ranges are designed for use on private networks. The ranges are 192.168.X.X, 10.X.X.X, and 172.16.X.X–172.32.X.X. Answers A, B, and C are all valid private IP address ranges.

50. **B.** Samba is an application that can be run on a Linux server that enables Windows clients to use the server as a file and print server without any additional client software. If there were a large number of users who required this functionality, installing Samba would be a suitable solution. If only one or two users required access, you would be more likely to use FTP, or install a Network File System (NFS) client on the Windows XP Professional systems. Either of these options would allow the client systems to copy files to or from the Linux server. The most commonly used network management systems are those that rely on the Simple Network Management Protocol (SNMP).

Installing Samba on the Linux server is unlikely to be part of a network management system installation. If you want to automate the allocation of IP addresses to client systems, you would install a DHCP server. You would not install Samba.

51. **B.** IANA is responsible for assigning IP addresses for systems on public networks—specifically, the Internet. Answer A is incorrect. IANA is responsible for assigning IP addresses for use on public networks (such as the Internet). Answer C is incorrect because domain names are administered by domain registry organizations. Answer D is incorrect because you don't need to apply for a network address for use on a private network.

52. **D.** A VLAN is implemented on a switch to create multiple separate networks. A proxy server (answer A) is used to control access to the Internet. Subnet masking (answer B) is not a valid method of creating separate networks. NAS (answer C) describes storage devices that are attached directly to the network media.

53. **A** and **C.** IP and IPX are responsible for network addressing. Answers B and D are incorrect because SPX and TCP are transport-layer protocols and are not responsible for network addressing.

54. **D.** In a typical configuration, a wireless antenna can be either omni directional or directional. An omni-directional antenna provides a 360-degree dispersed wave pattern. This provides an even signal in all directions. Directional antennas are designed to focus the signal in a particular direction. Omni dispersed and directional dispersed are not valid types of antennas.

55. **B.** The Internet Group Multicast Protocol (IGMP) is used by systems within the same multicast group to communicate registration information. The Internet Control Message Protocol (ICMP) works with IP to provide error checking and reporting functionality on a network. The Network News Transfer Protocol (NNTP) is used to access Internet newsgroups. The Lightweight Directory Access Protocol (LDAP) is a protocol used to access directory services systems.

56. **B** and **D.** Fiber-optic cable can use either SC or ST type connectors. RJ-11 connectors (answer A) are associated with telephone cable, RJ-45 (answer C) connectors are associated with UTP cable, and BNC connectors (answer E) are associated with thin coaxial cable.

57. **B.** USB interfaces have a number of connectors associated with them, but the most common are called Type A and Type B. FireWire interfaces use either a 4-pin or a 6-pin connector, neither are referred to as

Type A or Type B. RJ-11 is a type of connector associated with phone system wiring. Fiber optic interfaces use a wide range of connectors, but none are called Type A or Type B.

58. **A.** When a new NIC is installed on a Token Ring network, the speed of the card has to be set to match the speed used by the network. Answer B is incorrect because Token Ring networks operate at either 4Mbps or 16Mbps. Answer C is incorrect because full-duplex connections are not used on Token Ring networks. Answer D is incorrect because, although it is possible, a faulty card is not the most likely answer

59. **B.** The most likely explanation is that port 443, the HTTPS default port, is being blocked by a corporate firewall. Port 80 (answer A) is used by HTTP. All modern Web browsers support HTTPS automatically; therefore, answer C is incorrect. Port 110 (answer D) is used by POP3.

60. **A.** Class A subnets use the range 1 to 126 for the value of the first octet. Answer B is the loopback address, which allows the IP stack functionality to be tested. Answers C and D are both addresses in the Class B range (128–191).

61. **A** and **C.** Infrared and Bluetooth are wireless technologies commonly used to create personal area networks. They replace the need for peripheral cables. 802.11a is a wireless standard used for LAN-based networking and not designed for attaching peripheral devices. Ethernet wireless is not a wireless standard.

62. **A** and **C.** Systems that have APIPA assigned addresses will be able to talk to each other, but not with any other systems (answer B). Systems with APIPA assigned addresses will not be able to access the Internet, as the APIPA assigned information does not include default gateway information. Therefore, communication is limited to the local network. Answer D is incorrect because the systems with APIPA addresses will be able to talk to each other, even though they will not be able to communicate with any other systems.

63. **B, C,** and **D.** FTP, DHCP, and HTTP are all protocols in the TCP/IP protocol suite. AFP (answer A) is part of the AppleTalk protocol suite. NCP (answer E) is part of the IPX/SPX protocol suite.

64. **C.** SMTP is used for sending email. Answer A is not a valid answer. Answers B and D are incorrect because POP3 and IMAP are email retrieval protocols, not protocols for sending email.

65. **C.** The Service Set Identifier (SSID) is a unique identifier sent over the WLAN that acts as a simple password used when a client attempts to access an access point. The SSID is used to differentiate between networks; therefore, the client system and the AP must use the same SSID. WEP represents a form of wireless security, and the wireless channel is the band of frequency used for the wireless communication.

66. **A.** The MAC address is a 6-byte address expressed in six pairs of hexadecimal values. Because it is hexadecimal, only the letters A through F and numbers can be used. Answer B is incorrect because MAC addresses are expressed as six hexadecimal pairs. Answer C shows an example of an IPv4 address. Answer D shows an example of an IPv6 address. Answer E is incorrect because MAC addresses are expressed in hexadecimal; therefore, only the letters A through F and numbers can be used.

67. **C.** The Lightweight Directory Access Protocol (LDAP) is an application layer protocol that can be used to execute commands such as queries against LDAP compliant directory service systems such as Microsoft Active Directory or Novell Directory Services. NNTP is a protocol used to access Internet newsgroups. ICMP is a protocol that works with IP to provide error checking and reporting functionality on a network. SFTP is a secure implementation of the File Transfer Protocol (FTP).

68. **D.** A firewall can provide several services to the network, including NAT, proxy services, and packet filtering. NAS is not a function of a firewall server. Answers A, B, and C are all incorrect because NAT, packet filtering, and proxy functionality are all commonly implemented on firewall systems.

69. **C.** The output shown is from the `dig` command. `dig` is used on UNIX and Linux systems to run manual DNS lookups. The `nslookup` command also performs this function, but it produces different output. The `nbtstat` command provides information on NetBIOS name resolutions, and the `netstat` command shows what TCP/IP protocol connections have been established on a system. Both of these commands produce different output from `dig`.

70. **A.** The service to which a data packet is destined is determined by the port number to which it is sent. Answers B, C, and D are not valid.

71. **D.** The output displayed in this question is from the Windows `tracert` utility. Answers A, B, and C are all incorrect. These utilities produce output that is different from the output shown.

72. **A.** The physical layer of the OSI seven-layer model is responsible for placing the signal on the network media. The data-link layer (answer B) is responsible for physical addressing and media access. MAC and LLC (answers C and D) are sublayers of the data-link layer.

Practice Exam 2

This exam consists of 72 questions that reflect the material covered in this book. The questions are representative of the types of questions you should expect to see on the Network+ exam; however, they are not intended to match exactly what is on the exam.

Some of the questions require that you deduce the best possible answer. Often, you are asked to identify the best course of action to take in a given situation. You must read the questions carefully and thoroughly before you attempt to answer them. It is strongly recommended that you treat this as if it were the actual exam. When you take it, time yourself, read carefully, and answer all the questions to the best of your ability.

The answers to all the questions appear in the section following the exam. Check your letter answers against those in the answers section, and then read the explanations provided. You might also want to return to the chapters in the book to review the material associated with any incorrect answers.

1. As system administrator, you have been asked to implement name resolution on your network. The network uses both Windows and UNIX systems. Which of the following are you most likely to use?
   - ○ A. LMHOSTS
   - ○ B. DNS
   - ○ C. WINS
   - ○ D. DHCP

2. You are attempting to connect an Apple workstation to an existing TCP/IP network. The Apple system was previously used on a peer-to-peer network using the AppleTalk protocol. When the system is connected to your network, it cannot connect to the server. Which of the following could you do to connect the Apple workstation? (Select two.)
   - ○ A. Install the AppleTalk protocol on the server
   - ○ B. Install the TCP/IP protocol on the workstation
   - ○ C. Install NetBEUI on the workstation
   - ○ D. Install TCP/IP on the server

3. You have been employed by a small company to implement a fault-tolerant hard disk configuration. You have purchased four 40GB hard disks and intend on installing RAID 5 on the server. What is the storage capacity of the RAID solution?
   - ○ A. 120GB
   - ○ B. 40GB
   - ○ C. 80GB
   - ○ D. 160GB

4. You have been called in to troubleshoot a small network. The network uses TCP/IP and statically assigned IP information. You add a new workstation to the network, which can connect to the local network but not to a server on a remote network. Which of the following is most likely the cause of the problem?
   - ○ A. Incorrect IP address.
   - ○ B. Incorrect default gateway.
   - ○ C. DHCP server is unavailable.
   - ○ D. Duplicate IP addresses are being used.

5. You have been employed to configure a 10Base2 network. Which of the following technologies would you use? (Choose two.)
   - ○ A. UTP
   - ○ B. STP
   - ○ C. T-connectors
   - ○ D. RJ-11 connectors
   - ○ E. RG-58 cable

6. You are working as an administrator in a network using NetWare, Windows, and UNIX servers. You need to assign user permissions on the UNIX and Windows systems. Which of the following permissions are available on the Windows server but not on the UNIX server?

   ○ A. Read
   ○ B. Write
   ○ C. Execute
   ○ D. Change

7. You have just installed a new Windows 2000 server on your network. When first logging on to the system, which of the following is required to log on?

   ○ A. Username
   ○ B. Password
   ○ C. Context
   ○ D. Administrator's username

8. Which of the following topology types offers the greatest amount of redundancy?

   ○ A. Star
   ○ B. Bus
   ○ C. Ring
   ○ D. Mesh

9. You need to install a network printer and require the printer's MAC address to finish the installation. Which of the following represents a valid MAC address?

   ○ A. 192.168.2.13
   ○ B. 0x00007856
   ○ C. 00:04:e2:1c:7b:5a
   ○ D. 56g78:00h6:1415

10. You have been called in to replace a faulty ST connector. Which of the following media types are you working with?

    ○ A. RG-58
    ○ B. RG-62
    ○ C. Single mode fiber
    ○ D. SCSI

11. Your manager has asked you to recommend a secure way to copy files between a server on your network and a remote server in another location. Which of the following solutions are you most likely to recommend?

○ A. TFTP

○ B. FTP

○ C. SFTP

○ D. IGMP

12. You are setting up a wide area network between two school campuses and decide to use BRI ISDN. What is the maximum throughput of your connection?

○ A. 64Kbps

○ B. 128Kbps

○ C. 128Mbps

○ D. 64Mbps

13. You are troubleshooting a 10Base2 network and suspect that the maximum cable length has been exceeded. What is the maximum length of a 10BASE-2 network segment?

○ A. 25 meters

○ B. 100 meters

○ C. 185 meters

○ D. 500 meters

14. You have been given the task of installing Samba on a Linux server. What services does this product provide?

○ A. Web server services

○ B. Thin client services

○ C. File and print services

○ D. Proxy server services

15. What is the maximum cable length of a 10BaseT network?

○ A. 185 meters

○ B. 500 meters

○ C. 100 meters

○ D. 50 meters

16. While troubleshooting a DNS issue from a UNIX server, you suspect that the DNS record for one of your other servers is incorrect. Which of the following utilities are you most likely to use to troubleshoot this problem?

○ A. ipconfig

○ B. dig

○ C. netstat

○ D. nbtstat

17. A number of users have called to report printing problems. Upon investigation, you trace the problem to a network printer connected to a server system. You arrive at the printer to find that it is connected online and appears to perform a test print without any problems. You check the network connectivity, and that seems to be okay as well. Which of the following troubleshooting steps would you perform next?

    ○ A. Examine the log files on the server to determine whether there are any printing-related events.
    ○ B. Reboot the server that acts as the print server.
    ○ C. Remove and reinstall the printer drivers.
    ○ D. Change the network cable that connects the printer to the network.

18. You are experiencing problems with the network connectivity of a Windows 2000 system, and you suspect that there might be a problem with an incorrect route in the routing table. Which of the following TCP/IP utilities can you use to view the routing table? (Select two.)

    ○ A. tracert
    ○ B. nbstat
    ○ C. route
    ○ D. netstat
    ○ E. ping

19. Because of a promotion, you are moving one of the administrators to a new corner office. The administrator has a wireless connection to the network that has continued to operate consistently. After the move to the new office, the administrator can still access the network, but speeds are slower and periodically the connection fails altogether. What is the likely cause of the problem?

    ○ A. The SSID on the client system is incorrectly set.
    ○ B. IPSec has been configured to use high-level encryption
    ○ C. The administrators system has been moved too far from the AP.
    ○ D. The wireless channel is incorrectly set on the client station.

20. Which of the following services provides name resolution services for FQDNs?

    ○ A. DNS
    ○ B. DHCP
    ○ C. WINS
    ○ D. ARP
    ○ E. NTP

21. You are installing a 100BaseFX network and need to purchase connectors. Which of the following might you purchase? (Choose two.)

   ○ A. RJ-45
   ○ B. ST
   ○ C. BNC
   ○ D. SC

22. Which of the following network services or protocols is not associated with file sharing?

   ○ A. NFS
   ○ B. SMB
   ○ C. LPD
   ○ D. AFP

23. When designing a network, you have been asked to select a cable that offers the most resistance to crosstalk. Which of the following are you likely to choose?

   ○ A. Multimode fiber-optic
   ○ B. Shielded twisted pair
   ○ C. UTP
   ○ D. Shielded mesh

24. Which of the following are considered disaster recovery measures? (Select two.)

   ○ A. Backups
   ○ B. UPS
   ○ C. RAID 5
   ○ D. Off-site data storage

25. Which command produces the following output?

```
Interface: 24.77.218.58 --- 0x2
   Internet Address      Physical Address      Type
   24.77.216.1           00-00-77-99-a4-4c     dynamic
```

   ○ A. arp
   ○ B. tracert
   ○ C. ipconfig
   ○ D. netinf

26. A user with a newly created user account cannot access an application on the network, yet other users can. Which of the following troubleshooting steps are you likely to perform first?

   ○ A. Delete the application and reinstall it.
   ○ B. Delete the user account and re-create it.
   ○ C. Change the password of the new user account.
   ○ D. Check the file permissions for the new user account.

27. Because of a recent security breach, you have been asked to design a security strategy that will allow data to travel encrypted through both the Internet and intranet. Which of the following protocols would you use?

    ○ A. IPSec
    ○ B. SST
    ○ C. CHAP
    ○ D. FTP

28. As part of a network upgrade, you have installed a router on your network creating two networks. Now, workstations on one side of the router cannot access workstations on the other side of the router. Which of the following configuration changes would you need to make to the workstations to enable them to see devices on the other network? (Choose two.)

    ○ A. Change the IP address assignments on one side of the router so that the router is on a different IP network from the other one.
    ○ B. Update the default gateway information on all systems so that they use the newly installed router as the gateway.
    ○ C. Update the default gateway information on all systems so that they use a workstation on the other network as the default gateway.
    ○ D. Make sure that the IP address assignments on all network workstations are the same.

29. Which type of cable should be used in a 100BaseT network?

    ○ A. RG-58
    ○ B. Category 4 UTP
    ○ C. Category 5 UTP
    ○ D. Multimode fiber

30. Which of the following network types is easiest to add new nodes to?

    ○ A. Bus
    ○ B. Ring
    ○ C. Star
    ○ D. Mesh

31. Which of the following connectors is used with fiber-optic cable? (Choose three.)

    ○ A. SC
    ○ B. F-type
    ○ C. MTRJ
    ○ D. LC

32. You have recently installed a DHCP server to replace static IP addressing. You configure all client systems to use DHCP and then reboot each system. Once rebooted, they all have an IP address in the 169.254.0.0 range. Which of the following statements is true?

   - ○ A. The DHCP server has been configured to assign addresses in the 169.254.0.0 IP range.
   - ○ B. The DHCP must be rebooted.
   - ○ C. Client systems are unable to access the new DHCP server.
   - ○ D. Client systems are getting IP address information from the LMHOSTS file.

33. Placing a node on which of the following types of networks would require that you obtained an address from IANA?

   - ○ A. Private network
   - ○ B. Public network
   - ○ C. Ethernet network
   - ○ D. WAN

34. You are implementing a new network. From the network specifications, you learn that you will be using the 1000BaseCX standard. What type of cable will you be using?

   - ○ A. Multimode fiber
   - ○ B. STP
   - ○ C. Single mode fiber
   - ○ D. CoreXtended fiber

35. Which of the following network protocols can recover from lost or corrupted packets in a network transmission?

   - ○ A. L2TP
   - ○ B. TCP
   - ○ C. IPX
   - ○ D. ARP

36. A colleague decided to close all unused ports on the corporate firewall to further secure the network from intruders. The ports that were open were 25, 80, 110 and 53. Your colleague knew that 25 and 110 are required for email and that 80 is used for nonsecure Web browsing, so he decided to close 53, as he didn't think it was necessary. Which network service is now unavailable?

   - ○ A. Secure HTTP
   - ○ B. FTP
   - ○ C. Telnet
   - ○ D. DNS

37. You are working on a Linux system, and you suspect that there might be a problem with the TCP/IP configuration. Which of the following commands would you use to view the network card configuration of the system?

    ○ A. `config`

    ○ B. `ipconfig`

    ○ C. `winipcfg`

    ○ D. `ifconfig`

38. You have configured network clients to obtain IP addresses using APIPA. Which of the following IP ranges would be assigned to client systems?

    ○ A. `10.10.0.0–10.254.254.0`

    ○ B. `169.168.0.0–169.168.255.255`

    ○ C. `192.168.0.0–192.168.254.254`

    ○ D. `169.254.0.1–169.254.255.254`

39. Your manager has asked you to implement a fault-tolerant disk solution on your server. You have two 30GB hard disks and two controllers, so you decide to implement RAID 1. After the installation, your manager asks you how much storage space is now available for storing data. What do you tell her?

    ○ A. 30GB

    ○ B. 40GB

    ○ C. 60GB

    ○ D. 120GB

40. Which of the following statements best describes PRI ISDN?

    ○ A. PRI ISDN uses 128 B channels and two D channels.

    ○ B. PRI ISDN uses 23 B channels and one D channel.

    ○ C. PRI ISDN uses two B and one D channel.

    ○ D. PRI ISDN uses 23 D channels and one B channel.

41. Which of the following media types is used with the 802.3 1000BaseSX standard?

    ○ A. Coaxial

    ○ B. UTP

    ○ C. Single mode fiber-optic

    ○ D. Multimode fiber-optic

42. Which of the following user security models would you use if you were looking for the highest levels of security on your network? (Choose two.)

○ A. User-administered security

○ B. User-level security

○ C. Share-level security

○ D. Centrally administered security

43. A remote user calls you because he cannot dial in to the remote server. He says that the modem dials the number and negotiates the connection, but then the line is dropped. Which of the following two troubleshooting steps are you likely to try first? (Choose two.)

○ A. Change the modem IRQ assignments.

○ B. Run a remote diagnostic on the remote access server's modem.

○ C. Ask the user to verify that the username and password are correct.

○ D. Ask the user to verify that he is dialing the correct system.

44. At which layer of the OSI model does a NIC operate?

○ A. Physical

○ B. Network

○ C. Data-link

○ D. Transport

45. You are working with a Macintosh network. Which of the following AppleTalk protocols provides file sharing for the network?

○ A. SMB

○ B. Samba

○ C. NFS

○ D. AFP

46. You are implementing a 100BaseT network. Which logical topology does the network use?

○ A. Ring

○ B. Star

○ C. Mesh

○ D. Bus

47. Consider the following output:

```
Proto Local AddressForeign Address        State
TCP    laptop:2848   MEDIASERVICES1:1755   ESTABLISHED
TCP    laptop:1833   www.dollarhost.com:80 ESTABLISHED
TCP    laptop:2858   194.70.58.241:80      ESTABLISHED
TCP    laptop:2860   194.70.58.241:80      ESTABLISHED
TCP    laptop:2354   www.dollarhost.com:80 ESTABLISHED
TCP    laptop:2361   www.dollarhost.com:80 ESTABLISHED
TCP    laptop:1114   www.dollarhost.com:80 ESTABLISHED
TCP    laptop:1959   www.dollarhost.com:80 ESTABLISHED
```

```
TCP    laptop:1960    www.dollarhost.com:80    ESTABLISHED
TCP    laptop:1963    www.dollarhost.com:80    ESTABLISHED
TCP    laptop:2870    localhost:8431           TIME_WAIT
TCP    laptop:8431    localhost:2862           TIME_WAIT
TCP    laptop:8431    localhost:2863           TIME_WAIT
TCP    laptop:8431    localhost:2867           TIME_WAIT
TCP    laptop:8431    localhost:2872           TIME_WAIT
```

Which of the following commands produces this output?

- ○ A. arp
- ○ B. netstat
- ○ C. nbtstat
- ○ D. tracert

48. Which of the following protocols or services enables Windows-based clients to access resources on a Linux server?

- ○ A. IPSec
- ○ B. Samba
- ○ C. AFP
- ○ D. NFS

49. You are attempting to troubleshoot a remote connectivity problem for a user. Although the modem seems to be working properly within the computer, you cannot get the modem to dial a number. Working within a terminal software application, you attempt to communicate directly with the modem. From within the terminal application, which command would you issue to reset the modem?

- ○ A. ATD
- ○ B. ATI3
- ○ C. ATZ
- ○ D. ATI

50. Which of the following protocols maps Layer 2 addresses to Layer 3 addresses on a TCP/IP network?

- ○ A. ARPA
- ○ B. ARP
- ○ C. AARP
- ○ D. RARP

51. You have been asked to implement a server clustering strategy. Which of the following is a reason to use server clustering? (Select two.)

- ○ A. Increase data transmissions security over the LAN
- ○ B. Increase data transmission security over the WAN
- ○ C. Increase server service fault tolerance
- ○ D. Reduce network downtime

52. Which of the following is not a type of Digital Subscriber Line (DSL) technology?

    ○ A. VHDSL
    ○ B. RADSL
    ○ C. ADSL
    ○ D. XTDSL

53. You come into work on Monday to find that the DHCP server has failed over the weekend. Before you can fix it, client systems boot up and are able to communicate with each other. However, they are not able to directly access the Internet or a remote network segment. Given that the DHCP server has failed, how are systems able to communicate?

    ○ A. The DHCP service was recovered automatically using the Windows XP automatic restoration utility.
    ○ B. The DHCP addressing information was obtained from the client cache.
    ○ C. The client systems are assigned an IP address using APIPA.
    ○ D. The client systems are using static IP addressing.

54. Which of the following is a reason to implement a proxy server? (Select two.)

    ○ A. To centrally control Internet access
    ○ B. To protect the internal network from intruders
    ○ C. To provide NAT services
    ○ D. To provide automatic IP addressing on the network

55. Consider the following output:

    ```
    Name                 Type        Status
    - - - - - - - - - - - - - - - - - - - - - - - - - - - - - -
    LAPTOP       <00>  UNIQUE      Registered
    KCS          <00>  GROUP       Registered
    LAPTOP       <03>  UNIQUE      Registered
    ```

    Which of the following commands would produce this output?

    ○ A. nbtstat
    ○ B. netstat
    ○ C. ifconfig
    ○ D. arp

56. Which of the following wireless technologies are typically used to create a wireless personal area network?

    ○ A. Infrared
    ○ B. 802.11g
    ○ C. Bluetooth
    ○ D. 802.11c

57. Which of the following is a valid Class C address that could be assigned to a workstation on the network?

   ○ A. `200.200.200.200`
   ○ B. `200.200.200.255`
   ○ C. `143.67.151.17`
   ○ D. `203.16.42.0`

58. At which layer of the OSI model is flow control performed?

   ○ A. Network
   ○ B. Transport
   ○ C. Session
   ○ D. Data-link

59. Which of the following statements is true of IMAP?

   ○ A. IMAP leaves messages on the mail server, so they can be viewed and accessed from various locations.
   ○ B. IMAP is used for sending as well as receiving email.
   ○ C. IMAP can only be used for sending mail.
   ○ D. IMAP uses port `110`.

60. You are implementing a new network that will use 100BaseT with switches configured for full duplex. What is the maximum throughput that will be possible between two devices on the network?

   ○ A. 10Mbps
   ○ B. 20Mbps
   ○ C. 200Mbps
   ○ D. 100Mbps

61. Your manager has asked you to implement a RAID 5 fault-tolerant disk solution using four 40GB disks. He now wants to know how much data storage capacity will be lost by the implementation. What do you tell him?

   ○ A. 10GB
   ○ B. 20GB
   ○ C. 40GB
   ○ D. 120GB

62. A user calls you from a conference room. He needs to connect to the corporate RAS server, but the modem in his system is reporting a "no dial tone" error. When he plugs the telephone back in to the phone socket, he gets a dial tone and is able to dial out successfully. What is the most likely cause of the problem?

   ○ A. The phone line in the room is analog.
   ○ B. The phone line in the room is faulty.
   ○ C. The modem is faulty.
   ○ D. The phone line in the room is digital.

63. Which of the following is not a valid file permission on a Windows 2000 system?
    - ○ A. Read
    - ○ B. Attribute
    - ○ C. Execute
    - ○ D. Write

64. Which of the following utilities would you use to view the TCP connections that have been established between two systems?
    - ○ A. netstat
    - ○ B. nbtstat
    - ○ C. tracert
    - ○ D. ipconfig

65. Which of the following authentication systems uses tickets as part of its authentication process?
    - ○ A. HTTPS
    - ○ B. POP3
    - ○ C. Kerberos
    - ○ D. SSL

66. On an AppleTalk network, what is the function of AARP?
    - ○ A. It is a distance-vector routing protocol.
    - ○ B. It allows the resolution of AppleTalk addresses to MAC addresses.
    - ○ C. It allows the resolution of MAC addresses to AppleTalk addresses.
    - ○ D. It is a link-state routing protocol.

67. Which term describes the process of using parts of the node address range of an IP address as the network ID?
    - ○ A. Subnetting
    - ○ B. Supernetting
    - ○ C. Subnet masking
    - ○ D. Super routing

68. One of the network devices used on your network forwards packets only to an intended port. Which of the following devices does this describe?
    - ○ A. Hub
    - ○ B. Switch
    - ○ C. Gateway
    - ○ D. PPP

69. A user on your network can send data packets within the local subnet but cannot send packets beyond the local subnet. Which of the following is likely the problem?

   ○ A. Invalid permissions
   ○ B. Incorrect gateway information
   ○ C. No DNS server installed
   ○ D. No WINS server installed

70. You are the administrator for a network that uses TCP/IP. You are using a single registered Class C network address. You want to continue to use it because many of your systems are accessed from outside sources, but you also want to create more networks so that you can manage traffic and security more effectively. Which of the following strategies would help you achieve this?

   ○ A. Implement a 127.x.x.x addressing system throughout the network.
   ○ B. Use reverse proxy.
   ○ C. Use subnetting.
   ○ E. Use private addressing.

71. In a hardware loopback plug, which wire numbers are connected? (Choose the two best answers.)

   ○ A. 3 and 5
   ○ B. 1 and 3
   ○ C. 1 and 2
   ○ D. 3 and 4
   ○ E. 2 and 6

72. Which of the following wireless technologies operates at a 5GHz RF range?

   ○ A. 802.11a
   ○ B. 802.11b
   ○ C. 802.11g
   ○ D. 802.11

Answers to Practice Exam 2

Answers to Exam Questions

1. B	**16.** B	**31.** A, C, and D	**45.** D	**60.** C
2. A and B	**17.** A		**46.** D	**61.** C
3. A	**18.** C and D	**32.** C	**47.** B	**62.** D
4. B	**19.** C	**33.** B	**48.** B	**63.** B
5. C and E	**20.** A	**34.** B	**49.** C	**64.** A
6. D	**21.** B and D	**35.** B	**50.** D	**65.** C
7. A and B	**22.** C	**36.** D	**51.** C and D	**66.** B
8. D	**23.** A	**37.** D	**52.** D	**67.** A
9. C	**24.** A and D	**38.** D	**53.** C	**68.** B
10. C	**25.** A	**39.** A	**54.** A and C	**69.** B
11. C	**26.** D	**40.** B	**55.** A	**70.** C
12. B	**27.** A	**41.** D	**56.** A and C	**71.** B and E
13. C	**28.** A and B	**42.** B and D	**57.** A	**72.** A
14. C	**29.** C	**43.** C and D	**58.** B	
15. C	**30.** C	**44.** C	**59.** A	

Answers and Explanations to Exam Questions

1. **B.** DNS is used to provide hostname to IP address resolution on Windows and UNIX systems. A is wrong because the LMHOSTS file is used to resolve NetBIOS names to IP address. Answer C is wrong because WINS resolves NetBIOS names to IP addresses. D is wrong because DHCP is used to automatically assign IP information to clients' systems.

2. **A** and **B.** To communicate on a network, the server and the client must use the same protocol. In this scenario, installing AppleTalk on the server or TCP/IP on the client would allow the client to access the server. C is wrong because Apple systems do not use the NetBEUI protocol. D is wrong because TCP/IP is already installed on the server; to communicate on the network, the client must also have TCP/IP installed.

3. **A.** RAID 5 reserves the equivalent space of one partition in the array for parity information. In this scenario, there are four 40GB hard disks. With one reserved for parity, you have 160GB total space; and with 40GB removed for parity, there is 120GB of actual data storage.

4. **B.** To connect to systems on a remote network, the default gateway has to be correctly assigned. If this address is entered manually, the number might have been incorrectly entered. Answer A is incorrect. Because the system is able to connect to the local network, the actual address is correctly assigned. Answer C is incorrect because IP addresses are statically assigned. Answer D is incorrect because duplicate addresses will prevent the system from being able to log onto the network.

5. **C** and **E.** 10Base2 networks use BNC connectors including T-connectors and RG-58 cable (Thinnet coaxial cable). None of the other technologies are used in 10Base2 networks.

6. **D.** The change permission is available on Windows-based server systems but not on UNIX systems. All the other permissions are available on both platforms.

7. **A** and **B.** When logging on to a Windows server, all that is required is a valid username and password. C is incorrect because a context is associated with logging on to a NetWare network. D is wrong because you can log on using the administrator's username, but this is not required.

8. **D.** In a mesh topology, each device is connected directly to every other device on the network. Such a structure requires that each device have at least two network connections. All other network configurations do not offer the same level of redundancy as a true mesh network.

9. **C.** A MAC address contains six hexadecimal number sets. The first three sets represent the manufacturer's code, whereas the last three identify the unique station ID. A is wrong because the number represents a valid internal IP address. Neither C nor D are valid numbers.

10. **C.** ST connectors are a twist-type connector used with fiber-optic media. A is wrong because RG-58 (thin coax) uses BNC type connectors. B is incorrect because RG-62 (thick coax) uses vampire type AUI connectors. D is wrong because SCSI cables use a variety of connector types—none of which include ST connectors.

11. **C.** The Secure File Transfer Protocol (SFTP) allows you to copy files from one location to another. SFTP provides authentication and encryption capabilities to safeguard data. TFTP is a mechanism that provides file transfer capabilities, but it does not provide security. FTP provides basic authentication mechanisms, but it does not provide encryption. IGMP is a protocol associated with multicast group communications. It is not a file transfer protocol.

12. **B.** BRI ISDN uses two 64Kbps data channels. Combined, BRI ISDN offers a total of 128Mbps transfer rate. All of the other answers are invalid.

13. **C.** 10Base2 is an Ethernet network standard implemented using thin coaxial cable. The maximum length of a segment is 185 meters. A is incorrect. B describes 10BaseT. D describes 10Base5.

14. **C.** Samba is a product that provides file and print services to Windows-based clients. A is wrong because Web server services are offered through a variety of products; Samba is not one of them. B is incorrect because Samba does not offer thin client services. D is incorrect because proxy server services are offered through a variety of products; Samba is not one of them.

15. **C.** 10BaseT networks use UTP media, which have a maximum distance of 100 meters. A is not correct because 185 meters is the distance limitation of thin coax media used on 10Base2 networks. B is wrong because 500 meters is the distance limitation of thick coaxial media used with 10Base5 networks. D is wrong because 50 meters is not a valid cable distance.

16. **B.** The Dig command is used on UNIX and Linux systems to perform manual name resolutions against a DNS server. This can be useful in troubleshooting DNS related issues. The ipconfig, netstat, and nbtstat commands are all Windows-based commands, so they would not be used in this scenario.

17. **A.** Log files often record information about errors that can be vital to the troubleshooting process. It is also a step that has little or no impact on network services. B is wrong because rebooting the server is a last-resort troubleshooting step. C is incorrect because removing and rein-stalling the printer drivers might be a valid step, but it would not be the first choice of those listed. D is wrong because changing the net-work cable might be a valid troubleshooting step, but because it has been verified that the network connectivity is working, this should not be necessary.

18. **C** and **D.** Both the route and the netstat commands can be used to view the routing table on a Windows 2000 system. A is wrong because the tracert utility is used to track the route a packet takes between two destinations. B is incorrect because the nbtstat command is used to view statistical information for NetBIOS connections. E isn't correct because the ping utility is used to test network connectivity.

19. **C.** Wireless APs have a limited distance that they can send and receive data signals. Because the wireless client was recently relocated, the most likely explanation is that the system has moved too far away from the AP. SSIDs would not likely be the problem, as the configuration was correct before the move; and incorrect SSIDs would prevent net-work access, not cause intermittent access. Also, both the client and the AP need to use the same wireless channel for communication to take place. The IPSec protocol secures data transmissions over the network and would not cause intermittent connectivity problems.

20. **A.** The Domain Name Service system (DNS) resolves Fully Qualified Domain Names (FQDNs) to IP addresses. B is wrong because the Dynamic Host Configuration Protocol (DHCP) provides automatic IP address assignment. C is wrong because the Windows Internet Naming Service (WINS) provides NetBIOS computer name to IP address reso-lution. D is wrong because the Address Resolution Protocol (ARP) resolves IP addresses to MAC addresses. E is wrong because the Network Time Protocol (NTP) facilitates the communication of time information between systems.

21. **B** and **D**. 100BaseFX networks use fiber media, which can use either SC or ST connectors. A is wrong because RJ-45 connectors are used with UTP media. C is incorrect because BNC connectors are used with thin coax media on 10Base2 networks.

22. **C.** LPD, or Line Printer Daemon, is a network service associated with print serving. It is not associated with file sharing. LPD is typically associated with UNIX or Linux systems, but versions of LPD are available for all commonly used operating systems.

23. **A.** Unlike copper-based media, fiber-optic media is resistant to crosstalk, as it uses light transmissions. B is wrong because STP offers greater resistance to crosstalk than regular UTP, but is not as resistant as fiber-optic cable. C is incorrect because UTP cable is more susceptible to crosstalk than either STP or fiber-optic. D is wrong because shielded mesh is not a type of cable.

24. **A** and **D**. Both backups and offsite data storage are considered disaster recovery measures. B is wrong because a UPS is considered a fault-tolerant measure, not a disaster recovery measure. C is wrong because RAID 5 is considered a fault-tolerant measure, not a disaster recovery measure.

25. **A.** The output is from the arp -a command, which shows information related to IP address to MAC address resolutions. B is wrong because the tracert command displays the route a packet takes between two points. The output from the command is different from that shown in the example. C is incorrect because the ipconfig command displays the network configuration of a system. The output from the command is different from that shown in the example. D is wrong because there is no such command as netinf.

26. **D.** The problem is most likely related to incorrectly set file permissions, so this is the best course of action. A is wrong because this is unlikely to be the problem, as other users are able to access the application without a problem. B is incorrect because although this might be a solution to the problem, this would not be the first thing to try. C is wrong because if the user is able to log on, changing the password is unlikely to have any effect.

27. **A.** IPSec is a non-proprietary security standard used to secure transmissions both on the internal network and when data is sent outside the local LAN. IPSec provides encryption and authentication services for data communications.

28. **A** and **B.** The devices on one side of the router need to be configured with a different IP network address than when the network was a single segment. Also, the default gateway information on all systems will need to be updated to use the newly installed router as the default gateway. C is wrong because the default gateway address should be the address of the router, not another workstation on the network. D is incorrect because for systems to communicate on an IP network, all devices must be assigned a unique IP address. Assigning systems the same address will cause address conflicts, thus resulting in none of the systems being able to communicate.

29. **C.** 100BaseT is implemented using a minimum of category 5 UTP cable. A is wrong because RG-58 is a type of coaxial cable with a maximum speed of 10Mbps. B is incorrect because category 4 UTP cable is not intended for use on a 100BaseT network. D is wrong because multimode fiber is used in fiber-optic networks. The 100BaseT standard defines 100Mbps networking using UTP cable.

30. **C.** Each node on a star network uses its own cable, which makes it easy to add users without disrupting current ones. Adding a node to a bus network can sometimes involve breaking the segment, which makes it inaccessible to all other nodes on the network. This makes answer A incorrect. Answer B is incorrect because a true ring network model would require that the ring be broken to add a new device. Answer D is incorrect because a mesh topology requires that every device be connected to every other device on the network. It is, therefore, quite difficult to expand a mesh network.

31. **A, C**, and **D.** A number of connector types are associated with fiber-optic cabling, including LC, SC, and MTRJ. F-Type is a connector associated with coaxial cabling.

32. **C.** When a client system first boots up, it will look for a DHCP server. If the server cannot be found, Automatic Private IP Addressing (APIPA) automatically assigns IP addresses to the client systems. The addresses are not routable and cannot be used to access remote segments. The addresses assigned are in the 169.254.0.0 address range. All clients configured with the valid APIPA address will be able to communicate between each other.

33. **B.** The Internet Assigned Numbers Authority (IANA) manages the address assignments for public networks such as the Internet. A is wrong because on a private network, you can use any addressing scheme that is compatible with your network. C is incorrect because an Ethernet network can be either private or public. It does not directly

need an IANA assigned addressing scheme. D is wrong because a WAN can be either private or public. It does not directly need an IANA assigned addressing scheme.

34. **B.** The 1000BaseCX standard specifies Gigabit Ethernet over STP cabling. A is wrong because 1000BaseSX and 1000BaseLX specifies Gigabit Ethernet over two types of multimode fiber. C is incorrect because single mode fiber-optic cable is used with the 100BaseFX standard. D is wrong because there is no such thing as CoreXtended fiber-optic cable.

35. **B.** TCP is a connection-oriented protocol, so it can recover from failed transmissions. A is wrong because L2TP is used in remote access connections. C is incorrect because IPX is a connectionless transport protocol and cannot recover from lost packets. D is incorrect because ARP is part of the TCP/IP protocol suite that resolves IP addresses to MAC addresses.

36. **D.** The DNS service uses port 53. A is wrong because secure HTTP uses port 443. B is incorrect because FTP uses port 21. C is wrong because Telnet uses port 23.

37. **D.** On a Linux system, the ifconfig command shows the network card configuration. A is wrong because the config command shows the network configuration on a NetWare server. B is incorrect because the ipconfig command shows the network configuration information on a Windows system. C is wrong because the winipcfg command shows the network configuration information on a certain Windows systems such as Windows 95/98.

38. **D.** The Internet Assigned Numbers Authority (IANA) has reserved 169.254.0.1–169.254.255.254 for Automatic Private IP Addressing. APIPA uses a Class B address with a subnet mask of 255.255.0.0.

39. **A.** In a RAID 1 scenario (disk mirroring), one disk carries an exact copy of the other. Therefore, the total volume of one disk will be lost to redundancy. All the other answers are incorrect.

40. **B.** Primary Rate ISDN (PRI) uses 23 B channels for carrying data, and one D channel for carrying signaling information. C is incorrect because this statement describes Basic Rate ISDN (BR). D is wrong because PRI uses 23 B channels and one D channel.

41. **D.** The gigabit Ethernet standard, 1000BaseSX, specifies a multimode fiber optic cable. 1000BaseSX can be used up to 550 meters. Other gigabit Ethernet standards use single mode fiber-optic cable or UTP cabling. There are no gigabit Ethernet standards that use coaxial cabling.

42. **B** and **D.** The most secure security model commonly implemented on networks is user-level security that is administered centrally. A is wrong because user administered security is normally associated with peer-to-peer networks and is not robust, as there is more than one person administering security. C is wrong because share-level security is not as secure as user-level security.

43. **C** and **D.** In most cases, you should try the simplest solutions first. Information such as the username and password should be verified before any reconfiguration is attempted. A is wrong because if the modem is dialing the remote system and getting a response, it is most likely working correctly. B is incorrect because running a remote diagnostic on the modem is a valid troubleshooting step, but you should first verify that the correct connection information is being used.

44. **C.** Although it provides the physical connection to the network, a NIC is considered a data-link device. A, B, and D are wrong because a NIC is not said to operate at any of these layers.

45. **D.** The Apple Filing Protocol (AFP) allows clients using the AppleTalk protocol to share files across a network. SMB is a file sharing protocol used on Windows networks. Samba is a protocol that provides interoperability between Windows and Linux/UNIX systems. NFS is the file sharing protocol associated with Linux/UNIX networks.

46. **D.** The 100BaseT standard defines an Ethernet network using twisted pair cable, which would be configured in a physical star configuration. However, even in a star configuration, an Ethernet network still uses a logical bus topology.

47. **B.** The output shown is from the netstat command from a Windows-based system. A, C, and D are wrong because all of these commands produce a different output from that shown.

48. **B.** Running on a Linux/UNIX system, Samba allows Windows clients access to shared files and printers on a Linux/UNIX host. Samba also allows UNIX users to access resources shared by Windows systems.

49. **C.** The Hayes AT command set provides commands that allow you to communicate directly with the modem. The ATZ command is used to reset the modem. A is wrong because the ATD command is used to dial a number. B is incorrect because the ATI command is used to retrieve information from the modem. The ATI3 command shows the manufacturer and model of the modem. D is wrong because the ATH command is used to hang up a connection.

50. **D.** A layer 2 address is a MAC address. A Layer 3 address is a software-configured protocol address. Because a normal resolution is considered to be a Layer-3–to–Layer-2 resolution, the resolution the other way is considered a reverse resolution. On a TCP/IP network, such a resolution is performed by the Reverse Address Resolution Protocol (RARP). A is wrong because ARPA is not an address resolution protocol. B is incorrect because the address resolution protocol (ARP) resolves Layer 3 addresses to Layer 2 addresses. C is wrong because the AppleTalk address resolution protocol is used, on AppleTalk networks, to resolve AppleTalk addresses to MAC addresses.

51. **C and D.** Server clustering is a strategy using a grouping of servers to provide fault tolerance and failover service solutions for a network. In a clustered configuration servers constantly communicate with each other. If one should fail, the other will know and take over the functions of that server including the services that the failed server delivered. This provides fault tolerance for network services. Because the network can function in the event of a failed server, network downtime is reduced. Server clustering is not used to create data transmission security.

52. **D.** XTDSL is not a recognized form of DSL. A is wrong because Very High Bit Rate DSL (VHDSL) is a recognized version of DSL. B is wrong because Rate Adaptive DSL (RADSL) is a recognized version of DSL. C is wrong because Asymmetric DSL (ADSL) is a recognized, and arguably the most popular, version of DSL.

53. **C.** If a Windows client system cannot locate and obtain an IP address from a DHCP server, it will be assigned an address automatically using APIPA. Once assigned, all client stations with an APIPA address will be able to communicate with each other. However, APIPA addresses are meant for internal communication and cannot be used to access remote networks.

54. **A and C.** A proxy server acts as a centralized point for Internet access, thus making it easy to control a user's Internet use. Also, the proxy server provides network address translation services as requests are sent out to the Internet using the address of the external interface of the proxy server, not the system that sent it. B is wrong because this statement describes the function of a firewall. Although some proxy servers also offer firewalling functionality, they are separate operations. D is incorrect because this statement describes the function of DHCP.

55. **A.** The output shown is from an `nbtstat` command running on a Windows system. B, C, and D are wrong because all of these commands produce different output from that shown.

56. **A** and **C.** Infrared and Bluetooth are short range wireless technologies used to connect personal devices such as PDAs, printers, and other resources to a computer. These are called a Personal Area Network (PAN) because it is a small network designed for personal use. PANs are often seen in coffee shops, libraries, or other areas where users work remotely. The 802.11 wireless standards, including 802.11g, are used to create wireless LANs, which include more devices, users, and resources.

57. **A.** Although it looks odd, this is a valid Class C address that could be assigned to a system on the network. B is the broadcast address of the network `200.200.200.0`. C is incorrect because it represents a valid Class B address. D is wrong because it is the network address for the network `203.16.42`.

58. **B.** Flow control occurs at the Transport layer of the OSI model. A, C, and D are wrong because flow control does not occur at any of these layers.

59. **A.** Unlike POP3, IMAP does not directly download and then remove messages from the mail server. Instead, IMAP leaves the email on the server so that messages can be retrieved from various locations. B and C are wrong because IMAP is used only for retrieving email. D is wrong because IMAP uses port `143`. POP uses port `110`.

60. **C.** 100BaseT is a network standard that runs at 100Mbps. A full-duplex configuration in a switched environment gives a maximum throughput between two devices of 200Mbps. A is wrong because this would be the maximum speed of a 10BaseT network in half-duplex mode. B is incorrect because this would be the maximum speed of a 10BaseT network in full-duplex mode. D is wrong because this would be the maximum speed of a 100BaseT network in half-duplex mode.

61. **C.** In a RAID 5 implementation, the space equal to the size of one disk in the array is lost to the storage of parity information. D describes the amount of space available for the storage of data, not the amount of space lost to the storage of parity information.

62. **D.** Most modern phone systems are digital, and therefore, regular analog modems that require analog lines will not work. A is incorrect because if the phone line in the room were analog, the modem would probably work. B is incorrect because the phone line in the room is not faulty because the user can call you to report the problem. C is incorrect because if the modem can report a "no dial tone" error, it is most likely working correctly.

63. **B.** The attribute file permission is not a valid NTFS file permission. A, C, and D are all valid file permissions on a Windows 2000 system.

64. **A.** The netstat utility allows you to view the TCP/IP connections between two systems. The nbtstat utility (answer B) is used to see the status of NetBIOS over TCP/IP connections. The tracert utility (answer C) is used to track the path that a packet of data takes between two hosts. The ipconfig utility (answer D) is used to view the IP addressing configuration information on a system.

65. **C.** The Kerberos authentication system uses tickets as part of the authentication process. HTTPS (answer A) is an implementation of SSL. It does not use tickets. POP3 (answer B) is an email retrieval protocol. SSL (answer D) does not use tickets.

66. **B.** AARP is used to map the AppleTalk addresses to both Ethernet and Token Ring physical addresses. The distance-vector routing protocol used on AppleTalk networks is RMTP, which makes answer A incorrect. C is incorrect because AARP resolves AppleTalk addresses to MAC addresses—not the other way around. AARP is not a link-state routing protocol.

67. **A.** The term *subnetting* refers to the process of using parts of the node address range for network addressing purposes. *Supernetting* (answer B) refers to the process of borrowing parts of the network address portion of an assigned address to be used for node addressing. *Subnet masking* (answer C) describes the process of applying a subnet mask to an address. Answer D is not a valid term.

68. **B.** A switch is more efficient than a hub, as it forwards data only to intended ports. A is incorrect because a hub directs data packets to all devices connected to the hub. C and D are wrong because these are not network devices.

69. **B.** If the gateway information is not correctly set, the data packets cannot get beyond the local subnet. The other options are not going to prevent the user from transmitting data to remote hosts.

70. **C.** Subnetting allows you to create more than one network from a single network address by manipulating the subnet mask to create more network addresses. A is wrong because the 127.x.x.x address range is reserved for TCP/IP loopback functionality and cannot be used as an addressing scheme. B is incorrect because reverse proxy is used when a proxy server protects another server (normally a Web server), which responds to requests from users on the other side of the proxy server. D is wrong because private addressing might well solve the issues of security and traffic management, but without also using reverse proxy, systems on the internal network aren't available to outside users.

71. **B** and **E.** A hardware loopback plug connects the 2 and 6 wires and 1 and 3 wires to simulate a live network connection. Answers A, C, and D are not correct for the cable in a hardware loopback adapter.

72. **A.** Each of the 802.11 wireless standards specify radio waves as the media to transport data signals. 802.11a uses the 5GHz RF range for data transmissions. 802.11, 802.11b, and 802.11g all use the 2.4GHz RF range.

CD Contents and Installation Instructions

The CD features an innovative practice test engine powered by MeasureUp™, giving you yet another effective tool to assess your readiness for the exam.

Multiple Test Modes

MeasureUp practice tests are available in Study, Certification, Custom, Adaptive, Missed Question, and Non-Duplicate question modes.

Study Mode

Tests administered in Study Mode allow you to request the correct answer(s) and explanation to each question during the test. These tests are not timed. You can modify the testing environment *during* the test by selecting the Options button.

Certification Mode

Tests administered in Certification Mode closely simulate the actual testing environment you will encounter when taking a certification exam. These tests do not allow you to request the answer(s) and/or explanation to each question until after the exam.

Custom Mode

Custom Mode allows you to specify your preferred testing environment. Use this mode to specify the objectives you want to include in your test, the timer length, and other test properties. You can also modify the testing environment *during* the test by selecting the Options button.

Missed Question Mode

Missed Question Mode allows you to take a test containing only the questions you have missed previously.

Non-Duplicate Mode

Non-Duplicate Mode allows you to take a test containing only questions not displayed previously.

Random Questions and Order of Answers

This feature helps you learn the material without memorizing questions and answers. Each time you take a practice test, the questions and answers appear in a different randomized order.

Detailed Explanations of Correct and Incorrect Answers

In this mode, you'll receive automatic feedback on all correct and incorrect answers. The detailed answer explanations are a superb learning tool in their own right.

Attention to Exam Objectives

MeasureUp practice tests are designed to appropriately balance the questions over each technical area covered by a specific exam.

Installing the CD

The minimum system requirements for the CD-ROM are

➤ Windows 95, 98, Me, NT4, 2000, or XP

➤ 7Mb disk space for testing engine

➤ An average of 1Mb disk space for each test

To install the CD-ROM, follow these instructions:

 If you need technical support, please contact MeasureUp at 678-356-5050 or email support@measureup.com. Additionally, you'll find Frequently Asked Questions (FAQ) at www.measureup.com.

1. Close all applications before beginning this installation.

2. Insert the CD into your CD-ROM drive. If the setup starts automatically, go to step 6. If the setup does not start automatically, continue with step 3.

3. From the Start menu, select Run.

4. Click Browse to locate the MeasureUp CD. In the Browse dialog box, from the Look In drop-down list, select the CD-ROM drive.

5. In the Browse dialog box, double-click on Setup.exe. In the Run dialog box, click OK to begin the installation.

6. On the Welcome Screen, click MeasureUp Practice Questions to begin installation.

7. Follow the Certification Prep Wizard by clicking Next.

8. To agree to the Software License Agreement, click Yes.

9. On the Choose Destination Location screen, click Next to install the software to C:\Program Files\Certification Preparation.

 If you cannot locate MeasureUp Practice Tests through the Start menu, see the section later in this appendix titled, "Creating a Shortcut to the MeasureUp Practice Tests."

10. On the Setup Type screen, select Typical Setup. Click Next to continue.

11. In the Select Program Folder screen, you can name the program folder your tests will be in. To select the default, simply click Next and the installation will continue.

12. After the installation is complete, verify that Yes, I Want to Restart My Computer Now is selected. If you select No, I Will Restart My Computer Later, you will not be able to use the program until you restart your computer.

13. Click Finish.

14. After restarting your computer, choose Start, Programs, MeasureUp, MeasureUp Practice Tests.

15. On the MeasureUp Welcome Screen, click Create User Profile.

16. In the User Profile dialog box, complete the mandatory fields and click Create Profile.

17. Select the practice test you want to access and click Start Test.

Creating a Shortcut to the MeasureUp Practice Tests

To create a shortcut to the MeasureUp Practice Tests, follow these steps.

1. Right-click on your Desktop.

2. From the shortcut menu select New, Shortcut.

3. Browse to C:\Program Files\MeasureUp Practice Tests and select the MeasureUpCertification.exe or Localware.exe file.

4. Click OK.

5. Click Next.

6. Rename the shortcut MeasureUp.

7. Click Finish.

After you have completed step 7, use the MeasureUp shortcut on your Desktop to access the MeasureUp products you ordered.

Technical Support

If you encounter problems with the MeasureUp test engine on the CD-ROM, please contact MeasureUp at 1-678-356-5050 or email support@ measureup.com. Technical support hours are from 8 a.m. to 5 p.m. EST Monday through Friday. Additionally, you'll find Frequently Asked Questions (FAQ) at www.measureup.com.

If you'd like to purchase additional MeasureUp products, telephone 1-678-356-5050 or 1-800-649-1MUP (1687) or visit www.measureup.com.

Glossary

Numbers and Symbols

10Base2

An IEEE 802.3 specification for Ethernet at 10Mbps over thin coaxial cable. The maximum length of a 10Base2 segment is 185 meters (that is, 607 feet). 10Base2 operates at 10Mbps and uses a baseband transmission method.

10Base5

The IEEE 802.3 specification for 10Mbps Ethernet using thick coaxial cable. The maximum length of a 10Base5 segment is 500 meters (that is, 1,640 feet).

10BaseFL

The IEEE 802.3 specification for running Ethernet at 10Mbps over fiber optic cable. The maximum length of a 10BaseFL segment is 2,000 meters (6,561 feet).

10BaseT

The IEEE 802.3i specification for running Ethernet at 10Mbps over twisted-pair cabling. The maximum length of a 10BaseT segment is 100 meters (that is, 330 feet).

100BaseFX

The IEEE 802.3 specification for running Fast Ethernet at 100Mbps over fiber-optic cable. The maximum length of a 100BaseFX segment is 2,000 meters (6,561 feet), in full duplex mode.

100BaseT

The IEEE 802.3 specification for running Ethernet at 100Mbps over twisted-pair cabling. The maximum length of a 100BaseT segment is 100 meters (that is, 330 feet).

100BaseT4

The IEEE specification that allows the use of Fast Ethernet (100Mbps) technology over existing Category 3 and Category 4 wiring, using all four pairs of wires. The maximum length of a 100BaseT4 segment is 100 meters (that is, 330 feet).

100BaseTX

An IEEE 802.3u specification, also known as Fast Ethernet, for running Ethernet at 100Mbps over STP or UTP. The maximum length of a 100BaseTX segment is 100 meters (that is, 330 feet).

100BaseVG-AnyLAN

The IEEE 802.12 specification that allows data transmissions of 100Mbps over Category 3 cable, using all sets of wires. *VG* in 100BaseVG-AnyLAN stands for *voice grade* because of its capability to be used over voice-grade cable. The maximum length of a 100BaseVG-AnyLAN segment is 100 meters (330 feet) on Category 3 cable, 150 meters (492 feet) on Category 5 cable, and 2,000 meters (6,561 feet) on fiber-optic cable.

1000BaseT

IEEE 802.3ab standard that specifies Gigabit Ethernet over Category 5 UTP cable. The standard allows for full-duplex transmission using the four pairs of twisted cable

1000BaseX

The IEEE 802.3z specification, also known as Gigabit Ethernet, that defines standards for data transmissions of 1000Mbps (1Gbps). 1000Basex is most often associated with fiber or STP cable. 1000BaseX refers collectively to three distinct standards: 1000BaseLX, 1000BaseSX, and 1000BaseCX.

1000BaseCX

IEEE802.3ab standard that uses a special shielded copper cable. 1000BaseCX can be used up to a maximum distance of 25 meters.

1000BaseLX

IEEE 802.3z standard that specifies Gigabit Ethernet over fiber-optic cable. 1000BaseLX can be used up to 5,000 meters.

1000BaseSX

IEEE 802.3z standard that specifies Gigabit Ethernet over fiber-optic cable.

10GbE

Term commonly used to refer to the 10Gbps Ethernet networking standards such as 10GBaseER, 10GBaseLR, and 10GBaseSR. 10 Gigabit Ethernet is defined in the IEEE 802.3ae standard

10GBaseER

10Gbps Ethernet networking standard that can be used up to 40,000 meters.

10GBaseLR

10Gbps Ethernet networking standard that can be used up to 10,000 meters. 10GBaseLR uses single-mode fiber-optic cabling.

10GBaseSR

10Gbps Ethernet networking standard that can be used over relatively short distances, up to 300 meters.

A

Access Point

A transmitter and receiver (transceiver) device commonly used to facilitate communication between a wireless client and a wired network. Wireless APs are use with the wireless infrastructure network topology to provide a connection point between WLANs and a wired Ethernet LAN.

ACK

The acknowledgment message sent between two hosts during a TCP session.

ACL (access control list)

The list of trustees assigned to a file or directory. A trustee can be any object available to the security subsystem. The term ACL is also used with routers and firewall systems to refer to the list of permitted computers or users.

Active Directory

An X.500-compliant directory service used on Windows networks.

active hub

A hub that has power supplied to it for the purposes of regenerating the signals that pass through it.

active termination

A termination system used on a SCSI bus. Unlike passive termination, which uses voltage resistors, active termination uses voltage regulators to create the termination voltage.

address

A set of numbers, used to identify and locate a resource or device on a network. An example may be an IP address such as 192.168.2.1.

ad hoc topology

Defines a wireless network layout whereby devices communicate directly between themselves without using an access point. Sometimes called an unmanaged or peer-to-peer wireless topology.

administrator

A person who is responsible for the control and security of the user accounts, resources, and data on a network.

Administrator account

On a Windows system, the default account that has rights to access everything and to assign rights to other users on the network. Unlike other user accounts, the Administrator account cannot be deleted.

ADSL (Asymmetric Digital Subscriber Line)

A service that transmits digital voice and data over existing (analog) phone lines.

AFP (Apple File Protocol)

File sharing and access protocol implemented in Apple networks. AFP can be implemented over TCP/IP (AppleTalk over IP)

ANSI (American National Standards Institute)

An organization that publishes standards for communications, programming languages, and networking.

antivirus software

A software application that detects and removes virus programs.

APIPA (Automatic Private IP Addressing)

Technology implemented on certain Windows platforms through which a system will assign itself an IP address in the absence of a DHCP server. Addresses are assigned from the 169.254.x.x address range.

application layer

Layer 7 of the OSI model, which provides support for end users and for application programs that are using network resources.

Application log

A log file on a Windows system that provides information on events that occur within an application.

archive bit

A flag that is set on a file after it has been created or altered. Some backup methods reset the flag to indicate that it has been backed up.

ARP (Address Resolution Protocol)

A protocol in the TCP/IP protocol suite that is used to resolve IP addresses to MAC addresses. Specifically, the ARP command returns a layer 2 address for a layer 3 address.

ARP table

A table of entries used by ARP to store resolved ARP requests. Entries can also be stored manually.

array

A group of devices arranged in a fault-tolerant configuration. *See also* RAID.

attenuation

The loss of signal strength that is experienced as data is transmitted over distance and across the network media.

authentication

The process by which a user's identity is validated on a network. The most common authentication method is a username and password combination.

B

B (bearer) channel
In ISDN, a 64Kbps channel that carries data. *See also* D channel.

backbone
A network segment that acts as a trunk between other network segments. Backbones are typically high-bandwidth implementations such as fiber-optic cable.

backup schedule
A document or plan that defines what type of backups are made, when, and what data is backed up.

bandwidth
The width of the range of electrical frequencies, or amount of channels that the media can support. Bandwidth correlates to the amount of data that can traverse the media at one time, but other factors determine what the maximum speed supported by a cable will be.

baseband
A term applied to any media capable of carrying only a single data signal at a time. *Compare with* broadband.

baseline
A measurement of performance of a device or system for the purposes of future comparison. Baselining is a common server administration task.

baud rate
The speed or rate of signal transfer. Baud rate bandwidth is measured in cycles per second, or hertz (Hz). The word *baud* is derived from the name of French telegraphy expert J. M. Baudot.

binary
A base 2 numbering system that is used in digital signaling. It uses only the numbers 1 and 0.

Bindery
The name of the user account information database on NetWare servers up to and including NetWare 3.x.

binding
The process of associating a protocol with a NIC.

biometrics
The science and technology of measuring and analyzing biological data. Biometrics is used for security purposes to analyze and compare characteristics such as voice patterns, retina patterns, and hand measurements.

BIOS (Basic Input/Output System)
A basic set of instructions that a device needs to operate.

bit
An electronic digit used in the binary numbering system. Bit is a contraction of the terms *binary* and *digit*.

blackout
A total loss of electrical power.

Blue Screen of Death

The term for the blue-screen STOP errors that occur on and halt a Windows systems.

Bluetooth

A low-cost, short-range RF technology designed to replace many of the cords that are used to connect devices. Bluetooth uses 2.4Ghz RF and provides transmission speeds up to 16Mbps.

BNC (Bayonet Neill Concelman)

A family of connectors typically associated with thin coaxial cabling and 10Base2 networks. BNC connectors use a twist and lock mechanism to connect devices to the network.

bound media

A term used to describe any media that have physical constraints, such as coaxial, fiber-optic, and twisted pair. *Compare with* unbound media.

boundless media

See unbound media.

BRI (Basic Rate Interface)

An ISDN digital communications line that consists of three independent channels: two B channels, each at 64Kbps, and one D channel, at 16Kbps. ISDN BRI is often referred to as 2B+D. *See also* ISDN, PRI.

bridge

A device that connects and passes traffic between two network segments that use the same communications protocol. Bridges operate at the data-link layer of the OSI model. A bridge filters, forwards, or floods an incoming frame based on the MAC address of that frame.

bridging address table

A list of MAC addresses that a bridge keeps and uses when it receives packets. The bridge uses the bridging address table to determine which segment the destination address is on before it sends the packet to the next interface or drops the packet (if it is on the same segment as the sending node).

broadband

A communications strategy that uses analog or digital signaling over multiple communications channels.

broadcast

A packet delivery system in which a copy of a packet is given to all hosts attached to the network.

broadcast storm

An undesirable condition in which broadcasts become so numerous as to bog down the flow of data across the network.

brouter

A device that can be used to combine the benefits of both routers and bridges. Its common usage is to route routable protocols at the network layer of the OSI model and to bridge nonroutable protocols at the data-link layer.

brownout

A short-term decrease in the voltage level, usually caused by the startup demands of other electrical devices.

buffer

An area of memory in a device that is used to store data before it is forwarded to another device or location.

bus topology

A linear LAN architecture in which all devices are connected to a common cable, referred to as a bus or backbone.

byte

A set of bits (usually 8 bits) that operates as a unit to signify a character.

C

cable modem

A device that provides Internet access over cable television lines.

cable tester

A device that is used to check for electrical continuity along a length of cable. *Cable tester* is a generic term that can be applied to devices such as volt/ohm meters and TDRs.

caching-only server

A type of DNS server that operates the same way as secondary servers except that a zone transfer does not take place when the caching-only server is started.

carrier

A signal that carries data. The carrier signal is modulated to create peaks and troughs, which represent binary bits.

CDDI (Copper Distributed Data Interface)

An implementation of the FDDI standard that uses copper cable rather than optical cable.

Centronics connector

A connector that uses clips that snap into place to secure the connector. Used with external SCSI devices and some printer connections.

change control

A process in which a detailed record of every change made to the network is documented.

channel

A communications path used for data transmission.

checksum

A basic method of error checking that involves calculating the sum of bytes in a section of data and then embedding the result in the packet. When the packet reaches the destination, the calculation is performed again to make sure that the value is still the same.

CIDR (classless interdomain routing)

An IP addressing scheme that allows a single IP address to designate many unique IP addresses. CIDR addressing uses an IP address followed by a '/' and the IP network prefix. An example CIDR address would be 192.168.100.0/16. CIDR is sometimes referred to as Supernetting.

circuit switching

A method of sending data between two parties in which a dedicated circuit is created at the beginning of the conversation and broken at the end. All data transported during the session travels over the same path, or circuit.

Class A network

A TCP/IP network that uses addresses from 1 to 126 and supports up to 126 subnets with 16,777,214 unique hosts each.

Class B network

A TCP/IP network that uses addresses from 128 to 191 and supports up to 16,384 subnets with 65,534 unique hosts each.

Class C network

A TCP/IP network that uses addresses from 192 to 223 and supports up to 2,097,152 subnets with 254 unique hosts each.

client

A node that uses the services from another node on a network.

client/server networking

A networking architecture in which front-end, or client, nodes request and process data stored by the back-end, or server, node.

clustering

A technology that allows two or more computers to act as a single system to provide improved fault tolerance, load balancing and failover capability.

coaxial cable

A data cable, commonly referred to as *coax*, that is made of a solid copper core that is insulated and surrounded by braided metal and covered with a thick plastic or rubber covering. Coax is the standard cable used in cable television and in older bus topology networks.

config

A command that is used on a NetWare server to see basic information such as the server name, NDS information, and the details of network interface configurations.

collision

The result of two frames transmitting simultaneously on an Ethernet network and colliding, thereby damaging both frames.

collision domain

A segment of an Ethernet network that is between managing nodes, where only one packet can be transmitted at any given time. Switches, bridges, and routers can be used to segment a network into separate collision domains.

collision light

An LED on networking equipment that flashes to indicate a collision on the network. A collision light can be used to determine whether the network is experiencing a large number of collisions.

COM port (communication port)

A connection through which serial devices and a computer's motherboard can communicate. A COM port requires standard configuration information, such as an IRQ, an I/O address, and a COM port number.

communication

The transfer of information between nodes on a network.

concentrator

A device that combines several communications channels into one. It is often used to tie multiple terminals together into one line.

connectionless communication

Packet transfer in which delivery is not guaranteed.

connection-oriented communication

Packet transfer in which delivery is guaranteed.

connectivity

The linking of nodes on a network in order for communication to take place.

copy backup

Normally, a backup of the entire hard drive. A copy backup is similar to a full backup, except that the copy backup does not alter the state of the archive bits on files.

cost

A value that is used to encourage or discourage the use of a certain route through a network. Routes that are to be discouraged are assigned a higher cost, and those that are to be encouraged are assigned a lower cost. *See also* metric.

cracker

A person who attempts to break software code or gain access to a system to which he or she is not authorized. *See also* hacker.

cracking

The process of attempting to break software code, normally to defeat copyright protection or alter the software's functioning. Also the process of attempting to gain unauthorized access to a computer system. *See also* hacking.

CRC (cyclical redundancy check)

A method used to check for errors in packets that have been transferred across a network. A computation bit is added to the packet and recalculated at the destination to determine whether the entire content of the packet has been transferred correctly.

crimper

A tool that is used to join connectors to the ends of network cables.

crossover cable

A UTP cable in which the 1 and 3 wires and the 2 and 6 wires are crossed for the purposes of placing the transmit line of one device on the receive line of the other. Crossover cables can be used to directly connect two like devices—for example, two computer systems—or as a means to expand networks that use devices such as hubs or switches.

crosstalk

Electronic interference that is caused when two wires are too close to each other.

CSMA/CA (carrier-sense multiple-access with collision avoidance)

A contention media access method that uses collision-avoidance techniques.

CSMA/CD (carrier-sense multiple-access with collision detection)

A contention media access method that uses collision-detection and retransmission techniques.

cut-through packet switching

A switching method that does not copy the entire packet into the switch buffers. Instead, the destination address is captured into the switch, the route to the destination node is determined, and the packet is quickly sent out the corresponding port. Cut-through packet switching maintains a low latency.

D

D (delta) channel

The channel used on ISDN to communicate signaling and other related information. Use of the D channel leaves the B channels free for data communication. *See also* B channel.

D-shell connector

A connector that is shaped like a letter D and uses pins and sockets to establish connections between peripheral devices, using serial or parallel ports. The number that follows *DB* in the name of a D connector is the number of pins used for connectivity; for example, a DB-9 connector has 9 pins, and a DB-25 connector has 25 pins.

daemon

A service or process that runs on a UNIX or Linux server.

DAS (dual attached station)

A device on an FDDI network that is connected to both rings. *Compare with* SAS.

DAT (digital audio tape)

A tape recording technology that uses the helical scan recording method. This technology has been used in videotape recorders and VCRs since the 1950s.

Data field

In a frame, the field or section that contains the data.

datagram

An information grouping that is transmitted as a unit at the network layer. *See also* packet.

data-link layer

Layer 2 of the OSI model, which is above the physical layer. Data comes off the cable and goes into the data-link layer. The data-link layer has two distinct sublayers: MAC and LLC.

DB-9

A 9-pin connector that is used for serial port or parallel port connection between PCs and peripheral devices.

DB-25

A 25-pin connector that is used for serial port or parallel port connection between PCs and peripheral devices.

DDNS (dynamic DNS)

A form of DNS that allows systems to be registered and deregistered with the DNS system dynamically. DDNS is facilitated by DHCP, which passes IP address assignments to the DNS server for entry into the DNS server records. This is in contrast with the conventional DNS system, in which entries must be made manually.

DDS (digital data storage)

A format for storing computer data on a DAT. DDS-formatted tapes can be read by either a DDS or DAT drive. The original DDS standard specified a 4mm tape cartridge with a capacity of 1.3GB. Subsequent implementations of DDS have taken the capacity to 40GB with compression.

dedicated line

A dedicated circuit that is used in WANs to provide a constant connection between two points.

default gateway

Normally a router or a multi-homed computer to which packets are sent when they are destined for a host on a different network.

Delete or Erase

A right that is given to users, which allows them to delete a file or files in a directory or to delete a directory.

demarcation point

The point at which communication lines enter a customer's premises. Sometimes shortened to simply "demarc."

destination address

The network address to which the frame is being sent.

DHCP (Dynamic Host Configuration Protocol)

A protocol that provides dynamic IP addressing to workstations on the network.

dial-up networking

Refers to the connection of a remote node to a network using POTS.

differential backup

A backup of only the data that has been created or changed since the previous full backup. In a differential backup, the state of the archive bits is not altered.

directory services

A system that allows network resources to be viewed as objects which are stored in a database. This database can then be divided up and distributed among different servers on the network.Examples of directory services systems include Novell Directory Services and Microsoft Active Directory.

disaster recovery plan

A plan for implementing duplicate computer services in the event of a natural disaster, a human-made disaster, or another catastrophe. A disaster recovery plan includes off-site backups and procedures to activate information systems in alternative locations.

disk duplexing

A fault-tolerant standard that is based on RAID 1 that uses disk mirroring with dual disk controllers.

disk mirroring

A fault-tolerant standard that is defined as RAID 1 and mirrors data between two disks to create an exact copy.

disk striping

An implementation of RAID in which data is distributed across multiple disks in a stripe. Some striping implementations provide performance improvements (RAID 0), whereas others provide fault tolerance (RAID 5).

distance-vector routing

A type of routing in which a router uses broadcasts to inform neighboring routers on the network of the routes it knows about. *Compare with* link-state routing.

DLT (digital linear tape)

A high-performance and high-capacity tape backup system that offers capacities up to 220GB with compression.

DMA (direct memory access)

The process of transferring data directly into memory at high speeds, bypassing the CPU and incurring no processor overhead.

DNS (Domain Name Service)

A system that is used to translate domain names, such as www.quepublishing.com, into IP addresses, such as 165.193.123.44. DNS uses a hierarchical namespace that enables the database of host-name-to-IP address mappings to be distributed across multiple servers.

domain

A logical group of computers in a Windows NT/2000 network. Also, a section of the DNS namespace.

domain name server

A server that runs application software that enables the server to perform a role associated with the DNS service.

DoS (Denial of Service) attack

A type of hacking attack in which the target system is overwhelmed with requests for service, resulting in it not being capable of servicing any requests—legitimate or otherwise.

downtime

A period of time during which a computer system or network is unavailable. This may be because of scheduled maintenance or due to hardware or software failure.

drive mapping

A process through which an alias makes a network path appear as if it were a local drive.

DSL (Digital Subscriber Line)

A public network technology that delivers high bandwidth over conventional copper wiring over limited distances.

DSU (data service unit)

A network communications device that formats and controls data for transmission over digital lines. A DSU is used in conjunction with a CSU.

DTE (data terminal equipment)

A device used at the user end of a user network interface that serves as a data source, a destination, or both. DTE devices include computers, protocol translators, and multiplexers.

dumb terminal

A keyboard/monitor combination that allows access to a multiuser system but provides no processing or storage at the local level.

duplexing

In RAID, a RAID 1 mirror set in which each drive is connected to a separate controller to eliminate the single point of failure that the controller created.

dynamic routing

A routing system that enables routing information to be communicated between devices automatically and can recognize changes in the network topology and update routing tables accordingly. *Compare with* static routing.

dynamic window

A flow control mechanism that prevents the sender of data from overwhelming the receiver. The amount of data that can be buffered in a dynamic window varies in size, hence its name.

E

EAP (Extensible Authentication Protocol)

An extension of the PPP protocol that supports authentication methods more secure than a standard username and password combination. EAP is commonly used as an authentication protocol for token cards, smart cards, and digital certificates.

EMI (electromagnetic interference)

External interference of electromagnetic signals that causes a reduction of data integrity and increased error rates in a transmission medium.

encapsulation

A technique used by protocols in which header and/or trailer information is added to the protocol data unit as it is passed down through the protocol stack on a sending system. The reverse process, called decapsulation, is performed at the receiving system as the packet travels up through the protocol suite.

encryption

The modification of data for security purposes prior to transmission so that it is not comprehendible without the decoding method.

ESD (electrostatic discharge)

A condition that is created when two objects of dissimilar electrical charge come into contact with each other. The result is that a charge from the object with the higher electrical charge discharges itself into the object with the lower-level charge. This discharge can be extremely harmful to computer components and circuit boards.

Ethernet

The most common LAN technology. Ethernet can be implemented using coaxial, twisted-pair, or fiber-optic cable. Ethernet typically uses the CSMA/CD media access method and has various implementation standards.

Event Viewer

A utility that facilitates the viewing of log files on Windows server operating systems.

EXT2
The default file system used in Linux systems.

F

F-Type
Screw type connector used with coaxial cable. In computing environments, it is most commonly used to connect cable modems to ISP equipment or incoming cable feeds.

failover
The automatic switching from one device or system to another. Servers can be configured in a failover configuration so that if the primary server fails, the secondary server takes over automatically.

Fast Ethernet
The IEEE 802.3u specification for data transfers of up to 100Mbps over twisted-pair cable. *See also* 100BaseFX, 100BaseTX, 100BaseT, and 100BaseT4.

fault tolerance
The capability of a component, system or network to endure a failure.

FCS (Frame Check Sequence) field
A field of a packet that holds a CRC value to ensure that all of the frame's data arrives intact.

FDDI (Fiber Distributed Data Interface)
A high-speed data transfer technology that is designed to extend the capabilities of existing LANs by using a dual-ring topology and a token-passing access method.

FDM (Frequency-Division Multiplexing)
A technology that divides the output channel into multiple smaller-bandwidth channels, each of which uses a different frequency range.

fiber-optic cable
Also known as fiber optics or optical fiber, a physical medium that is capable of conducting modulated light transmissions. Compared with other transmission media, fiber-optic cable is more expensive, but it is not susceptible to EMI or crosstalk, is capable of very high data rates, and can be used over greater distances than copper-based media.

fibre channel
A technology that defines full gigabit-per-second data transfer over fiber-optic cable. Commonly used with storage area network (SAN) implementations.

firewall
A program, system, device, or group of devices that acts as a barrier between one network and another. Firewalls are configured to allow certain types of traffic to pass while blocking others.

FireWire

A high-speed serial bus technology that allows up to 63 devices to be connected to a system. FireWire provides sufficient bandwidth for multimedia operations and supports hot swapping and multiple speeds on the same bus.

fixed wireless

A technology that provides data communication capabilities between two fixed locations. Fixed wireless can be used as a private networking method but is also becoming increasingly common as an Internet access method.

flow control

A method of controlling the amount of data that is transmitted within a given period of time. There are different types of flow control. *See also* dynamic window, static window.

FQDN (Fully Qualified Domain Name)

The entire domain name that specifies the name of the computer as well as the domain in which it resides and the top-level DNS domain (for example, marketing.quepublishing.com).

fragment-free switching

A switching method that uses the first 64 bytes of a frame to determine whether the frame is corrupted. If this first part is intact, the frame is forwarded.

frame

A grouping of information that is transmitted as a unit across the network at the data-link layer of the OSI model.

Frame Length field

In a data frame, the field that specifies the length of a frame.

Frame Type field

In a data frame, the field that names the protocol that is being sent in the frame.

frequency

The number of cycles of an alternating current signal over a unit of time. Frequency is expressed in hertz.

FTP (File Transfer Protocol)

A protocol that provides for the transfer of files between two systems. FTP is part of the TCP/IP protocol suite and operates at layer 7 of the OSI model.

full backup

A backup in which files, regardless of whether they have been changed, are copied to the backup media. In a full backup, the archive bits of the files are reset.

full-duplex

A system in which data is transmitted in two directions simultaneously. *Compare with* half-duplex.

G

gateway
A hardware or software solution that enables communications between two dissimilar networking systems or protocols. A gateway can operate at any layer of the OSI model but is commonly associated with the application layer.

Gb (gigabit)
1 billion bits or 1,000Mb.

Gbps (gigabits per second)
The throughput of a given network medium in terms of 1 billion bps.

GFS (Grandfather, Father, Son)
A backup strategy of maintaining backups on a daily, weekly, and monthly schedule. Backups are made on a five-day or seven-day schedule. A full backup is performed at least once a week. On all other days full, incremental, or differential backups (or no backups at all) are performed. The daily incremental, or differential, backups are known as the *son*. The *father* is the last full backup in the week (the weekly backup). The *grandfather* is the last full backup of the month (the monthly backup).

Gigabit Ethernet
The IEEE 802.3z and IEEE802.3ab specifications that defines standards for data transmissions of 1Gbps. *See also* 1000BaseX.

guaranteed flow control
A method of flow control in which the sending and receiving hosts agree on a rate of data transmission. After the rate is determined, the communication takes place at the guaranteed rate until the sender is finished. No buffering takes place at the receiver.

H

hacker
A person who carries out hacking on a computer software program. *See also* cracker.

hacking
The process of deconstructing computer software in an effort to understand how it works and to improve it. *See also* cracking.

half-duplex
A connection in which data is transmitted in both directions, but not simultaneously. *Compare with* full-duplex.

handshake
The initial communication between two data communication devices, during which they agree on protocol and transfer rules for the session.

hardware address
The hardware-encoded MAC address that is burned into every NIC.

hardware loopback

A device that is plugged into an interface for the purposes of simulating a network connection and thus enabling the interface to be tested as if it is operating while connected.

High-Speed Token Ring

A version of Token Ring that has a maximum speed of 100Mbps. This is in contrast with other Token Ring standards, which have maximum speeds of 4Mbps or 16Mbps.

hop

The means by which routing protocols determine the shortest way to reach a given destination. Each router constitutes one hop; so if a router is four hops away from another router, there are three routers, or hops, between itself and the destination. In some cases, the final step is also counted as a hop.

host

Any computer system on a network. In the UNIX world, any device that is assigned an IP address.

host ID

An identifier used to uniquely identify a client or resource on a network.

hostname

A name that is assigned to a system for the purposes of identifying it on the network in a more user-friendly manner than by the network address.

HOSTS file

A text file that contains hostname-to-IP address mappings. All commonly used platforms accommodate static name resolution using the HOSTS file.

hot site

A disaster recovery term used to describe an alternate network site that can be immediately functional in the event of a disaster at the primary site.

hot spare

In a RAID configuration, a drive that sits idle until another drive in the RAID array fails; at which point, the hot spare takes over the role of the failed drive.

Hotspot

An area in which an access point provides public wireless broadband network services to mobile visitors through a WLAN. Hotspots are often located in heavily populated places such as airports, hotels, and coffee shops.

hot swap

The removal and replacement of a component in a system while the power is still on and the system is functioning.

HSSI (High Speed Serial Interface)

The network standard for high-speed serial communications over WAN links. Includes various T-carrier technologies.

HTTP (Hypertext Transfer Protocol)

An application layer protocol used by Web browsers to transfer pages, links, and graphics from the remote node to the user's computer.

HTTPS (Hypertext Transfer Protocol Secure)

A protocol that performs the same function as HTTP but does so over an encrypted link, ensuring the confidentiality of any data that is uploaded or downloaded. Also referred to as S-HTTP.

hub

A hardware device that acts as a connection point on a network that uses twisted-pair cable. Also known as a concentrator or a multiport repeater.

HyperTerminal

A Windows-based communications program that allows users to establish host/shell access to a remote system.

I

IANA (Internet Assigned Numbers Authority)

An organization that is responsible for IP addresses, domain names, and protocol parameters. Some functions of IANA, such as domain name assignment, have been devolved into other organizations.

ICMP (Internet Control Message Protocol)

A network-layer Internet protocol documented in RFC 792 that reports errors and provides other information relevant to IP packet processing. Utilities such as ping and tracert use functionality provided by ICMP.

IDE (Integrated Drive Electronics)

The most common type of disk drive used in PCs today. In these devices, the controller is integrated into the device.

IEEE (Institute of Electrical and Electronics Engineers)

A professional organization that among other things, develops standards for networking and communications.

IEEE 802.1

A standard that defines the OSI model's physical and data-link layers. This standard enables two IEEE LAN stations to communicate over a LAN or WAN and is often referred to as the internetworking standard.

IEEE 802.1X

An IEEE security standard designed for authenticating wireless devices. This standard uses the Extensible Authentication Protocol (EAP) to provide a central authentication server to authenticate each user on the network.

IEEE 802.2

A standard that defines the LLC sublayer of the data-link layer for the entire series of protocols covered by the 802.x standards. This standard specifies the adding of header fields, which tell the receiving host which upper layer sent the information.

IEEE 802.3

A standard that specifies physical-layer attributes, such as signaling types, data rates, and topologies, as well as the media access method used. It also defines specifications for the implementation of the physical layer and the MAC sublayer of the data-link layer, using CSMA/CD. This standard also includes the original specifications for Fast Ethernet.

IEEE 802.4

A standard that defines how production machines should communicate and establishes a common protocol for use in connecting these machines together. It also defines specifications for the implementation of the physical layer and the MAC sublayer of the data-link layer, using Token Ring access over a bus topology.

IEEE 802.5

A standard that is used to define Token Ring. However, it does not specify a particular topology or transmission medium. It provides specifications for the implementation of the physical layer and the MAC sublayer of the data-link layer, using a token-passing, media-access method on a ring topology.

IEEE 802.6

A standard that defines the distributed queue dual bus technology to transfer high-speed data between nodes. It provides specifications for the implementation of MANs.

IEEE 802.7

A standard that defines the design, installation, and testing of broadband-based communications and related physical media connectivity.

IEEE 802.8

A standard that defines a group, called the Fiber Optic Technical Advisory Group, that advises the other 802 standard committees on various fiber-optic technologies and standards.

IEEE 802.9

A standard that defines the integration of voice and data transmissions using isochronous Ethernet.

IEEE 802.10

A standard that focuses on security issues by defining a standard method for protocols and services to exchange data securely using encryption mechanisms.

IEEE 802.11

The original IEEE wireless standard defines standards for wireless LAN communication. It also specifies the original 802.11 wireless standard and offers speeds of 1 to 2Mbps using the CSMA/CA access method.

IEEE 802.11a

A wireless networking standard operating in the 5GHz band. 802.11a supports a maximum theoretical data rate of 54Mbps. Depending upon interference, 802.11a could have a range of 150 feet at the lowest speed setting. Higher speed transmissions would see a lower range. 802.11a uses CSMA/CA media access method and is not compatible with 802.11b and 802.11g.

IEEE 802.11b

A commonly deployed IEEE wireless standard that uses the 2.4GHz RF range and offers speeds up to 11Mbps. Under ideal conditions, the transmission range can be as far as 75 meters.

IEEE 802.11g

An IEEE wireless standard that is backward compatible with 802.11b. 802.11g offers a data rate of 54Mbps. Like 802.11b, 802.11g uses the 2.GHz RF range of 802.11b.

IEEE 802.12

A standard that defines 100BaseVG-AnyLAN, which uses a 1Gbps signaling rate and a special media access method that allows 100Mbps data traffic over voice-grade cable.

IEEE 1394

A standard that defines a system for connecting up to 63 devices on an external bus. IEEE1394 is commonly used with consumer electronic devices such as video cameras and MP3 players. IEEE 1394 is based on a technology developed by Apple Computers called FireWire.

IETF (Internet Engineering Task Force)

A group of research volunteers responsible for specifying the protocols used on the Internet and for specifying the architecture of the Internet.

ifconfig

A command used on Linux, UNIX, and OS/2 systems to obtain configuration for network interfaces.

IGMP (Internet Group Management Protocol)

Protocol used for communication between devices within the same multicast group. IGMP provides a mechanism for systems to detect and make themselves aware of other systems in the same group.

IMAP (Internet Message Access Protocol)

A protocol that allows email to be retrieved from a remote server. It is part of the TCP/IP protocol suite, and is similar in operation to POP but offers more functionality.

incremental backup

A backup of only files that have been created or changed since the last backup. In an incremental backup, the archive bit is cleared to indicate that a file has been backed up.

infrared

A wireless data communication method that uses light pulses in the infrared range as a carrier signal.

Infrastructure Topology

Wireless topology that defines a wireless network composed of an access point connected to a wired LAN. Wireless devices communicate with the wired LAN through the access point (AP).

inherited rights

The file system or directory access rights that are valid at a given point as a result of those rights being assigned at a higher level in the directory structure.

intelligent hub/switch

A hub or switch that contains some management or monitoring capability.

intelligent UPS

A UPS that has associated software for monitoring and managing the power that is provided to the system. In order for information to be passed between the UPS and the system, the UPS and system must be connected, which is normally achieved through a serial or USB connection.

interface

A device, such as a card or a plug, that connects pieces of hardware with a computer so that information can be moved from place to place (for example, between computers and printers, hard disks, and other devices, or between two or more nodes on a network). Also, the part of an application or operating system that the user sees.

interference

Anything that can compromise the quality of a signal. On bound media, crosstalk, and EMI are examples of interference. In wireless environments, atmospheric conditions that degrade the quality of a signal would be considered interference.

internal IPX address

A unique eight-digit hexadecimal number that is used to identify a server running IPX/SPX. It is usually generated at random when the server is installed.

internal loopback address

Functionality built in to the TCP/IP protocol stack that allows one to verify the correct functioning of the stack by pinging any address in the 127.x.x.x range, except the network address (127.0.0.0) or the broadcast address (127.255.255.255). The address 127.0.0.1 is most commonly used.

Internet domain name

The name of an area of the DNS namespace. The Internet domain name is normally expressed along with the top-level domain to which it belongs (for example, comptia.org).

Internet layer

In the TCP/IP architectural model, the layer that is responsible for addressing, packaging, and routing functions. Protocols that operate at this layer are responsible for encapsulating packets into Internet datagrams. All necessary routing algorithms are run here.

internetwork

A group of networks connected by routers or other connectivity devices so that the networks function as one network.

intrusion detection

The process or procedures that provide a warning of successful or failed unauthorized access to a system.

I/O (input/output)

An operation in which data is either entered into or taken out of a computer.

IP (Internet Protocol)

A network-layer protocol, documented in RFC 791, that offers a connectionless internetwork service. IP provides features for addressing, packet fragmentation and reassembly, type-of-service specification, and security.

IP address

The unique address used to identify the network number and node address of a device connected to a TCP/IP network. IP addresses are typically expressed in dotted decimal format, for example 192.168.1.1

ipconfig

A Windows NT/2000 command that provides information about the configuration of the TCP/IP parameters, including the IP address.

IPSec (IP Security)

A protocol used to provide strong security standards for encryption and authentication on VPNs.

IPv6 (Internet Protocol version 6)

The new version of IP, which has a larger range of usable addresses than the current version of IP, IPv4, and enhanced security.

IPX (Internetwork Packet Exchange)

A network-layer protocol normally used by Novell's NetWare. IPX provides connectionless communication, supporting packet sizes up to 64KB.

IPX/SPX (Internetwork Packet Exchange/Sequenced Packet Exchange)

The default protocol used in NetWare networks. It is a combination of IPX, to provide addressing, and SPX, to provide guaranteed delivery for IPX. IPX/SPX is similar in nature to its counterpart, TCP/IP.

IPX address

The unique address used to identify a node in a network.

IrDA

Wireless networking technology that uses infrared beams to send data transmissions between devices.

IRQ (interrupt request)

A number assigned to a device in a computer that determines the priority and path in communications between a device and the CPU.

IRTF (Internet Research Task Force)

The research arm of the Internet Architecture Board that performs research in the areas of Internet protocols, applications, architecture, and technology.

ISA (Industry Standard Architecture)

The standard of the older, more common, 8-bit and 16-bit bus and card architectures.

ISDN (Integrated Services Digital Network)

An internationally adopted standard for providing end-to-end digital communications between two points. ISDN is a dial-up technology allowing data, voice, and other source traffic to be transmitted over a dedicated link.

ISDN terminal adapter

A device that enables communication over an ISDN link.

ISO (International Organization for Standardization)

A voluntary organization founded in 1946 that is responsible for creating international standards in many areas, including communications and computers. This also includes the development of the OSI model.

ISP (Internet service provider)

A company or an organization that provides facilities for clients to access the Internet.

J

jumpered (or jumpering)

Refers to the physical placement of shorting connectors on a board or card.

jumperless

A term used to describe devices that are configured via a software utility rather than by physical jumpers on the circuit board.

K

Kb (kilobit)

1,000 bits.

KB (kilobyte)

1,000 bytes.

Kerberos

Network authentication protocol designed to ensure that the data sent across networks is encrypted and safe from attack. Its primary purpose is to provide authentication for client/server applications.

kernel

The core of an operating system. The kernel provides basic functions and services for all other parts of the operating system, including the interface with which the user interacts.

L

L2F (Layer 2 Forwarding Protocol)

A VPN protocol designed to work in conjunction with PPP to support authentication standards, such as Terminal Access Controller Access Control System (TACACS+) and Remote Authentication Dial-In User Service (RADIUS), for secure transmissions over the Internet.

L2TP (Layer 2 Tunneling Protocol)

A dial-up VPN protocol that defines its own tunneling protocol and works with the advanced security methods of IPSec. L2TP enables PPP sessions to be tunneled across an arbitrary medium to a home gateway at an ISP or a corporation.

LAN (local area network)

A group of connected computers located in a single geographic area—usually a building or office that share data and services.

laser printer

A type of printer that uses electrophotography as the means of printing images on paper.

latency

The delay induced by a piece of equipment or device used to transfer data.

LC

Media connector used with fiber-optic cabling.

LDAP

Protocol used to access and query compliant directory services systems such as Microsoft Active Directory or Novell Directory services.

learning bridge

A bridge that builds its own bridging address table rather than requiring someone to enter information manually. Most modern bridges are learning bridges. Also called a smart bridge.

legacy

An older computer system or technology.

line conditioner

A device used to stabilize the flow of power to the connected component. Also known as a power conditioner or voltage regulator.

link light

An LED on a networking device such as a hub, switch, or NIC. The illumination of the link light indicates that, at a hardware level, the connection is complete and functioning.

link-state routing

A dynamic routing method in which routers tell neighboring routers of their existence through packets called link-state advertisements (LSAs). By interpreting the information in these packets, routers can create maps of the entire network. *Compare with* distance-vector routing.

Linux

A UNIX-like operating system kernel created by Linus Torvalds. Linux is distributed under an open-source license agreement, as are many of the applications and services that run on it.

LLC (Logical Link Control) layer

A sublayer of the data-link layer of the OSI model. The LLC layer provides an interface for the network-layer protocols and the MAC sublayer.

LMHOSTS file

A text file used in a Windows network environment that contains a list of NetBIOS hostname-to-IP address mappings used in TCP/IP name resolution.

logical addressing scheme

The addressing method used in providing manually assigned node addressing.

logical topology

The appearance of the network to the devices that use it, even if in physical terms the layout of the network is different. *See also* physical topology.

loop

A continuous circle that a packet takes through a series of nodes in a network until it eventually times out.

loopback plug

A device used for loopback testing.

loopback testing

A troubleshooting method in which the output and input wires are crossed or shorted in a manner that allows all outgoing data to be routed back into the card.

LPD (Line Printer Daemon)

Service on a system (normally UNIX or Linux) that acts as a print server. Print jobs are submitted to the LPD application using a protocol such as LPR.

LPR (Line Printer Remote)

Network service that allows printing jobs to be sent to a remote print service such as LPD.

LTO (Linear Tape Open)

An open standard that allows both high storage capacity and fast data access in tape backup systems.

M

MAC (Media Access Control) address

A six-octet number, described in hexadecimal, that uniquely identifies a host on a network. It is a unique number that is burned into the network interface.

MAC layer

In the OSI model, the lower of the two sublayers of the data-link layer. It is defined by the IEEE as being responsible for interaction with the physical layer.

Mac OS X

Version 10 of an operating system designed for Macintosh computer systems. Mac OS X represents a complete shift in Apple operating systems, as it is based on UNIX code and, as such, can be managed using UNIX utilities and procedures.

MAN (metropolitan area network)

A network that spans a defined geographical location such as a city or suburb.

master name server

The supplying name server that has authority in a DNS zone.

MAU (media access unit)

A transceiver that is specified in IEEE 802.3. Not to be confused with a Token Ring multistation access unit, which is abbreviated MSAU.

Mb (megabit)

1 million bits. Used to rate transmission transfer speeds.

MB (megabyte)

1 million bytes. Usually refers to file size.

Mbps (megabits per second)

The number of millions of bits that can travel across a given medium in a second.

MDI (medium-dependent interface)

A type of port found on Ethernet networking devices such as hubs and switches in which the wiring is straight through. MDI ports are sometimes referred to as uplink ports and are intended for use as connectivity points to other hubs and switches.

MDI-X (medium-dependent interface crossed)

A type of port found on Ethernet networking devices in which the wiring is crossed so that the transmit line of one device becomes the receive line of the other. MDI-X is used to connect hubs and switches to client computers.

memory address

The label assigned to define the location in memory where information is stored.

metric

A value that can be assigned to a route to encourage or discourage the use of the route. *See also* cost.

MIB (Management Information Base)

A data set that defines the criteria that can be retrieved and set on a device using SNMP.

microsegmentation

The process of using switches to divide a network into smaller segments.

microwaves

A wireless technology sometimes used to transmit data between buildings and across vast distances.

mirroring

A fault-tolerant technique in which an exact duplicate of data on one volume is created on another. Mirroring is defined as RAID 1. *See* RAID.

modem (modulator-demodulator)

A device used to modulate and demodulate the signals that pass through it. It converts the direct current pulses of the serial digital code from the controller into the analog signals that are compatible with the telephone network.

MSAU (multistation access unit)

A device that is used in an IBM Token Ring network. It organizes the connected nodes into an internal ring and uses the RI and RO connectors to expand to other MSAUs on the network. Sometimes referred to as MAU.

MTBF (mean time between failure)

The amount of time, normally expressed in hours, that represents the average amount of time a component will function before it fails.

MTRJ

Media connector used with fiber-optic cabling.

MTTF (mean time to fix)

The amount of time it normally takes to fix a problem or swap out a component.

multicast

A single-packet transmission from one sender to a specific group of destination nodes.

multihomed

A term used to refer to a device that has more than one network interface.

multiplatform

A term used to refer to a programming language, technology, application or protocol that runs on different types of CPUs or operating systems.

multiplexing

Multiplexing is a technique of combining multiple channels over a transmission path and then recovering or de-multiplexing the separate channels at the receiving end. Examples include FDM, TDM, CDM, and WDM.

multiprocessor

A term that refers to the use of multiple processors in a single system.

multitasking

The running of several programs simultaneously. In actuality, during multitasking the processor is sharing its time between the programs, and it only appears as if they are running concurrently.

N

name server

A server that contains a databases of name resolution information used to resolve network names to network addresses.

NAT (Network Address Translation)

A standard that enables the translation of IP addresses used on one network to a different IP address that is acceptable for use on another network. This translation enables multiple systems to access an external network, such as the Internet, through a single IP address.

NBNS (NetBIOS name server)

A central server that provides name resolution for NetBIOS names to IP addresses. Commonly referred to as a WINS server.

nbtstat

A Windows operating system command-line utility that displays protocol statistics and current TCP/IP connections using NetBIOS over TCP/IP (NBT).

NCP (NetWare Core Protocol)

A protocol that provides a method for hosts to make calls to a NetWare server for services and network resources. NCP is part of the IPX/SPX protocol suite.

NDS (Novell Directory Services)

A standards-compliant directory services system introduced by Novell with NetWare 4.x. Subsequently renamed eDirectory.

NetBEUI (NetBIOS Extended User Interface)

A nonroutable, Microsoft-proprietary networking protocol designed for use in small networks.

NetBIOS (Network Basic Input/Output System)

A software application that enables different applications to communicate between computers on a LAN.

netstat

A Windows operating system command-line utility that displays protocol statistics and current TCP/IP network connections.

NLM (NetWare loadable module)

A service or process that runs on a NetWare server.

NLSP (NetWare Link Services Protocol)

A link-state routing protocol used on networks that use Novell's IPX/SPX protocol suite.

network card

See NIC.

network ID

The part of a TCP/IP address that specifies the network portion of the IP address. The network ID is determined by the class of the address, which in turn is determined by the subnet mask used.

network interface layer

The bottom layer of the TCP/IP architectural model, which is responsible for sending and receiving frames.

network layer

Layer 3 of the OSI model, which is where routing based on node addresses (that is, IP or IPX addresses) occurs.

network operating system (NOS)

An operating system that runs on the servers on a network. Network operating systems include NetWare, UNIX, Windows NT Server, and Windows Server 2003.

newsgroup

A discussion group that focuses on a specific topic and is made up of a collection of messages posted to an Internet site. Newsgroups are useful resources for support personnel.

NFS (Network File System)

File sharing and access protocol most commonly associated with UNIX and Linux systems.

NIC (Network Interface Card)

A hardware component that serves as the interface, or connecting component, between a network and the node. It has a transceiver, a MAC address, and a physical connector for the network cable. Also known as a network adapter or a network card.

NIS (Network Information Services)

The user, group, and security information database used in a UNIX internetwork.

NMS (Network Management System)

An application that acts as a central management point for network management. Most NMS systems use SNMP in order to communicate with network devices.

NNTP (Network News Transfer Protocol)

An Internet protocol that controls how news articles are to be queried, distributed, and posted. NNTP uses port 119.

noise

Another name for EMI. *See* EMI.

NTP (Network Time Protocol)

A protocol that is used to communicate time synchronization information between devices on the network. NTP is part of the TCP/IP protocol suite. NTP uses port 123.

O

operating system

The main computer program that manages and integrates all the applications running on a computer. The OS handles all disk interactions with the processor.

OSI (Open Systems Interconnect) reference model

A seven-layer model created by the ISO to standardize and explain the interactions of networking protocols.

OSPF (Open Shortest Path First)

A link-state routing protocol used on TCP/IP networks. *Compare with* distance-vector routing.

P

packet filtering

A firewall method in which each packet that attempts to pass through the firewall is examined to determine its contents. The packet is then allowed to pass or it is blocked, as appropriate.

packet sniffer

A device or an application that allows data to be copied from the network and analyzed. In legitimate applications, it is a useful network troubleshooting tool.

PAN (Personal Area Network)

A network layout whereby devices work together in close proximity to share information and services, commonly using technologies such as Bluetooth or infrared.

passive hub

A hub that has no power and therefore does not regenerate the signals it receives. *Compare with* active hub.

passive termination

A SCSI bus terminator that uses a terminating resistor pack placed at the end of the bus. This resistor relies on the interface card to provide it with a consistent level of power.

password

A set of characters used with a username to authenticate a user on a network and to provide the user with rights and permissions to files and resources.

patch

A fix for a bug in a software application. Patches can be downloaded from the Internet to correct errors or security problems in software applications.

patch cable

A cable, normally twisted-pair, used to connect two devices together. Strictly speaking, a patch cable is the cable that connects a port on a hub or switch to the patch panel, but today, people commonly use the term to refer to any cable connection.

patch panel
A device in which the cables used in coaxial or twisted-pair networks converge and are connected. The patch panel is usually in a central location.

PCAnywhere
A software program that allows users to gain control of a computer remotely.

PCI (Peripheral Component Interconnect)
A relatively new high-speed bus designed for Pentium systems.

PCMCIA (Personal Computer Memory Card International Association)
An industry group organized in 1989 to promote standards for credit card–sized devices such as memory cards, modems, and network cards. Almost all laptop computers today have multiple PCMCIA slots. PCMCIA cards are now generally referred to as simply PC cards.

peer-to-peer networking
A network environment that does not have dedicated servers, where communication occurs between similarly capable network nodes that act as both clients and servers.

permissions
Authorization provided to users that allows them to access objects on a network. The network administrators generally assign permissions. *Permissions* is slightly different from but often used with *rights*.

physical address
The MAC address on every NIC. The physical address is applied to a NIC by the manufacturer and except for very rare occurrences, is never changed.

physical layer
Layer 1 of the OSI model, where all physical connectivity is defined.

physical topology
The actual physical layout of the network. Common physical topologies include star, bus, and ring. *Compare with* logical topology.

ping
A TCP/IP protocol stack utility that works with ICMP and uses echo requests and replies to test connectivity to other systems.

plenum
The space between the structural ceiling and a drop-down ceiling that is commonly used for heating, ventilation, and air-conditioning systems as well as for running network cables.

plug-and-play
An architecture designed to enable hardware devices to be detected by the operating system and for the driver to be automatically loaded.

polling
The media-access method for transmitting data in which a controlling device is used to contact each node to determine whether it has data to send.

PoP (point-of-presence)

The physical location where a long-distance carrier or a cellular provider interfaces with the network of the local exchange carrier or local telephone company.

POP (Post Office Protocol)

A protocol that is part of the TCP/IP protocol suite and is used for retrieving mail stored on a remote server. The most commonly used version of POP is POP3. POP is an application layer protocol.

port

In physical networking terms, a pathway on a networking device that allows other devices to be connected. In software terms, a port is the entry point into an application, system, or protocol stack.

port mirroring

A process by which two ports on a device, such as a switch, are configured to receive the same information. Port mirroring is useful in troubleshooting scenarios.

POTS (Plain Old Telephone Service)

The current analog public telephone system. *See also* PSTN.

PPP (Point-to-Point Protocol)

A common dial-up networking protocol that includes provisions for security and protocol negotiation and provides host-to-network and switch-to-switch connections for one or more user sessions.

PPPoE (Point-to-Point Protocol over Ethernet)

Internet connection authentication protocol that uses two separate technologies, Ethernet and the Point-to-Point Protocol (PPP), to provide a method for multiple users to share a common Digital Subscriber Line (DSL), cable modem, or wireless connection to the Internet.

PPTP (Point-to-Point Tunneling Protocol)

A protocol that encapsulates private network data in IP packets. These packets are transmitted over synchronous and asynchronous circuits to hide the underlying routing and switching infrastructure of the Internet from both senders and receivers.

presentation layer

Layer 6 of the OSI model, which prepares information to be used by the application layer.

PRI (Primary Rate Interface)

A high-level network interface standard for use with ISDN. PRI is defined as having a rate of 1.544Mbps, and consists of a single 64Kbps D channel plus 23 T1 B channels for voice or data. *See also* BRI, ISDN.

primary name server

The DNS server that offers zone data from files stored locally on the machine.

private network

A network to which access is limited, restricted, or controlled. Most corporate networks are private networks. *Compare with* public network.

proprietary

A standard or specification that is created by a single manufacturer, vendor, or other private enterprise.

protocol

A set of rules or standards that control data transmission and other interactions between networks, computers, peripheral devices, and operating systems.

protocol suite

Any two or more protocols that work together, such as TCP and IP or IPX and SPX. Also known as a protocol stack.

proxy

A device, an application, or a service that acts as an intermediary between two hosts on a network, eliminating the ability for direct communication.

proxy server

A server that acts as a go-between for a workstation and the Internet. A proxy server typically provides an increased level of security, NAT, caching, and administrative control.

PSTN (public switched telephone network)

A term that refers to all the telephone networks and services in the world. The same as POTS, PSTN refers to the world's collection of interconnected public telephone networks that are both commercial and government owned. All of the PSTN is digital, except the connection between local exchanges and customers (which is called the local loop or last mile), which remains analog.

public network

A network, such as the Internet, to which anyone can connect with the most minimal of restrictions. *Compare with* private network.

punchdown block

A device that is used to connect network cables from equipment closets or rooms to other parts of a building. Connections to networking equipment such as hubs or switches are established from the punchdown block. Also used in telecommunications wiring for distributing phone cables to their respective locations throughout the building.

punchdown tool

A hand tool that enables the connection of twisted-pair wires to wiring equipment such as a patch panel.

R

RADIUS (Remote Authentication Dial-in User Service)

A security standard that employs a client-server model to authenticate remote network users. Remote users are authenticated using a challenge and response mechanism between the remote access server and the RADIUS server.

RAID (Redundant Array of Inexpensive Disks)

A method of storing data on multiple hard drives, allowing the overlapping of I/O operations. Depending on the level of RAID, there are either fault-tolerant or performance advantages.

RAID 0

A RAID configuration that employs data striping but lacks redundancy because there is no parity information recorded (*see* RAID 5). As a result, RAID 0 offers no fault tolerance, but it does offer increased performance. Requires a minimum of two disks.

RAID 1

A fault-tolerant method that uses disk mirroring to duplicate the information stored on a disk. Also referred to as disk duplexing when the two drives in a RAID 1 array are connected to separate disk controllers.

RAID 2

A fault-tolerant method that uses disk striping with error correction.

RAID 3

A fault-tolerant method that uses disk striping with a single disk for parity.

RAID 4

A fault-tolerant method that uses disk striping with a single disk for parity. Striping is done across the disks in blocks.

RAID 5

A fault-tolerant method that uses disk striping with distributed parity. Striping is done across the disks in blocks.

RAID 10

Also referred to as RAID 1/0, a RAID configuration in which stripe sets (RAID 0) are mirrored (RAID 1). This combination provides the fault-tolerant aspects of RAID 1 and the performance advantages of RAID 0.

RARP (Reverse Address Resolution Protocol)

A protocol, part of the TCP/IP protocol suite, that resolves MAC addresses to IP addresses. Its relative ARP resolves IP addresses to MAC addresses. RARP resides on the network layer of the OSI model.

RAS (Remote Access Service)

A Windows NT/2000 service that allows access to the network through remote connections.

RDP (Remote Desktop Protocol)

Presentation layer protocol that supports traffic between a Windows terminal client and Windows Terminal Server. RDP us also used for the Remote Desktop feature of Windows XP and Windows Server 2003.

read-only

An assigned right that allows the user to open a file and look at the contents or to execute the file if it is an application. The user cannot change or delete the file.

read-write

An assigned right that allows the user to open a file, to change a file, or to execute a file. The user cannot delete a read-write file in some network operating systems, but can in others. The user can create new files in the directory if he or she is granted read-write permissions to a directory.

remote control

In networking, having physical control of a remote computer through software such as PCAnywhere or Microsoft Systems Management Server.

remote node

A node or a computer that is connected to a network through a remote connection. Dialing in to the Internet from home is an example of the remote node concept.

repeater

A device that regenerates and retransmits signals on a network. Repeaters are normally used to strengthen signals going long distances.

resolver

A system that is requesting the resolution of a name to an IP address. This term can be applied to both DNS and WINS clients.

resource conflict

A problem that occurs when multiple devices are using the same IRQ or I/O address at the same time, usually causing the devices to fail and the program to halt.

restore

To transfer data from backup media to a server. The opposite of backup.

RFC (Request for Comments)

The process by which standards relating to the Internet, the TCP/IP protocol suite, and associated technologies are created, commented on, and approved.

RG-58

A designation for the coaxial cable used in thin coaxial networks that operate on the Ethernet standard.

RI (ring in)

A connector used in an IBM Token Ring network on an MSAU to expand to other MSAUs on the network. The counterpart to the RO, the RI on the MSAU connects to the media to accept the token from the ring.

rights

An authorization provided to users that allows them to perform certain tasks. The network administrator generally assigns rights. Slightly different from but often used with the term *permissions*.

RIP (Routing Information Protocol)

A protocol that uses hop count as a routing metric to control the direction and flow of packets between routers on an internetwork. There are versions of RIP for use on both TCP/IP- and IPX/SPX-based networks.

RJ-11 connector

A connector that is used with telephone systems and can have up to six conductors.

RJ-45 connector

An connector used with twisted-pair cable that can support eight conductors for four pairs of wires.

RO (ring out)

A connector used in an IBM Token Ring network on an MSAU to expand to other MSAUs on the network. The counterpart to the RI, the RO on the MSAU connects to the medium to send the token out to the ring.

root

The top level of a file system or a directory services structure. Also, the name of the default administrative account on UNIX and Linux systems. Also, the term used to describe the top level of the Domain Name Service namespace.

route

The entire path between two nodes on a network.

router

A device that works at the network layer of the OSI model to control the flow of data between two or more network segments.

RS-232

A communications standard that defines the flow of serial communications and the particular functions assigned to the wires in a serial cable.

S

sag

A momentary drop in the voltage provided by a power source.

Samba

Service that runs on a UNIX or Linux system that provides file and print services available to Windows clients without the need for additional client software. Samba is a variation of the Server Message Block (SMB) protocol.

SAP (Service Advertising Protocol)

A NetWare protocol used on an IPX network. SAP maintains server information tables, listing each service that has been advertised to it, and provides this information to any nodes that attempt to locate a service.

SAP (Service Advertising Protocol) agent

A router or another node on an IPX network that maintains a server information table. This table lists each service that has been advertised to it and provides this information to any nodes that attempt to locate a service.

SAS (Single Attached Station)

In an FDDI system, a device that is attached to only one of the two rings. *Compare with* DAS.

SCP (Secure Copy Protocol)

Basic file copying protocol that uses Secure Shell (SSH) technology to provide security to then transfer.

SCSI (Small Computer System Interface)

A technology defined by a set of standards originally published by ANSI for use with devices on a bus known as a SCSI bus. SCSI is commonly implemented to support high speed storage systems.

SCSI bus

The high-speed channel between the SCSI devices on a chain. The SCSI bus architecture contains a multithreaded I/O interface that can process multiple I/O requests at the same time.

SCSI bus termination

The use of a set of electrical resistors called terminators at the extreme ends of the SCSI bus to reflect the electrical impulses being transmitted across the bus.

SCSI ID

A number assigned to a SCSI device to identify the device and its priority when two or more devices are competing for the right to send data on the bus.

secondary name server

A type of DNS server that gets its zone data from another DNS name server that has authority in that zone.

Security log

A log located in the Windows NT 4/2000 Event Viewer that provides information on audit events that the administrator has determined to be security related. These events include logons, attempts to log on, attempts to access areas that are denied, and attempts to log on outside normal hours.

security policy

In general terms, a written policy that defines the rules and regulations pertaining to the security of company data and the use of computer systems. More specifically, the policy configuration on a server system or a firewall that defines the security parameters for a system.

segment

A physical section of a network.

server

A network node that fulfills service requests for clients. Usually referred to by the type of service it performs, such as file server, communications server, or print server.

server-based application

An application that is run from a network share rather than from a copy installed on a local computer.

server-based networking

A network operating system that is dedicated to providing services to workstations, or clients. *See also* client/server networking.

service pack

A software update that fixes multiple known problems and in some cases provides additional functionality to an application or operating system.

session

A dialog between two computers.

session layer

Layer 5 of the OSI model, which establishes, manages, and terminates sessions between applications on different nodes.

SFTP (Secure File Transfer Protocol)

A implementation of the File Transfer Protocol (FTP) that uses Secure Shell (SSH) technology to provide additional authentication and encryption services for file transfers.

shared system

The infrastructure component that is routed directly into the backbone of an internetwork for optimal systems access. It provides connectivity to servers and other shared systems.

shell

An interface, graphical or otherwise, that enables a user to access the functionality of an operating system.

SLIP (Serial Line Internet Protocol)

A protocol that uses encapsulation to enable TCP/IP to be transmitted over asynchronous lines, such as standard telephone lines. Previously used for most Internet access, SLIP has been largely replaced by PPP because of SLIP's lack of error-checking capabilities.

SMDS (Switched Multimegabit Data Service)

A data transmission system that uses public lines at speeds between 1.544Mbps (T1) and 44.736Mbps, using cell relay and fixed-length cells. Defined in IEEE 802.6.

SMB (Server Message Block)

Native file sharing and access protocol used on Windows platforms.

SMP (symmetrical multiprocessing)

The utilization of multiple processors on a single system.

SMTP (Simple Mail Transfer Protocol)

An Internet protocol that is used for the transfer of messages between servers, or between clients and servers.

SNAP (SubNetwork Access Protocol)

An Internet protocol that specifies a standard method of encapsulating IP datagrams and ARP messages on a network.

SNMP (Simple Network Management Protocol)

A protocol that provides network devices with a method to monitor and control network devices; manage configurations, statistics collection, performance, and security; and report network management information to a management console. SNMP is part of the TCP/IP protocol suite.

SNMP agent

A software component that enables a device to communicate with, and be contacted by, an SNMP management system.

SNMP trap

An SNMP utility that sends an alarm to notify the administrator that something within the network activity differs from the established threshold, as defined by the administrator.

socket

A logical interprocess communications mechanism through which a program communicates with another program or with a network.

socket identifier

An 8-bit number that is used to identify the socket and is used by IPX when it needs to address a packet to a particular process running on a server. The developers and designers of services and protocols usually assign socket identifiers. A socket identifier is also known as a socket number.

SONET (Synchronous Optical NETwork)

A U.S. standard for data transmission that operates at speeds up to 2.4Gbps over optical networks referred to as OC-x, where x is the level.

source address

The address of the host that sent the frame. The source address is contained in the frame, so the destination node knows who sent the data.

source-route bridge

A bridge used in source-route bridging to send a packet to the destination node through the route specified by the sending node.

spike

An instantaneous, dramatic increase in the voltage output to a device. Spikes are responsible for much of the damage done to network hardware components.

SPX (Sequenced Packet Exchange)

A protocol used in conjunction with IPX when guaranteed delivery is required. SPX is used mainly in NetWare network environments. SPX operates at the Transport layer of the OSI model.

SSH (Secure Shell)

An application, similar to Telnet, that allows a session to be opened on a remote host. SSH differs from Telnet in that it provides additional authentication methods and encryption for data as it traverses the network. SSH uses TCP/IP port 22.

SSID (Service Set Identifier)

A unique client identifier sent over the WLAN that acts as a simple password used for authentication between a wireless client and an access point. The SSID is used to differentiate between networks and therefore the client system and the AP must use the same SSID.

SSL (Secure Sockets Layer)

A method of securely transmitting information to and receiving information from a remote website. SSL is implemented through the HTTPS. SSL operates at the presentation layer of the OSI model and uses TCP/IP port 443.

STA (Spanning Tree Algorithm)

A standard defined by IEEE 802.1 as part of STP to eliminate loops in an internetwork with multiple paths.

static IP address

An IP address that is assigned to a network device manually, as opposed to dynamically via DHCP.

static routing

A routing method in which all routes must be entered into a device manually and in which no route information is exchanged between routing devices on the network. *Compare with* dynamic routing.

static window

A mechanism used in flow control that prevents the sender of data from overwhelming the receiver. The amount of data that can be buffered in a static window is configured dynamically by the protocol.

station IPX address

A 12-digit number used to uniquely identify each device on an IPX network. The station IPX address is derived directly from the MAC address of the network interface.

storage area network (SAN)

A subnetwork of storage devices, usually found on high-speed networks and shared by all servers on a network.

store-and-forward

A fast-packet-switching method that produces a higher latency than other switching methods because the entire contents of the packet are copied into the onboard buffers of the switch. CRC calculations are performed before the packet can be passed on to the destination address.

STP (Shielded Twisted Pair)

Twisted-pair network cable that has shielding to insulate the cable from EMI.

STP (Spanning Tree Protocol)

A protocol that was developed to eliminate the loops caused by the multiple paths in an internetwork. STP is defined in IEEE 802.1.

subdomain

A privately controlled segment of the DNS namespace that exists under other segments of the namespace as a division of the main domain. Sometimes also called a child domain.

subnet

A logical division of a network, based on the address to which all the devices on the network are assigned.

subnet mask

A 32-bit address used to mask, or screen, a portion of an IP address to differentiate from one another the part of the address that designates the network and the part that designates the hosts.

subnetting

The process of using parts of the node portion of an assigned IP address to create more network IDs. While subnetting increases the number of network IDs, it decreases the number of node addresses available for each network ID.

supernetting

The process of aggregating IP network addresses and using them as a single network address range.

Supervisor account

In a NetWare network, a default account that has rights to access everything and to assign rights to other users on the network.

surge

A voltage increase that is less dramatic than that of a spike but can last a lot longer. Sometimes referred to as a swell. The opposite of brownout.

surge protector

An inexpensive and simple device that is placed between a power outlet and a network component to protect the component from spikes and surges. Also known as a surge suppressor.

SVC (switched virtual circuit)

A virtual circuit that is established dynamically on demand to form a dedicated link and is then broken when transmission is complete.

switch

A layer 2 networking that forwards frames based on destination addresses.

SYN

A message sent to initiate a TCP session between two devices. The proper term is synchronization packet.

synchronous transmission

A digital signal transmission method that uses a precise clocking method and a predefined number of bits sent at a constant rate.

System log

A log, accessed through Event Viewer on Windows Server platforms, that provides information and warnings on events logged by operating system components and hardware devices. These events include driver failures, device conflicts, read/write errors, timeouts, and bad block errors.

T

T-line

A digital communication line used in WANs. Commonly used T designations are T1 (Trunk Level 1) and T3 (Trunk Level 3). It is also possible to use only part of a T1 line, which then becomes known as *fractional T1*. T-1 lines support a data transmission rate of up to 1.544 Mbps.

TCP (Transmission Control Protocol)

A connection-oriented, reliable data transmission communication service that operates at the transport layer of the OSI model. TCP is part of the TCP/IP protocol suite.

TCP/IP (Transmission Control Protocol/Internet Protocol)

A suite of protocols that includes TCP and IP. TCP/IP was originally designed for use on large internetworks but has now become the de facto protocol for networks of all sizes.

TCP/IP socket

A socket, or connection to an endpoint, that is used in TCP/IP communication transmissions.

TDI (Transport Driver Interface)

A kernel-mode network interface that is exposed at the upper edge of all Windows NT transport protocol stacks. The highest-level protocol driver in every such stack supports the TDI interface for still higher-level, kernel-mode network clients.

TDR (time-domain reflectometer)

A device used to test copper cables to determine whether and where a break is on the cable. For optical cables, an optical TDR is used.

Telnet

A standard terminal emulation protocol in the TCP/IP protocol stack. Telnet is used to perform terminal emulation over TCP/IP via remote terminal connections, allowing users to log in to remote systems and use resources as if they were connected to a local system.

Terminal Services

A service on Windows server platforms that allows clients to connect to the server as if it were a multiuser operating system. All the processing for the client session is performed on the server, with only screen updates and user input being transmitted across the network connection.

TFTP (Trivial File Transfer Protocol)

A simplified version of FTP that allows file transfers but does not offer any security or file management capabilities. TFTP uses TCP/IP port 69.

Thick Ethernet

The IEEE 802.3 standard 10Base5, which describes Ethernet networking using thick coaxial cabling. Also called ThickNet.

thick coaxial

The thick cable most commonly used as the backbone of a coaxial network. It is approximately .375 inches in diameter.

thin client

An application run from a back-end server system such as Microsoft Terminal Services. The processing tasks are all performed at the terminal server rather than on the client. In basic usage, only screen updates are sent from the terminal server, and only keyboard and mouse data is sent to the terminal server.

thin coaxial

Cable that is thinner than thick coaxial cable but still about .25 inches in diameter. It is commonly used in older bus topologies.

Thin Ethernet

The 802.3 standard 10Base2, which describes Ethernet networking using thin coaxial cabling. Also known as ThinNet.

TIA (Telecommunications Industry Association)

An organization that, along with EIA, develops standards for telecommunications technologies.

token

A frame that provides controlling information. In a Token Ring network, the node that possesses the token is the one that is allowed to transmit next.

Token Ring

An IBM-proprietary token-passing LAN topology defined by IEEE standard 802.5. It operates at either 4Mbps or 16Mbps, in a star topology.

Token Ring adapter

Traditionally an ISA or a Microchannel device with 4Mbps or 16Mbps transfer capability that is used to connect nodes to a Token Ring network.

tone generator

A device used with a tone locator to locate and diagnose problems with twisted-pair cabling. Commonly referred to as a fox and hound.

topology

The shape or layout of a physical network and the flow of data through the network. *See also* logical topology, physical topology.

trace route

A function of the TCP/IP protocol suite, implemented in utilities such as traceroute and tracert, that enables the entire path of a packet to be tracked between source and destination hosts. It is used as a troubleshooting tool.

transmit

To send data using light, electronic, or electric signals. In networking, this is usually done in the form of digital signals composed of bits.

transparent bridging

A situation in which the bridges on a network tell each other which ports on the bridge should be opened and closed, which ports should be forwarding packets, and which ports should be blocking packets—all without the assistance of any other device.

transport layer

Layer 4 of the OSI model. Protocols at this layer perform functions such as segmenting data so that it can be sent over the network and then reassembling the segmented data on the receiving end. The transport layer also deals with some of the errors that can occur in a stream of data, such as dropped and duplicated packets.

TTL (Time To Live)

A value that is assigned to a packet of data to prevent it from moving around the network indefinitely. The TTL value is decremented each time the packet crosses a router, until it reaches 0; at which point, it is removed from the network.

twisted-pair

A type of cable that uses multiple twisted pairs of copper wire.

U

UART (Universal Asynchronous Receiver/Transmitter)

A chip that is responsible for communications carried over a serial port; it converts between data bits and serial bits.

UDP (User Datagram Protocol)

A communications protocol that provides connectionless, unreliable communications services and operates at the transport layer of the OSI model. It requires a network-layer protocol such as IP to guide it to the destination host.

unbound media (or boundless media)

A term used to describe any media that do not have physical constraints. Examples of unbound media include infrared, wireless, and microwave. *Compare with* bound media.

UNC (Universal Naming Convention)

An industry naming standard for computers and resources providing a common syntax that should work in most systems, including Windows, UNIX, and NetWare. An example of a UNC name is *servername**sharename*.

unicast

Communication that takes place over a network between a single sender and a single receiver.

UPS (Uninterruptible Power Supply)

A system that provides protection against power surges and power outages. During blackouts, a UPS gives you time to shut down the network before the temporary power interruption becomes permanent. A UPS is also referred to as battery backup.

uptime

The amount of time that a device has been on and operating.

URL (uniform resource locator)

A name used to identify a site and subsequently a page on the Internet. An example of a URL is www.quepublishing.com/products.

USB (Universal Serial Bus)

A type of interface between a computer system and peripheral devices. The USB interface allows you to add or remove devices without shutting down the computer. USB supports up to 127 devices. USB supports auto detection and plug and play

user account

An account that an end user uses when logging in to a network. It contains the rights and permissions assigned to the user.

UTP (Unshielded Twisted Pair)

A type of cable that uses multiple twisted pairs of copper wire in a casing that does not provide much protection from EMI. The most common network cable in Ethernet networks, UTP is rated in categories including Category 1 through Category 5, as well as Category 5e and Category 6.

V

virtual memory

A process for paging or swapping from memory to disk that is used to increase the amount of RAM available to a system.

virus

A software program designed specifically to affect a system or network adversely. A virus is usually designed to be passed on to other systems with which it comes in contact.

VLAN (virtual LAN)

A group of devices located on one or more different LAN segments, whose configuration is based on logical instead of physical connections. This allows the devices to operate as if they were connected to the same physical switch, irrespective of whether or not they are connected to the same switch.

volume set

Multiple disks or partitions of disks that have been configured to read as one drive.

VPN (virtual private network)

A network that uses a public network such as the Internet as a backbone to connect two or more private networks. A VPN provides users with the equivalent of a private network in terms of security. VPNs can also be used as a means of establishing secure remote connectivity between a remote system and another network.

W

WAN (wide area network)

A data communications network that serves users across a broad geographical area. WANs often use transmission devices such as modems or CSUs/DSUs to carry signals over leased lines or over common carrier lines.

WAP (wireless access point)

A network device that offers connectivity between wireless clients and (usually) a wired portion of the network.

Web server

A server that runs an application and makes the contents of certain directories on that server, or other servers, available to clients for download, via a protocol such as HTTP.

WEP (Wired Equivalent Privacy)

Data encryption method used to protect the transmission between 802.11 wireless clients and Access Points. WEP security has come under scrutiny as it uses an insufficient key length and provides no automated method for distributing the keys.

WiFi

A voluntary standard that manufacturers can adhere to, which aims to create compatibility between wireless devices. WiFi is an abbreviation of the phrase WIreless Fidelity.

window flow control

A flow control method in which the receiving host buffers the data it receives and holds it in the buffer until it can be processed. After the data is processed, an acknowledgment is sent to the sender. *See also* dynamic window, static window.

WINS (Windows Internet Name Service)

A NetBIOS name-to-IP address resolution service that runs on Windows server platforms.

WINS database

A dynamically built database of NetBIOS names and IP addresses that is used by WINS.

Wireless Channel

Term used to refer to the band of frequency used for wireless communications. Each IEEE wireless standard specifies the channels that can be used.

wire crimper

A tool that is used to create networking cables. The type of wire crimping tool used depends on the cable being made.

wireless networking

Networking that uses any unbound media, such as infrared, microwave, or radio waves.

WISP (Wireless Internet Service Provider)

A service provider that specializes in offering users wireless access to the Internet, often including hotspot access.

WLAN (Wireless LAN)

A local area network created using wireless transmission methods such as radio or infrared instead of traditional wired solutions.

workstation

A client computer on a network that does not offer any services of its own but uses the services of the servers on the network.

WPA (Wi-Fi Protected Access)

Data encryption method used on 802.11 wireless LANs. WPA is an industry-supported standard designed to address security shortcomings of WEP.

Z

zone

A logical grouping of network devices in an AppleTalk network. Also, an area of the DNS namespace.

zone transfer

The passing of DNS information from one name server to a secondary name server.

Index

Caps Lock, 300

client connectivity authentication, troubleshooting, 303

Linux, 179

NetWare (Novell), 186-187

passwords, 227

 policies, 228

 sharing, 229

 strength of, 228-229

protocols

 CHAP, 169

 EAP, 170

 Kerberos, 170

 MS-CHAP, 169

 PAP, 169

 RADIUS, 170

 SPAP, 170

remote connectivity authentication, troubleshooting, 299-300

smartcards, 227

Windows servers, 192

wireless network communications, 22-23

automated virus scanning/updates, 248

B

backups

 differential backups, 258

 full backups, 258

 incremental backups, 259

 new tapes, 261

 offsite storage, 261

 strategy comparison table, 259-260

 tape drives, cleaning, 261

 tape rotation backups, 260

 tapes, labeling, 261

 verifying, 261

 virus protection strategies, 248

bandwidth, 36, 155

baseband transmissions, TDM (Time Division Multiplexing), 34

Bindery (NetWare), 187

biometrics, 227

blackouts, 257

Bluetooth wireless networks, 19-21

BNC connectors, 42

boot sector viruses, 245

BOOTP (Boostrap Protocol), 120

BRI (Basic Rate Interface) standard, 147

bridges, 64

 80/20 rule, 65

 bridging loops, 65

 IEEE 802.1d Spanning Tree protocol, 65

 OSI (Open Systems Interconnect) reference model maps, 93

 source route bridges, 65

 translational bridges, 65

 transparent bridges, 65

 troubleshooting, 328

bridging loops, 65

broadband Internet connections, 153

 FDM (Frequency Division-Multiplexing), 34

 remote network connections, 209

 security, 155

distance vector routing protocols, 68-69

distributed computing network models, 5

Distributed Print Services (Novell), 189

DNS (Domain Name Service) protocol, 132

HOSTS files, 132

networks services, 320

ping utility, 280

server addresses, 205

TCP/IP protocol suite, 102

documenting solutions (troubleshooting steps/procedures), 337-338

domain controllers, Windows servers as, 191

DSL Internet access. *See* xDSL

DSSS (direct sequence spread spectrum) chips, 20

dynamic addressing, 119

dynamic routing environments, 67-69, 90

E

E-carrier lines, 149-150

EAP (Extensible Authentication Protocol), 170

easy-to-guess passwords, 228

EFS (Encrypting File Systems), Windows servers, 194

electrical interference (wireless network interference), 24

email vetting (virus protection strategies), 248-249

EMI (electromagnetic interference), 35

coax (coaxial cable), 39

troubleshooting, 326

encryption, 23, 165, 229

network traffic, 230

PKI, 231

presentation layer (OSI reference model), 92

processors, 230

public key encryption

802.1x protocol, 168-169

SSL protocol, 166

WEP protocol, 167

WPA protocol, 168

supported operating systems, 231

unencrypted client requests, 231

enforcing password history, 228

environmental conditions (wireless network interference), 24

Erase permission (NetWare), 188

error control, LLC standards (IEEE 802 standards), 13

error messages

Destination Host Unreachable error message, 277

Expired TTL error message, 278

Request Timed Out error message, 277

Unknown Host error message, 278

Ethernet

5-4-3 rule, 48

CSMA/CD, 14, 17

permissions, 193

shares, 193

file sharing protocols, 184

file systems

inheritance, 188

Linux

NFS, 179

permissions, 180-182

Samba, 180

security, 181

Mac OS X server

file sharing protocols, 184

HFS+, 183

ISO9660, 183

MS-DOS, 183

NTFS, 183

permissions, 185

UDF, 183

NetWare (Novell), 187-190

file viruses, 246

Filescan permission (NetWare), 188

firewalls, 75

application gateway firewalls, 220

circuit-level firewalls, 220

firewalling proxy servers, 224

NAT, 218

packet-filtering firewalls, 219-220

private networks, 218

proxy servers, 224

FireWire as network connector, 46

floppy disks, boot sector viruses, 245

flow control (OSI transport layer), 91

foreign address information heading (netstat diagnostic utility), 282

foxes and hounds. *See* tone generators

fractional T, 149

FragmentFree-switching environments, 62

FTP (File Transfer Protocol)

commands list, 122-123

ports, 131

security, 122

full backups, 258

Full Control permissions (Windows Servers), 193

full-duplex dialog mode, 35, 62

G - H

gain (wireless antennas), 25

gateways, 69

default, 115-116

versus default gateways, 70

Gigabit Ethernet standards, 51

GSNW (Gateway Services for NetWare), 198

half-duplex dialog mode, 34

hard disks

boot sector viruses, 245

fault tolerance

RAID 0, 249

RAID 1, 250

RAID 5, 251-252

J - K - L

Q - R

How can we make this index more useful? Email us at indexes@quepublishing.com

X - Y - Z

Wouldn't it be great

if the world's leading technical publishers joined forces to deliver their best tech books in a common digital reference platform?

They have. Introducing
InformIT Online Books
powered by Safari.

POWERED BY **Safari**

InformIT Online Books

■ **Specific answers to specific questions.**
InformIT Online Books' powerful search engine gives you relevance-ranked results in a matter of seconds.

■ **Immediate results.**
With InformIt Online Books, you can select the book you want and view the chapter or section you need immediately.

■ **Cut, paste, and annotate.**
Paste code to save time and eliminate typographical errors. Make notes on the material you find useful and choose whether or not to share them with your workgroup.

■ **Customized for your enterprise.**
Customize a library for you, your department, or your entire organization. You pay only for what you need.

Get your first 14 days FREE!

InformIT Online Books is offering its members a 10-book subscription risk free for 14 days. Visit **http://www.informit.com/onlinebooks** for details.

informit.com/onlinebooks

informIT

www.informit.com

Your Guide to
Information Technology
Training and Reference

Que has partnered with **InformIT.com** to bring technical information to your desktop. Drawing on Que authors and reviewers to provide additional information on topics you're interested in, **InformIT.com** has free, in-depth information you won't find anywhere else.

Articles

Keep your edge with thousands of free articles, in-depth features, interviews, and information technology reference recommendations – all written by experts you know and trust.

Online Books

Answers in an instant from **InformIT Online Books'** 600+ fully searchable online books. Sign up now and get your first 14 days **free**.

POWERED BY
Safari

Catalog

Review online sample chapters and author biographies to choose exactly the right book from a selection of more than 5,000 titles.

CL

004.
6
BIR

5000426022

As an **InformIT** partner, **Que** has shared the knowledge and hands-on advice of our authors with you online. Visit **InformIT.com** to see what you are missing.

www.quepublishing.com